Born in Berlin and educated in England, John Weitz and his family fled from the Nazis in 1938. Thereafter he did sensitive work for American wartime intelligence. Author of the bestselling novel *Value of Nothing*, as well as *Man in Charge* and *Friends in High Places*, in 1988 he was decorated with the Order of Merit, the highest award a civilian can receive from the Federal Republic of Germany. John Weitz now lives in New York.

JOACHIM VON RIBBENTROP

HITLER'S DIPLOMAT

John Weitz

Introduction by Tom Wolfe

A PHOENIX GIANT PAPERBACK

First published in Great Britain
by George Weidenfeld & Nicolson Ltd in 1992
This paperback edition published in 1997
by Phoenix, a division of Orion Books Ltd,
Orion House, 5 Upper St Martin's Lane,
London WC2H 9EA

A CIP catalogue record for this book is available
from the British Library.

ISBN: 0 75380 003 9

Printed and bound in Great Britain by
Butler & Tanner Ltd, Frome and London

Contents

List of Illustrations	vii
Introduction by Tom Wolfe	ix
Preface	xiii
Acknowledgements	xvi

BOOK I

1. THE END — 3
2. WESEL TO LONDON, 1893–1910 – 'No Violin for Christmas' — 4
3. CANADA, 1911–1914 – 'The Wild West' — 12
4. WAR – 'The Hussar' — 18
5. BERLIN, 1919 – 'The Champagne Salesman' — 21
6. BERLIN – 'He Could Walk over Dead Bodies' — 26

BOOK II

7. HITLER TO 1934 – 'Hidden Fantasies' — 45
8. BÜRO TO EMBASSY, 1934–1936 – 'The German People's Supreme Judge' — 69
9. EMBASSY, 1936/1937/1938 – 'Our Fellows Look Terrific' — 113
10. EMBASSY–MINISTRY–MUNICH–KRISTALLNACHT, 1938–1939 – 'WILL MY ADORABLE AUSTRIA BECOME NAZIFIED?' — 139

BOOK III

11. WAR, 1940 – 'Is He Trying to Bore Us into Peace?' — 215
12. 1941–1942 – 'Unsung Heroes Doing the Reich's Dirty Work' — 241
13. 1943–1944 – 'Prussian Marshals Do Not Mutiny' — 267
14. 1945 – 'Justice from the Bomb Bay of a Boeing's Belly' — 286

Notes	307
Addendum	318
Select Bibliography	319
Index	327

For Susan and the kids.

Illustrations

Between pages 144 and 145

Ribbentrop aged just twenty-one (Topham)
Annelies as a young woman (US National Archives)
St Louis Post Dispatch, 18 October 1930
Hitler's own sketch of a Volkswagen (*Automobile Quarterly*)
Joachim and Annelies with Bettina in Dahlem around 1932–3 (US
   National Archives)
With Lord Rothermere in Berlin, 15 December 1934 (US National
   Archives)
The Special Adviser shakes hands with his delighted Chief, 1935 (US
   National Archives)
'Let us extend our hand to Germany': cartoon by David Low (Solo)
A Henkell advertisement in the *Berliner Illustrirte* (Ullstein Verlag)
On the way to Buckingham Palace, 27 October 1936 (Topham)
Via Mercedes to Buckingham Palace, 1937 (US National Archives)
The new Chief greets AA staff, 16 February 1938 (US National Archives)

Between pages 208 and 209

Reichstag, 20 February 1938: Goebbels, Frick, von Ribbentrop, Hess
   and Hitler (US National Archives)
The farewell visit to London, 9 March 1938 (US National Archives)
François-Poncet and Henderson at the French Embassy, 1 August 1938
   (*Der Spiegel*)
Stalin and von Ribbentrop, 23 August 1939 (Hulton-Deutsch Collection)
Returning from Moscow aboard the Führer's aeroplane, 25 August 1939
   (*Der Spiegel*)
In Königsberg after the Soviet treaty, 24 September 1939 (*Der Spiegel*)
'What no chair for me?': cartoon by David Low (Solo)
The final signing of the full Soviet–German Treaty, 28 September 1939:
   Shaposhnikov, von Ribbentrop, Stalin and Molotov (Ullstein Verlag)
Benito Mussolini and von Ribbentrop in Florence, 28 October 1940
   (Topham)
Berlin, June 1941: von Ribbentrop announces to the German and foreign
   press that Germany had invaded the Soviet Union (*Der Spiegel*)

Bettina with baby Barthold, Ursula, Adolf and Rudolf, probably early
    January 1942 (US National Archives)
Rudolf, Lt SS Leibstandarte, with Knight's Cross and First Class Iron
    Cross, around 1942 (US National Archives)
The War Crimes Trials in Nuremberg in 1945 (*Der Spiegel*)
Von Ribbentrop in his cell at the city gaol in Nuremberg (*Der Spiegel*)
Von Ribbentrop's body photographed at Nuremberg, 16 October 1946
    (*Der Spiegel*)
The Munich-Solln brook where the war criminal's ashes were scattered
    (Herlinde Koelble)

INTRODUCTION

―――

Tom Wolfe

In 1922 the great German caricaturist Karl Arnold drew a cartoon for the magazine *Simplicissimus* depicting four toffs in white tie and tails, two of them wearing monocles, lifting their champagne glasses: 'Between us, gentlemen: Long live His Majesty, the Kaiser – hurrah – pssst – hurrah – softly – hurrah!' By then Kaiser Wilhelm was already exiled quietly and permanently in Huis Doorn, the castle in Holland where he spent the last twenty years of his life. But among the upper orders in Germany, despite Germany's defeat in the late Great War, national glory and anti-republicanism remained, *sotto voce*, very fashionable notions. They elevated one above the bourgeoisie, above 'the ninnies', to use a term that had been borrowed, in the latest 1920s fashion, from the English. Foremost among the ninnies were the weak and incompetent middle-class ninnies who ran the Weimar Republic. On these three points – national glory, anti-republicanism and anti-ninnyism – the toffs wearing the evening clothes and monocles happened to agree with an obstreperous band of young radical socialists who called themselves the National Socialist German Workers' Party, or Nazis for short. This helps account for the presence among the leadership of the Third Reich of the unlikely figure of Joachim von Ribbentrop, the toff, the socialite, who became Hitler's Foreign Minister.

As we are about to see in John Weitz's portrait, von Ribbentrop, despite his 'von', was not an aristocrat. He was a wine-importer, champagne being his long suit. The 'von' he added himself. But the business took him to Paris, London and Rome, and he acquired a certain cosmopolitan polish. In the 1920s he and his wife became social climbers *par excellence* in Berlin at a time when the Berlin social climb was a glamorously *louche* competition. It was the time of the Cabaret, in Christopher Isherwood's memorable phrase, a time in which chic took on a sharp, aggressively decadent, adventurously amoral, bohemian edge. Smart women, most notably Marlene Dietrich, affected lesbian dress. Joachim von Ribbentrop affected the loud young Nazis; he picked them up on the night terrain of the Cabaret and presented them in his home as the antithesis of the ninnies, as 'the men who have a programme for Germany'. It was an example of what would later be called (if one can forgive the term) radical chic.

I can't think of any writer in a better position than John Weitz to bring the von Ribbentrop saga alive. Throughout the 1920s his father, Robert Salomon Weitz, and Joachim von Ribbentrop were part of the same world, and John Weitz himself grew up in its atmosphere. Bobby Weitz – English nicknames were also fashionable in the Cabaret period – was Jewish, but he felt confidently, even supremely, German. As a warrant officer in the 3rd Prussian Guards during the late war, he had been hit by shrapnel while advancing across an open field on the Russian front and had been awarded the Iron Cross. His wounds were so serious, he spent a year in hospital. To a degree that is hard to imagine today, wounded infantry veterans with the Iron Cross had a romantic cachet in post-war Germany. On top of that Bobby Weitz had money, good looks and great style. He and his wife, Hedy, entered into the Cabaret every bit as swimmingly as the von Ribbentrops.

Bobby Weitz was a rayon manufacturer, and Bobby and Hedy had an apartment in Berlin's equivalent of Manhattan's East Sixties and a country house in Kladow-Glienicke, south-west of Berlin. They spent their winters in St Moritz, the Italian Riviera, the French Riviera, San Remo and Lake Como. Bobby's clothes were made by Germany's most fashionable tailor, Knize; Hedy's, by France's most fashionable *couturière*, Chanel. They were chums of Die Dietrich and all the other swells of the nightclub and resort circuit. They had one child, John, and packed him off to a boarding school in England, St Paul's, which had been founded during the reign of Henry VIII and had John Milton and Samuel Pepys on its alumni roster. Even the Only Child was *comme il faut*. Small families were the thing. A house full of children made it hard to live the Cabaret life at top speed.

Bobby Weitz had done it all just right. Berlin was a city of 4.5 million souls, only 150,000 of whom were Jews. At the time, the 1920s, the social distance between Jews and non-Jews in Berlin was far less than it was in New York. The firmament in which Bobby Weitz starred was not Jewish society but Berlin society itself. He was a distinguished German, not a distinguished German Jew. For precisely that reason he found it impossible to believe that Hitler was actually serious in his anti-Jewish campaign. By 1936 it was obvious that the campaign was serious – but it couldn't possibly be aimed at *Jews like him*. Finally he took to adorning the lapel of his suit, every day, with the rosette that showed he had won the Iron Cross in the Great War. He was not *that other kind of Jew*. Bobby Weitz did not leave Germany until August of 1938, two months before the door closed forever, and all remaining Jews were sent off to the extermination camps. By then he was a broken man, not because he had lost everything he possessed but because he had lost his very identity ... as a proud German of the upper orders.

Joachim von Ribbentrop's journey from the Cabaret to the end of the night (to borrow Céline's phrase) was, if anything, more dreadful. At the outset the Nazis were his pet radicals. They lent his version of the Cabaret an exquisitely rowdy, *louche*, Low-Rent excitement. Before it was all over, however, he was the Nazis' pet toff. Hitler spoke of him with a teasing derision – to his face – as 'my little champagne salesman'. Like many others, von Ribbentrop did not seem to understand at first that the Nazis were precisely what they called themselves: socialists, members of the National Socialist German Workers' Party. Their contempt for the business mentality, for bottom-line greed, was breathtaking. Hitler saw to it that in Germany the historic destiny of socialism was fulfilled: absolute tyranny with a self-righteous homicidal cruelty rivalling even that of the Soviet Communists and the Khmer Rouge. To make sure, he borrowed the extermination camp and the euphemism for it, *concentration camp*, from the man who invented both, Lenin. The little champagne salesman's own destiny was to be hung as a war criminal in 1946.

John Weitz's personal history gives our story its final, fearsome symmetry. In 1944, now twenty-one years old and living in the United States, he took part in one of the OSS's most hazardous operations of the Second World War, to set up a liaison with the German resistance.* The identity that had meant so much to Bobby Weitz – noble German warrior – had turned out to be a bitter sham. His son clothed himself in the sham ... and had his vengeance.

But John Weitz was a warrior who was able to put vengeance behind him. In America today, of course, he is known as a fashion designer, author and former racing-car driver. In Germany he is also known as a man who for years has sought to bring about a reconciliation between the democratic Germany of today and the émigrés, Jewish and non-Jewish, who fled National Socialism in Germany two generations ago. His novel *Friends in High Places*, a portrait of an honourable and decent German who wound up as a Nazi Brown Shirt, became a cult book in West Germany, as a new generation of Germans began to look back at the National Socialist years. In 1986 he was awarded West Germany's highest honour for foreigners, the Order of Merit, and was offered renewed German citizenship, which, as a US citizen, he declined.

The pages that follow are John Weitz's *Rückblick*, his look back, upon a brutal drama that lies at the heart of a century of socialist madness now drawing to a close.

---

* OSS: Office of Strategic Services, forerunner of the CIA

Preface

I used to believe that my own fascination with the time of Adolf Hitler was due to my family's unhappy involvement with the Nazis and that the world had lost interest. I was wrong. Adolf Hitler has continued to rivet the attention of people worldwide. His name is still in constant use. His deeds are unforgotten (and unforgiven).

Joachim von Ribbentrop, a handsome young *arriviste*, was part of the jazzy, danger-filled Berlin of the late 1920s. He had made and married a lot of money, was quite well connected internationally, spoke excellent English and French, played good tennis and was socially ambitious. In many ways he resembled today's successful young big-city entrepreneurs, those familiar and beloved subjects of 'lifestyle' profiles in financial publications and magazines about instant success.

Then, in an attack of what Tom Wolfe might have described as radical chic, or perhaps to address some irrational insecurity he felt for Germany's future, von Ribbentrop threw in his and his family's lot with a group of revolutionaries, the Nazis. He joined forces with men who were known brawlers and killers and who advocated the end of all personal liberties in return for a supposed 'national cleansing and renewal'. The Nazi creed was every bit as frightening as the worst of Bolshevism, but the Nazis touted themselves as 'German', not 'foreign' like the Communists. This might have made them more acceptable to nationalists like Joachim von Ribbentrop, but other upper-class nationalist Germans were more cautious. They might have admitted some vague sympathies for the Nazis, but they were not as yet ready to embrace them.

Von Ribbentrop's own attachment seemed to be more personal. He became suddenly and thoroughly besotted with the man Adolf Hitler, and he made the quintessential deal with the devil. Perhaps he did so before he was fully aware of all its terms, but he was quite willing to continue once he knew the score. His Nazi time began as high adventure and the fulfilment of his daydreams. Later, if he had doubts, there remained neither the courage nor even the chance to quit. All he could do was to keep sufficient slack in the steel cable which tethered him to Adolf Hitler, else he would have fallen and been shredded by the jagged road.

At first it must have been heady stuff for the young von Ribbentrops. Before 1933 Joachim and Annelies were hoping for acceptance by the 'right' Berlin circles. Soon, as part of the Nazi entourage, they hosted prime ministers and kings and leading industrialists. The road from business executive to 'His Excellency' was short and swift.

He even achieved quick success in the game of international politics, when he negotiated some international treaties and obtained desirable terms for Germany. The world of diplomacy was glamorous, filled with titles and protocol, infinitely more gratifying for him than the importing of wines. The cost was high. Even he realized at the very end that his execution was the price which would have to be paid.

Von Ribbentrop provides a unique instrument for observing Hitler's times and events, because he was a familiar type. He was like the man in the next Concorde seat, a tennis-playing, well-groomed fellow with city and country houses, a well-born, well-dressed wife and several handsome children. With the exception of Schacht, Speer and von Schirach, most of the senior Nazis were malcontents and misfits, difficult to understand. Perhaps the professional therapist could read the motivations of a Goebbels, a Göring, a Hess or a Himmler, but lay members of today's world would find them obscure. Somehow the revolutionary life of these top Nazis seemed predestined, but what of von Ribbentrop? He was no more primed for revolution or revolutionaries than most of the members of an exclusive golf club or board room.

The von Ribbentrops began their Berlin lives as tireless aspirants to upper-class conventionality. They tried to arm themselves with all the machinery from aristocratic title to club memberships. Their fundamental and politically radical change of direction was baffling.

At first, it seemed an uphill task to write about the von Ribbentrops. Many knowledgeable people spoke of him as Hitler's parrot, a yes-man, a super-secretary, a vain, arrogant and stupid man of little character. Descriptions of his wife were equally pejorative. Several published biographical sketches echoed these views. Yet I knew enough about the time of the Nazis to beware these quick judgments. The man who negotiated the 1935 Naval Agreement with Great Britain, formed the propagandistic Anti-Comintern Pact and came up with the Soviet–German Non-Aggression Pact could not be dismissed so lightly. It is evidence of his power that both Göring and Goebbels, two men who had Hitler's ear, absolutely despised von Ribbentrop but could never unseat him. Until the last day in the Hitler bunker, he ranked among the remaining Nazi *altesses*.

Of course, the real key to the von Ribbentrop story was Adolf Hitler and the sum of his semi-educated, pseudo-political and historical notions. Probably overriding all else in Hitler's life was his hysterical hatred of Communism and his vastly inflated fear of the supposed power of 'world' Jewry. He was a dilettante boiling with hatred, yearning for revenge.

Von Ribbentrop managed to be there and to help his final steps to power. Then, once in control, the amateur Hitler achieved an immediate string of perceived successes all of which the experts had deemed impossible. These were then compounded into further daring acts which also succeeded, until both Hitler and almost all of those who had doubted him were convinced that he was infallible, a chosen man of destiny.

His final gamble proved that the experts who had doubted him were right. When Hitler stumbled, other Nazis tried to distance themselves from him, but von Ribbentrop kept his satanic bargain. His final payments involved infinite cruelty unleashed without a thought for the consequences.

Much of the research for this book was deeply painful work. Reading about so much cold-blooded and carefully reasoned murder sends the investigator into shock and often forces him, temporarily, to suspend further study. Not another word about bloodshed! Not another sum total of deaths!

This biography took me from the archives of Bonn's Foreign Ministry to archives all over Europe. I chased the ghost of von Ribbentrop from the mountains of Austria to London, Munich, Berlin, Nuremberg, Hamburg and Washington, DC.

I then assembled and wrote the final draft of this book against the background of the Gulf War. The nearby television screen provided a case study of dictatorship and its demands and what happens when the world says, 'No. Not another inch!' I was mesmerized by the effectiveness of the post-Cold War United Nations while I was chronicling the failures of its predecessor, the League of Nations. I even heard a small country, Kuwait, described as an 'artificial' patchwork, a phrase used to justify aggression. It was exactly what Hitler had called a small country called Czechoslovakia.

Acknowledgements

VERY SPECIAL THANKS TO:

Richard von Weizsäcker,
    President, The Federal Republic of Germany
Ambassador Leopold B. von Bredow,
    Federal Republic of Germany
Dr Peter Sympher,
    Director, Institut of Auswärtiges Amt
Eric Ambler
Tom Wolfe
Barbara Khoury

I ALSO WISH TO ACKNOWLEDGE THE FOLLOWING FOR THEIR GREAT HELP:

Katja Aschke
Prof. Valentin Berezhkov
Dr Ludwig Biewer
Rt Hon. Paul Channon, MP
Schuyler Chapin
Bob Daley
Elizabeth Diefendorf
René Dreyfus
Jacques Français
John Galliher
Gero Gandert
Dr Vartan Gregorian
Christa & Wolf Ulrich von Hassell
Dr Dieter Heckmann
Dr Hans-Jurgen Heimsoeth
Dolly Haas Hirschfeld
Mrs Ruth Hollander
Peter Howes
Prof. Dr Werner Knopp
Herlinde Koelbl
Jonathan Kranz

Dietrich Kraus
Frau Siegried Lüttich
Paul Makino
Henry Marx
Dr Mario Count von Matuschka
Dr Michael Mertes
Dr Franz Werner Michel
Gebhardt von Moltke
Bernhard von der Planitz
Karl Max Graf von Schaesberg
Lloyd S. Schaper (USAF, ret.)
Arthur Schlesinger, Jr
Frau Inge Sckirl
Peter M. F. Sichel
Reinhard Spitzy
Frau Margaret Spohn
Frau Anja Stehmann
Hugh Trevor-Roper
Prince George Vassiltchikov
Baroness Christina von Vietinghoff-Scheel

BOOK I

ONE

THE END

Men of the US Army's Graves Registration Service are usually quite matter of fact. Theirs is not the most admirable assignment, yet it is a very necessary one. No one interferes much with the way they do their job. On the chill evening of 16 October 1945, they waited snug in their pretty villa at Heilmann Strasse 25 in Munich-Solln.

They had been told to expect the ashes of eleven GIs who had been cremated for some reason or other. The villa, which had once belonged to a rich Bavarian businessman, was a comfortable headquarters for their uncomfortable job, except when things did not go as planned. The truck carrying the canisters with the remains, escorted by a guard car, finally arrived very late that cold night, and the US Graves Registration Service boys were peeved. Why couldn't the US Army avoid the usual SNAFUs (Situation Normal, All Fouled Up)? Since it was long past their bedtime, the GIs stored the ashes in the basement overnight.

The next morning they followed instructions. The ashes were to be scattered into the small stream, the Conwentzbach, which ran immediately behind and below the villa. The eleven shiny cylinders were carried down there, lined up in a row and then opened with axes or kicked open. The ashes were poured into the gurgling water by commissioned officers, according to regulations. One of these eleven shiny aluminium cans contained the ashes of His Excellency Joachim von Ribbentrop, once Hitler's mighty Foreign Minister. The rest were the remains of the other senior War Criminals. One, Hermann Göring, had committed suicide. The others had all been hanged, like von Ribbentrop.

The GIs of the US Graves Registration Service cared not one whit, one way or the other.

TWO

WESEL TO LONDON, 1893–1910

'No Violin for Christmas'

As the nineteenth century neared the twentieth, Wesel was still a small garrison town in the extreme north-west of Germany, a few miles from where the Rhine crossed the Dutch frontier. Today, Wesel is only a twenty-minute drive from the two fearful, fateful Dutch towns of Nijmegen and Arnhem, where so many British and American paratroopers lost their lives in 1944 during the oddly named Operation Market Garden.

Ulrich Friedrich Willy Joachim Ribbentrop (the 'von' came later) was born in Wesel on 30 April 1893, the second of three children. His brother Lothar was three years older, and his sister Ingeborg was born three years later, in 1896. Their father, Richard Ribbentrop, was a lieutenant in the Westphalian Field Artillery, a professional soldier. Their mother, Sophie, was a daughter of rich landowners in Saxony called Hertwig. Sophie was beautiful but doomed. She was tubercular, and at the turn of the century tuberculosis killed, almost without fail.

The Ribbentrops were all military people. Joachim's grandfather had won his Iron Cross First Class in the Brunswick artillery. His father Richard won his in the First World War, and so would Joachim. The Ribbentrops were typical Westphalians, usually considered tough and upright.

The Kaiser's officer corps was dominated by aristocrats, and an untitled commoner like Lieutenant Richard Ribbentrop had to be exceptionally good at his job. Officers also had to be rich or at least married to wealthy girls; they had to show a personal fortune of 90,000 gold Marks, otherwise they did not get permission to marry.[1] In the nineteenth century, the officer's world was a titled one, based on the dubious premise of hereditary leadership. The assumption that squires and counts, 'men on horseback', would inspire the dull burgher to do his military duty was widespread. Officers' messes in Britain, France and Germany were filled with the sons and grandsons of the regiments. Viscount followed earl, *marquis* followed *marquis*, and Baron followed Baron. Even the constant, ugly matter of duels could be resolved only among equals. Only a *Herr* could offer satisfaction to a *Herr*. Fortunately, Britain was exempt from this barbarity, but the German officer still thrived on it.

When Joachim was still a small boy, Lieutenant Ribbentrop was transferred to another small and beautiful garrison: Castle Wilhelmshöhe, near the Hessian town of Kassel where Wilhelm IX, Duke of Hessia, built his splendid *Schloss* and then, of course, named it after himself. Little Joachim's first recollections were of this castle and of the redbrick house near the castle gate where the Ribbentrops now lived. His father was commander of a battery of artillery. What a heroic view to have of one's father, dressed in splendid uniform, mounted on his charger and then to hear the massive boom of artillery pieces firing at ceremonial occasions, which either frightened little boys or thrilled them wildly. Probably Joachim felt a bit of each. Huge, noisy, live toy soldiers under the command of his father were every boy's dream.

Joachim's mother was bedridden. The children seldom saw her because then, as now, tuberculosis was highly infectious, and she wanted to protect them. It must have been heartbreaking for her. Despite her sacrifice, Lothar, her eldest, did become tubercular and would eventually die of it.

It is very likely that Joachim also was tubercular.[2] At eighteen, one of his kidneys had to be removed, probably to prevent the spread of the disease.[3] Handsome Joachim was also plagued by a drooping eyelid throughout his life, a sort of sad wink. Some German doctors believed that this was in some way connected with his infected kidney.

The two brothers Ribbentrop were very close. They depended on each other. Their father was easier to respect than to love, and there was no compensation from their self-quarantined mother, who was unreachable and untouchable. Still, they were 'military' children, and military kids were not as 'pampered' as civilian ones.

Joachim's very first contact with the British, who were to become his life-long love–hate affliction, came in Kassel, the Hessian town which had supplied Britain's George III with troops during the rebellion of the American colonies. One glorious, memorable day King Edward VII, the rotund sybaritic son of stern little Queen Victoria, visited Castle Wilhelmshöhe accompanied by his tall young cousin with the withered left arm, the German Kaiser Wilhelm II. There and then, young Joachim learned his first lesson in international relations: things are not always what they seem! *Everyone* 'knew' that the King of England and the Kaiser were feuding, although they were cousins. But there they sat, side by side in their open horse-drawn landau, smiling and chatting like the best of friends! Joachim and Lothar were disappointed and thoroughly puzzled. They had expected fisticuffs or at least scowls.

The two boys fell into line with the rigid honour guard drawn up at the castle entrance and saluted the Kaiser and the King with their toy swords. The jolly Edward VII waved and grinned. He was amused. Captain Richard Ribbentrop of the Imperial German Artillery was not, and two small bottoms were paddled later.

In 1901, Richard Ribbentrop was promoted to major and transferred from quiet, charming Kassel to Metz, the harsh garrison city in Lorraine. Metz was the scene of Prussia's greatest triumph and France's great military disaster. In 1871, the entire French garrison of 100,000 troops had surrendered to the Prussians, and now Metz was very Prussian indeed. Metz was the army, and the army was Metz.

A young artillery major, especially one without a title, could easily become invisible. Fortunately for him, Major Ribbentrop came to the attention of General Haeseler, a much feared eccentric, famous for his spartan ways and shabby, worn-out uniforms. He was the sort of general Richard Ribbentrop respected,[4] because he was ahead of his time, almost in the mould of the American West Pointers. To Richard Ribbentrop, being an officer was a beloved profession, not a playful semi-hobby. General Haeseler's successor also recognized Major Ribbentrop's talent and kept him as aide-de-camp.

How best to describe the brusque Major? In his second son's rather conventional words: he had a heart of gold, was well versed in politics and the arts, and insisted that the hand was 'for reaching out in friendship or grasping the sword. Nothing in between'.[5] Yet, for the time, the circumstances and his profession, he seemed unusually caring. For the sake of his sick wife he avoided the crowded central section of Metz and rented a house in quiet, suburban Queuleu.

The boys attended upper school in Metz. Joachim was quite confident he would dazzle everyone. There were fifty pupils in his class, but at the end of the winter term he ranked only thirty-second. He earned a paternal thrashing and forfeited his long-expected Christmas gift: a violin. Major Ribbentrop had made his point. Years later, Frau Meissner, wife of President Paul von Hindenburg's State Secretary, who had been a teacher in Joachim's upper school in Metz, said he 'was the most stupid in his class, full of vanity and very pushy'.[6] Others said he got away with everything thanks to his great charm. Both of these views would follow him throughout his public life. Many old-time Nazis resented his closeness to Adolf Hitler and his worldly, cosmopolitan ways. Many of the professional diplomats, mostly of aristocratic family, called him a parvenu, an *arriviste*, an amateur, a dilettante. Still, he succeeded quite remarkably and remained unscathed in the volatile and dangerous world of Nazi politics. It throws his reputation for supposed stupidity into doubt, though his reputation for arrogance might have been justified. No doubt he was very resentful and self-protective.

Joachim's mother was sinking fast. To please her and placate his father, he worked hard, and by Easter his school report was good. He was given his first, beloved violin. In his memoirs he said that music took a leading place in his heart. At thirteen, he played in several concerts and even thought of becoming a professional violinist.[7] 'My violin went with me everywhere, throughout my life. It never let me down as so many people did. Nuremberg proved that! My violin was always my comfort!' The would-be violinist was one day to join the would-be artist.

Later, much later, he was to own a Stradivarius,[8] bought for a fortune in gold Marks through Charles Evel, a famous Paris dealer in rare instruments, after the violin had been put up for sale by its Jewish owner. After von Ribbentrop's execution, it was stolen from his estate, probably by a soldier of the Allied occupation forces. It re-emerged for sale twenty years later, and according to some experts it turned out to be a fake, fabricated by Voller, a famed forger, in London.[9]

Sophie Ribbentrop died on 28 February 1902, when Joachim was nine. The children were devastated. She was buried on one of her father's Saxon estates in Groitsch, where the Ribbentrop children had often holidayed, learning to ride ponies and to hunt.

Now the Major and his children moved to Belle Isle Street in the centre of the city of Metz,[10] and the boys returned to the Kaiserliche Lyzeum (upper school). Richard Ribbentrop, a man who had done all he could for his invalid wife, now felt free to marry again. His new wife, Olga Margarete von Prittwitz und Gaffron, was a charming and cheerful woman, but the children seemed reluctant to let her take their dead mother's place. It was understandable. Their mother had been a dream, a myth, a vague presence in an upstairs bedroom, unscolding, unpunishing.

Joachim managed to finish *Obersekunda*,[11] the grade just below senior year. He never sat for his *Abitur*, the equivalent of the French *Baccalauréat* or the British A-level examination. This was not unusual. Many boys finished their schooling before the *Abitur*, particularly if they had no plans to enter university. Joachim had plans which were much more adventurous.

Richard Ribbentrop's dream of seeing both boys enter a *Kadetten-anstalt*,[12] a military academy, soon foundered. Lothar's health was much too delicate for this sort of rigorous schooling. Then Joachim cranked up his courage: he absolutely *refused*! He wanted to learn foreign languages and leave home and travel the world. Boys all over the world were gripped with the fever to travel, to explore. Each country had its new colonies; deserts were to be crossed, mountains to be climbed and jungles to be conquered. German boys were devoted to Karl May, the turn-of-the-century writer of adventure novels. This was probably the first link between Hitler and Joachim. They were both Karl May enthusiasts. Joachim's closest ally was an elderly relative, his 'aunt' Gertrud von Ribbentrop (from the titled side of the family), who often stayed with them in Metz. Sometimes one branch of a family received a title in multiple-principality empires like Germany, while the other branch stayed without a 'von'. In this case, Gertrud's father, Karl Barthold, had been Quartermaster General to the King of Prussia. According to the *Almanach da Gotha*, which records German titles, Karl Barthold von Ribbentrop was born in 1822 and died in 1893. He was elevated to his title in 1884 in Berlin. So Karl Barthold was indeed a *von* Ribbentrop, as was his daughter Gertrud Charlotte, who was born in Berlin in 1863 and died in Naumburg in 1943. (Naumburg was to be Major Richard Ribbentrop's retirement home.) 'Aunt' Gertrud was the boys' ally. She understood their sense of adventure. She had a small income and was willing to help them.

Much later, on 15 May 1925,[13] she was to be repaid for her early support. At Joachim's suggestion, she adopted the thirty-two-year-old Joachim and invested him with her 'von'. He was already a married man. In return, the newly named Joachim von Ribbentrop provided her with a life-long monthly pension of 450 Marks.[14]

So, with 'Aunt' Gertrud's help, the boys went to study French at a boarding school in Grenoble: Joachim had won his first battle with his strict father. In his memoirs he would say, 'I often wondered if this was the way to treat children and decided not to do the same to mine.'[15] Indeed, Joachim and Annelies von Ribbentrop seem to have been caring and generous parents to their three boys and two girls.

The newlywed Richard Ribbentrops attracted many new friends. They became favourite hosts and desirable guests in the tight military hierarchy of Metz. Richard Ribbentrop, now a lieutenant-colonel, was extremely patriotic and a great admirer of Prince Otto von Bismarck, the Iron Chancellor, the man who had forged the German Reich. At the same time, he admired his ambitious young Emperor Kaiser Wilhelm II, but when the Kaiser abruptly dismissed the patriarchal Prince Bismarck over some difference in policy, Richard Ribbentrop was deeply offended. This began many years of doubt about imperial policy. He felt he could not keep quiet. Despite his delicate assignment as senior aide to the commanding general of the garrison, he openly criticized the young Kaiser's military policies. In 1908, after an agonizing battle of conscience, he finally decided to resign his commission.[16]

In an unusual show of concern, his commanding general asked him to reconsider, or at least to postpone his decision. The German army could ill afford to lose a young staff officer of such talent. But Colonel Ribbentrop was adamant. He was the antithesis of the oft-caricatured, prototypical, tightly corseted, semi-literate Prussian officer–aristocrat. His resignation and its rationale caused a sensation in a city which was totally wedded to the army.[17] Military officers usually kept their political opinions to themselves.

The Ribbentrops were sad to leave their French friends in Alsace

Lorraine. Joachim always claimed special affection for the French, their ways and their language. Besides, Metz was wild about tennis. Joachim had played in all the tennis tournaments, some of which he had won. He would always love the game and through it met his wife. Later they built their own tennis court in Berlin-Dahlem, a rare luxury. From Grenoble, the boys joined the family in Arosa, the glossy Swiss ski resort. Now came Joachim's first taste of *la vie internationale*. He steered his bobsleigh, 'Meteor', manned by an English girl and an English clergyman, with papa Richard Ribbentrop at the brake, and this unlikely crew won several small races. The boys also took private English lessons and practised it on the many British and Canadian holidaymakers. Their tutor was an eccentric expatriate Englishman,[18] and they were completely fascinated by his lavish Edwardian style. He even introduced them to some of the British classics.

For the first time, Joachim found a way to relate to his father. He listened carefully to Richard Ribbentrop's political views, probably his first introduction to the subject. Since his father was a Bismarckian, Joachim was certainly treated to a full measure of the Prussian-guided pan-Europeanism of Prince Otto Edward Leopold von Bismarck-Schönhausen. It is odd that the young Joachim, who was probably force-fed Bismarck's anti-Austrian views, would one day become the virtual slave of an Austrian. During that winter in Arosa, the boys befriended a young Canadian girl and her family, who would be important to them later, on the other side of the Atlantic. Meanwhile, they daydreamed of seeking their fortunes in South or East Africa.[19]

In 1909 when Joachim was sixteen, the boys were invited to London by the family of Dr Grandage,[20] a famous surgeon and a friend of the senior Ribbentrops. The Grandages lived in garden- and park-ringed South Kensington. Both boys were deeply impressed by London and by the great kindness of their hosts. Before long, the Ribbentrop boys became devotees of the 'English way'. As Joachim was to write in his memoirs: 'The nonchalant ways of the British upper classes impressed my brother and me very much. Later, I found out that despite their nonchalance they were hard-working and committed, socially and politically.' His liking for England seemed real. Much later, having served in the war, he returned to England on business in 1920. He stayed at Brown's Hotel in Dover Street, a Victorian bastion of Englishness, and he still 'felt as much at home in London as if I had never left it'. Yet Ribbentrop never really learned the ways of the British, no matter how deeply he believed he had. He loved their style but often failed to see their substance.

Nevertheless, he wrote quite paradoxically that he was 'so sorry I never told Adolf Hitler what the British Empire meant. They say I gave him bad advice that the British are weak and degenerate. The opposite is true!

I always emphasized in my talks with Hitler the mighty power of their Empire and the heroic attitude of their ruling circles.'[21] Perhaps, since his memoirs were written in his jail cell in Nuremberg many months after the collapse of Nazi Germany, they reflect a revision of some of his earlier views, or perhaps he believed these things but could never persuade his Führer.

While the boys were in London with the Grandages, the rest of the Ribbentrops had remained in Arosa, enjoying their new freedom from the strict duties, constraints, snobbery and chauvinism of army life. Perhaps there were also some remaining tensions between the boys and their stepmother. Whatever the cause, late in 1910 the boys announced that, instead of coming to Arosa, they wished to find work in Canada. Surprisingly, there were no parental objections, though the boys were only nineteen and seventeen. Richard Ribbentrop seemed reconciled to his sons' independence.

By now Joachim was a handsome, blond young man with a fashionably bland face, blue eyes and a deep cleft in his chin. Years later, 'Chips' Channon, a well-known London wit of the 1930s, would say that the famed hostess Emerald, Lady Cunard 'fell in love with Ribbentrop's dimple'.[22] Lothar, the elder brother, was a charming, quiet boy who soon began to show the first signs of severe illness.

Why Canada? The answer is rather mysterious. Did the senior Ribbentrops accept Canada as a desirable option, a safer form of adventure than Africa? Was it the lure of the new world with its Indians and cowboys? Was it because they knew that they would see their Canadian friends from Arosa? Or was it perhaps because of the brothers von Alvensleben, later known as the 'notorious' Alvenslebens?[23]

Alvo and Eno von Alvensleben, from Berlin, were land speculators and adventurers who had set up an investment business in western Canada. In 1904, Alvo moved to Vancouver while Eno manned the Berlin office. There he planted the hooks into the 'fish' which Alvo reeled in, all the way across the Atlantic to British Columbia. As the sons of a former Imperial Ambassador to the Court of St Petersburg, they were certainly well connected and, though they had very little cash, they had a lot of imagination and boatloads of charm. Alvo had invested some of his family's money in the Vancouver area, and he made a large profit, which he advertised. Soon he became the talk of Berlin's financial circles. He then married a wealthy Canadian girl and became a fixture in Vancouver society.

Many prominent Germans like the future Chancellor Bethmann-Hollweg, Prussian cavalry hero General von Mackensen, Emma Mumm of the champagne Mumms and eventually even Kaiser Wilhelm himself soon invested with Alvo. Leading German families then began to pour their money and their youngest sons into western Canada. Finally, the von Alvenslebens got backing from German banks and collected an investment fund of ten million dollars, a huge sum of money at the time.

By 1911, German money, clubs and societies dominated Vancouver. The Deutsche Klub on Granville Street was one of the city's most fashionable venues, with members like millionaire yachtsman Hans von Grävenitz and one of von Mackensen's grandsons, Lieutenant von Tumplin, a dashing, sabre-scarred expatriate. There were also solid bankers like Johannes Wulfsohn.[24] Von Alvensleben then built an exclusive resort, a *Luftkurort*. Like many young Germans who read about them, the Ribbentrop boys seem to have been dazzled by the von Alvenslebens. They had seen the von Alvensleben advertisements and the adventure they promised. So many Germans were talking about them and dreaming about making their fortunes in Canada.

In the end, the Alvensleben enterprises would collapse, but it seems probable that Joachim eventually met Alvo von Alvensleben in Canada. Certainly they had much contact later, and Alvo was to be friendly with Joachim for years.

One autumn day in 1910 the brothers Ribbentrop set sail for Canada from England on a ship of the White Star Line.

THREE

CANADA, 1911–1914

―――

'The Wild West'

The newly arrived Ribbentrop brothers were immediately treated to a boisterous dose of North Americanism. Their Canadian friends, as Joachim explained, set out to 'cure them of their pre-World War London airs'. No more la-de-da 'How d'y' do?' or 'Don't y' know?' Several of their Montreal friends must have been visitors to Arosa, and some of them were probably Jewish. In his memoirs, Joachim von Ribbentrop protests that he is no anti-Semite[1] and that his 'Montreal friends could have given proof of that'. He loved Montreal 'and its diversions, poker, tennis, rugby and particularly ice hockey'. He was a handsome boy, so girls were no doubt part of the 'diversions'.

His first job was as a clerk at Molson's Bank.[2] Then he became a timekeeper on a vast reconstruction project of the great Quebec Bridge, which had collapsed with a tragic loss of life and was now being rebuilt. Documents about the project list contractors called M.P. and J.T. Davis,[3] who were probably Joachim's employers. Coincidentally, according to the boys a prosperous Montreal family named Davis 'adopted' them. If the Davises were Jewish, they probably were the friends who could prove he was no anti-Semite.[4]

The Ribbentrop name can also be found in John Lovell & Sons' Montreal City Directory every year from 1911 to 1914. 'Ribbentrop, Joachim, bds 103 Stanley' appears in each one, although he seems to have spent little time in Montreal after he had been hired by the Canadian Pacific Railroad as a clerk–timekeeper. This finally brought him to Vancouver and to his dream territory, the rugged and adventurous Canadian West. Lothar stayed in Montreal and, before leaving, Joachim arranged with the German Consul in Montreal to waive his own obligation to serve as a one-year volunteer in the German army.[5] Like most young men who had gone to upper schools, he had the right to volunteer for one year of duty and then to become an officer candidate, rather than to serve the full three conscripted years. His dispensation was not unusual – it was often given to Germans studying abroad.

At last, Joachim was in von Alvensleben country. Nowhere else in North America was there such an overwhelming German influence. Joachim drank German beer in the German Rathskeller in the Copp Building[6] on Hastings Street in Vancouver, surrounded by German loggers, roustabouts and vagabonds. For a while, life was how he had dreamed it should be in his boyhood. Then illness interfered. He developed a tubercular kidney[7] and returned to Montreal, where he was hospitalized and the kidney was removed. Strangely, as if to keep all blame from his late mother, he wrote later that he had contracted tuberculosis after 'eating some infected eggs'. While Lothar stayed in Canada, he returned to Germany to recuperate with his family at their new house in Naumburg. In 1913 he recrossed the Atlantic to New York, where he stayed a few weeks. A chance acquaintance introduced him to some 'prominent New Yorkers', and he seems to have done some freelance newspaper reporting, which 'taught him about the American mania for news, action and sensations'. His memoirs are sketchy about this time, and there are no witnesses. However, all who knew him speak of his good looks and charm, and it is obvious that he was what the French call a *débrouillard* and modern Americans an operator. He soon returned to Canada and Lothar. He had briefly visited Ottawa earlier and found the Canadian capital to have the sort of Anglo-North American mixture he loved. Besides, Lothar had gone to live there, and now Joachim joined him. The boys began a small wine import–export business, financed by a modest inheritance from their mother. This was Joachim's first taste of business. It tasted good.

Joachim also set about introducing himself to Ottawa society. Several things were in his favour: his blond, blue-eyed good looks and precise 'British' English, his love for dramatics and music, his tennis and, strangely, the fact that he was a German.

Ottawa social life revolved around Rideau Hall, the residence of His Majesty's Governor General, His Royal Highness the Duke of Connaught, the younger brother of King Edward VII. His Duchess was the former Princess Louise Marguerite of Prussia and, of course, a German. The Duke, like most of his generation of the English royal family, spoke English with a strong German accent, in good part because of his German father. The entire Connaught household spoke German, including the servants. It was easy pickings for a handsome young German boy.

In 1913, Joachim was introduced to Their Royal Highnesses by Sir Charles Fitzpatrick,[8] Lord Chief Justice of Canada. Sir Charles was the father of one of Joachim's lady friends, Patricia (later Lady Ramsey of London).[9] Joachim played violin for the Connaughts and tennis at the Rideau Club. He skated at the Minto Club, acted in amateur plays, attended costume parties, danced well and was, according to Ottawa's ladies, 'splendidly tailored'. He was a success. He also paid his own way because the German Mark was strong, and his little import–export business provided him with income. For him, the year 1913–14 would have been paradise if only Lothar had been in better health. From all contemporary accounts, the Joachim Ribbentrop of those days was a thoroughly likeable fellow. Canadian friends who saw him much later in London during the 1930s could not believe the change in him. The 'nice guy had turned into a stuffed shirt'.[10] But in 1914, before the outbreak of the First World War, he was greatly liked by both men and women, especially the latter. He even planned to marry a Canadian girl.

On 4 August 1914, Joachim played tennis with a young lady. Afterwards, he had dinner with her at Chateau Laurier, escorted her home and then took a train to neutral New York. War had broken out in Europe. He had to face the difficult choice of country or brother. Lothar was mortally sick. At his insistence, Joachim left for Germany, and Lothar was interned as an enemy alien at St Agathe Military Sanatorium in Montreal, where he was very well treated. He finally died four years later in Lugano, Switzerland.[11]

Joachim felt duty-bound to return to Germany and join up, though with only one kidney he was unfit: 'I knew every man was needed.' After arriving in New York, he tried every possible way to book a transatlantic passage, but it was not an easy task because many shipping lines refused to transport Germans on account of the tight British blockade. Then he discovered that the Holland–America Line had decided to sell passage to Germany to a group of returning Germans on one of their steamships, the *Potsdam*. He immediately bought a ticket.[12]

Most of the voyage was rather boisterous. There were a hundred wine-swilling German passengers, many of them reserve officers on their way home to join their regiments.[13] There was much bragging, joke-telling, gallows humour and gambling, accompanied by a flood of radio reports of early German victories. This set off even more idiotic celebrations. Everyone was drunkenly happy, but Joachim was worried. According to his memoirs, before embarking he heard in New York that the Ottawa papers had taken to calling him the sinister 'spy' Ribbentrop.[14] In fact, there were no such press reports.

There are several romanticized versions of his 1914 trip to Germany. Some were the product of the well-trained publicists of the Nazi era. For instance, he was said to have buried himself for days deep under the ship's coal supply at the risk of his life. The truth is that he chatted with a British army officer who came aboard when they entered British waters off Falmouth in order to check on the passengers. Joachim avoided suspicion by conveniently mentioning the Duke and Duchess of Connaught in fairly flawless 'Canadianized' English, and by a happy coincidence the very pukka British officer had once been the Duke's aide. When the British officer walked away, Joachim bribed a crew member to hide him in a coal locker below decks which was safe but dirty and was needed only until the Dutch-flagged *Potsdam* cleared British waters. Several other German passengers were taken ashore to be interned for the duration, a fate much better than death, though it ended any dreams they might have had of martial glory.

From neutral Rotterdam Joachim made his way to his father's house in Naumburg, a small town on the Saale river, south-west of Leipzig. Ever the patriot, Colonel Richard Ribbentrop had rejoined the army, and now Joachim volunteered to join the 12th Hussars, his maternal grandfather's old regiment based in Torgau on the Elbe river, fifty miles south of Berlin. (Forty-one years later, Russian and American soldiers would embrace at Torgau.) Probably making use of his family's connections with the regiment, and telling of his long trip across the Atlantic, he charmed his way past the medical examiners and was accepted. Among his new young regimental comrades was the eighteen-year-old Count Wolf Heinrich von Helldorf, who was to play an important part much later in Joachim (von) Ribbentrop's life. Helldorf became one of the great crooks of the Hitler years and ended his life hanged like von Ribbentrop, but hanged by Hitler's SS.[15]

His Canadian years had reinforced Joachim Ribbentrop's immature views of the British and, oddly, he never seemed to outgrow them. His adoration for the Empire seems to bear out the opinion of many of his contemporaries, that for all his allegiance to the revolutionary Nazi movement, in truth he was a royalist and an arch-conservative. It explains why he favoured nineteenth-century power-bloc thinking while Adolf Hitler thought in twentieth-century ideological and racial terms. At times, Hitler reluctantly found himself impressed by the world of the international aristocracy, trapped as he was by his own, humble, Austro-Catholic roots. Whenever this happened, he would soon regret it and then would delight in pointing a disdainful finger at the so-called upper crust (*feine Leute*). Since von Ribbentrop was often his nearest target, he became one of Hitler's favourite scapegoats. Whenever the Führer found himself distrusting or disliking something worldly or upper-class, it was 'typically Ribbentrop'.

The sum of early Ribbentrop delusions about the British after his years in Canada is quite startling. He admired the 'cleverness with which the Crown tied together the leading men of the far-flung British Empire through the system of *Knighthoods* and *Peerages*'.[16] He pointed at the Hudson Bay Company's Lord Strathcona, a Canadian, as a typical example of 'tying a colonial to the Crown'. Neither the First nor the Second World War, wrote Ribbentrop, was popular in the Dominions, but the Empire was willing to give its sons because of the personal appeal of the Crown. He added that he 'often told Adolf Hitler about the artful system the British used to forge their future, the harmonious blending of continuing old nobility with ambitious, newly created aristocrats, all anchored by the Crown'. He obviously saw 'Englishness' only in the top layer and had little understanding for the gut strength of Britain's working class. Hitler, he wrote, always listened attentively. Had things gone differently, Hitler 'might have adopted some of these ways'. In Ribbentrop's words: 'I cannot say if the Crown would ever have returned to Germany, but between 1933 and 1934 Adolf Hitler repeatedly told me: "Everything for a German Imperial House." '[17]

Annelies von Ribbentrop, who edited her husband's memoirs, noted:

> In the summer of 1933 [a few months after he became Chancellor] we once breakfasted alone with Adolf Hitler in the [Hotel] Kaiserhof [across the street from the Presidential Palace]. Hitler spoke of restoring the Hohenzollern monarchy, and he did so with great emphasis and warmth. He indicated that he was thinking of Prince August Wilhelm. At the celebration in the Potsdam Garrison Church, it was evident that, in the section reserved for the Imperial Family, the empty central armchair remained reserved for the [absent] Kaiser.[18]

Prince August Wilhelm, familiarly and disrespectfully known in Berlin society as Auwi, was the fourth of the Kaiser's six sons and the only one who became a devoted Nazi. At first, Hitler paid court to him but soon lost interest. Auwi, however, remained devoted to the Führer, probably hoping for an Imperial restoration. He was even made a stormtroop (SA) general (Obergruppenführer). After the Second World War, he served thirty months in jail as a 'co-conspirator', the technical term for those who had helped the Nazis perform war crimes.

The Potsdam occasion mentioned by Annelies von Ribbentrop was a charade staged by Hitler in an attempt to sanitize his raucous movement in the eyes of Germany's upper classes and the outside world.

On 21 March 1933, forty-nine days after his appointment as Reich Chancellor, he used the Potsdam Garrison Church, Prussia's most sacred symbol of aristocracy and of the officer corps, to stage the opening of the first Reichstag (Parliament) of his regime. It was a cynical display of seeming respect for the President of the Reich, the ancient Field Marshal von Hindenburg, and for 'Prussia's old, noble spirit'. Von Hindenburg and the aristocrats appeared, dressed in their Imperial uniforms, chests ablaze with old decorations. A demure Hitler, who wore a discreet civilian cutaway, stood by while von Hindenburg saluted the Kaiser's empty chair and laid a wreath at the grave of Frederick the Great. There were speeches by the old Prussian Marshal and the former Austrian corporal, who proclaimed the 'marriage of old greatness and new strength'. Finally, there was a twenty-one-gun salute and then a parade of army and party units. No one in the glittering diplomatic gallery of foreigners seemed altogether convinced that Hitler's attempt to make the Nazis respectable had succeeded,[19] but von Ribbentrop was willing to believe.

FOUR

WAR

—

'The Hussar'

In 1914 the 12th 'Torgau' Hussars were a typical semi-elite cavalry unit of the post-Bismarck era. German regiments were now numbered so that they became part of the 'new' pan-German Imperial Army, but they often retained local designations like 'Torgau' to celebrate pride and tradition. Other regiments were named after their princes or their commanders. The concept of a *German* army was still quite new, and there was a certain residual reluctance on the part of old regiments to de-Bavarianize, de-Hessianize or de-Saxonize themselves. The Prussian military spirit was dominant, but even Prussian regiments had their complaints. The Prussian Guards, for instance, could not use the prefix 'Royal', though certain Bavarian regiments had this privilege.

Field-grey uniforms for combat and fatigue duties had been introduced as recently as 1910.[1] Old soldiers shuddered at the sameness of grey. In 1914 all regiments adopted them for general use, albeit reluctantly. It Germanized the German army, although, as Ribbentrop pointed out, he became a 'blue' Hussar, a reference to the cornflower-blue tunics traditionally worn by the 12th 'Torgau'.[2] The Hussars were light cavalry, 'raiding' cavalry, recalling Attila and his wild, Mongol horsemen – the short, braided Hussar dress jacket was still known as the 'Attila'. The Hussars provided a very dashing way to soldier, and Joachim von Ribbentrop's memoirs related the usual story of the young gentleman who joins the cavalry and is told that while *he* may think he can ride he certainly cannot do it the army way.

While Joachim was receiving his equestrian come-uppance, in Bavaria hundreds of miles to the south a young Austrian volunteer named Adolf Hitler was learning soldiering in the 16th Bavarian Reserve Regiment of Infantry, known at the 'List' Regiment after its commanding officer. Hitler was no officer candidate, and his regiment was by no means elite, but both of these recruits would later win the Iron Cross First Class, and both awards, though undoubtedly deserved, are often questioned by historians. According to the historian Joachim Fest,[3] the Führer of the German Reich was never anxious to show that he was recommended for the decoration by his Jewish regimental adjutant, Hugo Gutmann. Von Ribbentrop simply reports that he served with the 12th 'Torgau' Hussars on the Eastern and Western Fronts as an officer and was wounded several times. His Iron Cross, according to his account, was awarded in 1917 before he was found unfit for further combat duty and assigned to staff work. It was suggested in the 1930s that he had applied for the decoration long after he was assigned to staff duty back in Berlin.[4] Of course, this was forcefully denied by his widow. But, even if it was true, it was by no means unusual. Many combat soldiers were decorated long after a specific act of courage. The rumour was probably circulated by Hitler's jealous 'old fighters', the Führer's paladins since the Days of the Struggle in the early 1920s. In their eyes Ribbentrop was a Joachim-come-lately, a *nouveau* National Socialist, a man with a high number on his party membership card, betraying his late (1932) conversion. Hitler's own number was 7. Von Ribbentrop's was 1,119,927.

There have also been rumours about the last year of the war, when First Lieutenant Ribbentrop did administrative work. Putzi Hanfstaengl, the Harvard-educated Munich art dealer, a former Hitler intimate who fell out with his Führer, claimed that Ribbentrop was absent without leave during his regiment's 1918 withdrawal to the east. A man called Douglas Glen even published a book in London in 1941 which claimed that in 1915 Ribbentrop recrossed the Atlantic on a U-boat and became an espionage associate of Franz von Papen, then an attaché at the German Embassy in Washington.[5] (Von Papen was expelled from the USA for his illegal espionage activity.) Glen also claims that Ribbentrop later worked for von Papen as an espionage agent in Constantinople. While he was supposedly doing this secret work, he was being accused of desertion, and it was von Papen who convened a court of honour to 'clear Ribbentrop of the charges'. However, all this is a most unlikely scenario. Cut off by the war, Glen probably had few ways of obtaining legitimate facts, so he invented them.

According to the most believable sources, the war ended somewhat differently for Joachim Ribbentrop. He was posted to Constantinople as one of German General Erich von Falkenhayn's assistants. The Turks spoke French, as did Lieutenant Ribbentrop, and he was needed to interpret at sensitive meetings. General von Falkenhayn had been assigned to convince the Turks, Germany's half-hearted allies, to attack Suez. Ribbentrop was sent to Berlin to deliver his general's report about 1918 conditions in Turkey to the War Ministry. This trip reinforced Ribbentrop's rightist views. He recalled that there were more than 20,000 deserters hiding out in Berlin yet the government did nothing and 'stuck its head in the sand [*Vogel Strauss Politik*][6] in order not to stir up a fuss'.

He returned to Constantinople, disgusted with what he had seen and overcome by a feeling of betrayal.

Then in October 1918 the Turks suddenly signed an armistice with the Western Allies, and German officers had twenty-four hours to leave Constantinople or face internment. They were given temporary shelter in the home of an acquaintance of Ribbentrop, the Jewish manager of a German bank.[7] They then crossed to the Asiatic side of the Bosphorus and tried to find a way home to Germany. During this time Ribbentrop slipped back across the Bosphorus once more to destroy confidential papers in their deserted Constantinople office.[8] This was quite daring. The Kaiser abdicated in November 1918. Ribbentrop and the others were eventually caught and interned in Turkey, but Swedish friends helped them get back to Berlin via Italy. While in Constantinople, Ribbentrop had met von Papen, who was also stationed there following his expulsion from Washington and who in 1932 was to play a major role in his political career.

After the Armistice in spring 1919, Ribbentrop rented a small room in Berlin's Meinicken Strasse, a small, fashionable street off the Kurfürstendamm. Berlin was in the midst of revolution. Mutinous troops roamed everywhere. Officers like Ribbentrop were instructed to remove their epaulets of rank. Lieutenant Ribbentrop, still in the army, was employed at the War Ministry as a language specialist and was soon assigned to General von Seeckt's delegation to the Peace Conference at Versailles. There were 180 people in the delegation, but no one seems to recall Lieutenant Ribbentrop.[9] In fact he resigned his commission before his departure for Versailles, so he never witnessed the signing of what he considered a shameful treaty.

FIVE

BERLIN, 1919

'The Champagne Salesman'

The newly demobilized Joachim Ribbentrop remembered Berlin in 1919 as a place where crooks flourished and young men tried to 'wipe away the memory of their useless sacrifice'.[1] Once more, he said, Germany was divided. Division was its inherited disease. 'Suddenly,' he wrote, 'everywhere there were Jews'[2] who took a 'less than pleasing' part in economic and cultural affairs. Nonetheless, according to Ribbentrop, there were 'many Jewish families who felt just like my Nationalist friends and suffered just as keenly about our loss'.

The defeated Germany of the First World War was not the defeated Germany of the Second World War: 1918 had brought very few obvious signs of defeat. Of course, there were those long lists of dead, wounded and missing, the military hospitals were filled with crippled soldiers, and hardly a family had escaped some grim news about its men in uniform. But, until the very last day of the war, the newspapers told of victorious combat actions. The German combat soldier was still on foreign soil, and not a single enemy had crossed into the sacred Vaterland. It seemed a stalemate. To the average *Bürger* this was not a signal for disaster.

Compare this with the Second World War: in May 1945 Germany's cities lay in smouldering ruins, half of Germany's soldiers were dead, wounded or captured in faraway places. What remained of Germany's battered troops had been kicked out of Russia, North Africa, France, Belgium, Holland, Norway, Denmark, the Baltics and Italy. They were back inside Germany, too beaten to mount a final defence. The Russians were in the suburbs of Berlin, the Americans were entering Munich's Englischer Garten, and the British were nearing Hamburg's Inner Alster. In 1945 most Germans were homeless, shocked and hungry, and all around them lay the bombed-out ruins of their great cities. The booming enemy artillery was within close, lethal reach. Adolf Hitler's death did not come as a surprise (he had promised to die fighting, but committed suicide). Germany's helpless, exhausted surrender was more than expected.

By contrast it can be understood that the announcement on 9 November 1918 of the Kaiser's abdication came as a deep shock to many Germans. (Oddly, Wilhelm II abandoned only his title of Kaiser. Perhaps he still had the curious notion that he could eventually return as the King of Prussia.) Revolution followed at once. Led by mutinous sailors from the north of Germany, Berlin's working classes mounted a red-coloured revolt, named *Spartakus* after the rebellious Spartan gladiator–prisoner of Rome. Compared with its Russian predecessor, the German Communist revolution was mild. There were few deaths. The titled gentlemen of the fashionable Union Klub on Schadowstrasse were ousted from their red-leather armchairs and harassed and insulted, but they were not physically harmed. The Imperial Guards at the various palaces and Imperial residences surrendered without a fight. Their Kaiser had fled. Their oath was void. It must have been an extraordinary sight when a venerable Imperial Court Chancellor signalled surrender from a balcony of Berlin's Imperial Palace by waving a small square of red cloth tied to an umbrella.

That week, red hammer-and-sickle flags flew all over working-class Berlin, but the Communist Spartakus revolution did not last more than a few days. A coalition for a democratic socialist republic under future President Ebert was assembled as early as 10 November 1918. Then came various attempted coups of the left and the right, and some vicious political assassinations like the murder of socialists Karl Liebknecht and Rosa Luxemburg. But somehow the new republic survived. It tried as best it could to deal with the pressing social and economic hardships of a beaten country which was being further battered by the demands of her harsh victors. Many small businesses suffered, and unemployment grew. Germany's starchily inflexible lower-middle class lacked the guts and the wit to help themselves. They had always been professional underlings.

Meanwhile, entrepreneurs, new and old, who understood the international market, made fortunes in property and war-surplus goods. Companies which exported, like Siemens, the giant AEG and Daimler Benz, did very well, as did international banking houses. There were many profiteers. One man's loss becomes another man's profit when the seller is desperate and the buyer has 'hard' currency.

Post-war Berlin had not changed very much. Its famous sense of humour and its tolerance were strained but still in place. Joachim Ribbentrop did not take long to find his way. Berlin never was a stuffy city, in part because of the early influence of the eccentric Frederick the Great, the Prussian soldier–king (1712–86). 'Fredericus Rex' preferred to speak French, loved flute concerts, encouraged French Huguenot immigration and even made life easier for his Jewish subjects (all the better if they made the *beau geste* of converting to the Protestant faith). At his superb castle, Sans Souci, in Potsdam he played host to revolutionary thinkers like Voltaire and Rousseau. This liberal tradition guaranteed Berliners a certain sense of freedom from the powers 'above'.

Besides, those who lived in the city on the Spree river were a strange mixture of Slavic, Celtic, Nordic and Frankish. Berlin always welcomed the new, the exotic, the strange. All through the Hitler years (and to this day), Yiddish and French expressions were part of the language – an aristocratic young man might complain that a girl he has met was *mies* (Yiddish for ugly) or a cab driver might talk about his *Miljö* (milieu). The Berlin of 1919 was raucous and dynamic. As Europe's youngest capital city, it lacked the ancient traditions of London, Paris and Rome, but it had elasticity and great recuperative power.

The 1919 revolution shed blood but was not bloodthirsty. In 1920 there were still riots in the streets, and shots were exchanged between political demonstrators, the police and hastily assigned troops, but Berlin's West End had its cafés and cabarets, its *thés dansants* and dinner parties. Rich women went to their dressmakers and coiffeurs, and straying husbands visited their mistresses in cosy little Charlottenburg flats. Most upper-class Berliners were not suffering financially. Their main complaints were that Germany had lost the war ('How could it happen to *us*?') and that the government seemed a disorganized shambles compared with the years of Imperial and aristocratic security. For upper-middle-class Germans, not knowing exactly what to expect was extremely painful. Even Berliners longed for 'order'. As Stendhal wrote, 'For the Germans, truth is not what exists but what ought to be true according to their system.' In this one respect, Berliners were typical Germans. After all, the reassuring Imperial government had been right there in Berlin. This was the Berlin Ribbentrop found in 1919.

One July day in 1919 Dr Paul Schwarz, a long-time member of Germany's elite Foreign Service, the Auswärtiges Amt, was lunching with Ottmar Strauss and some others. Strauss, a prominent industrialist and a Jew, introduced him to a recently demobilized officer named Ribbentrop, who spoke German with a slight English accent. The young man explained that he had studied in London and had lived in Canada. He had been sent to meet Strauss by Mathias Erzberger, the Minister of Finance. Ribbentrop was pleasant company. He spoke several languages and was descended from an old military family. He was also looking for a job. He was very courteous, very 'correct'. He said he had heard Schwarz's name mentioned by German diplomats in Turkey who told him about his Iron Cross First Class and how he won it as a civilian. Schwarz played it down. Then someone ordered Henkell *Sekt* (champagne), and Ribbentrop said, 'You must admit there's no comparison with the real, French stuff.' This irritated some of the patriots at the table, but his host

Ottmar Strauss agreed. He said, 'I just can't *get* the real stuff.' Ribbentrop promised to find him a price list for French champagne. Schwarz thought him rather a bore. Besides, the food at the restaurant was poor.

Thereafter Schwarz met the modest, well-mannered young Ribbentrop at several dinners given by Ottmar Strauss at the Hotel Esplanade. (He had provided both Strauss and Schwarz with the promised wine price list.)[3] One evening, Strauss said he had told Ribbentrop's patron, Erzberger, not to worry about his protégé. 'He won't need a job.[4] He'll be marrying Otto Henkell's daughter, Annelies!'

By coincidence, the Henkells were friends of Dr Paul Schwarz, and he had spent much time at the champagne family's home in Wiesbaden. Before long Otto Henkell asked him about Joachim Ribbentrop, and Schwarz said that Ribbentrop was well dressed, well brought up and kept his word.

Joachim Ribbentrop's first post-war business deal in August 1919 was the sale of six cases of Moët et Chandon champagne, vintage 1911, to Ottmar Strauss, his frequent host and first client. The cases came from a British officers' mess (the mess sergeant had been bribed). Ribbentrop made a small profit.[5]

In October 1933, eight months after Adolf Hitler became Chancellor, Ottmar Strauss needed a favour from von Ribbentrop, though he was still a nonentity among the Nazis. He said that von Ribbentrop still treated him warmly, addressing his letters 'My dear friend' and still using the very familiar *Du*. Later, in 1937, when Strauss was in Zurich and von Ribbentrop was Ambassador to the Court of St James and 'special, personal adviser to the Führer', he asked von Ribbentrop for help. 'Joachim behaved like a swine. After all, hadn't I done everything for him in the old days when *he* needed help? I never expected this. A secretary of the Consulate General in Zurich just called me up and informed me that Herr von Ribbentrop is unable to answer your letter.'[6] This treatment of old friend Ottmar Strauss is one of many such examples of Joachim von Ribbentrop's ambivalence, his fluctuating attitude towards Jews, which he exhibited throughout his life. It is the anti-Semitism of the socially ambitious and the insecure: when one fears being snubbed, one often finds someone to snub.

Even demonstrably anti-Nazi officials of the time often failed to recognize Jews as fellow German citizens. On 22 April 1933, three months after the Nazi takeover, Ernst von Weizsäcker, who was later von Ribbentrop's stubbornly opposed Chief of Staff (*Staats Sekretär*) and who was clearly anti-Hitler, wrote, 'It is extremely difficult for foreigners to understand anti-Jewish acts because they themselves did not get swamped by Jews.'[7]

In many ways, von Ribbentrop's life had none of the normal stages of most men's lives: no before-and-after school, before-and-after the army, before-and-after marriage. The drama of Joachim von Ribbentrop had only two acts: before Hitler and after Hitler. The longer he took part in the second act, the more he lost those things which he had felt and learned during the first act. Most men build on the foundation of their youth. Von Ribbentrop dismantled his. Most men's careers follow a certain logical progression. A few film stars or athletes achieve sudden international prominence when they are still young, but few businessmen, having gained the sort of mature success, wealth and local position which they can consider their final goal in life, are then suddenly launched on to the world's centre stage. Joachim and Annelies von Ribbentrop were highly successful big-city people, but before Hitler comparatively few people knew them. They had many friends in international business circles and had even made brief forays into international society or to the edge of politics, but on the scale of international renown they ranked near zero. Then with the sudden and irreversible power of an avalanche, the whole world began to see them, read about them, gossip about them and fear them. Kings and prime ministers flattered them and catered to them, while unseen others berated, ridiculed and condemned them.

The von Ribbentrops – and eventually they must be judged as a couple – did much to deserve obloquy and indeed adversity because of the bestiality which they helped to sustain by exploiting Nazi tyranny in the interests of their own deep-seated fears and ambitions. How this banal business couple marketed grief, their own and that of millions, lies at the core of their story.

SIX

BERLIN

———

'He Could Walk over Dead Bodies'

Although ex-Lieutenant Ribbentrop had made some money selling champagne to his friends, he needed a job, and he found one in the Berlin office of a Bremen cotton importer. He liked his kindly and understanding 'typically Hanseatic'[1]* employers but did not enjoy the textile field. He decided to stick with it only because he needed the money. Many of his brother's hospital bills in Lugano remained unpaid, though his father had tried unsuccessfully to tackle them and had even mortgaged his house in Naumburg.[2] Joachim soon settled them in full and also paid off his father's mortgage.

He wanted to start a business of his own, much like his little wine-importing firm in Canada, and he did so with a loan from a Jewish banker named Herbert Guttmann of Dresdner Bank,[3] who was a friend of Ottmar Strauss.

There are several versions of how Joachim met the wealthy Annelies Henkell, of the famous champagne family. The year was 1919. Some say he contacted the Henkells through his new wine business and was invited to their splendid home in Wiesbaden, where he then met Annelies. As Ribbentrop remembers it, he was holidaying at Bad Homburg, the smart spa, and they met during a tennis tournament. After a short engagement they married on 5 July 1920 at the Henkell villa in Wiesbaden.

Twenty-six years later, shortly before his execution, Joachim von Ribbentrop wrote of his warm love for his wife: 'my wife gave me over twenty-five years of immeasurable happiness and gave me "our five", our three sons and two daughters. It is more than a mere mortal may ask from the Fates.' Indeed, theirs was a closely bonded marriage. Many of his contemporaries agree that this may have been the cause of his down-

---

* Cities of the medieval Hanseatic trading league like Bremen, Hamburg and Lübeck were famed for their relaxed unhurried ways.

fall. The ambitious Annelies Henkell has even been described as his Lady Macbeth,[4] but there were never any complaints from her husband.

Shortly after the wedding, Joachim Ribbentrop was offered a partnership in the Berlin sales agency which represented Henkell. Contrary to many reports, he was never offered a partnership in the Henkell firm,[5] nor was he ever associated with the management of Henkell. There were many reasons for this arm's-length relationship. Annelies was a rebellious young woman, keenly aware of her parents' poor opinion of her handsome new husband.

Annelies was often pain-ridden and depressed.[6] Many called her difficult. One reason may have been that throughout her life she suffered from severe and chronic sinus infections. The headaches made her moody and irritable even as a young woman. Later, several operations scarred her forehead and produced a permanent frown. As a young woman she was attractive, though not as beautiful as her sister Fänn Artzen. People called Annelies chic, but no one thought her a great beauty.

Joachim was quite content with Otto Henkell's partnership offer and the chance to live in Berlin, which was at the centre of his plans. In Berlin they could lead the life they chose and keep their independence from the powerful senior Henkells.

There was never much love between the Henkells and the Ribbentrops. Otto Henkell once told a friend how sorry he was that Annelies had ever met Joachim.[7] Even Annelies' sister Fänn detested her brother-in-law. There was much strain. It was reported that later Ribbentrop sued Otto Henkell for being in arrears on payments promised to Annelies.[8]

Annelies' brother Stefan Karl, who was killed in the war, had married a rich Dutch girl, Fentner van Vlissingen, a Shell Oil heiress, who was very anti-Nazi. After her husband's death in combat, she made many anti-Hitler remarks and was finally jailed. Neither her sister-in-law Annelies nor Joachim von Ribbentrop, then a major Nazi official, ever came to her aid.[9]

Joachim Ribbentrop's new parents-in-law were an extraordinary couple. Otto Henkell was worldly and witty. His wife Käthe was born a Michel, one of Mainz's oldest wine-growing families. She was an eccentric, a fearless, monocle-wearing dowager who either loved or hated with no shadings in between. At the family mansion on Beethoven Strasse in Wiesbaden she conducted a powerful salon of politicians, artists, academics and men of industry. She said, 'Annelies is wilful and capricious. I tried to prevent her marriage to that adventurer. I detest him! He terrifies me. He could walk over dead bodies. He does not fit into our family. And that trick of getting himself adopted!' She was referring to the 'von' which he added to the Ribbentrop name when he was adopted by his 'Aunt' Gertrud in 1925. 'He is a laughing stock! His so-called society friends are laughing! I am a Michel of Mainz, the daughter of Geheimrath

[Privy Counsellor] Michel. Our family pokes fun at our "titled" son-in-law. He is a nasty fool and a dangerous fool.'[10]

But Annelies and Joachim von Ribbentrop clung together in rebellious union. Between his new job and her Henkell dowry they had plenty of money. They bought a superb home and property in garden-filled, suburban Dahlem at Lenzeallee 7–9, and added a tennis court and swimming pool; in the 1920s, these were a rare luxury, even in prosperous Dahlem. The mansions of Berlin's old, aristocratic families were in the Tiergarten district or near the Imperial Palace along Unter den Linden, but much of its new society, its successful industrialists and professionals, lived in Dahlem, where streets were quiet and tree-lined, and houses were called villas. Each villa had its butlers, chauffeurs and upstairs and downstairs maids. Dahlem's Protestant church was one of Berlin's 'smart' churches, and its pastor, Martin Niemöller, a former U-boat captain, was the 'society' pastor. Today's Dahlem is virtually unchanged, although the von Ribbentrop villa at Lenzeallee 7–9 is no more.

Joachim and Annelies seemed to have a sound marriage. Handsome Joachim was a bit of a boulevardier, and there are reports of his early and solitary philanderings in Berlin's heated round of *thés dansants*, parties and cabarets. He was often seen alone, and he was a *serious* dancer. He treated dancing almost as an art form, and he wore white tie and tails with great flair. One of his constant comrades on the dance circuit was a young Russian Jewish immigrant called Hoffelmann,[11] and they were known as 'Ribb and Hoff' or 'Hoff and Ribb'. One of the reasons for Joachim Ribbentrop's lonely forays was that Annelies was mostly pregnant. She bore two children in quick succession. Rudolf was born in Wiesbaden on 11 May 1921 and Bettina in Berlin on 20 July 1922.

When the young Ribbentrops were out as a couple, it was usually with the *nouveau riche*. Despite the superb villa and their great wealth, they had not yet found their place in 'upper' Berlin.

Given the political turmoil, the mood of Berlin between 1920 and 1930 was strangely light-hearted and full of humour. After the failed left-wing Spartakus revolt, there followed some right-wing attempts. In March 1920 came the Kapp *putsch*, which was named after its perpetrator, a prominent East Prussian reactionary. It was supported by small units of mutinous Reichswehr called the Ehrhardt Brigade led by a Captain Ehrhardt. The brigade moved into Berlin and installed itself near the Brandenburg Gate. An armoured train arrived at Anhalter station. The government decided to leave Berlin for Stuttgart, several of the senior Reichswehr generals having declared that 'Reichswehr will not shoot at Reichswehr.' Despite the reluctance of the legal government's generals to defend the new constitution, the Kapp *putsch* failed. It was simply not supported by the majority of Berliners, who protested by mounting a massive general strike.

Most Berliners showed sang-froid during this Berlin brand of insurrection. One socialist Cabinet member switched the doorplates from the offices of the socialist deputies to the reactionary German nationalist offices. 'The hell with them,' he said about the expected invaders, 'let them wreck the other party's typewriters!'[12] Minister of the Interior Heine would not leave Berlin – he refused to run. When the Cabinet returned to the capital after the *putsch*, he greeted them with a booming, 'Oh, it's you again?' and soon resigned.

Another right-wing blow was struck by a group of reactionary nationalist ex-officers who assassinated Walter Rathenau, the Foreign Minister, on 24 June 1922, as he was being driven to his office in an open car. Rathenau had ignored several threats and refused to take special precautions. The assassins objected to his attempt to use simple logic to prove to the Allies that Germany could not pay the Versailles reparations. The reactionary nationalists also hated him for signing the Rapallo Treaty of co-operation with the young Soviet Union. On 16 April 1922, Rathenau for Germany and Tchitcherin for the Soviet Union agreed to waive all mutual war claims, to unfreeze each other's holdings and to co-operate in future. (Obviously, they were more principled than the Nazis would be in 1939 when such a pact was signed by von Ribbentrop.) Finally, they hated Rathenau, who had given up a leading post in German industry to join the government for being a Jew.

In 1925, stolid President Ebert died, and old Field Marshal Paul von Hindenburg, the darling of the conservative nationalists and royalists, was elected president. He was a towering figure, physically and metaphorically, who remained unalterably the Junker, the quintessential Prussian officer.

Berlin was reviving as an international diplomatic centre. After the war, the decisions were being made in London, Paris and Washington. The first of many heads of state to visit the newly republican city was the exotic oriental potentate, King Aman-Ullah of Afghanistan. Every Berlin street boy learned to say his name: Amanulla! It rolled easily off the tongue and had a certain ring. At one state ceremony, the teetotaller Muslim King drank the republic's health in water. He then wanted to present a decoration to the President of Parliament who, regretfully and apologetically, had to turn it down. 'We are a republic, sir. You, sir, do not drink alcohol, and we cannot accept titles or decorations.' However, the magnificent red Afghan coat which accompanied the decoration was accepted and passed on to State Secretary Weissmann, a playboy and *bon vivant* who sported it a few nights later. The Berlin street wits promptly dubbed him *Weissmannulla*.

Next came the pragmatic King Fuad of Egypt, who in French-accented German said, 'During the mornings I work at the King-business. During the afternoons I work for myself, the banks, *les maisons*, the estates.'

King Faisal of Iraq appeared in civilian clothes. He was a modern monarch who wished for no fuss.

The first post-war US ambassador to Berlin was the very wealthy and much-liked Fredrick Sackett, a great party-giver with a beautiful wife. They invited many young Berliners and even received acceptances from certain Prussian aristocrats who, as a matter of principle, snubbed most invitations to the embassies of their former enemies, particularly the French.

The spirit of Berlin was reviving in other ways. In 1919, for the first and only time, the German Derby, usually run in Anglophile Hamburg, was moved to Berlin's Grunewald Race Track. The winner was German-bred Gibraltar and ironically, his jockey was named Kaiser, giving much fodder to those who found the comparison with their runaway monarch irresistible.* (In 1924 on the same track a horse named Pan Robert won at odds of 2248 to 10.) Most of Berlin's horse-breeding families belonged to the Grunewald Jockey Club and several of them were Jewish. Joachim and Annelies were always happy to be invited to the Club. Jockey Club Jews were not so Jewish.[13]

Post-war Berlin was as bewitched by theatre, film and music as were the other capitals of the world, but nowhere else was there such single-minded mania for sports. The Sportpalast, a large, indoor arena, Berlin's equivalent of New York's Madison Square Garden or London's Olympia, was always filled to overflowing with spectators. Everyone was there, from society people in evening clothes to workmen out for the night in their sweaters and plus-fours. Six-day bike races, boxing, horse shows were invariably sold out. During Sportpalast intervals, if Berlin's great singing stars like the monocled Richard Tauber or Hungary's blonde diva Gitta Alpar were in the audience, they could always be persuaded by the crowd to sing their most famous melodies. It was all in the family! Small wonder that later Hitler often requisitioned the Sportpalast for his most important speeches. He was very smart to exploit a Berlin mecca.

Berlin's sports heroes of the twenties were Paavo Nurmi, the Finnish runner, Arne Borg, the Swedish swimmer, America's Bill Tilden of tennis, Norway's Sonja Henie of skating, foreigners all, but immediately and affectionately adopted by Berlin's street people. Everyone 'knew' that Tilden's racquets were strung with *purple* gut. Tiny Sonja Henie became 'Häseken', the 'baby hare'. Nurmi's name was part of the Berliner's language. Any thief who was chased by the cops 'ran like Nurmi!'

And what was Berlin without film? Nowhere else was there such an undying love affair between a big metropolitan city and its film people. The premières of *Blue Angel, The Cabinet of Dr Caligari, All Quiet on*

---

*   Kaiser Bill, as he was street-dubbed in Britain and America, was living in comfortable exile in a half-million *Guilder* mansion named House Doorn. It was purchased from the van Heemstra–de Beauforts, the family of film star Audrey Hepburn.

the Western Front, Mädchen in Uniform and *The Congress Dances* became events of tremendous importance and, in the case of *All Quiet on the Western Front*, of political rioting. The Nazis considered the war novel by Remarque and the film which followed it to be 'pacifist treason to the brave men who fought and died' and an 'unpatriotic slander to their sacred memory'. The cinema had to cancel some performances to avoid riots. Peter Lorre, Luise Rainer, Elisabeth Bergner, Marlene Dietrich, Conrad Veidt, Pola Negri, Emil Jannings and even the young Swede, Greta Garbo, were all launched in Berlin, as were directors Ernst Lubitsch, George William Pabst and Billy Wilder.

In the theatre Reinhardt, Piscator, Brecht, Weill invented new, often jarring ways to present famous pieces. Bertolt Brecht's *Threepenny Opera* and *Mahagony*, once called monstrous and repetitious, have become classics. The Bauhaus and its multinational stars stunned the world of architecture. Mies, Gropius, Mendelssohn shaped new offices and dwellings from concrete and glass. The world still is influenced by Bauhaus architects, although Hitler, an amateur architectural dilettante, damned flat roofs as 'oriental' and the use of glass and cement as 'foreign'. Berlin's painters of that time were usually 'political'. Grosz, Kollwitz, Dix, Schadt were all pacifists and bitter critics of Germany's upper strata. Their vernissages were usually political events. (In the long run, however, the non-political artists of the time became more famous: Kokoschka, Klee, Nolde.) Conductors Furtwängler, Otto Klemperer and Bruno Walter, composer Schönberg and the Berlin Philharmonic brought music lovers of the world to Berlin. There was also a mediocre violinist called Albert Einstein.

In the Berlin of the 1920s and 1930s the motorcar was king, just as it was in New York, London and Paris. But Berlin was also married to motor sports. Great racing drivers became the spoiled, much invited darlings of Berlin society. Every schoolboy knew the German champion 'Karatsch' (Caracciola, a German despite his Italian name) and his personal white two-seater supercharged SSKL Mercedes, licence number 1A-4444. Twice each year the AVUS road, normally a wide pre-Autobahn highway to the wealthy suburbs, became a motorcar race track, and over 100,000 Berliners flocked to watch 'Karatsch' and the other German aces race against the French, the Italians (Signor Ferrari was the team manager for Alfa Romeo) and the English.

Mercedes-Benz was the 'prestige' car, preferably the big Kompressor (supercharged) type with its tubular, outside exhausts, unless one was rich enough to own an American Packard, which was considered *prima* (as Berliners called, and still call, something splendid). In fact, most American and English fads or stars were *prima*, from Josephine Baker to 'Yes, We Have No Bananas!', the New York song which was whistled by everyone. In the Berlin of the 1920s the Charleston was danced, cocktails were offered and the very worldly, the very rich and the dissolute sniffed cocaine. The Berlin versions of New York's vaudeville or London's revues were Berlin's *Variété*, complete with long-legged English chorus girls. Berlin loved the English. To excuse anything lopsided, Berliners said, 'Lopsided is English, and anything English is modern!' Many Berliners bought cheap cars, Opels and DKWs, and they got them *auf stottern* (literally 'stuttering') or in instalments. No matter how precarious the economy, Berlin's roads were always jammed on weekends as people streamed out of the city to *das Grüne*, the beloved outdoors. Working-class families made day excursions to the nearby lakes and woods. The rich owned villas on the beautiful lake Wannsee where they played tennis, danced, sailed, played golf and partied. (Leisurely, lovely Wannsee gave its name to the most brutal meeting of modern times, the Wannsee Conference for the 'Final Solution of the Jewish Problem'.)

Later, Berlin's mania for motorcar racing was turned into one of Adolf Hitler's favourite propaganda tools. His regime gave massive subsidies to Germany's two all-conquering Grand Prix teams, Mercedes-Benz and Auto Union (the old Auto Union four-ring symbol is still used today by one of its former brands, Audi). Foreigners were impressed by German might and efficiency, and millions of Europeans got their first close-up of Blitzkrieg-style action by watching Germany's 600-horsepower Mercedes or Auto Union's racing cars thunder past their cowed opponents.

Later, in 1938, a blue French Delahaye driven by French champion driver René Dreyfus (the symbolic Jewish name) beat Mercedes in a race at Pau in front of a delirious French crowd. But no one around Hitler took the sportsmanlike view. It was one of the few times German racing cars lost. At the British-organized International Grand Prix at Donington Park on 2 October 1937, the Germans came, they saw, they conquered. The British crowds were awed; they had never seen such a display of massive power. Hitler was even involved with car design. The original drawings for the Volkswagen were Hitler's own sketches, and he asked that the engineering be done by Prof. Porsche, his favourite motorcar designer.

Like all Berliners, Joachim von Ribbentrop was a motorcar addict. In 1936 when he became Ambassador to the Court of St James, the German Foreign Office shipped over a behemoth seven-litre, supercharged, black Mercedes-Benz limousine. The car slurped a gallon of fuel every three miles, and even short trips became adventures in refuelling. Yet London crowds were impressed by that long black Mercedes with its swastika flag and London licence plate CYF 3 pulling into Buckingham Palace, arriving at Westminster Abbey or at 10 Downing Street. Londoners might not have appreciated the Nazi Ambassador, but they loved fine cars.

Berlin's playful revival of the 1920s could not hide its economic ills. A

1923 edition of *Berliner Illustrirte*, an early equivalent of *Time* or *Newsweek*, includes a 'medical' essay on the illnesses of Europe:

> Britain: two million unemployed. France: excessive military costs and a decrease in the birth rate. Spain: troubles in Morocco and a vast deficit. Italy: border disputes and weak currency. Switzerland: recession. Austria: negative trade balance. Czechoslovakia: economic crisis. Hungary: constitutional crisis. The Balkans: political confusion. Greece: near civil war. Turkey: depression from ten years of war. Poland: currency problems and internal conflicts. Russia: economic collapse, epidemic and hunger. Lithuania, Latvia and Estonia: baby countries with severe teething problems. Norway, Sweden and Denmark: recession. And Germany? In the middle of it all lies the carrier of the infection, Germany, which has been inoculated with the pestilential bacillus of Versailles.* No one wishes to administer the necessary antidote, yet everyone wonders why they can hear a death rattle all over Europe.

Newspaper photographs in 1923 show long queues even for the most staple of foods. The elderly waited in the snow in front of Salvation Army soup kitchens, and crippled Berlin veterans marched for their rights. Much of Europe was in trouble, and even across the Atlantic angry American war veterans were massing in front of the White House. Perhaps to these hopelessly hungry and unemployed citizens of Europe and the USA, the Soviet option seemed like a very appealing one, but the democratic standpoint was not ignored. On 7 November 1927, *Berliner Illustrirte* commented on the tenth anniversary of the Soviet Union: 'The Soviet Union started with the bloody torso of the Russian Colossus. Finland was lost. Poland was lost, also Estonia, Latvia and Lithuania which had depended economically on Russia while providing her with access to the sea. Another loss was the repossession of Bessarabia by Romania. Lost also was the concept of "Russia".' The article then expresses its admiration for Soviet achievement against these odds, but it also points out the obvious penalties of the Leninist system: 'loss of personal freedoms without proportional increases in the standard of living and the economic and intellectual penalties of ideological isolation'.

The threatening spectre of a Soviet-sponsored revolt continued to haunt middle- and upper-class Germans. Other nations like Britain and the USA were also confronted with depression, unemployment, hunger, strikes and demonstrations, but the Western nations had developed certain democratic skills and had few delusions about their system of government. They knew that the democratic system was often harsh and disappointing and that it tested the patience of even its most enthusiastic advocates.

---

* The Versailles Treaty.

Most Germans knew little about the discipline and patience required by a democracy under economic attack. Unlike their grandchildren of today, Germans had never tasted the rewards of a successful capitalist republic, nor did Germany's conquerors have twentieth-century minds. The Treaty of Versailles was written with a nineteenth-century pen.

In the late 1920s, Joachim von Ribbentrop (he was now using the new 'von') was a very successful young entrepreneur who had built up a wide circle of business friends abroad. He never missed the opportunity during these trips to 'convince foreign friends of the senselessness and dangers of the Versailles Treaty'. He complained that 'Only a few foreigners understood. They hid behind those concepts which felt comfortable for the victors.' He also met some foreign diplomats through business friends and invited them to Dahlem, where he could 'speak unencumbered by an official position'.[14]

In 1924, Weinhandlungsgesellschaft, his Berlin firm, had a practical monopoly on the sale of Henkell champagne, or *Sekt* as it was called in Germany. He had persuaded Baron de Mumm of Pommery French champagne and Sir Alexander Walker of Johnny Walker Scotch whisky to appoint his firm as their exclusive agent. Von Ribbentrop's senior partners were two men called Muther and Schonberg. Muther died in 1924, and Schonberg, a congenital gambler, soon got into trouble. Otto Henkell paid off Schonberg's debts, with the proviso that Joachim von Ribbentrop should become a senior partner. Now the name of the firm was changed to Schonberg und Ribbentrop, IMPEGROMA (acronym for 'Importers of Great Brands' in German).

After 1 January 1924, when Germany lifted all import restrictions, the firm had prospered.[15] Eventually, on 17 October 1931 the partnership was dissolved, and von Ribbentrop became the sole owner. Even in the midst of diplomacy, he stayed the businessman. When France fell in 1940, de Mumm of Pommery became head of the French Champagne Group – Ribbentrop believed in old business friendships. IMPEGROMA, run for him by a Henkell family member, lasted well into the Nazi era, securing the von Ribbentrop fortune even while he held major government positions.

In the Berlin of the late 1920s, the von Ribbentrops were still battling for their place in society. Annelies von Ribbentrop was the driving force. She was determined that her family should be accepted as full members of Berlin's highest circles. It is astonishing how many people who knew them or were part of their circle insist that Annelies was the 'power behind', the 'evil influence behind', the 'grim secret behind' Joachim von Ribbentrop's final desperate journey through life.

Trying to create contacts among Berlin's foreign diplomats, they met the much liked US Ambassador Jacob Gould Schurman, who introduced them to Lord D'Abernon, the lofty British Ambassador. Invitations to the British Embassy were considered a supreme compliment, and they badgered the British envoy by leaving their cards. D'Abernon finally had them assigned to the rather widespread 'R' list (Receptions only).[16]

Von Ribbentrop explained his new 'von' to many old friends with varying degrees of success. To a French business friend, Count Polignac, he hinted that it had been given retroactively as a reward for bravery in the war, an unlikely explanation in a republican Germany which accepted his 'von' only as an addition to his name without any implication of nobility.[17]

Von Ribbentrop's first attempt to join Berlin's exclusive Union Klub on Schadow Strasse foundered when he was blackballed, probably because of the adopted 'von'. The Union Klub's membership ranged from royalty to untitled bankers, and the members were Protestant, Catholic and Jewish. But it preserved its beloved taboos. Among these was adding a 'von' for social advancement instead of inheriting it. Finally, von Papen, his old acquaintance from Turkey, persuaded the Admissions Committee to reverse its decision.[18] Ever the businessman, von Ribbentrop made a point of cultivating some of the distinguished Jewish bankers who were members, such as the Weinbergs, Oppenheims, Goldschmidt-Rothschilds, von Friedlander-Fulds and Herzfelds. Among the other members, he already knew the Guttmanns through business, and Ottmar Strauss had been one of his early patrons after the war. At one point, the von Ribbentrops had so many Jewish friends that Count Oskar von Platen-Hallermund, a former chamberlain to the Kaiser, said to the amusement of a dinner party, 'Ribbentrop, it seems I'm the only Christian friend you have!'[19]

At the Klub, von Ribbentrop also met some of the young, titled members of the Foreign Service, the *Attachés*, as the junior ranks were called in the Auswärtiges Amt, the Foreign Ministry.

Von Ribbentrop's anti-Semitism in his pre-Hitler days is a moot question. It seems most improbable that he was an anti-Semite early in his Berlin career days or early in his marriage.[20] The Henkells, like most international business families, had close Jewish connections. A surviving member of the family reports that Otto Henkell's sister was married to a Rhineland Jew called Opfermann, who was a director of Henkell. Opfermann, a First World War veteran with an Iron Cross, was a great German patriot. After the Nazis seized power, he committed suicide. The Henkell family lawyer, Dr Oppenheim, was also a Jew, as was von Ribbentrop's personal family secretary, Susie Fried, who remained his secretary all through the Nazi period. After the war, she worked for the Michel branch of the family, and she died in Freiburg about 1960. 'I have no idea', said a relative, 'if Annelies was ever aware that Susie Fried was Jewish!' Although there were only 150,000 Jews among Berlin's four million citizens, it was almost impossible in the 1920s and early 1930s to live the life of a socially ambitious couple without developing some Jewish contacts.

Among the city's most charming couples were Freddy and Lali Horstmann. Freddy, a professional diplomat and a long-time member of the Auswärtiges Amt, had held many key posts abroad. He was independently wealthy and an avid collector of art, *objéts* and attractive people. Lali, née von Schwabach, was the daughter of a banker friend of the Kaiser who was an honorary British consul and one of the few foreigners to wear the British Order of the Garter. The von Schwabachs were Jewish. In his foreword to Lali Horstmann's memoirs, Harold Nicolson wrote that at a time when Prussia's pouting aristocrats and military people had refrained from entertaining foreigners, the Hortsmanns' Berlin home was an international haven of civilized dining and conversation.[21] Their mansion on the Tiergartenstrasse was the scene of memorable parties. Horstmann, a former Minister to Belgium and Portugal, headed the British desk at the Foreign Ministry, and many foreign diplomats were devoted to him and to Lali. The Horstmanns also owned an exquisite country estate.

They entertained the most beautiful women, the most charming men, the greatest wits, the most creative writers and artists. The younger set were invited after dinner to dance to the latest American tunes, and a white-gloved footman attended to the wind-up record player. The young Russian Princess 'Missie' Vassiltchikov, who lived in Berlin during the Nazi years, tells of evenings of 'subtle defiance' of the 'Brown Regime', after Freddy Horstmann had resigned his post at the Foreign Office in silent protest.[22]

Freddy Horstmann's life ended in tragedy. Bombed out of Berlin and their country estate, Kerzendorf, the Horstmanns hid in the nearby woods while the Russian army approached. At Freddy's insistence, Lali escaped towards Berlin, but he refused to leave his treasures. He was captured by the Russians and finally starved to death in captivity. Lali escaped to England with the help of her many Western friends.

Somehow, the young von Ribbentrops got themselves invited to the Horstmanns', where they finally met some of those elusive Berliners they had longed to know. But it was a debt that was not to be repaid. Bubi von Schwabach, Lali's brother, later wrote to Ambassador Joachim von Ribbentrop in London, begging for help – he wanted to leave Germany. He received no reply. Von Ribbentrop told his secretary, Reinhard Spitzy, 'You know how the Führer feels about such things! I can't speak to him about Jews.'[23] Von Schwabach was one of many old friends who were let down by a Hitlerized von Ribbentrop.

At the very beginning of the Nazi takeover, von Ribbentrop often seemed to misjudge Hitler's purpose and aims. He even told worried

Jewish acquaintances and business friends, 'Don't take Hitler's anti-Semitic talk too seriously! It's only a *political gesture*. It's aimed at the *Eastern* Jews, not at German Jews. Everyone knows that German Jews lost a higher percentage of men during the war than Germany's aristocrats!'[24] The day after the first anti-Jewish boycott of 1 April 1933, when stormtroopers stood in front of Jewish stores bullying 'Aryans' not to buy from Jews, von Ribbentrop, still essentially a businessman with tenuous Nazi connections, invited several Jewish social and business friends to a 'reassurance' lunch at the Adlon Hotel. He was immediately denounced by people who saw him there and Hitler summoned him and harshly reprimanded him for his 'offence'. Von Ribbentrop emerged from that meeting with his Führer in complete shock.

In 1930, three years before Hitler seized power, von Ribbentrop was still much involved with Jews both socially and in business, so when Count von Helldorf, his old regimental friend and now a Nazi bigshot, suggested he join the Nazi Party, he could not do so without risk to his business. So he did not join at that time, but he had discovered the thrilling and dangerous world of radical politics. Here, in his own words, was his reasoning:

Since 1929 the German economy had been approaching a crisis. The screws of the Versailles reparations were too tight. Gold reserves shrank, and our balance of payments slid. There were millions of unemployed, and investment capital fled abroad. By 1930 it looked as if Germany would fall to the Communists. I was convinced only National Socialism could save us. I watched the collapse of the moderate political parties. I suspected that you got nowhere without force. Only when catastrophe brewed did we get concessions. I did not wish to involve myself in politics but was forced to help in forming a coalition between my party, the DNVP [the right-wing German People's Party he had joined in the late twenties] and the NSDAP [Nazi Party].

Putting this rationale aside, it is difficult to guess the true background to von Ribbentrop's hunger for right-wing politics. No doubt some of it was a matter of personal conviction. After all, he was a former officer, the son of an Imperial officer and the grandson of an Imperial officer, and he deeply resented the lost war and Germany's lost international prestige. But there was also opportunism and self-promotion. By touting anti-Communism, one could be guaranteed the attention of the 'best' people. The von Ribbentrops began what one of their former neighbours described as a 'political salon'. Many prominent Berliners, some friendly with the von Ribbentrops, others only casual acquaintances, were invited to their villa on Lenzeallee 7–9 in Dahlem, where they met and listened to various right-wing politicians of all shadings who offered their plans for a new 'cleansed and pure' Germany, a strong and rearmed Germany, a Germany with its 'pre-war honour' restored. Their simplistic theories promised an end to the years of submission, compromise and empty debate, an end to the harsh penalties. The war would have been won but for a 'stab in the back'. (The 'stab in the back' or *Dolchstoss* legend was a favourite nationalist explanation for Germany's seemingly inexplicable collapse in 1918, although it is generally acknowledged that Germany was near bankruptcy and unable to continue fighting for more than two weeks when it agreed to an armistice.) This 'new' Germany would regain its rightful place among Europe's great powers. Most of all: beware of the Bolshevist plague!

The von Ribbentrops became important hosts. Along with a serving of right-wing politics, their guests had an attractive evening in a civilized household. On summer weekends there was tennis and swimming. Some of the speakers seemed a little radical, but they often made their point!

It was not the first or the last time that insecure people had used political radicalism to further their own social ambitions.

Meanwhile, the wine business prospered, their two children were a joy, the house was filled with interesting guests, and, if the family in Wiesbaden was still reluctant, that could not be helped. Annelies had proved her point. In her eyes, Joachim and she had made a success of their life.

On 29 October 1929, the *New York Times* front-page headline read: 'Europe is disturbed by American action on occupation debt', and immediately to the right of that: 'Stock Prices Slump $14,000,000,000 in Nation-wide Stampede to Unload: Bankers to Support Market Today'. There were other stories that day: 'French troops withdraw from the Rhineland after a settlement in the Hague!'; 'Arabs attack Jews in Palestine after an argument over use of the Wailing Wall!'; 'Hitler appoints Heinrich Himmler to head the SS'; 'Russia, Poland, Rumania, Estonia and Latvia sign a pact condemning war . . .'

A few months later in 1930 Germany suffered the consequences of this disaster on New York's Wall Street. The American bill would have to be paid, and all the world's countries rowed on the same monetary lake. The wave set off by the New York stock-market crash upset the precarious financial balance of war-battered Europe. That included the struggling, vulnerable new republic of Germany.

In the 1930 Reichstag elections, Hitler's NSDAP (Nazis) won 107 seats, the largest single bloc, though not a majority. To control them, President von Hindenburg chose conservative Catholic Chancellor Brüning, hoping he could form a coalition government of the right.

German patience was wearing thin. After years of upheaval, everyone wanted a solution. Both the Nazis and the Communists promised such solutions, but the Nazis looked for support from Germany's powerful upper class by playing on their fear of Bolshevism. Many Germans, unskilled in self-determination, were unwilling to stick with a democratic system which foisted all ultimate responsibility on to the individual citizen. Britain and France were long accustomed to the laborious and slow grinding of the wheels of representative government, and the United States had never known any other system. But in twentieth-century Germany, an immature, forty-three-year-old Bismarckian empire had been replaced by an even less mature republic. Germans who felt betrayed by the Kaiser were not yet willing to trust their new republic. They were still accustomed to leaders who were strong and decisive, the 'soldierly qualities'. As the old Cavalry song said: 'On the field of battle man still has worth!'

Can one generalize about that generation of Germans? Should one? And yet, so many male German university graduates of the time proudly wore their duelling *Schmiss*, the facial scars attesting to supposed 'courage when faced with cold steel'. University duelling (*Schlagen*), a barbarous anachronism still in existence, was conducted in an almost token manner: only the cheeks could get cut, fighting stopped at first blood, and cuts were specially treated to produce scars. The duelling societies, called *Brüderschaften* (fraternities), were a form of Teutonism which also appealed to certain German Jews. Many Jewish university graduates had scarred cheeks.

At the extreme, Teutonism even produced bitter anti-Semitism among Jews. A Berliner named Max Naumann, a decorated World War officer and a Jew, was a member of the DNVP (the same nationalist organization to which von Ribbentrop belonged), and agitated for the total assimilation of Jews into the body of Germany, if they were pure German Jews. He formed an organization called the League of Jews of German Nationality, which advocated the expulsion of 'Eastern' Jews from Germany as 'harmful bacteria in the body of the nation'. In 1935, the Gestapo eliminated his organization as 'enemies of the State'. Naumann died in Berlin in 1939.

The Berlin of 1931 in which the von Ribbentrops were advancing to a certain prominence was now the seat of the Brüning government. Friedrich Brüning was a controlled, introverted man who headed the Catholic Centre Party. Von Hindenburg unrealistically expected that Brüning could block the Nazis while holding off the Communists. Abroad, Brüning was supposed to arrange an end to the heavy Versailles reparations. Economically, Brüning was expected to stem the shock wave of the 1929 earthquake which had begun on Wall Street. Few men would have been equal to the task. Brüning was cool and judicious, unemotional and rational, qualities which raised neither popular support nor enthusiasm. To stem the economic downturn, he took all the right emergency steps, but the medicine tasted too bitter. To deflate the heated economy, he reduced wages and pensions, infuriating the workers and the fixed-income, lower-middle-class pensioners. Price control angered the farmers. Controls over banking upset the financial community. His wish to break up the subsidized and debt-ridden Junker landholdings into smaller, individually farmed parcels angered the landed gentry, who were part of von Hindenburg's own set. Brüning could not last.

For the 1932 presidential election Hitler, who had finally become a German citizen on 25 February,* decided to challenge von Hindenburg for the presidency: the Austrian corporal against the Prussian Field Marshal. Von Hindenburg was narrowly re-elected on 13 March. The slim margin came as a shock. Worse, his opponent, Adolf Hitler, was now supported by the very same right-wingers who had originally installed von Hindenburg himself. The Marshal could not have won without co-operation between the liberals ... and the hated Communists. What uncomfortable allies these were for von Hindenburg! Nevertheless, Brüning, ever the unemotional intellectual, was pleased. He had preserved his patron. But the Nazis then won majorities in the next regional elections (Prussia) and the President would no longer support Brüning. On 30 May 1932, at five minutes before noon, Brüning resigned.

The great French statesman and wit, André François-Poncet, who was then the French Ambassador in Berlin, explained:

> Brüning's errors were typically German. He did not realize that the praise he got abroad rendered him suspect at home. He never realized to what pitch of blind fanaticism nationalist passion might rise, a frenzy too fierce to be assuaged by any victories he might have won. He tried the velvet glove. The Germans preferred the mailed fist. He was repelled by the drastic and brutal methods which would have saved him. He had two excellent opportunities to smash the Nazis: they were twice discovered planning treason and insurrection. Arms were found and plans for a coup d'état. Everything could be proved. But Brüning would not smash his opponents.[25]

General Gröner, the Minister of War, had no such scruples. He persuaded the President to let him ban the Nazi SA (stormtroopers), and he did so on 13 April. His troops also raided their barracks. But Gröner found no support from his own military people, and von Hindenburg soon reversed himself. On 14 June the SA troopers were back on the streets in all their vulgar, brown-uniformed strength. While Brüning had tried to govern Germany, the right-wingers had consolidated. On a raw,

---

* The State of Bruswick appointed him State Counsellor, thereby bestowing citizenship.

autumn day in October 1931 in the old Harz mountain spa of Bad Harzburg a fierce assembly of nationalists had come together for the first time. Leading the factions were the arrogant Hitler and his storm-troops. Then came the nationalist Steel Helmet. There was also flotsam: the Pan-German League with their boss, Clars, a lawyer, and the right-winger General von der Goltz and his obscure, folkish agrarian party.

But there were also individuals of great prestige: the banker Hjalmar Schacht, the steel industrialist Poensgen, white-moustached General von Seeckt, the founder of the Reichswehr, and also a group of Nazi-prone royals – the Duke of Saxe-Coburg, Prince William of Lippe and Prince Eitel Friedrich, a son of the Kaiser. This was the first time that men of such seeming substance had endorsed Adolf Hitler's plans for Germany by their presence.

The months between this 'Congress of Harzburg' in 1931 and Brüning's resignation in 1932 had set the stage: Adolf Hitler's coming was now imminent. The end of democracy was at hand. In his Nuremberg memoirs von Ribbentrop wrote: 'To my foreign friends I said: give Brüning a chance and he may succeed. Scuttle him and we will be Nazi or Communist.'

Like millions of their countrymen, the von Ribbentrop family was about to face drastic changes. Their pre-Hitler days were over.

BOOK II

SEVEN

HITLER TO 1934

'Hidden Fantasies'

Brüning was gone, and von Ribbentrop's old friend von Papen was Chancellor. He had known von Papen since Turkey and had been sponsored by him for the Union Klub.

Von Papen was the classic Catholic–aristocrat–squire, a man whose style pleased von Hindenburg. The President was sure von Papen could do it all: block Hitler, get the support of industry, repulse the Bolshevists, deal with the French and the English. Von Papen had formed a Cabinet, snidely known as the Barons' Cabinet since its members were almost all titled. Taken seriously by no one, they were ignored by friend and foe alike.[1] These were not the right men to grapple with the monstrous problems facing Germany. Von Hindenburg had misjudged, badly.

There was one man in the Cabinet whose firm hand could have saved the day, Reichswehr (Defence) Minister Kurt von Schleicher, an able man, a soldier–politician and the natural 'next' choice for von Hindenburg. Von Papen was keenly aware of the challenge, and, being vain and ambitious, the gentleman–squire was about to make a compromise with the devil to keep his chancellorship. He asked his old protégé von Ribbentrop to 'go down to Bavaria to see if this fellow Hitler could be talked into some sort of coalition'. Von Ribbentrop was then a member of the DVP (Deutsche Volks Partei), a conservative right-wing party. Because of the economic turmoil, he wrote in his memoirs, 'I did not want to involve myself in politics but found myself wishing that I could help to form a coalition.'

It all sounded understandable, rational and even laudable. He knew von Papen and owed him favours. Besides, he was probably flattered that the Chancellor of the German Republic should ask him, a business executive, to undertake this delicate mission. Like most Germans, he knew a good deal about the external Hitler, the man with the Austro-Bavarian accent who expressed in harsh terms the simplistic solutions everyone wanted. Many Germans of the working class and lower-middle class found in him a 'German' option to Communism, which seemed foreign because its red heart beat in Moscow. Among the higher German social echelons, Hitler raised the secret chills people feel when they admire brutal solutions. He appealed to the hidden thug which can be found behind many civilized façades.

In all probability, von Ribbentrop set out for Berchtesgaden with a certain amount of snobbish disdain for the semi-educated, ex-lance corporal he was to meet. After all, von Ribbentrop was more anxious than most to guard his own social status, and he was going there to speak for a rather lordly Chancellor.

He travelled to Munich and then up into the mountains to a chalet called Haus Wachenfeld which Hitler had bought with the help of his admirers. Wachenfeld was a pretty place, formerly a holiday villa in the Bavarian farm style, near Berchtesgaden, with stunning views of the high mountains and valleys below. It was soon to become the centre of the compound known as the Berghof, which can still be seen in so many photographs of the Hitler era.

Von Ribbentrop's mission for von Papen was to persuade Hitler to join the Chancellor's Cabinet as Vice Chancellor. This would block the threatening General Kurt von Schleicher, the Defence Minister. It would also mean that von Papen had formed the conservative coalition he had promised the President and he would be able to control Hitler by having him close at hand.

Von Ribbentrop had never met Hitler face to face, and no one knows exactly what happened to change the life of a man as seemingly assured as von Ribbentrop. After all, from boyhood to Canadian entrepreneurship, from life as a young Prussian officer to wealthy Berlin cosmopolitan, Joachim von Ribbentrop had taken good care of his own fate and fortune. His own explanation was that he was 'convinced' by Hitler.

And it was a very angry Hitler who greeted him. Von Ribbentrop was immediately told that the NSDAP leader wanted no part of a deal with von Papen. Instead, he believed in von Schleicher because 'one can trust a German general.'[2] Politics or the truth? Was he threatening von Papen with von Schleicher, or did he really believe in the General? Any doubts in von Ribbentrop's usually cynical mind were removed by a classic Hitlerian technique. Somehow, Adolf Hitler frequently found the energy to explain himself to listeners by pouring out his views, his dreams, his arguments in a massive and hours-long, drama-filled barrage of words. These 'lectures', dissertations, verbal assaults were always aimed, quite instinctively, at the vulnerable core of the audience, which might range in size from 10,000 to the one person sitting in front of him. No matter how often people have tried to describe their personal impressions of

Hitler, they invariably speak of his powers to persuade through this mixture of seeming logic and brute force.

Von Ribbentrop had never dealt with anyone who so touched the best and also the worst in him. Hitler must have reached the hidden fantasies, both brutal and vainglorious, which Joachim von Ribbentrop had harboured but was too embarrassed, too 'mannerly' and too conservative to express. After two hours of Adolf Hitler's verbal pounding, he was convinced, converted and devoted.

Hitler finally said he might be willing to join a coalition and to become Vice Chancellor.

When von Ribbentrop brought this answer back to von Papen in Berlin, the Chancellor rushed to sell the idea to President von Hindenburg. He failed abysmally. The old man snorted, 'That Bohemian corporal?' and refused even to consider it. Despite von Ribbentrop's failure in Berchtesgaden to obtain an *absolute* promise to join a coalition, Hitler had convinced him he was the right man for the future of Germany.[3] Von Ribbentrop, 'drunk' with Hitler's ideas, donated 6,000 Marks to the NSDAP[4] and finally joined the party on 1 May 1932, once more at the urging of his old regimental comrade, Count von Helldorf. The handsome von Helldorf was a crook, one of several black-sheep aristocrats who had become part of the Nazi coterie after his service in the 12th 'Torgau' Hussars, where he had been one of the regiment's youngest officers. After the Armistice, like many other unemployed ex-officers, he joined one of the roving Freikorps, the semi-military groups which attached themselves to right-wing political parties. Naturally, he took part in the Kapp *putsch*. When that failed, he joined the SA, the stormtroopers of the NSDAP, where he quickly reached high rank. The proletarian SA and its brawling chief Röhm always tried to recruit ex-officers and aristocrats, who helped to gloss over its reputation for thuggery. After the Nazi takeover, von Helldorf blackmailed several Jews and then gambled away the money on horses at the Jockey Klub in Berlin.[5] Göring, who appreciated scoundrels, helped him to become President of the Berlin Police in 1935. It is even possible that von Helldorf, on Göring's instructions, took part in the 1933 planning of the infamous Reichstag fire.[6] Eventually, towards the end of the Second World War, always ready to desert the losing side, he made contact with the officer resistance who planned to assassinate Hitler. He was caught and then hanged by his former Nazi cronies in August 1944.

In May 1932 he was delighted to help the new Hitler convert, von Ribbentrop, become a party member. It was von Ribbentrop's first open public commitment to the Nazi movement, made despite his many Jewish business connections and acquaintances.

To von Ribbentrop's disappointment, his new hero Hitler now ignored him. After all, Joachim and Annelies von Ribbentrop were people to be reckoned with in the higher Berlin circles, and his membership of the

Nazi Party constituted something of an endorsement. Nevertheless, there was nothing but silence from the man in Bavaria.

Annelies, who was pregnant, hated von Helldorf, who had often borrowed money from them,[7] and she wished that they had better contacts with the party. The breakthrough came after a small stag dinner at the home of Prince Wied, where von Helldorf introduced von Ribbentrop to Count Vico von Bülow-Schwante, another titled reprobate and Hitler satellite. Von Bülow-Schwante had been forced to resign from the Foreign Ministry after he and a wealthy well-known lady, much his senior, were found *in flagrante delicto* in a curtained compartment on the train to Salzburg.[8] It happened in broad daylight, and the embarrassing discovery was made by a border policeman who had entered to check their passports. Gossip followed. The lofty Foreign Ministry was not pleased, and von Bülow-Schwante departed from that aristocratic enclave on the Wilhelmstrasse. He then became another member of the coterie of chic delinquents Hitler seemed to have at his paid disposal. Many a third son had broken contact with his family and joined the one right-wing party which was bound to send fathers into apoplexy.

One day Hitler complained to von Bülow-Schwante that he wanted to read the London and Paris papers, but there was no one to translate them. Von Bülow-Schwante, probably expecting munificent thanks from the rich von Ribbentrops, suggested to Hitler that the right man was von Ribbentrop. Not only did Joachim speak foreign languages, but the von Ribbentrops were a wealthy, worldly couple with many connections abroad. They were part of Berlin's upper crust and could introduce the party and its Führer to the city's more elevated circles. Even more importantly, they could introduce the Führer to influential Londoners and Parisians. He showed Hitler some of the circular letters about the new Germany von Ribbentrop had been distributing to his friends and acquaintances abroad. Hitler was impressed. (Later, in Nuremberg at the War Crimes Trials, von Bülow-Schwante claimed that he had introduced von Ribbentrop to Hitler at a Prince Wied dinner in 1930,* two years earlier. However, the 1932 encounter in Berchtesgaden seems more likely to have been von Ribbentrop's first meeting with his Führer.)

Von Bülow-Schwante's idea worked. At last Hitler showed some interest in von Ribbentrop and accepted several of his invitations to small, intimate dinners *en famille* in Dahlem. While Joachim held forth on the ways of influential London and Paris, Annelies gently coached the gauche Austrian Nazi Führer in the art of table manners. She usually refrained from inviting other guests because Hitler 'was not someone you could invite anyone with!'[9] For Hitler, it was a glimpse into a new world. He

---

*   Prince Wied was head of a mini-principality and anxious to gain influence. His family once held the Albanian crown for less than a year. He was one of Hitler's aristo-paladins.

often succumbed to a lower-middle-class craving for the 'better' things. He relished the well-run household, the tasteful furnishings, the carefully trained servants and the beautiful grounds. He was delighted with the *kultivierte* atmosphere. He agreed with von Bülow-Schwante that the von Ribbentrops might be important to the future of the movement.

Finally, Annelies invited a few carefully selected guests to meet Adolf Hitler: the von Bülow-Schwantes were there, as was Joachim's father, Colonel Richard Ribbentrop. Colonel Ribbentrop was not impressed by Hitler's pomposities. The Henkells were never invited.[10] Joachim and Annelies probably feared, and rightly, that the imperious Käthe Henkell would have turned the evening into a shambles. One of the few genuine society couples they asked were Count and Countess Alexander Dörnberg. The Countess was a schoolfriend of Annelies, and the red-haired Count, known as '*der lange Sandro*' (Tall Sandro) or the 'Red Tower', was related to many royals, including the Mountbattens (Battenbergs). The von Dörnbergs became part of the von Ribbentrops' entourage for years, and joined them on the Embassy staff in London.

Whenever he visited Lenzeallee 7–9, Hitler probably sensed that he occasionally deserved better from life than the crude, beer-brawling world of his old Nazi cronies. Besides, Annelies spoiled him with special fruit from Rollenhagen, the Fauchon or Fortnum & Mason of Berlin, and with the kind of flower arrangements Hitler loved.[11]

Six years later, the Foreign Ministry's Chief of Protocol, Vico von Bülow-Schwante (the job was his eventual reward from Foreign Minister von Ribbentrop) fell foul of his chief over the minor matter of the costume Hitler was obliged to wear during a state visit to Italy. Von Bülow-Schwante was fired, and his place was then taken by Tall Sandro, Count Alexander von Dörnberg. Von Bülow-Schwante is said to have complained: 'I introduced Joachim to the Führer, and now he's Foreign Minister, and I'm out of a job!'[12]

What Hitler magic had bewitched Joachim von Ribbentrop? Some men never succumbed to it, among them Sir Nevile Henderson, Britain's Ambassador to the Reich during the fateful late 1930s. Henderson wrote,

> Many Germans, women in particular, used to descant to me upon the radiance of his expression and his remarkable eyes. I must confess he never gave me any impression of greatness. He was a spellbinder for his own people. To the last, I continued to ask myself how he had risen to what he was and how he maintained his ascendance over the German people.[13]

Others were completely enthralled, but in truth there was hardly a secure, intelligent person who fell *completely* under Adolf Hitler's spell. His closest associates seemed flawed almost without exception. Some others, like Hjalmar Schacht, the banker, stayed rational in the presence of Hitler and used him opportunistically. Still others were less snake-charmed than plain frightened. This is how the wise statesman André François-Poncet, the French Ambassador in Berlin whom Hitler courted, describes the German Führer:

> A pale face, globular eyes, the faraway look of a medium or a somnambulist. At other times, animated, colourful, swept away with passion and violence. Impatient of control, bold, cynical, energetic. Sometimes a 'Storm and Assault' face, the face of a lunatic! At other times naive, rustic, dull, vulgar, easily amused, a thigh-slapper, a face like a thousand other faces.
>
> Sometimes he was all three in one conversation. He ranted on for ten minutes, a half hour, three-quarters of an hour. Then he was exhausted. At that time one could speak, and he would even smile. He was no normal human being, but a morbid, quasi-mad Dostoevsky figure, a man possessed. He was an Austrian with a passionate love for Germany, wildly romantic, full of half-baked theories of Houston Stewart Chamberlain, Nietzsche, Spengler. He wanted a new Germany to replace the Holy Roman Empire, a purified race, an elite. He lived Wagner!
>
> A dreamer but a cold-blooded realist and schemer. He was LAZY and hated regular work. He wanted oral information, not written reports. He allowed great freedom but knew every move his collaborators made. He willed or tolerated every excess, all crimes. He used intuition for the sudden power of decision. He was tied to the masses and had contempt for them. He lulled opponents by signing treaties while planning to wriggle out of them.[14]

André François-Poncet believed that Hitler eventually failed because of 'Pride, swollen out of proportion by success and flattery. His success since the beginning persuaded him that Providence protected him. He was anti-religious but the elect of the Almighty. The stars had told him that he would have success and then suffer disaster. He counted on only ten years.'

This was the man Joachim von Ribbentrop had first met in Berchtesgaden. Now he thought he and Annelies had 'tamed' him and had made a pliable pupil of him. They were not the last people who mistakenly thought they had secured Adolf Hitler's admiration, his thanks and good will. At the end, of all the dozens of these men who were closest to their Führer, only Goebbels would be there in the bunker under the Chancellery to share his fate. The others all made the error of thinking that Adolf Hitler cared for them, and they finally learned that he cared for no one, not even the German people. He wanted to consign them all to death for not wishing to follow him to a fiery Wagnerian end. His last orders were to destroy everything and to flood the Berlin subways, where tens of thousands had taken shelter. During those final apocalyptic days in April 1945, he even ordered his beloved SS bodyguard, the Leibstandarte Adolf Hitler, to strip off their identification tape. They were no longer worthy of his name.

Following Brüning's resignation in May 1932, it is unlikely that von Ribbentrop saw more than the surface ripples of the ocean of intrigues, backstage politics and strange, short-lived alliances of the second half of 1932. Brüning's first successor, Franz von Papen, the elegant squire and clubman married to wealth, was chosen for his conservative views, his promise to control the Nazis, his assurance that he would deal with the insufferable reparations of the Versailles Treaty. Besides, the Catholic von Papen protected the staunchly Protestant von Hindenburg from any accusations of anti-Catholicism. But von Papen had failed to retain the President's confidence. The stormtroopers, once banned under Brüning, were legitimized once more by von Hindenburg at the suggestion of von Papen. He negotiated with the French and came up with a treaty to pay French reparations in a few discounted lump sums rather than in a full schedule of instalments, which raised unending protests. His promised battle against Nazi influence seemed unnecessary after the Nazis suddenly lost votes in the November 1932 elections. Von Papen's own Cabinet soon disowned him, and von Hindenburg reluctantly dismissed him. His farewell present was a signed, framed photograph of the Marshal inscribed with the first words of the old German soldier's lament: *Ich hatt einen Kameraden* (I once had a comrade).

Next to be appointed was General Kurt von Schleicher, von Papen's former Reichswehr Minister who was half soldier, half politician. Since 1920, the General Staff had nominated him as their political expert, and he had developed his own plans for the future of Germany. After the Nazis lost votes in November 1932, he approached one of Hitler's more moderate rivals in the Nazi Party, Gregor Strasser, hoping that he could split the Nazis. He also tried to attract the co-operation of the trade unions. Then, on 3 December 1932, he took charge himself. He, too, would not last. Hitler kept a firm hold over his Nazis, and the unions defected from a coalition with the General. Like many European republics, the Weimar Republic* was ruled by prime ministers (chancellors) who depended on coalition governments, which could be challenged by no-confidence motions in the Reichstag and often had to resign. The American system appoints governments for fixed terms even if the constituency does not support them.

Early in 1933, von Schleicher admitted defeat and resigned. Once more the path seemed clear for von Papen and his new ally, Adolf Hitler. All

---

* Named after the 'poets' town' of Weimar, where it was formed in 1919.

machinations ended on 30 January 1933 when Hitler was legally appointed Chancellor. Democracy had failed a people without the patience, the skill or the will to fight for individual freedom. The German people chose a dictator and, like most nations, they probably got the government they deserved.

During those final, fitful days of the Weimar Republic, almost without knowing how, the von Ribbentrops suddenly became useful commodities to Hitler. Their new 'friendship' with the Führer, their old relationship with von Papen and the discreet and convenient location of their Lenzeallee villa now formed the stage for some historic meetings during the January of 1933.

The sequence of events was launched by a speech given on 16 December 1932 by von Papen at the Herrenklub, the right-wing political gentlemen's club in Berlin. Hungry to return to power, he again hinted at a coalition with Hitler, for which he had dispatched his friend von Ribbentrop to Berchtesgaden. One of the club's members, a banker called Kurt von Schröder, took the hint and translated it into a meeting on 4 January 1933 between von Papen and Hitler at his home in Cologne.

Before going to Cologne, Adolf Hitler invited Hanussen, the stage clairvoyant, to Berchtesgaden, and Hanussen prophesied that the Cologne meeting would bring the long-awaited chancellorship. He even predicted the date: 30 January 1933.

Hitler, deeply superstitious, ever one to believe in destiny, was now sure.[15] They all met in Cologne, trying to preserve secrecy, unsuccessfully as it would turn out. The participants: Hitler, Rudolf Hess, Heinrich Himmler, von Papen and von Schröder, the host. From the outset, the sly von Papen did not speak of Hitler as sole chancellor. Instead, he offered to negotiate between Hitler and von Schleicher for NSDAP participation in von Schleicher's Cabinet. Like a Cantonese menu, he offered many combinations. Perhaps a shared von Schleicher–Hitler co-chancellorship? Or eventually a von Papen–Hitler tandem? There was also the hope that Germany's major industrialists would now finally subsidize a conservative–Nazi coalition. But it was not to be. The meeting was inconclusive.

Many leading industrialists had been invited, but they stayed away just as they had in October 1931 from the Congress of Harzburg. Germany's industrial capitalists, though they have often been accused of being Hitler's earliest financial 'angels', were actually most reluctant to participate. In 1932, according to leading German historian Heinz Höhne, Friedrich Flick (coal and steel) donated a token 50,000 Marks to the Nazi Party. In contrast, that same year he donated 1,800,000 Marks to conservative political causes, most of it to help re-elect von Hindenburg as president in preference to Hitler. In fact, von Papen had met with the leading industrialists, including Gustav Krupp von Bohlen und Halbach, on 7 January 1933 in Düsseldorf and found little enthusiasm. They were not inclined to contribute funds towards a collaboration between von Papen and the Nazis, and they had suggested that instead von Papen should ally himself with some of the less radical nationalist parties. Carl Duisberg and Carl Bosch of the Dye Trust (I.G. Farben) and Carl Friedrich von Siemens of the Siemens Concern had actually resisted Hitler.

On 5 January, the newspaper *Tägliche Rundschau* reported the supposedly secret Cologne meeting of 4 January. Von Papen returned to Berlin on 9 January. Of course, Chancellor von Schleicher was furious. He had seen photographs of the conference taken by a former army officer.[16] (Von Schleicher's dentist had procured these after hearing about the conference. When he warned von Schleicher, he received a lecture about 'the honour of men towards each other' for his pains.)

When von Schleicher confronted him, von Papen strenuously denied any self-promoting machinations, blaming the 'unbridled press'. But von Schleicher's suspicions were well founded. Von Papen still lived in the old Chancellor's apartment in the Wilhelmstrasse, from where it was easy to meet secretly with the President, whose office was but a few steps away across a garden. According to Alexander Stahlberg, one of von Papen's young assistants, von Papen still preferred to be addressed as 'Herr Reichskanzler' (Chancellor), though he was now *ex officio*.

Stahlberg's memoirs also attest to his own immunity to Hitler-hypnosis. As a twenty-year-old, part-time assistant to von Papen, he was 'not unprepared' for his first meeting with Hitler: 'I had been told that his eyes were so "incredibly fascinating". Hitler stopped in front of me and fixed me with his blue eyes, but I felt at once that this "look" was fake, nothing but a pose, studied in front of the mirror.'[17] Stahlberg was then asked to hang up Hitler's trenchcoat; thinking it unusually heavy, he looked in the pockets and found two large pistols, manufactured by Walther, finished in chrome.

On 10 January 1933 history chose Joachim and Annelies von Ribbentrop to host at their home the crucial meetings which preceded the *Machtergreifung* – the seizure of power on 30 January.

At 9 p.m. on 10 January, the von Ribbentrop family chauffeur, Fritz Bohnhaus, collected Franz von Papen from his apartment on the Wilhelmstrasse.[18] Bohnhaus was dressed in civvies, not in his chauffeur's livery, to avoid 'looking official'. With the exception of Landgraf, the butler, all the von Ribbentrop servants were quarantined in the villa's upstairs servants' quarters. Hitler and his group arrived at 10 p.m. Landgraf served refreshments while chauffeur Bohnhaus patrolled the grounds.

This meeting also went badly. Hitler demanded the post of Chancellor for himself. Von Papen, who had assured von Hindenburg this would not be, was in a dilemma, and he told Hitler that von Hindenburg would never consent. They began to argue angrily and Hitler threatened to leave. Still, he agreed to another meeting on 12 January. However, he cancelled it later, 'in order to await the outcome of the regional elections in the State of Lippe'. The previous November, the Nazis had lost many votes in the larger states, and Hitler now saw a chance to reverse the slide.

The Nazis made gigantic efforts to win the voters of tiny Lippe, village by village, town by town. They presented this election as a weathervane. As Heinz Höhne has said, 'It was grotesque. Lippe was a midget state. The fate of 70 million Germans was to be decided by 100,000 voters!' The Nazis won 39.5 per cent of the vote, after using a sledgehammer to kill a fly, and they trumpeted their 'fantastic reversal of fortune'. Hitler now called a meeting of his party's leaders on 16 January in Weimar to rid himself of his critics, including Gregor Strasser, whom he never forgave for his 'treachery' with von Schleicher.

Now von Ribbentrop persuaded a much reassured Hitler to return to Dahlem. On 18 January, von Papen, Hitler, Röhm and Himmler met again at Lenzeallee, and this time von Papen was persuaded that there was no way around Hitler's demands. The propaganda value of his victory in tiny Lippe was bound to bring popular enthusiasm. Von Papen would have to reassure the President that he could load the Cabinet with conservatives who could control Hitler. The next meeting was scheduled for 22 January. The two men von Papen invited specifically to help to persuade the old Marshal were his son, Colonel Oskar von Hindenburg, and his State Secretary, Otto Meissner. André François-Poncet wrote acid portraits of these two men: von Hindenburg's son was 'tall, brutal, semi-educated with none of his father's nobility'. Meissner was 'a strange factotum, too tightly encased in his clothes, who served *all* regimes!'

At 9 p.m. on the 22nd von Papen arrived at Lenzeallee, again in the von Ribbentrop car. Next, at 10 p.m., came Hitler, Wilhelm Frick, Göring and Körner, a friend of Göring's. Frick, an early Hitler paladin, was a rabid Nazi ideologue.

Oskar von Hindenburg and Meissner had begun the evening in a box at the opera. They then left between intermissions, unnoticed in the dark, and took a taxi to Dahlem, arriving at 10.30 p.m. They even used the back entrance through the garden. When they entered the villa, Hitler paid no attention to Meissner. He walked up to Oskar von Hindenburg and took him to a neighbouring room, where they spent two straight hours behind locked doors, until long after midnight. When they emerged, von Hindenburg seemed convinced. In the taxi back to the city he turned to Meissner and said that Hitler now had to be taken seriously as a future Chancellor.

What had been said during those two hours? Hitler had obviously made promises and used persuasion and charm, but it is also possible that there was a much harder edge. Two things made the von Hindenburgs vulnerable: certain matters concerning their magnificent estate Neudeck in East Prussia, and the *Osthilfe* scandal. The von Hindenburgs were an old Prussian family, but they owned no land. To tie the old Marshal to his fellow Junkers, a group of estate-owning aristocrats led by the East Prussian Junker von Oldenburg-Januschau had persuaded heavy industry to underwrite the purchase of the vast Neudeck estate in West Prussia, which was then donated to von Hindenburg in 1927, on his eightieth birthday, 'by a grateful nation'. However, the estate was registered in the name of Oskar von Hindenburg, his son, in order to cheat the government out of eventual death taxes. Although this was known in some quarters, it was not a fact to be widely publicized.

The other matter, *Osthilfe* (which meant 'Eastern Help'), was potentially a much greater scandal. In 1930, Germany's heavy industry had approved subsidies to the agricultural east of Germany. The purpose, supposedly, was to strengthen this agricultural area as a consumer market. Billions of Marks flowed into what soon turned into a bottomless pit. Much of the money went into the coffers of the richest landowners in Germany, who bought luxury cars, yachts and horses, and gambled away fortunes in Monte Carlo. The figures speak for themselves: in 1932, 12,000 small farms received a total of 69 million Marks, and 722 large landowners received a total of 60 million Marks. Hermine, the wife of the former Kaiser, one of the richest landowners, claimed and received *Osthilfe* while she was living in faraway Berchtesgaden. Von Oldenburg-Januschau, the very man who had arranged the gift of the Neudeck estate to the von Hindenburgs, collected 621,000 Marks, with which he added a fourth estate to the three he already owned.[19] Heavy industry finally cancelled *Osthilfe* and put its money into exports.

No matter what he threatened in those two hours, Hitler must also have made some promises: Oskar von Hindenburg was promoted from colonel to general shortly after Hitler came to power, and thousands of acres were added to the Neudeck estate.

The day after this 22 January meeting brought more convoluted twists and turns in alliances and proposals. Von Schleicher suddenly realized his ruling days were ending. He received a flat no from von Hindenburg when he asked for emergency powers. He now knew that he was being undermined by von Papen and also by his own chief, the old Marshal. Von Hindenburg had no further trust in a Prussian general who wanted to reach out across all strata of German society even to the socialists and who had failed to favour his own Junker brethren in the *Osthilfe* scandal. Suddenly von Schleicher saw everything clearly: Field Marshal Paul von Hindenburg, the President and symbol of upright manliness who was General von Schleicher's idol, had been disloyal. This was not the first time. He had scuttled Brüning and von Papen, and now he was scuttling von Schleicher. Outraged, von Schleicher accused the old man to his face of disloyalty. Von Hindenburg made only a mild response: 'My dear young friend, soon I shall be up there, looking down. Then I'll see if I was right or wrong. . . .'[20]

The hysterically insecure Hitler still swerved between arrogant demands and hopeless depression while his Nazi associates as well as von Papen tried to persuade him to accept a government of national unity, a coalition cabinet incorporating Nazis as well as more moderate National-ist Conservatives, under Hitler as Chancellor. Meanwhile, von Papen secretly explored his own options, which even included an alliance with von Schleicher. Or could he form a cabinet with Hugenberg, the National-ist Conservative Hitler hated? Hugenberg and his nationalist movement were not to be denied. They insisted on a place in the Cabinet. Von Schleicher, no longer Chancellor, thought he might return to the Cabinet post of Reichswehr Minister, but von Hindenburg had already selected a new man: General von Blomberg, a rival of von Schleicher.

Von Schleicher then called together the senior generals. Was now the time to arrest von Hindenburg before he handed full power to Hitler? On the afternoon of 29 January they sent Werner von Alvensleben, the same von Alvensleben who in the eyes of the young von Ribbentrop had once given glamour to Canada, to warn Hitler that the army was ready to launch a *putsch* from its lair in Potsdam to 'clean out the whole mess in government'. They wanted to scare Hitler into withdrawing, but they miscalculated. Von Alvensleben found Hitler's group having afternoon coffee and cake at Goebbels' apartment on the square called Reichs-kanzlerplatz (later Adolf Hitler Platz, now Theodor Heuss Platz). The alarmed Hitler ordered Count von Helldorf, now the head of the Berlin stormtroopers, to mobilize his thugs from every *Kneipe* (pub) and beerhall. Hitler warned Meissner, and an immediate date was set for the swearing-in of the coalition government Hitler had wanted to avoid. Hitler would be Chancellor, with only two Nazis in his Cabinet. The other Ministers would be conservatives.[21] The time for the swearing-in was fixed for 11 a.m. on 30 January. Rumours of a military revolt increased. The Presidential Reichswehr guards were alerted. Escape plans were made. A plane was ordered to stand by. Oskar von Hin-denburg himself went to the railway station to intercept the new Reichswehr Minister von Blomberg, who was arriving from the Geneva disarmament conference. Von Blomberg was told to avoid his new offices at army headquarters in the Bendlerstrasse, because he might be arrested there. Instead, von Blomberg walked to the Presidential Palace.

Hitler, Göring, Goebbels and Röhm were at the Kaiserhof Hotel across the street from the Chancellery. The superstitious Hitler was driven the few yards in his usual large black Mercedes. He wanted to make an impressive entrance. Waiting in Meissner's office for the swearing-in, the other candidates for office argued and haggled until Meissner told them it was time. In fact, they had already kept the old President waiting fifteen minutes. Shortly after 11.15 a.m. they walked through a dusting of snow to the presidential reception hall.[22] Von Hindenburg was ill tempered, so the ceremony was brief.

Hitler's anxious group peered through field glasses from the Kaiserhof and waited for Hitler to emerge. When he came out of the Chancellery, he looked sombre. A few minutes later he was among them. There were tears in his eyes. He was Chancellor!

The group of enthusiastic Nazis in front of the hotel were ecstatic: 'Heil! Heil Hitler!'

Only half an hour earlier, von Papen's wife had looked across her wintry garden at the line of men following each other towards the presidential ceremony. She turned to young Alexander Stahlberg and with a shaking voice said, 'Oh my God, oh my God, I am afraid!'

That night was the first of many occasions when Dr Joseph Goebbels, Hitler's propaganda genius, would mask Germany's face.[23] There was to be a huge torchlight parade through the Brandenburg Gate to celebrate the appointment of Adolf Hitler.

Von Papen, the new Vice Chancellor, had rented a balcony suite at the luxurious Adlon Hotel, overlooking the square in front of the Brandenburg Gate. His family and friends were there to view the parade of stormtroopers through the gate's immense arches and in front of the 'jubilant crowds'. The torchlight parade did indeed take place, but the crowd was slim and somewhat apathetic. The suite underneath von Papen's was rented by Hans Albers, Germany's dashing blond film hero, who appeared in full evening dress on his balcony, flanked by two beautiful girls in low-cut gowns despite the chill. They were all drinking champagne, toasting the sparse crowd and waving.

The world has often seen photos and films of that torchlight parade, but the marchers they saw did not parade on the night of 30 January 1933. It was much too dark that night, the marchers were ragged, and no searchlights had been positioned. The whole parade was restaged a day later by Goebbels, with floodlights and cameras in place and film directors to channel the brown-shirted, torch-carrying marchers. It was the first typical Third Reich propaganda fabrication.

And what about the von Ribbentrops, now that Joachim's new idol and pupil would decide the future of Germany? Joachim had waited at the Kaiserhof Hotel with Göring, Röhm and Goebbels, but no one had paid any attention to him. Feeling snubbed, he returned home to Dahlem.

At first, Joachim and Annelies were pleased, hoping that once the first rush of events had died down they would be asked into the new Chancellor's circle to be thanked for their friendship and help and then shown some tokens of respect and distinction. They waited in vain. Others had previous claims, mainly Hitler's 'old fighters', who were sure they would now be rewarded with important posts. These old Nazis, the real revolutionaries, had their own vision of a Nazified Germany. The last thing they had in mind was that a bunch of arrogant aristocrats would continue to run the army and the government. There were millions who wore SA and SS uniforms and who now considered themselves Germany's true soldiers. As the 'Horst Wessel Lied', the party's anthem, proclaimed: 'Hold high the flag, close your ranks! The SA is marching!'* The SA's chief, Ernst Röhm, would see that his men got their due.

The next claims made on Hitler came from the military, the Foreign Ministry and heavy industry precisely because of these street brawlers. The General Staff of the Reichswehr wanted to be reassured, and the titled gentlemen of the Foreign Ministry wanted to be reassured, and the heads of heavy industry wanted to be reassured, and, last but not least, the outside world also wanted to be reassured. Ambassadors from all over the world had to report these German events to their governments. Some were openly cynical. Some were cautiously optimistic. The French, British, American and Italian Ambassadors, whose countries had all been signatories to the Versailles Peace Treaty, now had to deal with a man who had sworn to wipe away the treaty and its reparations. Fascist Italy was still close to Great Britain. Benito Mussolini viewed Hitler with the tolerance of a master for a pupil, but he was soon taken aback by the brutal anti-Semitism and fierce methods of the Nazis. He was hoping and waiting for moderation and hoping for the best. In 1933, only the Soviets needed no clarification. Joseph Stalin knew exactly where he stood: he knew he was hated and so was his country.

The von Ribbentrops had only secondary claims to attention. They would have to wait their turn. Joachim von Ribbentrop was unable even to contact his former dinner guest, and he pouted. According to von Papen, von Ribbentrop then approached him, asking that he be proposed for the job of state secretary (chief of staff) of the Foreign Ministry. He suggested that von Papen could discuss the matter with Baron Konstantin von Neurath, the Foreign Minister. At von Hindenburg's insistence, von Neurath had remained in the Cabinet, and his State Secretary, von Bülow, was a respected professional.

If, indeed, von Ribbentrop had proposed himself for this post, it was an absurd notion. In the structure of German ministries, a state secretary has to possess great administrative, legal and diplomatic skills. He must be a professional. Von Papen had the habit of bending the facts, and it is unlikely that Joachim von Ribbentrop, even if goaded by Annelies,

---

* Horst Wessel was a Berlin pimp who joined the SA, was killed in a brawl and then raised to Nazi sainthood by party propagandists.

would have had the temerity to confront the professionals of the Wilhelm-strasse.

Baron von Neurath, a tall, corpulent, impeccably tailored *bon vivant*, had been Ambassador in London under Brüning. He was then appointed to von Papen's 'Barons' Cabinet' as foreign minister. His contemporary, André François-Poncet, offered a full catalogue of adjectives for him: 'good humoured, simple, dignified, polite, south German'. Also 'not frank and a liar, no moral courage and ... lazy'. Nevertheless, von Hindenburg trusted and admired him. Von Neurath, a German diplomat of the old school, cheered the old man's Junker heart, even though 'he was from the south'. Prussians usually considered south Germans jolly but slack and not dependable.

Von Neurath had met von Ribbentrop briefly, and from the very beginning no love was lost between the mature, opportunistic diplomat and the ambitious, younger wine merchant. At the Foreign Ministry, the Auswärtiges Amt, they were aware that Adolf Hitler had been listening for months before his appointment to the von Ribbentrop notions of foreign policy during the private dinners in Dahlem. Hitler was never reluctant to play off one adviser against another, and he must certainly have quoted the opinions of 'Herr von Ribbentrop' to von Neurath, raising some hackles. But the professionals in the Auswärtiges Amt were not the only ones to show disdain for Joachim von Ribbentrop. Old Nazi Party cronies had watched with alarm while 'their' Adolf became a constant visitor at Lenzeallee. They feared that Adolf Hitler would be diverted from his revolutionary course and led into the ways of the *haute bourgeoisie*. Things like champagne, tennis courts, swimming pools and butlers went counter to the true National Socialist ideal. Their anthem, the 'Horst Wessel Lied', referred to those who had become the victims of 'Communism and the reactionaries'. Besides, von Ribbentrop's fairly recent entry into the party rendered him suspect, an opportunist, a fake Nazi. In the years to come, the old party members never lost their disdain for Joachim von Ribbentrop. It drove him to ever greater efforts to prove that he was a *true* National Socialist, an impulse which caused him to make some of his greatest errors of judgment.

To obviate criticism, he sooned joined the black-uniformed SS and stayed a member for the rest of his life – at the time of his death he held the honorary rank of SS general. Throughout his career in the service of Adolf Hitler, there were only two 'party' portraits on his desk: one of the Führer and one of Heinrich Himmler, the head (Reichsführer) of the SS and one of the few old party men with whom von Ribbentrop exchanged the familiar appellation 'Du', the mark of close friendship among Germans. But in 1933 at the head of the Hitler hierarchy stood Göring, Hess, Frick, Goebbels, Röhm, Himmler and then the *zweite Garnitur*, the second level just below them. Von Ribbentrop did not rate.

In 1933 the elite, black-uniformed SS was still young. The real party troops were the 'brown grenadiers', the SA stormtroopers, under their brutal leader Ernst Röhm. Ex-Captain Röhm was the classic mercenary, a scar-faced, thick-bellied and snub-nosed man who stood on stubby legs. He looked more like a drill sergeant than an officer, and the gentry who commanded the Reichswehr shuddered at the sight of him. They were also alarmed by Röhm's vast army of brawling, jack-booted Brown Shirts, who had been recruited from the millions of unemployed workers. (The Brown Shirts were really 'Tan Shirts': the uniforms were cheap copies of British Colonial khaki shirts and riding breeches, including the 'Sam Browne' belt and shoulder strap. The outfit was completed with store-bought riding boots and a vague version of the French Army *képi* head-gear, usually worn with chinstrap down. The whole effect was supposed to be 'tough'. In party propaganda illustrations, the SA man always had a boxer's broken nose and a thick neck.)

The Reichswehr's commanders were aware that Röhm saw himself as the commander of Germany's *real* army. Plain, old-fashioned snobbery aside, the vulgar Röhm represented a real danger and much more than a mere embarrassment in the *Offiziers Kasino*, the officers' mess.

Only two months after Hitler became Chancellor the SA mounted a brawling boycott of Jewish stores. Armed with nightsticks, they planted themselves in front of shop entrances, daring anyone to walk past them. They carried placards which proclaimed, 'Germans, defend yourselves! Do not buy from Jews!' Stars of David were smeared on to display windows, and billboards were plastered everywhere which repeated their shouted threats. It was the first such public outrage. The police stood by benignly, because the SA had just been legalized as 'auxiliary' police by decree of Hermann Göring.

The news soon reached the United States, but Americans were more concerned with the Depression, hoping the newly elected Franklin D. Roosevelt could bring back the 'Happy Days' his campaign song had promised. The America of 1933 was still racially segregated, *de jure* below the Mason Dixon line and *de facto* everywhere else. Americans freely used terms like 'Wop', 'Mick', 'Polack', 'Kike' and 'Nigger'. The country was widely anti-Semitic. Many clubs, apartment houses, residential areas, resorts and hotels were 'restricted', a euphemism for 'Jews not wanted', and they were often advertised as such.

America's Jewish population was deeply divided between the descendants of German Jews who had immigrated in the early and mid-nineteenth century and the more recent arrivals from the ghettoes of Russia, Poland and the Balkans.

The German Jews had brought their Germanism with them. They loved order, decorum, *kultur*. They were bankers and merchants who founded their own clubs, built their own apartment houses. Their rigidly structured world was dominated by Kuhns, Loebs, Lehmans and Schiffs. They snubbed 'eastern' Jews whom they considered pushy and vulgar. Their attitude was not unlike that of the old Jewish families in pre-Hitler Germany.

The bad news from Nazi Germany left many of America's 'German' Jews strangely apologetic. Cyrus Adler, President of the German-dominated American Jewish Committee, said, 'There is too much public discussion [about the Nazi acts]. Our Christian fellow citizens will get tired of us.'

When a large number of American 'eastern-descended' Jews demanded an immediate trade boycott of Germany, the American Jewish Committee objected. Despite them, Rabbi Stephen Wise, a powerful American Jewish leader with direct access to Franklin D. Roosevelt, called an anti-German protest meeting. He packed 20,000 into Madison Square Garden, and another 35,000 had to stand outside.

Many newspapers headlined Berlin's brown-shirted barbarities. Both the tiny *Poughkeepsie News* and the influential *Chicago Tribune* reported the beatings of Jews and Reichstag deputies, the existence of concentration camps and the newly coined term 'protective arrest'. On 15 April 1933, H. R. Knickerbocker of the *New York Evening Post* wrote about the atrocities as did the *Toledo Times* and *August (Maine) Journal*. Others, like the *Columbus Journal* and the *St Louis Post-Dispatch*, were still ambivalent while the *Washington Post* was incredulous.* During the first Hitler months of 1933, US reporters in Berlin were often urged by American diplomats to moderate their stories.†

On 27 March 1933, Hitler issued a statement through his new foreign press aide Putzi Hanfstaengl that 'all allegations of brutalities are base lies'. Foreign Minister von Neurath and Hitler's banker, Hjalmar Schacht, issued similar denials.

The first tenuous moment of American anger at Nazi Germany had quickly come and would soon have disappeared. But American journalists like Louis Lochner, William Shirer and H. R. Knickerbocker kept reporting the ugly facts from Berlin.

On the day of the boycott, an embarrassed von Ribbentrop, known for his Nazi sympathies but regarded as a moderate, 'civilized' Nazi, invited several Jewish business associates to that calming lunch at the Adlon Hotel,[24] with the unpleasant result mentioned earlier. Thereafter, he thought twice before he dealt with Jews again. By now his old friend Count von Helldorf was the head of Berlin's SA, but von Ribbentrop was 'safely' in the SS, like so many doctors, lawyers and businessmen who shuddered at the proletarian SA. In 1933 the SS was a small, elite

---

* LBI Yearbook, 1984, Secker & Warburg, London, 1984, p. 29.
† *Ibid.*

section of the SA. It had a distinctive uniform (black breeches, tunic and cap), and most of its members had an upper-school or university education. At first, the SS functioned as a politicized 'weekend soldier' organization, a vicious version of London's cheerful Honourable Artillery Company or New York's snobby Squadron A. Full of fanciful Teutonic lore and ideas, the SS was a haven for upper-strata National Socialists.

In broad outline the SS had three 'faces'. There was the 'weekend' (*Algemeine*) SS which von Ribbentrop had joined. Second, there were the SS units under Obergruppenführer Reinhard Heydrich, which included the Party Police (SD or Sicherheitsdienst), the Gestapo and, eventually, the SD's Einsatzkommandos (Action Squads) which pillaged and murdered in the wake of the army's Polish, Baltic, Balkan and Russian campaigns. General Walter Schellenberg, who headed foreign espionage for the SS, also came under Heydrich. Equally frightening were the Death's Head (Totenkopf) units, which ran the concentration camps and were under the command of Oswald Pohl, who equalled Heydrich in rank. Finally, with the war came the Waffen SS (SS at arms), virtually a combat-ready army spawned from Hitler's guard battalion, the Leibstandarte. The Waffen SS had its own infantry, artillery, armour, cavalry and signals. It also recruited from the police, the Death's Head concentration camp units and from foreign countries. There were Waffen SS divisions of Latvian, Estonian, Lithuanian, Norwegian, Ukrainian, Dutch, Belgian and even Indian troopers. Young Rudolf von Ribbentrop served in the division which grew from the Leibstandarte.

The sense of horror all SS uniforms usually conveyed was often due to the second category: Police, Gestapo and Death's Head units and Einsatzkommandos. With the beginning of the war the general SS lost importance, although for the AA (Austwärtiges Amt) there remained a certain opportunistic symbiosis. At the end the AA entered a time of self-protective and sycophantic co-operation with Heydrich's SD although Heydrich despised von Ribbentrop.

In 1933 the first concentration camp was opened at Oranienburg near Berlin for 'political re-education'. It was run by the SA in the most brutal way. The original concentration camps were used for political revenge, not for racial 'cleansing'. The inmates were mostly the Nazis' old political enemies, Communists and Social Democrats. Gangs of stormtroopers raided the Communist Party offices and also arrested socialists, trade unionists and anyone who had ever shown open opposition to the Nazis, had written an article about them or ridiculed them from a cabaret stage. A large number of innocent citizens were in constant danger of being beaten up and incarcerated as stormtroopers started settling their personal scores. Any SA man who had ever been fired, dispossessed or dunned now took his revenge. Any supposed insult was 'righted' with rubber truncheons and steel knuckle dusters. The streets of Berlin became dangerous for anyone who had dark hair and eyes and who would not give an immediate Hitler salute to a roving squad of shouting and singing SA, either on foot or in one of their open swastika-flagged trucks. Incident followed incident. A British Embassy member was beaten up because he did not salute, despite his diplomatic papers.[25] A few months later, the Portuguese Consul General in Hamburg was set upon by an SA squad and had to be hospitalized, mainly because of his 'Jewish appearance'.

Those who were sympathetic to the new regime insisted that 'these brutal things were done without the knowledge of Adolf Hitler'. Later, when Nazi terror was much more widespread and more organized, many people in Germany still said, 'Wenn der Führer das nur wüsste!' (If the Führer only knew!) Eventually everyone would learn that Adolf Hitler knew all. He was the very force which powered the monstrosities.

There is no way that the von Ribbentrops could have failed to see what was happening on the streets of Berlin. All Berliners were aware of the SA thugs and avoided confrontations. To pre-empt any negative reports abroad through Berlin's foreign embassies, State Secretary Bernhard von Bülow immediately instructed all German heads of missions in capitals all over the world to 'exert a calming influence'.

The Nazis had always accused Jews of 'dominating' the scene. For instance, 'everyone' had a Jewish doctor. The fact is that in 1933 when Hitler came to power, Jews made up less than 1 per cent of the total population, 550,000 out of 62 million. In Berlin, they numbered 150,000 out of 4 million, or less than 4 per cent. In all of Germany, there were 9,000 Jewish or part-Jewish doctors out of Germany's 52,000 doctors, or about 17 per cent.

While the SA rampaged through the city of Berlin, Adolf Hitler with his two Nazi Cabinet members quickly demonstrated to von Papen and the other conservatives in the Cabinet that he would not be harnessed by them. On 1 February 1933 he dissolved the Reichstag. On 4 February he dissolved the provincial and municipal assemblies. With the aid of his fellow Nazi Frick, now the Minister of the Interior, and Göring, now the Prussian Minister-President, he fired the top police officials and installed three Nazis: Diels, Lewetzow and Daluege. The SA had already been sworn in as auxiliary police.

On 27 February, the Reichstag building was burned down. Of all the possible explanations that have since been put forward, the most likely is that the fire was started by a mentally retarded Dutch Communist called van der Lubbe and was then spread by a group of SA troopers who used the old underground passageway between Göring's new official residence and the Reichstag building. Count von Helldorf was again at the centre of trouble. Later, he claimed to have been involved. An SA officer named Kruse, an aide of Röhm's, said that he and twenty-three SA troopers were the actual arsonists.[27] In retrospect, one wonders how the burning of any building, no matter how important, could so disrupt the political process. The burning of the Houses of Parliament or the Capitol would not shatter Britain or the USA, but Germans had less trust in their system and were more easily shaken. Two notes of murderous finality trailed after the Reichstag fire. Berlin's Fire Chief, Gempp, was arrested and 'found shot' in his cell. It is assumed he knew too much. Then Hanussen, the nightclub clairvoyant, who had once advised Hitler before the Cologne meeting and was said to have 'recruited' van der Lubbe for his friend von Helldorf, was found shot to death in the woods near Berlin.

On 7 March, using the second emergency decree since his appointment on 30 January, Hitler ordered 5,000 people in Prussia and 2,000 in the Rhineland to be arrested 'for the defence of the state'. On 16 March, he convinced von Hindenburg that the country needed a Minister for Enlightenment and Propaganda, and Dr Joseph Goebbels joined the Cabinet. Then came Goebbels' invention, that hypocritical Potsdam 'Act of State'. It was he who insisted that the old Prussian Junkers and the military appear on 20 March at Potsdam's old Garrison Church in full-dress uniforms with decorations and swords and sashes, while Hitler wore a modest black civilian cutaway coat and striped trousers. It was time to lull the conservatives and the world by making a calming, obedient 'statement'.[26] Hitler made a restrained speech, dwelling on his deep respect for Prussian tradition. He then pledged peace and shook hands – respectfully – with the old Marshal. The Reichswehr gave an outstanding display in the parade which followed.

On 23 March, the Reichstag was reconvened and met at the lavish Kroll Opera House, heard Hitler address the assembly, which was packed with SA and SS uniforms and presided over by Göring. The Führer promised to respect property and individual initiative, grant a debt moratorium to farmers, aid the middle class, work to change joblessness, give special attention to the Reichswehr, and work for peace.

Then he demanded absolute power to carry out his programme without presidential endorsements. Courageously, the senior Social Democratic delegate, Weiss, refused to vote for the full powers Hitler demanded. Then the Chancellor launched a vicious attack on him. The political party which was supposed to provide some equilibrium, the Catholic Centre Party under Monsignor Kaas, was deferential and unwilling to fight Hitler, who was now accorded full powers by 441 votes to 94. He no longer needed President von Hindenburg's signature to enact laws.

The fake humility of Potsdam had been a solemn swindle.[27] Almost instantly all unions were disbanded, the socialists were outlawed and, ironically, the right-wing nationalist Stahlhelm (Steel Helmet) organisation which had backed Hitler since the Harzburg Conference in 1931 was abolished. Three Nationalist Conservative Cabinet members, von

Neurath, the Foreign Minister, Count Schwerin von Krosigk, the Minister of Finance, and Franz von Papen, the Vice Chancellor, quickly abandoned fellow Cabinet Minister Hugenberg, the chubby head of the Stahlhelm. He was out.

Meanwhile, Hitler's round of domestic brutalities continued. Following on the heels of the anti-Jewish riots of 1 April, baited by the Nazis' favourite vulgarian anti-Semite, Julius Streicher, severe anti-Jewish laws were enacted. Streicher, a former schoolteacher, was one of Hitler's old comrades. Then on 14 July came new laws for the sterilization of those with hereditary illnesses and incurable diseases. As André François-Poncet wrote: 'Nazism is debasing Germany and isolating her from civilized societies.'[28] At villages and small towns all over Germany the local SA commanders hoisted banners over the roads leading into each municipality which bore the slogan, 'Jews not desired.' Restaurants and hotels posted similar signs.

This was the Hitler the von Ribbentrops finally managed to entice back to Dahlem for dinner. They need not have counted it a victory. Adolf Hitler always did exactly what was right for himself. He now faced decisions about foreign policy, and he refused to rely only on the guidance of Foreign Minister von Neurath and his Foreign Ministry experts. As usual, Hitler wanted several sources and opinions, all from rivals for his favour, and it was now von Ribbentrop's turn. Between bites of his specially prepared vegetarian meal, Hitler declared that he wanted peace, but Germany had to become 'an equal among nations'. He wanted revisions of the Versailles Pact. Most urgently, he wished to establish connections with England. He declared his friendship for Italy and his disdain for France, and he was fanatical in his hatred for Soviet Russia. To Annelies, as an aside, he confessed he was sorry he had ever 'signalled' any of these views on foreign policy in *Mein Kampf*. During that whole evening, he made no mention of the Jews, and von Ribbentrop, not willing to face another rebuff, did not bring up the subject.

Later, in the library after dinner, Hitler proclaimed his fascination for Great Britain. He asked von Ribbentrop to tell him how Britain's leading circles viewed National Socialism. Von Ribbentrop 'could not report much that was favourable'. Yet he 'sensed Hitler's admiration for Britain'[29] and claimed that 'our mutual feelings about the English became the basis for our mutual trust'. Von Ribbentrop's memoirs, which he wrote shortly before his execution in Nuremberg, continue:

Hitler stated facts others simply had to accept. He was very self-possessed, a man without compromise. He could be courteous and warm, but there was a certain distance he could not help. I am sure it troubled him at times. He could speak freely and amusingly about his army days or his own beginnings, and when he spoke of architecture, one could sense the artistic side of his nature. He could be enormously charming and supremely convincing when he tried to persuade someone. Many men went to 'tell him the real truth' and reappeared totally convinced of *his* view. I also fell under his spell although he called me his 'most difficult' subordinate because I would calmly defend my ideas after he thought he had convinced me. He could be incredibly loyal, but he could also be unreasonably suspicious. He could hurt people deeply. I never understood this split in him. 'Divide and Conquer' was used by him so frequently that there was constant conflict among his collaborators. Particularly in the matter of foreign policy, everyone thought he could participate!

Adolf Hitler had a quick temper, often out of control. At Godesberg [1938] he wanted to break off the Chamberlain talks when the Czechs mobilized. He jumped up with his face tell-tale red. The same at Hendaye with [Generalissimo] Franco, when Suner [Franco's Foreign Minister] said some clumsy things. Same with Henderson [British Ambassador 1937–9] in the Poland crisis, when Henderson slammed his hand on the table. Every time it happened I managed to calm things down. He said to me much later, 'You know I just can't control myself!'

Von Ribbentrop continued, 'No one got close to him except, possibly, Göring. When Göring was in a meeting, I barely seemed to exist. ... Perhaps he was even a bit frightened of Göring! When I once offered to speak to Göring about giving up command of the Luftwaffe in 1944, when it had failed, Hitler said, "God help us, no, Ribbentrop! You should have seen how angry Göring just got when I spoke to him!"' But even Göring lost Hitler's loyalty in the end.

Clearly, Joachim von Ribbentrop wanted to be involved in forming Germany's foreign policies. He felt qualified by virtue of his years of travel, his knowledge of the international world, his service in the war, his inherited sense of political participation. After all, his father had sacrificed his career for political principle. Why, then, should the Foreign Ministry's languid aristocrats and clubmen be more able to advise Adolf Hitler than he?

Von Ribbentrop was not the only one. There were three other men who were sure they could help to guide their Führer to formulate Germany's future *Aussenpolitik*, its foreign policy: one was an international businessman named Lüdecke, another was a Munich millionaire art dealer called Hanfstaengl, and then there was Hitler's long-time associate, Alfred Rosenberg.

Kurt Lüdecke, a right-wing exile, had led an adventurous, cosmopolitan life as a dealer in aircraft and tyres, mostly in Latin America. He held a Mexican passport but was renaturalized when Alfred Rosenberg asked him to return to the 'new' Germany. For a short time, he became press attaché at the Embassy in Washington, but he returned to Berlin to help Rosenberg advise Hitler. Somehow he fell foul of Göring and was sent to a concentration camp, but escaped. By the end of 1933, he was no longer in contention.

'Putzi' Hanfstaengl, towering over the other top Nazis at six foot three inches, was a rich young man from Munich (his family owned a famous art gallery and his mother was a Boston Back Bay Sedgwick) and a Harvard graduate. He was an early backer and follower of Hitler and, since 1930, had been the Nazi Party's foreign press 'expert'. Adolf Hitler often solicited his views, particularly about America and Britain. Somehow, rich Putzi, the Harvard man, became the favourite target of the party Old Guard. They subjected him to unending pranks and practical jokes. He was a born raconteur, amateur bar pianist and court jester, and he never seemed to object to his tormentors.

Eventually, the pranks became more serious. When he was sent out on a plane and 'warned that he might be ejected without a parachute', supposedly a joke, he began to fear for his life. He fled to England and remained there, comfortably in exile. It is possible he was in a position to have blackmailed certain senior Nazis. His son attended London's St Paul's School while German Ambassador von Ribbentrop's son, Rudolf, was at Westminster School, but for obvious reasons the boys' parents avoided contact. Clearly, Hanfstaengl had ceased to be a rival.

The third and most serious contender for the unofficial post of foreign policy adviser was the strange Alfred Rosenberg. Born in Latvia of German parents, Rosenberg, an architect, was a man who brought a religious fervour to his belief in racism and the 'purity' of the National Socialist creed. His book, *The Myth of the Twentieth Century*, a confused jumble of racist philosophy and political theories, became the second bible of National Socialism. The first, of course, was Hitler's *Mein Kampf*. To Rosenberg, National Socialism became an overpowering religion. He was the only senior Nazi who objected to the 1939 Soviet pact on ideological grounds, as 'a betrayal of the National Socialist revolution'. He had studied in Riga and Moscow, was an expert on Russia and had witnessed the Russian Revolution. His contacts among White Russian émigrés were worldwide. It was he who 'unearthed' once more the oft-discredited and poisonous *Protocols of the Elders of Zion*, a slanderous anti-Jewish fraud which 'exposes' Jewish 'plans for world domination'. Although even Hitler was inclined to dismiss his single-minded theories about the world of superior Aryans and inferior non-Aryans, he agreed with some of Rosenberg's basic contentions about the 'inferiority' of certain 'bloods'.

Rosenberg had his chance at foreign policy. In mid-1933 he was sent to England by the party, at his suggestion. He promised he could 'forge certain links' for his Führer and convince leading British circles that

Germany's fight against Communism would benefit all Western civilization. He was invited by F. W. Winterbotham, who was actually (unknown to Rosenberg) a British Intelligence agent, and introduced to June Barlow, Prime Minister Ramsay MacDonald's secretary. He also met Lord Hailsham, the Secretary of War, and some senior RAF people. Towards the end of his trip, Rosenberg placed a wreath at the foot of the Cenotaph, London's main war memorial. Unfortunately, the wreath was bedecked with swastika pennants, and was soon snatched from the memorial by a British officer and thrown into the Thames. (The officer was fined 40 shillings and was delighted to pay the fine.) Rosenberg neither made friends nor influenced anyone, and the story of the wreath caused much laughter about the anti-Nazi incident. Of course, he had no idea that he was being used by British Air Intelligence.

His blunders eventually eliminated him from contention. In mid-1933 Hitler had asked von Ribbentrop to help Rosenberg formulate ideas for the London trip. For lack of a better offer, a reluctant von Ribbentrop had agreed. Then came Rosenberg's failure. At last, von Ribbentrop seemed to have the field to himself. He was given rooms in the offices of the Führer's party deputy, Rudolf Hess, across the street from the Reich Chancellery. So began the Ribbentrop Büro (office), later enlarged, on 24 April 1934, into the Dienststelle Ribbentrop (the Ribbentrop Organization). It was financed by the party and responsible only to the party's Führer, Adolf Hitler. For the next four years it would plague Germany's Foreign Minister von Neurath and his Ministry.

EIGHT

BÜRO TO EMBASSY, 1934–1936

'The German People's Supreme Judge'

As late as December 1933, at a dinner given by André François-Poncet, von Ribbentrop complained that he still had no job in government.[1] He even expressed some doubts about the Nazi Party's future.

But the Büro's small beginnings changed all that. The new 'adviser to the Führer' quickly learned that Adolf Hitler was a man of action, and often precipitate action. Since February 1933, Hitler had shown his anger at the lack of progress made by the Geneva disarmament conference after the departure of the German delegate, General von Blomberg, who was now Hitler's Reichswehr Minister in Berlin. General von Blomberg's former aide in Geneva told friends that his General was not a great Hitler enthusiast and had accepted the Reichswehr Ministry only out of respect for von Hindenburg.[2]

Two party bigwigs visited Geneva to attend the conference as part of the German team. One of them, Reinhard Heydrich, appeared with the 'simulated' SS rank of major-general. At first he kept quiet, but he grew more presumptuous as the days passed. He even insisted that a swastika flag be raised over the hotel where the delegation was housed. Nadolny, the Foreign Ministry official who headed the German Mission, put Heydrich in his place, and the SS 'General' and his assistant, Kruger, soon left Geneva. Nadolny then reported the contretemps to Berlin and was told that Hitler approved his actions. Then Nazi leader Ley and Danzig Nazi chief Forster appeared in Geneva. Ley was mostly drunk and behaved badly. When the South Americans would not accept his credentials, he called them monkeys. But this time Hitler stuck with his man. He insisted that Ley's credentials must be accepted, and Ley then returned to Berlin in triumph. Next, Goebbels came to Geneva. The delegation was soon calling him the 'tricky dwarf'.

It was clear that the party did not intend to take the Geneva disarmament conference seriously. Nevertheless, Hitler stated publicly on 17 May that he did 'not aim to change the face of Europe by force'. The

French then proposed a probationary period during which an international team would inspect German arms facilities. The next meeting of the conference was scheduled for 18 October 1933 but four days before Germany withdrew from the conference and on the 19th, from the League of Nations. Hitler declared that the conference's proposal for international inspection was 'against Germany's national honour'. The sudden withdrawals sent shock waves through Europe's governments. Neither were they greeted with joy by von Neurath at the Auswärtiges Amt or by von Blomberg at the Reichswehr Ministry.[3] As if to advertise his disdain for the League of Nations, Hitler now urged von Neurath to initiate a German–Polish treaty of non-aggression without consulting the League. This was concluded on 25 January 1934.

Hitler decided the time had now come for von Ribbentrop to 'go on patrol' for his Führer. On 2 February 1934 von Neurath advised the German ambassadors in Paris and London ('in strictest confidence') to receive a gentleman called Joachim von Ribbentrop[4] at the suggestion of Chancellor Hitler. A few days later, the British Ambassador in Berlin, Sir Eric Phipps, wrote to the Foreign Secretary, Sir John Simon, about von Ribbentrop: 'No doubt the man is a friend of Hitler's. However, I doubt if he has the influence he claims. Ribbentrop and his wife are self-promoting people, nationalists who deserted the sinking ship of the Republic and in 1933 [sic] joined the Party just in the nick of time.' Phipps' view was no doubt reinforced by Foreign Minister von Neurath, who told him on 5 February that von Ribbentrop was 'insufficiently acquainted with our policy to speak with authority'.[5]

On 20 February, Anthony Eden, Lord Privy Seal, visited Hitler in Berlin to discuss disarmament and the forthcoming Saar plebiscite. Earlier that month von Ribbentrop had met with Phipps and had proposed various plans for armaments and troop parity. There was to be an army of 300,000 men but a maximum of 50,000 stormtroopers. The German air force was to be gauged against the combined French and British air forces. A naval agreement was to allow 35 tons displacement to every hundred British. These were no doubt some of the bases for Eden's discussions with Hitler, although Jacobson, the German historian of record, does not mention von Ribbentrop's presence at the meetings.

Von Ribbentrop continued to dabble. On 7 March German Ambassador Köster in Paris reported that the puzzled French Foreign Minister, Barthou, had on Sunday, 4 March, met a Herr von Ribbentrop, introduced by a mutual friend. Von Ribbentrop was charming, knowledgeable about music and tried to initiate matters of diplomacy.[6] Barthou wanted clarification about von Ribbentrop's role. Meantime, he had suggested to von Ribbentrop that these questions should be handled through normal diplomatic channels. Köster asked for instructions from his chiefs at the Auswärtiges Amt. State Secretary von Bülow said in reply that von

Ribbentrop was 'an old party member [sic], a special intimate of the Chancellor with wide international connections who was travelling with the knowledge of the Auswärtiges Amt to clarify the position of the German government'. He explained that 'Historically, such agents had been used in the past',[7] although he admitted that President von Hindenburg 'did not find it advisable'. Von Ribbentrop had an equally uncertain reception in London. Through his friend Ernest W. Tennant, a Berlin-based British businessman, he met with the former Prime Minister Stanley Baldwin (then serving in Ramsay MacDonald's coalition Cabinet) at the house of J.C.C. Davidson, Chancellor of the Duchy of Lancaster, a friend of Tennant's. Baldwin courteously deferred to Sir John Simon, the Foreign Secretary, who was present, which prevented von Ribbentrop from handing over an unofficial note from Hitler. In contrast, the French Foreign Minister, Barthou, had been quite sarcastic. However, he sent von Ribbentrop a book on Richard Wagner, inscribed: '*En mémoire d'une conversation dans laquelle Wagner a joué le rôle de rapprochement.*'*
Von Ribbentrop considered Barthou a bitter foe of Germany. He was sure that his British and French missions had failed because of reports then circulating in London and Paris that an anti-Hitler *putsch* was about to take place.

Von Ribbentrop had already made some private trips. One was to London late in 1933. He had breakfasted with Stanley Baldwin, introduced by E.W. Tennant, and then met with him in the afternoon at 10 Downing Street, where the Prime Minister Ramsay MacDonald joined them. Von Ribbentrop had emphasized Adolf Hitler's desire for friendship and arms parity. He believed that Baldwin's speech in Parliament the following day showed he had been favourably impressed. Von Ribbentrop also took credit for having persuaded Hitler to give a conciliatory interview to the Paris paper *L'Information* and its foreign editor, Count Fernand de Brinon. Finally, von Ribbentrop was sure he had influenced Adolf Hitler to consider giving up German claims to Alsace Lorraine, the province where von Ribbentrop had spent so much of his Francophile boyhood.

On 20 April 1934, at the urging of Adolf Hitler, President von Hindenburg appointed von Ribbentrop 'Plenipotentiary for Matters of Disarmament'. (The old man had asked, 'What, that wine merchant?', but Meissner had reassured him by saying that von Ribbentrop was from 'an old military family'.)[8] Von Ribbentrop was supposed to report officially to von Neurath. In practice, his reports went directly to Adolf Hitler. At last, von Ribbentrop had his first governmental title. He was a man with some official status.

By obtaining the appointment for him, Adolf Hitler had completed one of his typical manoeuvres. Raising von Ribbentrop to the flimsy, sub-

---

* 'To remind us of a conversation in which Wagner played the role of peacemaker.'

ambassadorial rank of plenipotentiary, Hitler had rattled the aristocrats
at the Foreign Ministry, startled foreign governments and also propped
up the vanities of the ambitious von Ribbentrops. At the same time, he
had signalled to his overbearing old Nazi cronies his special regard for
von Ribbentrop.

The diplomats who ran the Foreign Office now made a protective move
of their own. They appointed one of their brightest young men, the thirty-
one-year-old Erich Kordt, an expert on disarmament, to act as their
liaison on an attachment to the new emissary. Strangely, the normally
suspicious von Ribbentrop was pleased with the appointment. Perhaps he
realized he would need expert guidance. At the same time, von Ribbentrop
widened his fledgling Büro by recruiting a staff of advisers. He requested
and was assigned his own suite of offices opposite the Foreign Ministry
at Wilhelmstrasse 64, one floor above street level in the old Bismarck
Palais. The Büro was small and so dark that the conference room was
called the 'Blue Grotto'.

Erich Kordt described his new chief, the forty-year-old Plenipotentiary
for Disarmament.

> Elegantly dressed, greying hair, watery eyes with one half-closed, a tic
> in the cheek muscles. Trying to look energetic. Nothing natural about
> him. He walks up and down, keys in pocket clinking. Then lunch at
> the Dahlem house: elegant, in the English style, much good art. Frau
> von Ribbentrop seemed ill. I hear she had many operations, constant
> headaches.[9]

The first four staff to join the Büro ranged from a shipbuilder to a
prince, each chosen for his speciality. Soon there were thirteen of them.
The following year there were thirty-three, and at its peak in 1936 the
enlarged Büro, now called Dienststelle (Agency),[10] had a staff of 150 and
a budget of 10 million Marks, paid for by the Nazi Party, not by the
government. To assist the party, heavy industry was 'induced' to produce
some of the money. Roland Brauweiler, the head of the union of industrial
companies, complained of the party's 'bottomless shnorring', using the
Yiddish term for 'begging'.

In May, von Ribbentrop returned to London as plenipotentiary.
Bypassing German Ambassador von Hösch, von Ribbentrop and Kordt
tried several hotels and finally found rooms in the Savoy through one of
von Ribbentrop's business friends. The evening papers headlined:
'Mystery Emissary from Hitler has arrived!' On 10 May he had a meeting
with Sir John Simon, Anthony Eden, Lord Stanhope (the First Lord of
the Admiralty) and Sir Robert Vansittart (Permanent Under Secretary at
the Foreign Office). Once more he assured them of Hitler's warm feelings
for Britain and asked them to postpone the German disarmament conference. They told him, courteously, that it was impossible. To Kordt's

dismay, von Ribbentrop's report to Berlin nevertheless implied that he had achieved the postponement, and on his return on 15 May he was greeted at the door of the Chancellor's anteroom by a happy Adolf Hitler.[11] Kordt was sure that von Ribbentrop had ruined himself. He was wrong. Von Ribbentrop had a believing patron in Berlin.

On 18 May, von Ribbentrop went to Rome, staying with the German Ambassador, von Hassell. He called on Mussolini on the 19th, hoping to use his influence to bring about the postponement of the disarmament conference.

Despite all his efforts, the conference began on 20 May. What were the feelings at the Auswärtiges Amt, the AA, among the professionals who were now being bypassed by this new 'shadow' ministry backed by the Nazi Chancellor and by his Nazi Cabinet ministers? Kordt wrote, 'They are highly critical of the Nazis, but mostly they are loyal officials.' Also, a few real Nazis had recently joined the AA, and one needed to be careful of them. All over Germany that most hidden of attitudes, 'inner emigration', now began to form. For the next thirteen years people hid within themselves, withdrew and became silent.

The first true Nazi in the AA was Prince Josias zu Waldeck und Pyrmont. He was assigned to the Ministry's Personnel Department. As a Nazi, this gave him dangerous control over those to be hired, fired or jailed. There was also an old department called Referat (Department) Deutschland, originally the liaison office between AA and the various political parties, so innocuous it was manned by one official. It was now expected to monitor the political side of AA and spy on it. Its new head, protesting at this unsavoury mission, was denounced by Prince Waldeck und Pyrmont and was arrested by the Gestapo on 30 June 1934. After he had been freed, he was 'cured' of any further urge to criticize.

Von Ribbentrop, not an old party comrade nor part of the AA establishment, made sure he stayed close to the Reich Chancellery and to Adolf Hitler. By 1934 a bizarre Nero's court had developed around the Führer. Kordt, who visited the Chancellery frequently, wrote these impressions:

To enter the Chancellery, one had to pass police, army guards, then SS guards. One finally entered a big anteroom which was constantly filled with twenty or thirty hangers-on and permanent private emissaries from the various top Nazis like Göring. Dietrich, the Press Chief of the Chancellery, was always there. Some people were waiting for special audiences. Everyone mumbled in subdued, respectful tones or read the blue AA reports which contained the foreign news not published in the press. These reports were known as the 'Blue Plague'. Then a voice boomed, 'The Führer is coming!' and silence would fall and certain gentlemen who had been loitering now disappeared in a hurry.

Hitler loved to keep people waiting in order to humiliate them. Some people waited for days in that anteroom, losing prestige in the eyes of the others with the passage of each day.

Von Ribbentrop developed into a skilled anteroom 'waiter'. He listened to Hitler's statements, repeated by people who had just seen the Führer, and then reported arrogantly, or resignedly, what Hitler had said about this or that. If people agreed with Hitler and things went wrong, said Kordt, the Chancellor never got angry. He assumed there was no other solution except his own. Professional yes-men were usually happy. If you disagreed or failed to agree with him and things went wrong, then he lashed out at you.

On 5 June a sudden rumour made the rounds that Ernst Röhm, head of the SA, tired of the Reichswehr's conciliatory attitude to the Geneva arms talks, wanted to take over the army to install himself as Reichswehr Minister. General von Blomberg, who held that post, and the top army and navy people were 'ready to shoot'. Erich Kordt and his brother Theo met two of von Blomberg's aides at a friend's house. One of them, the naval aide, hoped that there would soon be a test of strength. The rumours died down after a few days, but they presaged disaster for Röhm.

In mid-June 1934, von Ribbentrop made his own attempt to persuade the French to change their stance on the harsh disarmament terms of the Versailles Treaty. Several important French, Belgian and Luxemburg industrialists and bankers were in Berlin for a conference. He invited them all to a dinner, using the connections of Reichsbank President Hjalmar Schacht and the prestige of Count Schwerin von Krosigk, the Minister of Finance, both of whom were also asked to attend. The guests were senior people from Arbed, the French–Belgian–Luxemburg steel company and also from the Banque d'Industrie et du Commerce. Using these and other contacts, including Lazard Frères, he went to Paris on 16 June and was introduced to the influential French politician Daladier, under the sponsorship of the pro-Nazi Count Fernand de Brinon of the newspaper *L'Information*. Daladier said that French–German relations were '*dans un état lamentable*'. After all, on 6 June Hitler had ordered the tripling of the Reichswehr from 100,000 to 300,000 men. Von Ribbentrop also met again with Barthou, the Foreign Minister, at the Quai d'Orsay. However, arranging a meeting with the Prime Minister, ex-President Doumergue, proved to be less simple. Protocol demanded a formal diplomatic introduction, and von Ribbentrop was below ambassadorial rank. Embarrassingly, he had to turn to German Ambassador Köster who gleefully prepared the audience and sent along an Embassy official as chaperone. In Doumergue's anteroom, the rumour was that the 'mystery visitor' was probably Schuschnigg, the Austrian politician, since von Ribbentrop had left his Austrian-made Habig hat in the Prime Minister's cloakroom during the meeting.[12]

A rush of events would soon make it difficult to explain Germany to foreign observers. On 16 June, Franz von Papen, the Vice Chancellor, began the sequence with an uncharacteristically open speech at Marburg University in Hessia. He lamented the suppression of German Christianity and described the single-party system as only a temporary necessity. He asked how Germany expected to fulfil its mission in Europe by removing itself from the realm of Christian nations. He hinted at the lack of character, the self-seeking arrogance, the vulgarity and the untruthfulness which was behind this German revolution.[13]

After the speech, Edgar Jung, one of von Papen's associates and the man who had written the speech for him, had only thirteen days left to live. He was to be murdered by SS police. Von Papen's office in the Voss Strasse was raided by SS police and the Gestapo. His press aide, Herbert von Bose, was also shot at his desk. This was only the beginning.

Next came rumours which shook the Nazi regime and sent shock waves abroad. They focused on Ernst Röhm, one of Adolf Hitler's closest friends and long-term comrades. Röhm had expressed his complaints and ambitions quite openly. He despised the 'decay' of the National Socialist revolution and its compromises with 'reactionary elements' in the army and the aristocracy. He visualized a new, aggressive Germany led by a revolutionary people's army, under the command of men who had emerged from the National Socialist 'gut' of Germany. He despised the army's theoreticians and 'old fogeys'.[14] He commanded 500,000 SA men, and he had even made an appeal to a small group of opportunistic young Reichswehr officers. In February 1934 Röhm confronted General von Blomberg with demands which would have turned over all national defence to him and his stormtroops. Von Blomberg appealed to Hitler and during a meeting on 28 February Hitler negotiated a compromise. The Reichswehr would be the nation's only army, while the SA would train men before and after they had served in the Reichswehr. After leaving the room, Röhm shouted that he would never stick to this 'ridiculous agreement' and that 'the Corporal would now have to go on leave. If we can't get there with him, we'll get there without him!'[15]

One of his top aides, SA General Lutze, denounced Röhm to Himmler, head of the SS and one of Röhm's oldest Nazi comrades. Himmler turned to Reinhard Heydrich, one of the new, young SS leaders, a fierce former navy officer who eventually executed the brutal plan for removing Röhm and his group. Heydrich, cashiered by the navy for offences against the code of honour, had already shown his style at the Geneva disarmament conference. He would soon become the coldest, most brutal man in the cold and brutal SS. Himmler also induced Röhm's rival, Göring, to co-operate.

The rebel Röhm and Hitler had further stormy meetings. Then on 8 June the party newspaper, *Völkischer Beobachter*, suddenly announced that Röhm had to take several weeks' sick leave at a Bavarian spa called Bad Wiessee and that the entire SA would go on one month's furlough beginning 1 July. Röhm seemed beaten. But this quashed Heydrich's plans to accuse Röhm and his SA leaders of insurrection and then to slaughter them.

Until the Röhm trouble, Hitler had been playing his usual hand. He wanted the SA to act as a counter-balance to the army, and he wanted the army to keep Röhm in check. This was now no longer possible. The army was fed up, and Hitler could wait no longer. The SS Leibstandarte's chief, Sepp Dietrich, a street brawler turned SS general, drew weapons from the acquiescent army for his SS men. Hitler then ordered all SA chiefs to meet him on 30 June for a special conference at Bad Wiessee, the spa where Röhm was taking the cure.

After he had been fed two false rumours that an SA insurrection was scheduled for that very day, a nervous, shaking Hitler flew to Munich in his Junkers 52 plane. Munich's SA chiefs were immediately arrested. He then drove on to Bad Wiessee through the early-morning mountain mist. At 6.30 a.m. he entered the inn where Röhm and his men were staying, pushed his way past a startled, awestruck innkeeper and then burst into the sleepy Ernst Röhm's room, gun in hand, backed by SS and police. He ordered Röhm arrested.

Other SA chiefs, one with his male lover, were dragged out of their beds, told harshly to get dressed and then sent to Stadelheim jail in Munich. The SS now embarked on a bloody campaign of terror all over Germany. Six senior SA leaders were immediately shot in the Munich prison yard. Several senior civilian officials in Munich were also murdered. Others who had been an enemy or a seeming enemy were shot. This included former Chancellor General von Schleicher and his wife, dozens of senior SA leaders, Gregor Strasser, Hitler's old comrade and rival, and even Captain Ehrhardt of the Kapp *putsch*.

Now afraid that Göring and Himmler would become too powerful without Röhm, Hitler almost spared the SA chief, but Göring and Himmler both insisted on Röhm's death. (On 29 June in Dahlem during dinner, Annelies von Ribbentrop had asked Heinrich Himmler what had happened to Röhm. She had not seen him around Berlin. Himmler told her that Röhm was 'as good as dead'.)[16]

The half-naked, sweating Röhm was finally shot in his Munich cell by three minor SS officers after scorning the chance to kill himself. In all, eighty-three people were murdered.[17] Hitler told the Reichstag: 'In this hour I was the German people's supreme judge.'

Later, beside accusations of treason and sedition, Hitler evinced 'righteous disgust' about Röhm's homosexuality, though he had known about it since the early Nazi days. In 1925 Röhm had sued a Berlin gigolo for theft. The man claimed he had refused Röhm when the Nazi chief wanted to perform homosexual acts. He then stole a suitcase from Röhm which contained compromising love letters.[18] Then in 1932 a Munich newspaper, the *Münchener Post*, published a story stating that Röhm was homosexual. The Nazis did not sue. They knew they had no chance.[19] In 1934, the Cardinal of Cologne confronted Hitler with evidence of Röhm's homosexuality. Hitler denied it and said it was a malicious lie.[20] Until 30 June 1934, Hitler said that Röhm's preference was a 'private matter', but this was hardly true, because SA chiefs supplied their commander with young men. Among SA headquarters troops, Röhm's sexual appetites were a very public matter.

Foreign newspapers headlined these events in Nazi Germany. The cruelty of the bloodbath, the display of Hitler's callousness towards his former comrades, the murder of the two von Schleichers and of Gregor Strasser, who were all known among influential foreigners, caused waves of revulsion abroad. German diplomats in London, Paris, Rome and Washington suddenly seemed to confront a frigid world. Those foreigners who had shown sympathy for the 'new' Germany now kept an embarrassed silence.

For the second time since the 1933 anti-Jewish boycott, Joachim von Ribbentrop was face to face with events which went against his very nature. He was a rational, conventional man, of conservative background, an international businessman who cared about his own and his family's place in German and foreign society. He had always worried about the reputation of his country as an equal among nations, and Annelies was a woman of good family and careful upbringing.

The mass murders of Hitler's former Nazi associates and friends and of the von Schleichers, a former Chancellor and his wife, could not have been part of the normal world of the von Ribbentrops, and one can imagine how these things were seen by the Henkells in Wiesbaden, or for that matter by the von Ribbentrops' many friends in Paris and London.

Then, as if to shake off any doubts he might have had, Joachim von Ribbentrop made a violent symbolic gesture: Erich Kordt reports that 30 June, the day of the Röhm affair, was the first time he had seen von Ribbentrop dressed in full SS uniform. The die was cast. The bridges were burned. It is inconceivable that Annelies von Ribbentrop failed to approve.

Germans were presented with a *fait accompli*. The *Völkischer Beobachter* dateline Munich, 1 July 1934, ran this front-page banner headline:

'RÖHM ARRESTED AND DEPOSED. Thorough cleansing of the SA. The SA spirit is victorious. Röhm excluded from Party. The Führer orders Lutze to become the SA's new Chief of Staff.' There was no explanation for Röhm's fall, but another article implied that Röhm's 'unfortunate tendencies' had brought the Führer a 'crisis of conscience'. Elsewhere in the same paper, there are articles about the 'harsh treatment of Austria's workers by their government' and, ominously, a piece about the 'cruelty of Austrian Chancellor Dollfuss' police'. These were typical Goebbels signals of things to come.

(Among the advertisements, there was a half page from Horn's, a Munich men's clothing store, which offered SA uniform shirts in first class poplin with two spare collars, colour SA brown, fadeproof, for 5.25 Reichsmarks and breeches in the new SA olive brown or in black, 9.00 Reichsmarks.)

Should the Goebbels message of 1 July have failed to penetrate, the 14 July edition, now datelined Berlin, carried the following banner headline: 'DEATH IS CERTAIN FOR ANYONE WHO RAISES HIS HAND AGAINST THE STATE!' Sub-headlines read: 'The German Reich is no longer a geographic term but a political unit.' 'A war we have been fighting for one and a half years.' 'The whole people stands behind the Führer.' 'The only ones to carry arms in the Reich are the armed forces, and there is only one carrier of political ideas: the party.' 'He broke his faith to me, and I had to make him pay the consequences.' In effect, the entire newspaper was turned over to these statements from an Adolf Hitler speech to the Reichstag of Friday, 13 July. There was no mention of the murders of the von Schleichers, Gregor Strasser or von Papen's assistant, Jung, although men in von Ribbentrop's position could not help but know all these facts, and Berlin gossip was rampant. As André François-Poncet liked to point out: 'Germans are talkative. Danger excites them. Despite censorship, police and denunciations, they love to gossip!'

The *Völkischer Beobachter* of 14 July listed the senior Nazis in attendance at the Reichstag, but von Ribbentrop was not among them. In 1934, he was still nowhere near the party's top echelon. The other top Nazis were unimpressed by him, with the exception of Heinrich Himmler, head of the SS. Himmler wanted to enlist the co-operation of the Berlin 'society businessman' who seemed to appeal to Hitler. In May 1934 he created him a colonel in the 'weekend' SS. Von Ribbentrop now took advantage of Himmler's friendship and declared himself part of the victorious and newly powerful fraternity by wearing his black uniform quite frequently. To reward it for its cruel actions in Bad Wiessee, Hitler had elevated the SS to independent status.

On 24 July, William Dodd, the new American Ambassador, was a guest in Dahlem. The von Ribbentrops tried to allay his obvious doubts, but what was to follow should have given serious pause to any foreign diplomat who had to deal with the German government.

Neighbouring Austria, the country of Hitler's birth, was governed by the nationalist Engelbert Dollfuss. The Austrian head of state was so tiny he was known among Vienna wags as the Millimetternich. To counteract the Nazis and still satisfy conservative Austrian appetites, he banned the Communist Party and virtually abolished representative government. He introduced a neo-Fascist regime based on close friendship with Austria's big neighbour, Mussolini's Italy. Dollfuss had begun to heal Austria's ailing economy by arranging major loans from France and Britain, but the money was tied to a Franco-British understanding that Austria would stay completely independent of Germany. Dollfuss' neo-Fascist party, the Vaterländische Front, seemed to pre-empt an internal takeover by Austrian Nazis, which would lead to unification with Germany.

Then, on 25 July 1934, Dollfuss was murdered by Austrian Nazis. Despite instant denials from Berlin and the immediate recall and firing of the German Ambassador to Vienna Dr Rieth, the Western world blamed Adolf Hitler for Dollfuss' murder.

An astonishing commentary on the way Adolf Hitler had changed Germany is to be found in a story told by Franz von Papen, then still Vice Chancellor in name, but totally estranged from Hitler following his controversial Marburg speech and the murder of his speechwriter, Jung.[21] A few days after the death of Dollfuss von Papen and his son were at his country estate when there was a sharp knock on the front door. The von Papens drew pistols. They assumed that the SS had come to arrest them, and they were not surprised when they opened the door and found three SS men.

'Herr von Papen, the Führer wishes to speak to you on the phone at once! He is in Bayreuth.' Von Papen feared that he would be shot while he was on the telephone, but an immediate connection was nonetheless made with Hitler, who came straight to the point: 'I want you to go to Vienna as ambassador.' Von Papen, who had been in transit, as yet knew nothing about the Dollfuss murder. He asked why Hitler had called him after all that had happened between them. A shaken, nervous Adolf Hitler told him about Dollfuss and said, 'You must go to Vienna. [Ambassador] Rieth has behaved in an impossible manner and should actually be put before a military tribunal. You are the only man for the job! We're confronting a new Sarajevo!' This last was a reference to the murder of Austria's Crown Prince which was said to have caused the First World War. Von Papen asked Hitler how he could be expected to accept the assignment 'after the events of 30 June'. However, characteristically, he did not say no to Adolf Hitler. Von Papen always landed like a cat.

Most Western diplomats and journalists were sure that the Dollfuss murder had been engineered in Berlin. Even von Ribbentrop, who was still a semi-private observer, could have had few doubts about that, and many of his foreign friends had probably asked him for clarification. The rumours were spreading all over the world.

Reactions from London and Paris were extremely negative. While the 30 June SA purge could possibly have been considered 'an internal matter', a Berlin-directed, Nazi-executed Dollfuss murder was meddling in a foreign country's affairs. Reports in the French and British press ranged from dismay to condemnation. There was equal anger from Rome. Mussolini had been repelled by the 30 June SA massacre.[22] He had called Hitler a 'cruel and ferocious character, an Attila'. The Dollfuss murder brought a much harsher reaction, because Austria was Mussolini's ward, which he wanted kept independent.[23] On 28 July, Rome newspaper *Il Messaggero* declared that 'only fools fall into the same trap twice', a comment on Mussolini's earlier show of trust for Hitler. Italian troops were rushed to the Austrian border. Mussolini issued a guarantee of Austrian independence to right-winger Prince Starhemberg, Austria's Vice Chancellor. Mussolini was bitterly disappointed when France and Britain failed to do the same.[24] Nevertheless, Hitler seemed in full retreat. He even fired Habicht, the Nazi Party's chief in Austria.

Although von Ribbentrop had to assume that German embassies everywhere were bound to report negative reactions to the AA in Berlin, he made it his business to calm the Führer, which was exactly what Adolf Hitler wanted and needed. Even though the Disarmament Plenipotentiary's voice was not a major one, at least it was positive, and that was most welcome. Adolf Hitler often grasped at the straws of pleasant fiction in an ocean of unpleasant truth.

On 3 August, after the Dollfuss débâcle, Hitler closed the Austrian branch of the Nazi Party. Two days later he gave an interview to George Ward Price, senior correspondent of Lord Rothermere's London *Daily Mail*, in which he tried to calm the troubled waters: 'No colonies ... no thoughts of Austrian Anschluss ... possible return to the League of Nations ... end of war psychosis'.[25]

The last great brake on his arbitrary ways was about to be released. On 1 August, unwilling to wait for the actual event, the Cabinet decided to combine the offices of President and Chancellor after von Hindenburg's death. In future, no more presidential approval would be needed by Adolf Hitler. The law was to take effect a day after the old President's death.

The following day von Hindenburg died! Always prepared to clothe the unconstitutional in respectability, the new unification of presidency and chancellorship was 'put to the popular vote' two weeks later. On 19 August the German people voted to approve the measure by a predictable 89.9 per cent.

For two weeks, no last will of von Hindenburg could be located. Then on 15 August Oskar von Hindenburg handed von Papen an envelope with five red seals which he had 'found'. Von Papen brought it to Hitler at the Berghof. It turned out to contain a 'will' in which the old Junker praised Hitler extravagantly and put the fate of Germany into the hands of the man he had often disdainfully called the 'Austrian corporal'. It was generally believed to be bogus,[26] the work of von Papen, Oskar von Hindenburg and State Secretary Meissner. A grateful Hitler rehabilitated von Papen and promoted Oskar von Hindenburg to general. Meissner remained as State Secretary to the Führer and Chancellor.

Another act of obedient surrender took place when Reichswehr Minister von Blomberg ordered that the Reichswehr would take their oath of allegiance not to the German Reich any longer, but to the person of Adolf Hitler. Unlikely though it may seem from today's perspective, in later years many disgusted and disillusioned German officers shied away from assassinating Hitler precisely because of this personal oath.

Later in August, von Ribbentrop was invited to England by Lord Rothermere, the newspaper publisher, whose *Daily Mail* had just interviewed the Führer. The invitation impressed Hitler, and von Ribbentrop's stock continued to rise. He now became Adolf Hitler's advance man in the battle for an alliance with Britain. Other clever men in Hitler's circle might have been assigned more strategic work, but von Ribbentrop was given a very specific task to go with his title. He was to begin by signing some form of arms agreement with Great Britain and he was to continue to enlist sympathetic British men of influence. The arms agreement could be focused on land, sea or air.

It was unusual for Hitler to assign one task to one man. Often several competitors were assigned the same job. Each thought he had the most important responsibility and his Führer's total trust and attention. No doubt Joachim von Ribbentrop felt, exactly as they all did, that he was Hitler's most trusted adviser.

In November von Ribbentrop, accompanied by Erich Kordt, set out for London for another meeting with Sir John Simon and Anthony Eden. This time the subject was an Anglo-German naval agreement. He launched an initiative to establish 'close and warm relationships' in Britain. His informal arrival at Brown's Hotel signalled an unexpected display of British amity. All the evil of the bloody purge of 30 June and the murder of Dollfuss now seemed to have been forgotten in Britain as 'not our business'. Von Ribbentrop was entertained by Lord Londonderry,[27] the Earl of Athlone, the Archbishop of Canterbury and the Labour MP Arthur Henderson. In turn, he invited to breakfast the Lords Lloyd and Stonehaven, Norman Davis of the US Embassy, Major Astor and Mrs Greville, a major Cunard shareholder. There were invitations to London's best clubs and to various hunts. The press was equally anxious to have his ear. Von Ribbentrop spent time with Aubrey Kennedy of *The Times*, Gordon Lennox of the *Telegraph* and Sir Roderic Jones of Reuters. Of course, Lord Rothermere was his original patron, as was one of the senior foreign editors, George Ward Price, now the 'expert' on Hitler.

Von Ribbentrop was not quite so well received at a dinner party given by Lord Cecil, where Austen Chamberlain expressed his anti-German feelings and George Bernard Shaw vented his Irish spleen by telling von Ribbentrop to 'stop talking peace! Talk attack, mayhem and bloody battle, and these English will give you anything you want!'

Also somewhat reluctant was Lord Lothian,[28] one of the architects of the Versailles Treaty. Lothian, now feeling somewhat guilty about the harsh Versailles terms, said he had no objection to German rearmament if 'they could convince the world of their peaceful intentions!' Kordt thought that Lothian regarded von Ribbentrop as more of a courier than a diplomat.

One of the key men von Ribbentrop saw during this trip was Oxford-educated Philip Conwell-Evans, an expert in German history who had lectured in German at Königsberg University. Conwell-Evans was one of the men who believed passionately in Anglo-German friendship and who viewed the Nazi movement's debauches as the temporary mistakes of a young revolutionary movement. He was essentially democratic and by no means anti-Semitic – indeed he often tried to help Jews who were trapped in Germany. His patient attempts to help von Ribbentrop were well meant. He became rather a tragic figure in his pursuit of the impossible. At the end, even he knew that Hitler's Germany and its sins could not be defended.

Banker and Nazi sympathizer E. W. Tennant, a cousin of Lady Oxford, had prepared von Ribbentrop's first unofficial meeting with Stanley Baldwin in 1933. He claimed that Baldwin said he 'liked von Ribbentrop's face' after their first breakfast conference, although Tennant's friend, J.C.C. Davidson, at whose home the meeting took place, denied this.[29] Von Ribbentrop also managed to intrigue the press lord Esmond Harmsworth. He planned to hold a dinner on 19 December 1934 with Hitler in Berlin for both Rothermere and Harmsworth, along with George Ward Price and Ernest Tennant.

British journalists were also invited to the annual Nazi Party rallies at Nuremberg, the first of which took place in September 1933. Hundreds of thousands of men and boys in uniforms from Hitler Youth to storm-troopers and SS filled an immense field which had once been the landing base for dirigibles called the Zeppelinwiese. The party transformed it into the world's largest parade ground. From a platform sixty feet above the massed formations of ardent followers, their Führer preached his fierce sermons, sending his message to his people and to the whole world. At night, hundreds of anti-aircraft floodlights surrounding the field were beamed straight up towards the sky, a 'temple surrounded by pillars of ice', as its designer Albert Speer, Hitler's favourite young architect, called the venue. At one end of the field, facing the participants, stood a Greek revival structure a quarter of a mile long, fronted by the speaker's platform and backed by a thirty-foot cement swastika straddled by its hovering eagle. These party rallies were part Wagnerian opera, part pagan ritual. To the thunder of massed kettle drums, uniformed Nazi legions swore allegiance, shouting their oaths with deep-throated synchronized roars.

Reich Propaganda Minister Goebbels made strenuous efforts to ensure good reports from the foreign press. Certain British freelance journalists were paid to write enthusiastic articles, among them the alcoholic Clifford Sharp of the *New Statesman* and Graham Seton Hutchinson,[30] and James Murphy, who translated *Mein Kampf* into English. Murphy eventually became an employee of Goebbels' Propaganda Ministry in Berlin. Schoolmasters were also approached. H.E. Lewington, German master at the John Ruskin School in Croydon, co-authored a glowing schoolboy biography of Adolf Hitler. Dr Robert Birley, headmaster at Charterhouse School, told Harold Nicolson that Dr Goebbels had arranged a trip to the rally for some Charterhouse pupils.

At first von Ribbentrop could count on some sympathy. Historian Richard Griffiths points out that ever since the 1929 economic crisis some leading British Conservatives had expressed doubt about the moral value of representative capitalist democracy, regretting its materialism and greed. The idea of corporate government, in which a country was run by a 'board' of capable appointees, as demonstrated by Mussolini's Fascism, had great appeal in some surprising quarters. Fascism seemed to show true concern for the working man without brutalizing the bourgeoisie and upper classes like Communism. Ramsay MacDonald, Austen Chamberlain and even Winston Churchill had all expressed praise for Mussolini. Writing from Rome for *The Times* on 21 January 1927, Churchill said of Mussolini, 'If I were an Italian, I'd follow you against Lenin. But we in England have not had to fight this danger and have other ways of doing things.'[31] In 1927, George Bernard Shaw wrote in a letter, 'Mussolini is more socialist than the British Labour Party.' Many voices of doubt about democracy came from unlikely quarters. In 1932, H.G. Wells wrote the pessimistic *After Democracy*. In 1933, the socialist Harold Laski authored *Democracy in Crisis* and J.R.B. Muir asked *Is Democracy a Failure?* in 1934.

Many new non-democratic governments had emerged in countries other than Italy, including Mussolini in Italy in 1922, Mustafa Kemal in Turkey in 1923, Horty in Hungary in 1920, Pilsudski in Poland in 1926, Primo de Rivera in Spain between 1920 and 1930; imperial Japan and Salazar's Portugal were also run by decree. All were non-Communist countries, friendly with the Western democracies. At first the emergence of Hitler's Nazi government following Germany's 'incompetent republic' seemed a natural development. Then came the anti-Jewish boycott, the blood purge of Röhm and the murder of Dollfuss, and many pro-Fascists, including British Conservatives, began to draw sharp distinctions between 'constructive' Fascism and the 'animal brutality' of the Nazis. The Fascists were 'moral and upright'. The Nazis were 'brutal and barbarian'.

Despite this, in 1934 von Ribbentrop could nonetheless count on the pacifism and isolationism of a Britain which had shed so much blood in the trenches of the Great War. Moreover the well-meaning seekers after some new form of 'moral' government, and those who believed in 'peace at any cost', were joined by the many who responded to reports of Nazi cruelties with 'What concern is it of ours?' Von Ribbentrop's efforts and even his early blunders were treated generously by many of Britain's upper class, even though they were not Nazi sympathizers. British hunger for peace misled both von Ribbentrop and his master until five minutes before midnight.

The list of those Britons whose sympathies might be engaged by von Ribbentrop in 1934 is immensely varied. At one end stood the lunatic fringe, the racists, the chauvinists, the haters. Most successful of these was Sir Oswald Mosley, a baronet of great charm and imagination who was described by Harold Nicolson as 'a romantic, his greatest failing'. He began his political life as a Conservative MP before switching to the Labour Party. Concerned by Labour's inability to help working people, he then founded the New Party. The New Party began as a parliamentary party but was soon accused of Fascism and lost many of its former Labourite members. Then the New Party formed a group of 'fisticuffers' much like Hitler's SA to combat any rowdy opposition. In 1931 they lost badly in the elections.

Mosley visited Mussolini in February 1932 and then wrote a laudatory article in the *Daily Mail*. By April 1932, the New Party no longer believed in parliamentarism. It began trying to take over the small British Fascist Party and then tried to merge it with the Imperial Fascist League.

On 1 October 1932 Mosley founded his British Union of Fascists (BUF), with all the requisite black-shirted, hand-raising 'thunder and lightning' trappings. Mosley's attitude was that the 'drama was necessary and efficient' and that the working classes had no sense of the ridiculous. In 1933 his wife died. She had been of American Jewish descent. He was now free of this 'blemish'.

Newspaper magnate Esmond Harmsworth was a believer, declaring that within five years Mosley would be the power in the land. By 1934, the BUF had lost many of its intellectuals but had attracted some upper-middle-class conservatives and some working-class members. When Joachim von Ribbentrop made his first real efforts in Britain, many BUF members tended to distance themselves from Nazism as 'too barbaric and pagan'.[32]

Then on 7 June 1934 the BUF held a major rally in Olympia, using it as a London Sportpalast. Extreme violence broke out between supporters and their opponents in the hall. BUF goon squads duplicated the worst of the SA's brutality. This finished BUF for many who now saw it as nothing but a British Nazi Party.[33] It also brought an end to any support from Lord Rothermere's papers, and many earlier Mosley supporters defected, in part because of Mosley's 'ranting' attacks on Jews. However, to conservative Fascists this was more a matter of style than of content.

That same year some ultra-conservatives formed the January Club, chaired by Sir John Squire, an editor and writer and an admirer of Mussolini. The club was first supported by Dr Forgan, a Fascist who had tried to help Mosley to take over the other Fascist organizations, by Captain H.W. Luttman-Johnson and by the writer Francis Yeats-Brown, the romantic idealist, born in Italy. (Yeats-Brown had soldiered in India; his most famous work, *Bengal Lancer*, was later made into a film.) The naive Yeats-Brown, whose name appeared and reappeared in Fascist and right-wing connections until the outbreak of war, was another devotee of the 'pure' idea of Fascism which envisages an elite administering a benign dictatorship.

The January Club, which began as a study group, provided a forum for 'men interested in modern systems of government'. It gave a largely upper-class platform to the Fascist and corporate-state points of view and also allowed Fascists to listen to those who were not Fascist. Among the speakers were contributors to the *English Review*, which was a stage for Fascist views.

The BUF provided the January Club with Mosley, William Joyce, Sir Donald and Lady Makgill and the newly remarried Mosley's sister-in-law, Lady Ravensdale. Other BUF members at the club were Lady Alexandra Metcalfe, wife of 'Fruity' Metcalfe,[34] who was also a member of the BUF and a close friend of the Prince of Wales. Others who attended included Lord Iddlesley, Lord Francis Hill, Lord and Lady Russell, Sir Philip Magnus and General the Hon. Charles Bruce. Among these participants, surprisingly, there were also some Christian Zionists, who believed in the establishment of a Jewish homeland. When Harold Laski debated with Yeats-Brown and a Miss Currey, both early admirers of Fascism, they pointed out that the Chief Rabbi of Italy was a Fascist and a Mussolini supporter[35] and that there was no anti-Semitism in Fascist Italy.

The BUF still attempted to appear respectable. Dr Forgan insisted that 'what happened under Nazism would not necessarily happen here [in Britain] under Fascism.' One of the few British speakers actually to empathize with the glory of Nazi Germany was Commandant Mary Allen of the London police, who had in January 1934 been an honoured guest of Hitler's and had been eulogized by him as the 'perfect new woman'.

Mosley's third sister-in-law, Unity Mitford, also spoke glowingly about Germany. She had met Hitler during her Munich school days, had then attended the 1933 Nuremberg Party Rally, and was completely besotted with Adolf Hitler and the Nazis.

By July 1934 the BUF had changed. It decided not to accept Jews as members and claimed that it was 'under attack from an international conspiracy'.[36] On the 14th Lord Rothermere finally declared himself in the *Daily Mail*. In an open letter to Mosley he said he was against Fascism, dictatorship, the corporate state and anti-Semitism. Other conservatives now agreed. Even the anti-Semitic Yeats-Brown was 'sick of' Mosley.

British anti-Semites ranged from those who believed in some vague conspiracy theory to the usual, banal sort of social ostracism and stereotyping exemplified by T.S. Eliot's poem 'Bleistein with a Cigar' who turned out to be 'Chicago Semite Viennese', and the popular Bulldog Drummond books by Sapper in which it was said that a certain villain's 'hooked nose proclaimed his race'.[37] Anti-Semitic writer Gordon Bolitho said in 1934 that the 'reason we hear Jews first is that they wail more loudly' and P. Wyndham Lewis, a warm Nazi sympathizer, wrote in 1931 that anti-Semitism is a 'mere bagatelle' which must stand in no one's way. Rolf Gardiner declared in a book published in Berlin in 1933 that the 'smell of Asia was in Ghetto beards' and that every country 'had the Jews it deserved'.

Though Germany's anti-Semitic acts went against the grain of most fair-minded Britons, apologists for Nazi Germany or isolationists existed everywhere and at the highest levels. Griffiths quotes Robert Bruce Lockhart's diary of 13 July 1933: 'The Prince of Wales [said] to Prince Louis Ferdinand of Hohenzollern that "it's no business of ours to interfere in Germany's internal affairs."' Many, like M.G. Balfour of Magdalen College, Oxford, were guilt-ridden by the Versailles Treaty. 'After all,' he wrote in 1936 in a letter to *The Times*, 'we brought the Germans their problems.'

There were two violently anti-Semitic, pro-Nazi MPs: Edward Doran of Tottenham North and Arthur Bateman of North Camberwell. Doran said in a speech in front of the Palace of Westminster that 'we have lost London to the Jews and we will have to make war on them like Germany.'[38] Doran was furious because he had been defeated in an election for Sheriff of the City of London by Councillor Isidore Jacobs. In 1935 Doran and Bateman both lost their seats in Parliament, having badly misjudged their constituents. Apparently anti-Semitism was not the way to the British voter's heart.

At the absolute extreme end of the British Nazi scale stood the Imperial Fascist League, headed by a surgeon, Arnold Leese. He rejected fusion with Mosley's BUF on the ground that Mosley's first wife, Cynthia Curzon, was the granddaughter of Levi Leiter, a grain dealer from

Chicago. Mosley insisted that Leiter was a Dutch Calvinist. Leese then called Mosley a 'kosher Fascist'. Leese even proposed gas chambers to end the Jewish problem.

In 1933, pacifists headed by Dr Margarete Gürtner, who was neither Fascist nor Nazi, founded the Anglo-German Group. She persuaded Lord Allen of Hurtwood to become chairman. This group was composed of left-of-centre pacifists with strong Labour Party, Quaker and League of Nations connections. Among them were Lord Noel Buxton, Charles Roden Buxton, Philip Noel Baker, Horace Alexander, Carl Heath, Sir Walter Layton (who chaired the *New Chronicle* and the *Economist*), John Wheeler-Bennett, Vyvyan Adams MP and W. Arnold-Foster – all men of good will, anxious to find some *modus vivendi* with Nazi Germany. Lord Lothian, the Liberal peer, and von Ribbentrop's friend Philip Conwell-Evans, formerly Lord Noel Buxton's private secretary, also joined.

There was also some exchange between British and German war veterans, mainly pilots. Sir Nigel Thomas, who owned Heston airfield, invited a group of German pilots to England. The whole event was shepherded by F.W. Winterbotham, a British secret agent who had earlier created contacts with Alfred Rosenberg, the Nazi Party's star ideologist who had bungled his trip to England. The Guards Flying Club gave a cocktail party for the Germans, who included one of Germany's top military pilots, Bruno Lörzer, one of the architects of the new Luftwaffe, still illicit under the terms of the Versailles Treaty. Winterbotham was extremely anxious to foster these air force veterans' exchanges to learn as much as he could about the rebuilding of German military aviation, but to von Ribbentrop it must have looked like a welcome development.

In 1934 several semi-important Britons were guests at the Nuremberg Party Rally, among them the Archdeacon of Gloucester. His superior, the Bishop of Gloucester, was a well-known Nazi sympathizer.

At that time the British Royal Family was still firmly under the command of its paternal monarch, King George V, who would soon chastise his heir Edward, the Prince of Wales, for too friendly a speech to the German war veterans in June 1935. 'Chips' Channon (Sir Henry Channon, MP), one of London society's most vivid chroniclers, told how as a result of the scolding the Prince of Wales 'was in a foul mood' at a ball the following night and looked 'like a pouting twelve-year-old'. In January 1935, another of the King's sons, the Duke of Kent, had approached the Air Ministry for a briefing about the German leaders 'for the King' and had been put in touch with a certain Baron William de Ropp, a Baltic-born, naturalized British subject who was one of *The Times'* political writers in Berlin. De Ropp had ingratiated himself with some senior Nazis like Alfred Rosenberg and was frequently 'used' by secret Air Ministry agent Winterbotham. According to Rosenberg, de Ropp told Hitler and Rosenberg that 'the King wishes to know more about the leaders of Germany.' It is probable that the Duke wished the briefing for himself, and used his father as a pretext. Von Ribbentrop, with his naive early notions about the political influence of the British Crown, probably misinterpreted the Duke of Kent's interest and also the Prince of Wales's sympathetic speech to the German war veterans. These were the sort of ideas von Ribbentrop still harboured when he became Ambassador to Great Britain in 1936. He was never able to shake off his schoolboy view of Britain, almost unchanged since his boyhood visit to London, or his Ottawa-born theories about the British Empire and the political power of its aristocracy. He would follow the progressive fate of Edward from Prince of Wales to King to Duke of Windsor with the self-delusions of a film fan about his favourite star. Later, when Edward was ex-King, and he and his Duchess were in exile in Spain, von Ribbentrop was sure Edward could be persuaded to take the throne after a German victory and did his best to arrange the opportunity.

One of the most overrated groups to be assigned a pro-Nazi role was the one loosely described as society. It began with the wildly eccentric, American-born Emerald, Lady Cunard, who conducted a potent salon. Sir Henry Chips Channon, also born American, called her a 'twittering, bejewelled bird'. Channon claimed that it was her influence which in June 1935 encouraged the young Prince of Wales (who the following year was briefly to become Edward VIII) to make a British Legion speech which his father George V angrily judged to be too pro-German. She also introduced Mrs Simpson to the Prince of Wales. The witty, flirtatious Emerald Cunard saw Joachim von Ribbentrop (and his dimpled chin, according to Channon) as a delicious 'real, live Nazi' to be served on a platter to her friends, ironically not unlike the von Ribbentrops' own Dahlem Nazi presentations of 1932.

Her greatest rival, Mrs Ronnie Greville, also a rich widow, the daughter of a brewer, had married into London society. She was a devotee of the Nazi cause and had great personal influence on the Foreign Secretary Sir John Simon, who was said to have once been her lover. In 1934 the so-called 'Cliveden set' had not yet assembled.

For many British society people, Nazi Germany was the latest tourist attraction, where 'one was invited and escorted everywhere by uniformed Nazis'. They told exciting tales of being received by von Ribbentrop and then meeting Hitler. A thrilling safari into deepest Naziland. Harold Nicolson described the Cunard–Greville syndrome and the Londonderry–Astor salons which were to follow: 'The harm which these silly, selfish hostesses give is immense. They convey to foreign envoys the impression that foreign policy is decided in their own drawing rooms. They convey an atmosphere of authority and grandeur when it is only flatulence of the spirit!'

British banker Ernest Tennant, von Ribbentrop's old Berlin friend, in

1935 created the Anglo-German Fellowship, and its German equivalent the Deutsch-Englische Gesellschaft, which in 1935 boasted many influential London members, ranging from devoted Nazi sympathizers to left-of-centre pacifists: Conwell-Evans, the Lords Arnold, Eltisley, Brocket, Londonderry, Lothian and Hollenden, F. C. Tiarks of the Bank of England, the MPs Sir Thomas Moore, Sir Ashton Pownall and Norman J. Hubbert, Sir Murray Sueter, Sir Ernest Benner, Sir Alfred Knox and the Duke of Wellington.

The Fellowship, which came into existence at a period when von Ribbentrop was spending much time in London, began by promoting good will and creating trade connections, but it soon became a platform for a flood of Nazi propaganda. Before long, the Berlin branch, which was near the Foreign Ministry, became so deserted that von Ribbentrop's and the Ministry's officials used it as a sort of private club. Eventually, even von Ribbentrop admitted, in a rare display of humour, that the only Englishman there was Edward VIII, whose picture was on the wall.

Probably the most secure and long-lasting pro-Nazi in the AGF (Anglo-German Fellowship) was Admiral Sir Barry Domville, an eccentric racial theorist, who was later to found the *Link*, the last pre-war, pro-German group in England. Domville, a former head of Naval Intelligence and President of the Royal Naval College until 1934, was suspicious of what he called 'Judmas', a form of Judeo-Masonic conspiracy he had invented. Yet during a 1935 visit to Germany, he told Himmler that the banners in front of villages saying 'Jews not desired' were 'in poor taste' and 'bad for foreign visitors'.

On 13 January 1935 came the next Hitler shock. The inhabitants of the Saar district, which had been under French mandate, voted to return to Germany, with 90.67 per cent in favour. The vote had taken place under a provision of the Versailles Treaty which stated that after fifteen years the Saar could choose to which country it wished to belong. France's new Foreign Minister (Barthou had been assassinated) was Pierre Laval, who seemed unmoved by the Saar's defection, since it was legal. He had just signed an agreement with Mussolini which cleared Italy's 'economic way' into Ethiopia, though this would eventually not be enough for Mussolini. George Ward Price of the *Daily Mail* conducted another interview with Hitler in which the Führer now threatened that anyone who tackled Germany 'would reach into thorns and thistles'. Hitler was on one of his mood-swings. Meeting Lord Allen of Hurtwood he mentioned a plan for creating a 35/100 tons parity between the German and British fleets. Late in January, Hitler met with Lord Lothian, von Ribbentrop, Hess and Conwell-Evans, and again discussed this 35/100 warship parity. He was tightening the screws.

To put some pressure behind these proposals, Hitler decided to lift the cover of secrecy from his new Luftwaffe. Germany now admitted to having 2,500 planes.

The British government soon published a White Paper which accused Germany of secret rearmament. Probably as a result of this official blast, von Neurath, the Foreign Minister, informed the British government early in March that a planned visit by Sir John Simon and Anthony Eden would have to be postponed. The official explanation was that the Führer 'had a cold' and had to 'recuperate in Bavaria'.

France now extended its period for compulsory military service from one to two years to bolster the size of its military. The very next day, Hitler reintroduced compulsory military service to Germany, which until then had only the professional 100,000-man Reichswehr. The plan was to raise an army of 580,000 men. On 18 March, the British protested against this new breach of the Versailles Treaty. On the 21st the French and Italians made their own protests. But there was no doubt: Hitler was raising the stakes.

On 25 March, despite protest and postponement by Hitler, Sir John Simon and Anthony Eden came to Berlin to discuss the state of armament with Hitler, von Neurath and von Ribbentrop. Hitler told them that Germany now had air parity. Hitler's constant *faits accomplis* taught von Ribbentrop lessons in modern statesmanship, conducted the Nazi way.

On 11 April in Stresa, Britain, France and Italy condemned German rearmament, conscription and other treaty breaches. The League of Nations issued a similar protest. Von Ribbentrop could well gloat over his Führer's string of successes, despite the Stresa condemnation. It seemed that Germany's best diplomacy was the mailed fist.

The time had come to modify the Nazi 'blood' laws for diplomatic convenience. Probably with Japan in mind, the German Ministry of the Interior, which administered the racial laws, issued a decree on 18 April which declared that, provided they were not Jews, those who were of foreign blood could be treated as 'Aryans' and exempted from the racial laws if it was found to be 'in the interest of foreign policy'.

Two economic agreements were signed by Germany in April 1935. One gave Soviet Russia long-term credit; the other, with Italy, concerned foreign currency. Von Ribbentrop was learning further lessons, though the ones relating to Britain must have been almost painful for so devoted an Anglophile. A man does not like to discover the clay of his heroes' feet. It must also have embarrassed him to admit to Adolf Hitler that the British were 'just another weak democracy' after his Anglophile tales of admiration. He probably now experienced his first anger and disdain for Great Britain.

In May, Sir Oswald Mosley met Hitler in Berlin for the first time, ushering in the transformation of the BUF from Fascism to National

Socialism. On 11 May 1935 the *Frankfurter Zeitung* published a telegram from Mosley to Streicher, the party's greatest Jew-baiter and vulgarian. The telegram thanked Streicher for congratulating Mosley on an anti-Semitic speech he had delivered in Leicester.

The new Mosley commitment probably heartened the von Ribbentrops. If a British baronet married to the daughter of another noble house was so completely convinced by National Socialism and by the people who led the movement, it would make it easier to overcome certain of his own doubts. These doubts must surely have assailed the conventional von Ribbentrops from time to time, and no amount of wearing of his black SS Standartenführer uniform could have completely silenced the tiny, complaining, inner voice of his upbringing. During these early Nazi years Joachim von Ribbentrop's father was a silent and probably disapproving spectator. Colonel Richard Ribbentrop's natural loyalties were to the embarrassed senior army officers whose few dissenting voices were the first of any consequence to be heard. As for the Henkells of Wiesbaden, they kept a deep silence. The respected Henkell in-law and director Opfermann, a Jew, had recently committed suicide in sorrow over the Nazis.[39]

Whatever doubts Joachim von Ribbentrop might have had seemed to be quickly shed when he was named Ambassador Extraordinary of the German Reich on Special Mission. The pompous title was bestowed for several reasons. Von Ribbentrop had often protested about his lack of ambassadorial rank in dealing with foreign ministers, and he was frequently snubbed by Germany's ambassadors in London and Paris. He could no longer tolerate these humiliations and had frequently and bitterly complained to his Führer. Von Ribbentrop had also won the right to bypass the conventional AA channels. Usually, ambassadors reported to the Foreign Minister, von Neurath. Von Ribbentrop could now report directly to Hitler while submitting a parallel 'courtesy' report to von Neurath: so all his dispatches were addressed to 'Führer and Foreign Minister' in tandem. It was part of Hitler's usual system to duplicate missions and foster rivalries.

The main purpose of the appointment was to arm von Ribbentrop with rank for his London negotiations on the Naval Agreement. The British signalled that such an agreement was acceptable. Only the actual numbers were still undecided, although German demands could have come as no surprise to the British. The figure 35/100 tons had been openly mentioned on several occasions both by Hitler and by von Ribbentrop. According to Dr Paul Schwarz, a former AA official, both von Neurath in Berlin and Ambassador von Hösch in London had called the terms impossible and had declared that they would never be accepted by the British. Hitler insisted that von Ribbentrop could close the agreement, and he was right. Three days before the actual signing, Ambassador von

Hösch, while attending a ball in London, heard his own Naval Attaché, Captain Wassner, confirm that the deal was as good as made.

At this time two nations changed leaders. In Britain Stanley Baldwin succeeded Ramsay MacDonald as Prime Minister; and in France Pierre Laval became Prime Minister. The two men were of entirely different character: Baldwin extremely steadfast, Laval forever the opportunist.

On 2 May 1935, a Franco-Russian mutual assistance pact was signed, giving Hitler both offence and excuse. He relished these pretexts for sudden acts of policy. The pact would be ratified later in February 1936 with instant consequences from the German side. To keep the pot bubbling, Hitler now called an emergency meeting in Munich on 8 June to discuss Danzig, the free-port city on the Baltic, once German and Hanseatic, and then mandated to the Poles after the war. The participants were Hitler, Göring, von Blomberg, Schacht and the two Nazi Party heads in Danzig, Forster and Greiser. With things churning in Germany, von Ribbentrop was once more on his way to London, this time for the naval negotiations. He climbed into a big Junkers plane emblazoned with the letters D-AMY which was to be his private transport for years to come. Travelling with him in other planes were Kordt and Ambassador Paul Schmidt, the AA's brilliant chief interpreter. The thirty-six-year-old Paul Otto Schmidt was a Foreign Ministry professional who predated the Nazis. He was the AA's head interpreter and the man whose face appears in nearly every photograph of Hitler with foreign dignitaries. Schmidt was completely fluent in English, French and Italian, and in the case of Turkish or Japanese he would use the common alternate language. (The Turks spoke French. The Japanese spoke English.) However, he was even more valuable because of his uncanny memory. Both German and foreign negotiators knew they could rely on Schmidt to give an accurate account of the verbal record. Schmidt held senior diplomatic rank and was often delegated to conduct AA business for the RAM (Reichs Aussen Minister), though he did not become a party member until 1943. Also in the party were Admiral Schuster and Captain Kiderlen, Dr Woermann, 'British' expert in the AA, Count Karlfried von Dürckheim (later shelved for being non-'Aryan'). Others came several planeloads later, forty in all. They took two floors of the Carlton House Hotel, and five Mercedes cars were shipped over for them. Von Ribbentrop insisted that the swastika flag be hoisted over the Haymarket entrance of the hotel, causing no small sensation. The treaty had already been prepared down to the smallest detail by Captain Wassner, the Naval Attaché at the German Embassy in London, whom some considered the real architect of the agreement.

First, however, came the celebrations for the Silver Jubilee of King George V and Queen Mary. Each man in the delegation had been issued with a full-dress suit, white tie and tails, for the many London Jubilee balls, including one at Londonderry House.

Dr Paul Schwarz described a party to watch the parade on 3 June given by German Ambassador von Hösch on the terrace of the German Embassy, which had the best view in London, overlooking Pall Mall. The party had divided into three distinct groups: British society guests, then von Hösch, his staff and Diplomatic Corps friends, and finally the von Ribbentrop delegation. The latter raised their arms in the Hitler salute when the royal family passed. There was obvious tension between von Hösch and von Ribbentrop, but von Ribbentrop made some friendly gestures which paid dividends. The newly mollified von Hösch, a wealthy, witty and charming bachelor who was much liked in London society, ensured that von Ribbentrop was invited to a dinner given by Emerald Cunard where he was introduced to the Prince of Wales and Mrs Simpson.[40] Having met Wallis Simpson, von Ribbentrop always made it a routine to send her seventeen roses. No one ever knew why. Diplomats gossiped and even Hitler asked but got no explanation. The recipient seemed equally perplexed. It certainly was not a romance.

On 4 June, treaty discussions started at the Foreign Office. Von Ribbentrop was blunt. He began by saying that the Führer had instructed him to insist on the 35/100 formula without any further negotiation. According to chief Foreign Ministry interpreter Schmidt, whose memory was renowned, these were the actual words: 'If the British government does not accept this at once, we see no purpose in continuing these discussions. We must ask for an immediate decision!' Sir John Simon, taken aback by this undiplomatic opening, red-faced and uncharacteristically angry, excused himself and left. The meeting continued.

After returning to the hotel, the ever-suspicious von Ribbentrop insisted that all Carlton House conversations be held in a whisper and in the centre of each room to avoid any microphones planted in paintings or mirrors by the wily British Security Service. But all was not lost. The next day Sir Robert Craigie of the Foreign Office came to the Carlton House and invited the delegation to meet at the Admiralty at ten o'clock the next morning, 5 June, for 'a pleasant surprise'. Afterwards there would be a luncheon at 10 Downing Street. The following morning the Germans were conducted into the legendary board room of the Admiralty, where for hundreds of years the First Lords of the Admiralty and their associates had made their most important naval decisions.[41] The First Sea Lord, Sir Bolton Eyres-Monsell, informed von Ribbentrop that the proportional strength of 35/100 tons was deemed acceptable. The British Cabinet had agreed after a short discussion, thereby scuttling part of their Stresa protests of six weeks earlier. Privately, Kordt, a Foreign Ministry professional who predated the Nazis, was furious. He believed that if Brüning, the old Weimar Chancellor, had so rapidly received acceptance for breaches of the Versailles Treaty, Germany would have remained a democratic republic.

The success of the crude new Nazi tactics were confirmed by a luncheon in von Ribbentrop's honour at 10 Downing Street, attended by Baldwin, Chancellor of the Exchequer Neville Chamberlain, Eyres-Monsell, Eden and others. Kordt, Schmidt and the other professional German diplomats must have been shaken by the discarding of everything they had deemed acceptable international custom.* Von Ribbentrop soon got into the habit of putting his cards on the table – 'Take it or leave it.' He was now convinced Hitler was right. Schmidt wrote, 'Perhaps von Ribbentrop's rough methods worked! I often remembered that later whenever I had to translate certain distasteful statements made by Hitler or von Ribbentrop which would once have been considered a slap in the face by our pre-1933 diplomats.'

D-AMY flew von Ribbentrop directly to Munich to report his triumph to his Führer at Berchtesgaden's Haus Wachenfeld, as the Berghof was still called. This was where he had first met Hitler. The chalet's front door became one of the most famous photographic 'sets' of the Hitler era. Chamberlain, the Duke of Windsor and David Lloyd George were all photographed stepping out of a 7.7 litre 'Grossen' Mercedes and climbing up these stairs with their SS guard. The step on which Hitler stood to greet them denoted his respect for the visitor. If he descended the entire flight and stood at the bottom, the visitor was of great importance to him. After waiting for a day in Munich, von Ribbentrop and his group were invited to proceed to Berchtesgaden and were greeted as returning heroes. The delegation then returned to London to finalize the formal Naval Agreement, which was completed on 18 June. From London, von Ribbentrop flew to meet Hitler in Hamburg, where he assured his delighted Führer that a wider Anglo-German treaty was now feasible. Twenty million Marks were alloted as a reward to the Ribbentrop Büro, which then became the Dienststelle Ribbentrop, the Ribbentrop Agency, although everyone still called it the Büro.

There were instant protests from France about the Naval Agreement. Laval complained that the Versailles Treaty seemed to have become a private matter between Germany and England. Eden had to fly to Paris to soothe ruffled feelings. Meanwhile, Mussolini had his own surprises for the world. He decided to expand Italy's influence in Africa and threatened war in Ethiopia. Erich Kordt reported the following exchange between Dr Paul Schmidt and Conwell-Evans at the beginning of the Ethiopian crisis which was then brewing. They outlined the perils of appeasement before the political term was invented.

---

* 35/1000 proportion of tonnage led Hitler to order the building of two 'pocket' battleships (maximum armament for minimum tonnage).

Conwell-Evans (ever the pacifist): 'No one wants war, only sanctions.'
Schmidt: 'If you won't fight a small war, you'll have a big one.'
Conwell-Evans: 'But we must think of the Empire and not get involved in Europe.
Schmidt: 'Then you'll lose Europe now and the Empire later!'

July 1935 was a glorious month for von Ribbentrop. He basked in his success and now became Hitler's star adviser in all matters of international diplomacy. At a 3 July meeting in Berlin with Colonel Beck, Poland's Foreign Minister, officially listed in order of attendance, were von Ribbentrop, Göring, von Neurath and Lipski, the Polish Ambassador. That same day, von Ribbentrop stated that he was now responsible for the conduct of colonial policy. On the 11th, he met with US Ambassador Dodd about German–Japanese relations. Von Ribbentrop's star was on the rise. He was taking part in meetings which had once been reserved for Foreign Minister von Neurath. The rumour that he had Hitler's ear caused many foreign statesmen to bypass normal channels.

That July a group of veterans of the British Legion led by Major Fetherston-Godly was received by Adolf Hitler. Von Ribbentrop had persuaded the head of the Berlin Quaker office, Corder Catchpool, to contact Colonel George Crossfield of the British Legion to arrange this visit.[42] Eden had warned Crossfield that they would be used for Nazi propaganda, which of course they were. Following a visit to the 'sanitized' Dachau concentration camp of those early days, Heinrich Himmler hosted a 'small, family dinner for them all'. The veterans found much to admire.

The Dachau of 1934 and 1935 was not the crematorium-armed hell of the 1940s. The Nazis used it as a demonstration facility for distinguished foreign visitors. 'This is how we re-educate our criminals.'

The opening of the 1935 party rally in Nuremberg took place on 10 September. Looming over Europe was Mussolini's threat of war in Ethiopia; in response, the League of Nations planned sanctions against Italy. But in Adolf Hitler's Germany, the world's attention focused on the Nuremberg rally, and that vast parade ground. Its 1935 theme was 'Freedom'. In ironic contrast, Hitler simultaneously proclaimed the new racial laws, technically known as the Reich Citizenship Law and the Law for the Defence of German Blood and German Honour. These were later known throughout the world as the Nuremberg Laws, although they were signed in Berlin by Minister of the Interior Dr Frick on 15 September 1935.

The original version was comparatively mild. It replaced the notion of race with that of blood in the following words (the convoluted Nazi-style German sounds equally clumsy in translation):

German blood does not of itself form a race. Instead, the German people is composed of the members of differing races. However, what all of these races have in common is that their blood is mutually compatible, and that a mixture of these bloods, in contrast to bloods which are not of a related sort, will not cause any inhibitions or tensions.

This bypassed the untenable notion of a 'pure' German race and instead, spoke of compatible 'German-bloodedness' (*Deutsch-blütigkeit*). The laws specifically excluded Jews, gypsies, Negroes, Mongolians or anyone whose blood was 'not akin [*artverwandt*] to German bloods.'[43] The original law was so structured that it was supposed to eliminate Jews without 'causing hardship'. These were mutually exclusive terms since the lawyer, architect, government official or businessman who could not be accredited or licensed by the state would face extreme hardship. Here is the original explanation given in 1935 by Reichsminister Dr Frick:

The Reichscitizenship law and the Law for the Protection of the Blood as well as the attached regulations shall not have the purpose of lowering the standing of members of the Jewish people because of their [exclusion from] membership in the national community. Instead, the exclusion of Jews from official German life and the prevention of racial mixing are imperatively necessary to secure the continuation of the German people's existence. Jews in Germany shall not be prevented from pursuing a livelihood. However, the fate of Germany shall in the future be solely in the hands of the German people.[44]

These original regulations were endlessly changed, modified and brutalized during the coming years. They became unspeakably cruel in major matters, and were also seeded with endless chicanery in minor matters. For instance, three years later: 'In conformity with Paragraph 3 of the Reichscitizenship laws of 1938, certification of all Jewish physicians shall be cancelled as of 30 September 1938.' This eliminated the 9,000 Jewish doctors, of whom 3,152 still practised in Germany in 1938. 709 of them, all decorated for gallantry in the (First) World War, retained a form of temporary certification as 'medical practitioners' with permission to treat Jews and certain non-Jews. These racial laws which ruined so many lives and cost so many more seeped into the most unlikely quarters and even in their least virulent form destroyed human decencies.

As an example, a young AA official, an honorary SS officer called von Thadden, wished to marry. He came from a distinguished, titled military family and had been assigned his SS rank by decree of his ministry. In the routine pre-nuptial 'racial purity' investigation, the SS found that he had a Jewish great-great-grandfather on his maternal side. They refused permission for his marriage and began proceedings to throw him out of the SS, which would have ruined his career in the Foreign Service. Von

Thadden set out to prove that he was really the illegitimate great-great-grandson of a Russian prince and therefore Aryan. The SS accepted his illegitimacy. Von Thadden could now marry and also continue his career, ironically, in the Jewish Affairs department of the AA. In the Third Reich it was better to be an illegitimate Aryan than to be of distinguished family and have a Jewish great-great-grandfather, in this case a man named Ludwig Epenstein, the great-uncle of Dr Hermann von Epenstein who was Hermann Göring's godfather. In fact, it was Göring who had interceded for young von Thadden. These are the first small tragicomic manifestations of the vast evil which was to follow.

Meanwhile, Joachim von Ribbentrop was enjoying his new role. On 27 September 1935, accompanied by Kordt, he paid a visit to Belgium. He met with Belgian Prime Minister van Zeeland and informed him that Germany was dropping its claims to Malmédy and Eupen, two towns which had been discussed by Germany with a view to laying claim to them. He also assured the Belgians that Germany was 'their last bulwark against Communism', his usual sales-line. He received a rather unexpected answer. Van Zeeland said, 'If one improves living standards, there is a decreased danger of Communism and we have managed to do that!' They also talked inconclusively about some former German colonies, then under Belgian mandate.

Next the 'strange blood but still compatible' theory was brought into play.[45] Von Ribbentrop began the first move in one of his favourite game-plans: he made friends with Japan's Military Attaché in Berlin, Lieutenant-Colonel Oshima, son of the German-trained War Minister of Japan. The first flickerings of the Anti-Comintern Pact now showed on the horizon.

Von Ribbentrop had been a busy diplomat since the Naval Agreement, and Konstantin von Neurath, the Foreign Minister, did not fail to notice. He was also aware that the Führer of the Reich had great distrust and even disdain for the slow, meticulous, judicious, titled diplomats at the AA in its traditional home at Wilhelmstrasse 76. To Hitler they seemed inflexible, unimaginative, snobbish and overbearing. On 25 October, the very *ancien régime* von Neurath angrily offered his resignation to Adolf Hitler. It was refused. Hitler was not yet ready to depend on his own duo of von Ribbentrop to the West and Rosenberg to the East. Rosenberg, an Estonian who had studied in Riga and Moscow, was for a short while Hitler's personal Russian expert, despite his failures in England. Rosenberg's power would end with the forthcoming pact with the Soviets. Nor did he want Göring or Goebbels to attempt to elbow their way into the field of foreign policy. He liked things the way they were, with everybody around him hating and mistrusting everybody else while he enjoyed their contest. Von Neurath's resignation would have cost him the entire apparatus of professional German diplomats and their relationship with foreign diplomats. He need not have worried. Despite his threat, von Neurath did not resign. He liked to present himself as the classic aristocrat, diplomatist and grand seigneur, but often enough he showed his true, opportunistic colours. Here is a letter of 30 October 1934 to Hess, Frick and Goebbels, about a directive he had sent to the German Ambassador in London. (Ambassador von Hösch probably sympathized with the Jews.)

> About negotiating or dealing with any Jewish organizations, such a gesture should be an expression of our strength and not of our weakness. The Jewish question must only be addressed from a position of strength and not as a result of any economic or political pressure. To give in on the Jewish question would not lead to a satisfactory resolution of any political situation, nor would it satisfy our Jewish enemies. Instead it would undermine the ideological position of National Socialist Germany. The worse their economic position, the less should we compromise on the Jewish question.

On 28 November 1935 Ernest Tennant's and Conwell-Evans' Anglo-German Fellowship held its first official meeting in London under the chairmanship of Lord Mount Temple, but before the end of the year the appeasers would have to face a new British Foreign Secretary who was a stern critic of Nazi Germany. Two days before Christmas, Anthony Eden replaced Sir Samuel Hoare, who had himself briefly replaced Sir John Simon. The change must have upset Sir Samuel's friend, Mrs Ronnie Greville, whom Harold Nicolson called a 'fat slug filled with venom'. She had complained that there was no British Ambassador at the 1935 Nuremberg rally 'When they did attend Mayday in Moscow!' Anthony Eden would certainly not accommodate her in 1936.

For Joachim and Annelies von Ribbentrop the beginning of 1936 was filled with triumphs, to be followed by setbacks. The year began with a group of German war veterans who visited London on 4 and 19 January. These events was completely overshadowed by the illness of old King George V, who died on the 21st. No doubt von Ribbentrop, after a proper Anglophile moment of mourning for the old King, was gladdened by the seemingly Germanophile new King, Edward VIII. Edward was by then deeply in love with Wallis Simpson and most friendly with some German sympathizers like Emerald Cunard. It was at Emerald Cunard's that von Ribbentrop had first met the new King and his Baltimore-born mistress, and in 1935, Edward had made the controversial speech to the visiting German war veterans. The father who had criticized him now lay in state in Westminster Hall, guarded by four immobile officers with heads bowed and by several gentlemen at arms.

It probably did not cheer von Ribbentrop that von Neurath, a childhood friend of the King's widow, Queen Mary, represented Germany at the state funeral, or that von Neurath then met informally with Anthony Eden.

The following month von Ribbentrop was absorbed by Hitler's anger about the Franco-Soviet pact, which was ratified by the French Chambre des Députés on the 27th by 353 to 164 votes. On 14 June, von Neurath, von Ribbentrop, Göring and von Blomberg met with Hitler, who told them of his plan to send German troops into the demilitarized Rhineland in revenge. This would be the first military move of the many still to come. Hitler also briefed General von Fritsch, Chief of Staff of the Wehrmacht. The reactions of his advisers were half-hearted. Von Neurath and Göring urged caution, as did von Blomberg. It is probable that von Ribbentrop sat on the fence until he could gauge Hitler's true intentions. Eventually, the discussion narrowed to the Führer and the army's Chief of Staff. General von Fritsch said, 'Don't!' But Hitler insisted, 'It's my responsibility.'

On 7 March, using the 'breach of the Locarno Pact [the Franco-Soviet Treaty] by France' as an excuse and trumpeting that Germany's borders were 'threatened by France, indirectly through its new ally Russia and directly by Russia's ally, Czechoslovakia', Hitler sent German troops into the demilitarized Rhineland.

There are few eye-witnesses, but rumours have it that the night of 6–7 March, while his troops were on their way west, had Hitler in fits of nervous hysteria. The troops had orders to withdraw if there was any sign of French resistance. It would have been an enormous international embarrassment if Hitler's nineteen battalions of infantry and thirteen artillery sections, about 35,000 men, had had to turn tail. In the Rhineland, jubilant people greeted the German soldiers. And France made no move.

The Franco-Soviet Treaty was only one item on a list of international developments which primed Hitler's seemingly paranoid Rhineland move. The first was when Soviet Russia doubled its military budget in January 1936. Then in February the socialists were voted into power in Spain. In March, Léon Blum, a socialist and a Jew, became French Prime Minister. To Hitler, the whole left-wing world was now conspiring against Germany.[46] Following a speech by him to the Reichstag justifying the Rhineland move, Bolshevism became the next leitmotif of every conversation held by von Ribbentrop in France or Britain, as justification for the new Luftwaffe, and for the introduction of conscription. Did the Führer not warn the French in his interview with *Paris Midi* (Bertrand de Jouvenal, 21 February) to consider the consequences of their Soviet Pact? There was 'no arch enmity between Germany and France'. De Jouvenal had asked, 'What about your anti-French statements in *Mein Kampf!*' and Hitler replied, 'I'll correct those in the great book of history!'

On 10 April D-AMY and von Ribbentrop bounced their way back across the Channel to London. This time the Plenipotentiary Extraordinary was carrying a very full peace plan to be handed to Anthony Eden. This was Hitler's way: hit them and then propose peace. The proposal contained nineteen points, among them a twenty-five-year non-aggression pact with France and Belgium,[47] no reinforcing of the troops now in the Rhineland, no gas warfare, no bombing of open cities, and the scrapping of tanks. The proposals went on and on. Eden promised to 'study them carefully'.

Nevertheless, the General Staffs of Britain, France and Belgium went ahead with a previously scheduled joint conference, which von Ribbentrop had hoped to see postponed because of Hitler's peace offer. And there was no immediate response to the proposals. A furious von Ribbentrop climbed into D-AMY and returned to Berlin.

One month later, on 7 May, Sir Eric Phipps, HM Ambassador in Berlin, handed the AA a lengthy questionnaire which asked for clarification of many details of the Hitler proposals. Hitler probably deemed it a typical exercise in British sarcasm. The questionnaire was completely ignored by the angry Führer, who called it 'an insult'. Recognizing that Hitler's offer was bogus, the British questionnaire was indeed ironic and terse. The easily affronted Hitler was not amused.

But Adolf Hitler had occupied the Rhineland and explanations, such as they were, had to be rendered to the League of Nations and to the signers of the Locarno Treaty. A meeting was convened in London to demand clarification from Germany. Von Ribbentrop was chosen to represent his country.

In London, there already existed a certain degree of understanding. After all, some people said, the Rhineland *is* German, and Baldwin and Eden calmed the House of Commons. This, they explained, was no hostile move. While the French shared a common frontier with Germany, Britain did not. The French saw things quite differently. The Rhineland had been demilitarized for the sake of French security so that no surprise attack could ever again be launched against France.

Von Ribbentrop appeared before the Council of the League of Nations accompanied by Kordt and Dieckhoff of the AA and Dr Woermann, the AA legal expert, as well as a team of fifty from the Büro. This time, Hitler had expressed the desire to go to London himself and to present his case to the League, but knowing the Führer's mercurial temper von Neurath and von Ribbentrop, unusual allies, had dissuaded him. Now Hitler wished von Ribbentrop to help smooth the way in front of the Council by hinting at an offer by Germany to re-enter the League. The venue for the meeting was beautiful, tan-coloured old St James's Palace. Von Ribbentrop stood up and made his statement in defence of the Rhineland move – the usual accusations against France, Russia, Czechoslovakia and the supposed Soviet plans of aggression. The Council then retired to consider their verdict.

Meanwhile, von Ribbentrop was invited to Sir Robert Vansittart's country house, probably at the suggestion of the much liked Ambassador von Hösch, who was also a guest. Von Hösch knew that Vansittart, the Permanent Under Secretary for Foreign Affairs, and his American wife were no admirers of von Ribbentrop, but he thought he could ease the way for him.

The Council of the League of Nations delivered their verdict: condemnation of Germany. Eleven out of twelve voted in favour. Only Chile abstained. The Versailles Article deemed to have been breached was no. 43. Von Ribbentrop, after some meetings with sympathizers[48] in London, including the Lords Rothermere, Camrose and Kemsley, all men of the press, returned to Berlin to reassure his Führer that despite the League's verdict he need expect no further repercussions from the Rhineland move. To reassure himself further, Hitler asked the German people for a vote of confidence. On 29 March the vote was cast: 98.8 per cent in favour of their Führer. Germany and the League were still going their separate ways.

On 10 April Ambassador Leopold von Hösch died in London. In his memoirs, von Ribbentrop says he mourned him deeply, but according to former diplomat Paul Schwarz, von Ribbentrop did not even attend von Hösch's funeral in Berlin and eventually even had the grave of von Hösch's little pet dachshund in the London Embassy garden levelled.

April 1936 also marked the beginning of the sad and misunderstood career of Charles Lindbergh as a political figure and an unwilling ally of Nazi Germany. It began at the American Embassy in Berlin, on the Tiergartenstrasse, a few miles from the Foreign Ministry.

Major Truman Smith, the American military attaché, frustrated by his inability to learn the secrets of the budding Luftwaffe, invited US Army Reserve Colonel Charles Lindbergh to help him on a patriotic basis. The Lindberghs had withdrawn to rural England, following the kidnapping and murder of their baby in America.

Lindbergh agreed to accept an invitation from the vain Hermann Göring and was indeed shown most of the Luftwaffe's secrets. He made several trips to Germany and Göring even 'surprised' him by decorating him during a dinner at the American Embassy. Lindbergh had never met Hitler and, according to Major Smith, had a low opinion of the Nazis and their racial policies. He was, however, dazzled by the Luftwaffe's fighting power. Lindbergh was certain that neither Great Britain nor the United States stood a fighting chance against Nazi Germany.

He joined the America First Committee, the most powerful and quasi-respectable of the anti-war groups. It was backed by General Robert E. Wood of Sears Roebuck, Douglas Stuart of Quaker Oats, World War ace Captain Eddie Rickenbacker, Henry Ford of Detroit, New York Congressman Hamilton Fish, Senator Burton K. Wheeler, Colonel McCormick of the *Chicago Tribune*, William Grace and Avery Brundage of the American Olympic Committee. Lindbergh became their star.

In a typical speech on 16 September 1941 in Des Moines, Iowa, he said that if America became engulfed in war, it would be 'because of the British, the Jews and Franklin Roosevelt'. These were his views. Were they anti-British, anti-Semitic and anti-Roosevelt, or did he simply single out the three most obvious pro-war factions?

After Pearl Harbor, Lindbergh did courageous war duty, but much of America never forgave his seeming treachery.

The America First Committee, according to J. Edgar Hoover, was secretly supported by Berlin with annual donations of one million dollars.* Another substantial foreign contributor was Swedish magnate Axel Werner Gren.

That August Hitler appointed von Ribbentrop to be von Hösch's successor as Ambassador to the Court of St James. Von Ribbentrop had visited London often, alone or with Annelies, at first on private business and then, after 1933, on the semi-official and official business of Nazi Germany. But he had barely touched the surface of the cynical, poisonous, charming and witty world of London society. The von Ribbentrops probably thought they could cope because, after all, they had learned to deal with Berlin's fierce snobberies. But they were wrong.

The diary of Chips Channon documents the set of mind of that time and the traps which awaited the insider as well as the outsider. Everyone was treated with even-handed venom. He wrote of Emerald Cunard: 'Ribbentrop rang up, the arch-Hitler spy of Europe. She told him the French Ambassador had declared him perfectly charming and his voice dropped with surprise. I asked Emerald whether the Frenchman had ever said such a thing. She laughingly admitted she'd invented it on the spur of the moment.' Von Ribbentrop's friendship with Lord Londonderry gave him the nickname of the 'Londonderry Herr'.

On 7 November 1936 when von Ribbentrop had been in residence as Ambassador for a few months, Channon wrote:

> My feeling is that they will not be a social success in London, though at first I prophesied great things for them; but for all their ambition, they have not the well-bred ease which Londoners demand and Frau von Ribbentrop really dresses too dowdily. She will be the liability, though he has not started off well, either.

This was written after the Channons had been the von Ribbentrops'

---

* Charles Higham, *American Swastika* (New York: Doubleday, 1985), p. 14.

delighted guests in Berlin during the 1936 Olympics, before von Ribbentrop had taken up his post in London.

On 23 November, the Channons hosted a dinner to say goodbye to the much liked Prince and Princess Otto Bismarck, the Prince having served as Chargé d'Affaires until the von Ribbentrops' arrival. Of course, the von Ribbentrops were the 'protocol' guests of honour. Annelies von Ribbentrop described her own sad fate. She told Channon, 'I know that in five years I shall be liked in London, but I am going to have a lonely five years until that happens.' The von Ribbentrops stayed in London just two years. Channon's response was, 'She dresses very badly, with high-fronted evening gowns.'

None was safe: Jew, Nazi, pretender, King, they were all skewered by London society's tongues. This should not have been a matter of import to world history, but in the case of the ambitious, insecure von Ribbentrops, it was. Once they realized they were frequent targets, they despised most cordially the social punishment they were suffering and, most of all, the London people who were their torturers.

Probably because of their London trials, they felt great bitterness towards the British and all things British. Those who were on their side, Conwell-Evans, Tennant and even the Lords Rothermere and Mount Temple, could not protect them from the sting of these rampaging social hornets.

Now there were two separate false assumptions. Adolf Hitler thought the von Ribbentrops were his perfect emissaries to the highest British circles, which was not so. The von Ribbentrops found a much more subtle world than they had ever faced and wrongly believed they were capable of coping with it.

Joachim, the impoverished young provincial ex-officer, had married an influential, rich and assertive wife and had then succumbed to a powerful national leader. Now he was to be overwhelmed once more, this time by a coterie of London society's insiders.

This was painful to the von Ribbentrops but only indirectly to Germany. Much more dangerous to Germany were Robert Vansittart and Duff Cooper, two influential men who were opposed on principle to any form of alliance between the British Empire and Adolf Hitler's Nazi Germany.

The more powerful of these was Sir Robert Vansittart, since 1930 the Permanent Under Secretary for Foreign Affairs. This position was technically like that of von Bülow, the AA's State Secretary, but it carried much more weight. Churchill would speak of getting information from 'Bobby Vansittart's spies in Berlin', and he was not far from the mark. Vansittart was a player to be counted when one rated British foreign policy. He was deeply suspicious of Germany, shocked by Nazi brutality, disdainful of Hitler and pessimistic about the future of European peace.

He was also the brother-in-law (their wives were sisters) of Sir Eric Phipps, the British Ambassador in Berlin, who had become totally disenchanted with the Nazis. Phipps was so filled with dislike for them that he was eventually replaced with a seemingly more 'pliable' diplomat, Sir Nevile Henderson, when the last pre-war Prime Minister, Neville Chamberlain, took power.

Vansittart's respect and liking for Britain's wartime allies, the French, brought him a reputation for unquestioning Francophilia.[49] He opposed those who wanted to co-operate with Germany. Eventually he became the victim of those who assumed that Hitler's appetites could be satisfied, and he was removed 'upstairs' into the powerless job of Chief Diplomatic Adviser. One of his few misjudgments was his assumption that returning Germany's colonies was necessary and even fair. But, although Hitler often talked about the 'lost' colonies and von Ribbentrop claimed to be in charge of all German colonial policy, Hitler actually seemed uninterested in their return. He used them as playing cards while bargaining for entirely different and much bigger stakes, the freedom to do as he pleased in Eastern Europe while Britain ruled the oceans and her own Empire. The colonial world seemed too exotic, removed and strangely 'Britannic' for Hitler. The born Austrian understood Eastern Europe, because it was Austria's backyard. People said, 'The Balkans begin at the Ringstrasse.'

By 1936, von Ribbentrop found Vansittart a rock of opposition, blocking any approach. William Manchester called Vansittart 'arrogant, sometimes wrong, but dead right about Nazi Germany'. Sometimes it seemed as if Vansittart was the only man in the British government to have read *Mein Kampf*. For instance, he alone predicted Hitler's move into the Rhineland. His Germanophobia went deep. He felt that 'nothing but a change of German heart can avert another catastrophe and that was unlikely to come from within, for the true German nature has never changed'.[50]

Vansittart complained that his brother-in-law Ambassador Phipps' reports from Germany had 'too much wit and not enough warning! They did not alarm the Cabinet enough!'[51] Sir Robert's views of von Ribbentrop were scathing: 'A Commissioner for Questions of Disarmament of which there was no question!' 'He [Ribbentrop] had to flatter himself until he found others to do so for he suffered from the sore vanity of a peacock in permanent moult.' 'He was not beneath contempt. That depends anyhow where you pitch it.' 'He was successful in Mayfair, his course eased by the first-rate Hösch.' 'Neurath was his other oily predecessor.'[52] About the 1935 Naval Agreement, Vansittart wrote: 'Von Ribbentrop had his way with our perilous shortages. We had to buy time and if the Germans kept their word for awhile, we were ahead for that time.'[53]

The other enemy lying in wait was Alfred Duff Cooper and his beautiful wife Diana. They were more worldly than Vansittart and also a part of society which was deceiving, because their 'salon' life did not inhibit their influence. Alfred Duff Cooper, ex-Oxford, ex-army officer, ex-MP, was Secretary for War from 1935 to 1937, First Lord of the Admiralty from 1937 to 1938 and, from 1940, Minister of Information. Lady Diana Duff Cooper, daughter of the Duke of Rutland, was a famous beauty and a stage actress. The Duff Coopers were powerful wheels in the machinery of London society, and known for their Francophilia and anti-Nazi stand. In the case of Alfred Duff Cooper, it was almost manic. Chips Channon described a dinner at Lympne, Sir Philip Sassoon's mansion, in August 1936: 'There was the usual German argument after dinner with Philip and Duff attacking the Nazis with the violence born of personal prejudice.'[54] In the case of Sassoon, obviously because he was Jewish. In the case of Duff Cooper, everyone in London society simply expected it.

The Duff Coopers were often guests at homes which had also invited the von Ribbentrops and that made for some tense evenings, although Lady Diana's legendary charm often managed to smooth things over.

The Duff Coopers disapproved of anyone in London society who accepted von Ribbentrop's invitations to the 1936 Berlin Olympics. It was a 'show' year. For the foreign visitors' sake, there was reduced anti-Semitic display. 'Jews not desired here' signs were hidden and there was less anti-Western talk. Of course, this was all only temporary. Throughout the subsequent flush of British admiration for Hitler's Olympics, the Duff Coopers remained steadfast anti-Germans.

At dinner on 8 November 1936 the hostess, Venetia Montague, in her small house in Onslow Gardens, had 'the cleverest, worldliest, quickest people in London'. Greatly influenced by his recent Berlin Olympics visit Chips Channon said that 'for the first time [the company] seemed boring, and worse, out of date'. He felt that 'they do not know what it is all about now and they are all too pro-Semite.' Channon reports that Crinks Jonstone, a capitalist and a gourmet, began dinner by saying, 'Here's death to Ribbentrop.' Diana Cooper turned on him, but Duff Cooper laughingly said, 'I only hope he dies in pain!' Then, according to Channon, 'the usual long, anti-German tirade began'.[55] Channon had become one of the new breed of Nazi accommodators, but it was not to last. He, too, would eventually become their enemy when Hitler finally invaded Prague and war approached.

The Duff Coopers never changed. Their anti-German influence went far beyond the dinner table all the way into the War Office, the Admiralty and then the Ministry of Information, Britain's propaganda branch, when Duff Cooper headed those ministries. It is strange to recall that Duff Cooper was a warm friend of Edward VIII, later the Duke of Windsor, who was accused of Nazi sympathies.

In July 1936 world attention had shifted to Spain. On the 17th and 18th, General Francisco Franco launched the Spanish Civil War from

Morocco at the head of Spain's rebel colonial army. This suited Adolf Hitler's anti-Communist paranoia. Here was an attack on one of the two supposedly Communist-influenced and Moscow-friendly regimes in the south-west sector of Europe. The other nation was France. Actually, the legal Spanish government was headed by the moderate socialist republican Negrin, and the French government by the very similar Léon Blum. Hitler, as usual, began to fear a flood of red. He insisted that Germany was being 'squeezed' between Czechoslovakia (through its Russian allies) and France and Spain.

Von Ribbentrop seemed to disagree. He was Hitler's guest at the Bayreuth Music Festival when word of the Spanish war reached them. Hitler, who was himself a guest of the Wagner family, told von Ribbentrop he had decided to help Franco. Franco had requested transport planes to shuttle troops from North Africa, and Hitler would provide them. In his memoirs, von Ribbentrop said he had suggested to the Führer that Germany stay out of Spain, that there were 'no laurels to be gained', and that German intervention would provoke negative reactions in England, but Hitler insisted he would not tolerate a Communist Spain. He had already ordered the planes for Franco. Von Ribbentrop wrote, 'Hitler rejected my objections. He said Spain's Prime Minister Negrin was a Communist, that his weapons came from Moscow and that there was a close connection between him and Léon Blum in France.'

Von Ribbentrop continued, 'I saw things differently. I tried to argue with Hitler but found it too difficult. He reacted nervously and cut off the conversation. He said he had made his decision. This was a matter of deep principle, and not of my sort of mundane foreign diplomacy.' Again Hitler was the ideologist while von Ribbentrop attempted diplomacy. According to von Ribbentrop, the Spanish matter 'disturbed [his] mission' later as ambassador to London.

Hitler's unfriendly rejection depressed him deeply. He went into a black mood whenever he fell foul of Hitler. His subordinates called it his Tango Nocturno and he took to his bed. But he was soon cured.

Apparently, Hitler's anger did not last either. The day after their disagreement over Spain, von Ribbentrop was ordered into his Führer's presence. As von Ribbentrop tells it, Adolf Hitler then named him state secretary of the AA to succeed Bernhard von Bülow, who had died in June. Hitler congratulated him.[56] Von Ribbentrop later said he had told Hitler it would be wiser to send him to England as ambassador than to appoint him state secretary in Berlin. 'Despite Hitler's sceptical view of the possibilities of a bond with Britain, it seemed important to keep the Führer fully informed about the London situation. Also, although British kings had little political influence, Edward VIII was friendly to Germany.' This was written after Hitler's death, when his recognition of Edward VIII's lack of influence might have been achieved by hindsight.

Others viewed von Ribbentrop's London appointment quite differently.

Typically, ex-Foreign Ministry official Dr Paul Schwarz wrote that von Neurath wanted to get rid of von Ribbentrop, who was a thorn in his side as long as he was in Berlin.[57]

Erich Kordt's holiday in Greece was interrupted by a frantic phone call, and von Ribbentrop sent D-AMY to bring him at once to Bayreuth. As a member of the Foreign Ministry, Kordt knew that von Neurath was very anxious to see the back of von Ribbentrop and probably had prevented his appointment as state secretary. Von Neurath again threatened to resign, this time because he 'could not personally work closely with von Ribbentrop'. Now von Ribbentrop wanted Kordt to negotiate with von Neurath, to ensure that he, von Ribbentrop, in addition to his London post, would remain ambassador at large and would report directly to Hitler. The Foreign Minister agreed hastily and on 27 July he sent a request for *Agrément* (acceptance of a proposed ambassador) to London. It was granted on 30 July, with unusual speed. Kordt claimed that many countries preferred Nazi ambassadors to foreign service professionals. Belgium turned down a top professional who had some Jewish blood, because a 'Nazi' ambassador would guarantee the direct attention of Adolf Hitler.

At first von Ribbentrop declined to announce his London appointment, which probably confirms the Schwarz and Kordt views. Hitler then refused to receive von Ribbentrop's English guests invited for the Olympics. His adjutant told von Ribbentrop, 'You announce the appointment, and the Führer will receive your guests,' and that was exactly what happened. Von Ribbentrop's announcement of his appointment to London opened the doors to Hitler's receptions for his guests.[58] Dr Paul Schmidt, the AA interpreter, told how von Ribbentrop, on being congratulated after the announcement, responded with 'a sour laugh'.[59]

An apocryphal story of the day was that Göring told Hitler, 'You cannot send von Ribbentrop to London!' Hitler insisted that von Ribbentrop was the right man because he 'knows the top people in England'. Göring laughed and replied, 'The trouble is that *they* also know *him*!'

The Dienststelle Ribbentrop remained intact, despite the bitter dislike of the AA professionals, who called it 'full of overpaid playboys with London wardrobes and big expense accounts'.

Von Ribbentrop's eventual entourage for the London Embassy was 120 strong, many of them lower-rank SS men, some of whom did the flunkey work and guard duty. The regular AA officials at the Embassy were paid extra to bring their salaries up to the level of the newly imported SS officers. This money came from the mysterious, so-called Sonderfond des Führers, the Führer's Special Fund, and it was flown in weekly from Amsterdam, where German Marks had a good market.[60]

Meanwhile, von Ribbentrop had 'previous commitments' which kept him away from England in the immediate weeks ahead, and the Embassy in London was left without an ambassador for a discourteously long period of time. First, the von Ribbentrops planned a vast party in Dahlem to entertain foreign visitors and leading Germans during the Berlin Olympic Games. The von Ribbentrop fête was one of three such stellar events. The other two were given by Hermann Göring and Joseph Goebbels.

Another matter of priority was an anti-Comintern alliance with Japan, the 'Aryans of the East', as Hitler called them. 'Comintern' stood for the Communist International, composed of the world's Marxist leaders who met annually at the Comintern's headquarters in Moscow. Originally, there was some danger that such a pact would seem like a near-declaration of war on Soviet Russia. Then in November 1936, a clever legal expert at the Ribbentrop Büro, Dr Hermann von Raumer, found a convenient technicality: Soviet Russia had denied responsibility for certain controversial statements made by the Comintern's headquarters in Moscow. Thereby, Soviet Russia removed herself officially from certain directions she probably endorsed unofficially. This 'loophole' allowed von Ribbentrop to formulate an anti-Comintern pact without officially involving Soviet Russia. The path was clear for von Ribbentrop's first attempt at power-bloc politics and *Realpolitik* with Japan. The whole subject of 'race' and 'congenial blood' soon came to haunt the conduct of such politics. It caused problems for von Ribbentrop and his parvenu Büro, and it also became an irritant for the supposedly principled and distinguished Auswärtiges Amt. Certainly with the approval of the opportunist Konstantin von Neurath, the notorious AA department called Deutschland, its most Nazified wing, suggested to the Nazi Party that it should retain its racial policies in principle, but avoid 'damage in matters of foreign policy' (17 November 1936). The suggestion was turned down by the party on 28 April 1937.[61] Therein lies one of the secrets of Nazi Germany. Its evil men were usually more committed than those who considered themselves principled and decent.

The Olympic Games opened on 1 August 1936. The huge party Joachim and Annelies von Ribbentrop had planned was at hand. Earlier in the year, on 14 July, the Duke and Duchess of Brunswick, both convinced Nazis, came to England for an Anglo-German Fellowship dinner. The doubly ducal Brunswick had given up the British dukedom of Cumberland to declare himself the complete Nazi German. To schedule the dinner for Bastille Day, 14 July, was probably a deliberate anti-French provocation. The event was chaired by Lord Mount Temple, who had a Jewish wife (a daughter of banker Sir Edward Cassel). There were the usual Germanophile speakers, the Lords Revell and Lothian and General Sir Frederick Maurice of the British Legion.

Many of these AGF guests were invited by von Ribbentrop to Berlin for the Olympic Games, as were Admiral Eyres-Monsell of Naval Agreement fame, the press Lords Rothermere and Beaverbrook and Chips Channon and his wife. The least likely guests were Sir Robert and Lady Vansittart. She probably came mainly to visit her sister, Lady Phipps. A startled von Ribbentrop said he was particularly happy to see them.[62]

All guests were assigned Mercedes cars and drivers from the SS or the NSKK, the Nazi Party Motor Corps, also in uniform. Everyone was very impressed indeed. Channon thought the 'Horst Wessel Lied' had 'rather a good lilt'.[63]

In total, the von Ribbentrops had asked 600 people to Dahlem. A huge tent was put up over the gardens and the tennis court. There were water lilies in the swimming pool and rhododendrons everywhere. Milling among the guests were Göring, Hess and their wives, and Himmler, who, as an American guest wrote, 'wove his mincing, quiet and menacing way through the crowd. There was a small crisis of protocol when the President of the International Olympic Committee, Count Balliet Latour, appeared uninvited. They finally solved the dilemma of where to place him. After all, it was the Olympic week and his reign.'[64]

Barnabas von Geczy, one of Berlin's best dance orchestras, was hired to play and the Vansittarts foxtrotted and tangoed and were among the last guests to leave. Von Ribbentrop remembers asking himself if that was a good sign. The next day he had his answer. He lunched with Vansittart at the Kaiserhof Hotel, and tried to convince the British official of Hitler's peaceful intentions and that the Führer was ready for an agreement with Britain.[65] He faced 'a blank wall. There was no response, no reaction, only banalities.' It was clear there was no approaching Vansittart. So much for late dancers!

The Göring party which followed was an event of positively operatic proportions, and the Goebbels soirée was lavish and voluptuous. But the von Ribbentrops were well pleased with their own efforts in Dahlem and with its results (with the exception of Sir Robert Vansittart).

In his Nuremberg prison memoirs, von Ribbentrop insists that it was not true that Vansittart's anti-German views were the result of Adolf Hitler's policies. On the contrary, Hitler's views were the result of Vansittart's 1936 policies. Writing in his cell, after he had been condemned to death, von Ribbentrop insisted, 'I am certain Adolf Hitler would have kept any pact with England,' and 'It is Vansittart who is largely to blame for the red incursion into Europe.' After all the broken pacts, the broken promises, with Germany in ruins, Hitler's spell still held his disciple, Joachim von Ribbentrop.[66]

Like many other guests at the von Ribbentrops' Olympics party, Martha Dodd, the daughter of the US Ambassador, had congratulated von Ribbentrop on his appointment to the London Embassy and he 'accepted with a sort of pained graciousness, disdain and bored *savoir faire*'.[67] Obviously it was not his favourite subject. Then Miss Dodd heard

Hitler's unique attitude to sports, sportsmanship and the human race. One of von Ribbentrop's young assistants told her that Adolf Hitler considered Jesse Owens and other black American athletes unfair competition because 'blacks were animals, non-humans, and to enter them in competition against whites was like entering fleet-footed deer, gazelle or other species of speedy animals, and totally unsportsmanlike and unfair'.

After the Olympics, the von Ribbentrops had to plan their move to London. First Joachim and Annelies separately went to see Pastor Niemöller, the decorated former First World War U-boat Commander who now presided over the Dahlem congregation, one of the most fashionable Protestant parishes in Berlin. Niemöller was a German nationalist but a fierce opponent of National Socialism. He frequently preached sermons against the government's anti-religious and anti-Semitic acts. Because he was a world-renowned clergyman, Joachim wanted Niemöller to accept him back into the Church he had left. He explained that the English 'would expect that of him'.

Niemöller told him that that was not sufficient reason for confirmation and turned him down.[68] Separately Annelies had asked Niemöller to baptize her third child, Adolf (named after the Führer), who was born on 2 September 1935, but Niemöller again refused, unless von Ribbentrop returned to the Church for God's sake and not for British society's.[69] Niemöller was denounced by Annelies for his anti-Hitler attitude and eventually sent to Dachau. Little Adolf von Ribbentrop was baptized elsewhere. Despite all their misguided ambition, both von Ribbentrops were good parents.

In the meantime, the superb John Nash buildings which housed London's German Embassy were gutted, leaving only the façade in place. Annelies brought a Dahlem construction and furniture man called Martin Luther to London. He was hired to supervise the work of hundreds of imported German workmen. Luther, an old-time Berlin Nazi Party factotum, would remain a close associate of von Ribbentrop and soon became his liaison with the 'old party fighters'. Years later it was Martin Luther who represented the AA at the notorious Wannsee Conference for the Final Solution of the Jewish question, and it was Martin Luther who would eventually land in a concentration camp for betraying von Ribbentrop.

A story went the rounds of London during the Embassy reconstruction that any German workman whose wife back in Germany gave birth to a male child could collect a 300 Mark bonus if the baby was named Joachim. It was said there were seven Joachims born during those months.[70]

While the construction work was carried out, the Embassy was temporarily moved into 17 Carlton House Terrace, and a Chamberlain family house on Eaton Square was rented as the von Ribbentrops' private residence.

The same Dr Hermann von Raumer who had found the loophole for the Anti-Comintern Pact, reported that this was the pre-London briefing given to von Ribbentrop by Adolf Hitler:

> Ribbentrop, bring me England into the Anti-Comintern Pact. That is my greatest wish! I'm sending you as the best horse in my stable. See what you can do. ... But if all efforts come to nothing, well then I'm prepared for war, though I'd regret it a lot, but if it has to be. ... But I believe it would be a short war and I'd offer generous terms to England, an honourable, mutually acceptable peace. Then I'd still want England to join the Anti-Comintern Pact. Ribbentrop, you hold all the trumps. Play them well. I'm prepared for an air agreement any time. Do well! I shall follow you with interest![71]

Another event which preceded the London move was the visit of Lloyd George to Berchtesgaden, brought about by the well-meaning pacifist Conwell-Evans. It took place on 4 and 5 of September, and it was meant to be a symbolic token of understanding between the Führer and Germany's old enemy, now its new admirer, the white-maned former Prime Minister Lloyd George. Adolf Hitler produced a flood of charm and flattery. He greeted his British guests at the very bottom of the famous long stairway in front of the Berghof.

Also present were Lord Dawson, the King's physician, who happened to be in Germany, and Dr T. Jones, a close adviser of Stanley Baldwin. On the German side were the two von Ribbentrops, State Secretary Meissner and Baron Geyr von Schweppenburg, the intellectual Military Attaché in London, one of the few to emphasize to Hitler that England was in reality a tough nation.

The out-of-power Lloyd George was overwhelmed and impressed. Later he called Hitler the George Washington of Germany, but it mattered not at all. Lloyd George's influence was minimal, though Hitler took him quite seriously, hoping for forceful advocacy in Parliament of Germany's anti-Soviet offers of friendship.

Meanwhile, preparation of the Anti-Comintern Pact with Japan went forward through the Japanese Ambassador Viscount Mushanokoji and his Military Attaché, Lieutenant-Colonel Oshima. Several things still stood in the way. The Japanese government was reluctant to commit itself too deeply. To Japan the three-year-old Nazi government was still a 'new' friend, while the governments of Britain and America were a well-known and familiar quantity. Another problem was China. Germany was trading with China and there was still a German military mission in China which was training Chiang Kai-shek's army.

Von Ribbentrop's ally in the pursuit of a treaty with Japan was the famous geopolitical scientist Professor Karl Haushoffer, a former Tokyo resident, Japanophile and the guru of Hitler's deputy, Rudolf Hess.

Haushoffer's political views impressed Hitler, who now conveniently discovered the similarities between the mythical knightly Wagnerian spirit of National Socialism and the Bushido warrior's way of the Japanese Samurai. While the von Ribbentrops were preparing themselves for London, the Büro carried out the other von Ribbentrop function as Ambassador Extraordinary at Large and Special Adviser to the Führer. For von Ribbentrop the Japan connection was an exercise in old-time power politics as well as good business. For Hitler it was bathed in ideological blood and thunder, but above all it was anti-Communist.

Surprisingly, on 5 September, a few days before the party rally in Nuremberg, Germany decided to participate in a Non-Intervention Committee which had been formed in London to ensure that no outside powers would intervene in the Spanish Civil War. This after Germany had loaned planes to Franco!

The 1936 party rally was named Day of Honour. Among Ribbentrop's Kindergarten, as they were dubbed in Nuremberg, there were many British visitors,[72] including Lady Redesdale, mother of the Mitford girls, two of whom, Lady Mosley and Unity Mitford, were quite at home in Nuremberg. Lady Redesdale was there as a guest of Prince Bismarck, the former Chargé d'Affaires in London. The others were Lord Mount Temple, Admiral Domville, Sir Frank and Lady Newnes of *Country Life* magazine, Lord Apsley, Sir Frank Sanderson, Sir Thomas Moore, Sir Arnold Wilson and Admiral Sueter. Some of the British newspapermen were impressed. Beverly Nichols in the *Sunday Chronicle* of 12 September 1936 wrote, 'Such moral strength! So much that is beautiful!' The party rally was deemed a post-Olympic success. However, the diplomatic corps of the Western nations did not attend.

Just before the von Ribbentrops arrived in London, the Duke of Saxe-Coburg and Gotha, a grandson of Queen Victoria and an enthusiastic Nazi, arrived there with a delegation of German war veterans. At the same time, Duff Cooper was in Paris making a speech cleared by the Foreign Office in which he warned that Germany 'was a danger common to Britain and France'. King Edward VIII expressed strong disapproval[73] of his friend's words.

The von Ribbentrops could also expect amity from several publications. The first was Lady Houston's crackpot *Saturday Review*, which had petitioned the King on 6 June to become a benevolent dictator. Much more powerful were the *English Review*, centre of pro-German journalism with contributors like Evelyn Waugh, and the *New Journal*, with articles by Lloyd George and the Oxford-trained historian, Sir Raymond Beazley.

Then, at long last on 26 October 1936, the von Ribbentrops assumed their post in London. The official announcement of his position as ambassador to the Court of St James *and* ambassador at large (to avoid von Neurath's control) had been made on 11 August.

NINE

EMBASSY, 1936/1937/1938

―――――

'Our Fellows Look Terrific'

On 13 September 1936 his friend, Heinrich Himmler, promoted Joachim von Ribbentrop to the honorary rank of general (Gruppenführer) in the SS. So far, von Ribbentrop's year had gone extremely well. His Führer seemed to trust him. Perhaps it was a disappointment that the Berlin post of state secretary had escaped him, but Adolf Hitler had persuaded him that he was the 'best horse in the stable', sent out despite British intransigence and power and tradition to form an alliance. Friendship with Britain seemed to matter immensely to Adolf Hitler, ever the ideologue, trapped by his own 'instinctive' ways of looking at the world and of making decisions. He was cynical about many things and most people, but he fed himself many naive half-truths to bolster his self-assurance. Hitler's Austrian soul probably considered the 'Aryan brethren' across the Channel as even more 'desirably Nordic' and coldly unreachable than his own adopted Germans had once seemed. He wanted them. The short, dark-haired Hitler lusted for the brotherhood of the blond and the tall.

Joachim von Ribbentrop, SS Gruppenführer, Ambassador Extraordinary to the Court of St James, Special Adviser to the Führer and victor of the skirmishes at the British Admiralty in 1935, was ready to do battle. If there were any nagging doubts about his own lack of standing inside the Nazi Party, his absence from 'court' in Berlin or his possible rejection by Britain's people of influence, he hid them behind a newly assumed mask of gravity and purpose. As his battle flag he carried the unvarying message against Bolshevism. As his armour he had the memory of that recent day when he told the British to 'take it or leave it', and they had taken it. Besides, he had never lacked for the company of titled Englishmen whenever he was in London. Von Ribbentrop felt that they respected him and the new Germany. And then, he always had Annelies by his side. Her taste and talent for entertaining would surely charm even the most unbending Londoners. She had already worked wonders at the old Embassy at Carlton House Terrace. Albert Speer, Hitler's favourite architect, was asked to help with the interiors of the shelled-out old John Nash structure. The famous Professor Troost was designing special furniture. Martin Luther acted as contractor. Annelies even brought over some of her own valuable works of art from Dahlem. There were well-trained waiters, footmen and guards, all SS men. Erich Kordt estimated that the total cost of the rebuilding was five million Marks.[1]

Germany would be proud of its London Embassy and its new ambassadorial family. The Ribbentrops had brought along their four children, Rudolf, Bettina, Ursula and little Adolf. Feelers were put out to test the suitability of Eton for Rudolf, who was fifteen, but instead they decided on Westminster, the centuries-old London public school. Bettina was enrolled in a boarding school in Cornwall. Ursula, who was a delicate child, stayed in London, and Adolf was only a year old.

Rudolf had joined the Jungvolk (the Cub Scouts of the Hitler Youth) at the age of ten in Berlin. At fourteen he became a member of the Hitler Youth. His Fähnleinführer, a sort of Hitler Youth scoutmaster, a young man called Thorner, came to London with the von Ribbentrops as a secretary–aide to the Ambassador, paid by the Büro.[2]

It must have been a wrenching change for young Rudolf to trade the hard-edged, stiff Hitler Youth, its brown uniform and shouted slogans for the relaxed, top-hatted drawl of London's Westminster School. Thorner reported that Rudolf had several shouting matches at Speakers' Corner near London's Marble Arch, where all one needs to this day is a soapbox and a political cause. Rudolf howled 'Bolshevist!' at several speakers, who probably were just that.[3] The Austrian Reinhard Spitzy, also a secretary to von Ribbentrop, said that Rudolf sometimes complained about his father to him, probably as the result of arguments with his schoolmates at Westminster.[4] (The SS later discovered that Thorner had some Jewish blood.)

By the time the von Ribbentrops and their entire entourage, *Kind und Kegel*, as the Germans would say, arrived at Victoria station on 26 October 1936, all seemed well in hand, organized and calm. Then Joachim von Ribbentrop, the new Ambassador, decided there and then to apply the crude technique he had learned from Adolf Hitler and which he had used in the naval negotiations. On the station platform, dignitaries and Embassy staff expected no more than the banal and customary ambassadorial greetings. Instead, Joachim von Ribbentrop launched into an animated speech inviting Great Britain to join Germany in a crusade against 'the greatest danger of the century, the Bolshevist menace'.[5] Copies of the speech were then handed out in mimeographed form to the press.

It was a supremely tactless way for a new ambassador to attempt to 'manage' his host country's policy. Within the week, the influential Austen Chamberlain wrote an article in the conservative *Daily Telegraph*, complaining bitterly about this crude attempt to interfere in British affairs.

He wrote, 'Neither the Nazi nor the Soviet faiths, both strange to Britons, are worth one British Grenadier's bones.' He added, 'While von Ribbentrop spoke of an anti-Communist alliance, Göring and Goebbels made speeches proclaiming that Britain had stolen Germany's colonies.'

It was not an auspicious beginning.

As an opening gesture, probably anxious to demonstrate his adherence to the new Germany's ways, von Ribbentrop then quickly decreed that the German Embassy's ladies would no longer curtsey to royalty and that all future Embassy invitations would be worded in German, instead of the customary language of the host country. An SS guard was then posted in a sentry booth at the Embassy entrance, also an unheard-of discourtesy. With one eye on Berlin, von Ribbentrop awaited the party's approval of the new Germany's style he was introducing to stuffy old England. Nazi jargon such as 'manly, direct, soldierly, forthright' was supposed to spring to mind. Instead, he had already been slammed by the distinguished Austen Chamberlain and then dubbed 'Brickendrop' by the widely respected cartoonist David Low (*Evening Standard* and *Manchester Guardian*). Upon hearing that only the raised-arm salute would henceforth be used by the Embassy staff, Low drew a cartoon of a schoolroom full of pupils. One little boy who looks exactly like von Ribbentrop has his arm raised in a Hitler salute and the teacher says, 'Yes, von Ribbentrop, you may leave the room.' A year later, during the Coronation of George VI in crowded Westminster Abbey, the ushers were instructed to guide anyone who raised an arm to the cloakrooms, 'except His Excellency the German Ambassador'.

The Ambassador's urge to 'Germanize' went far beyond the Embassy. For many years a former German called Baron Bruno Schröder,[6] a naturalized British subject and London resident, had financed London's German Hospital. The Hamburg-born Schröder, a non-Nazi cousin of the Cologne banker Kurt von Schröder who had called the 1932 meeting with Hitler and von Papen, devoted himself and his money to this charity clinic which employed some Jewish physicians and had Jewish patients. Despite von Ribbentrop's personal urging, Baron Schröder refused to fire the Jewish doctors or discharge the Jewish patients. But to retain the appellation 'German' Hospital, it had to fly the swastika flag, although there was still a small kosher kitchen for religious Jewish patients.

The new Ambassador had the good fortune of having excellent staff members, since he needed frequent and professional help. Erich Kordt was appointed First Secretary, and Ernst Woermann, another AA professional, became deputy to the Ambassador and Chargé during his frequent absences.

The Ambassador refused to pay certain formal visits which were decreed by custom. One of these was the courtesy visit to the Financial Secretary of the Admiralty, someone he deemed beneath his notice. The customary written self-introductions to other ambassadors were now in German too, contrary to protocol. Said von Ribbentrop, 'I don't care one whit about what used to be customary.' As a joke, the Turkish Ambassador responded in Turkish.[7]

On 30 October von Ribbentrop, in morning dress, submitted his credentials to King Edward VIII.* The King was deep in the throes of his romance with the recently divorced Mrs Simpson, which was about to produce a crisis of major proportions. How could a British sovereign, head of the Church of England, marry a foreign, multiple divorcée? What would happen if the German-friendly British King were forced to abdicate his throne? Von Ribbentrop hated the idea of losing the man whom he considered a powerful ally. The dilemma presented itself to Adolf Hitler in these simplistic terms: a young, war-veteran King, a liberal, is prevented from marrying the woman of his choice by a 'clique of reactionaries and Jews'. Hitler thought the King should 'tell these plutocrats and Marxists' that nothing would keep him from marrying a 'girl of the people'.[8] This was Hitler's lower-middle-class naivety at its most conspicuous. In a misguided effort to show sympathy for the embattled King, he prevented the German press from reporting the entire matter. One wonders how Wallis Warfield Simpson of the International Best-Dressed List would have reacted to the appellation 'girl of the people'.

The new German Ambassador's blunders were to be chided but not punished. Despite an astonishing amount of careless and overbearing behaviour, prominent Londoners, with few exceptions, were not willing to show anger. Only the press saw where von Ribbentrop was aiming and refused to follow. He stumbled on, over-anxious to please faraway Berlin and still impressed by his own recent negotiating success using the fist-on-table method. As a new senior diplomat, he was completely unsure of himself, so he adopted the weak man's way of bluffing: press on until someone calls a halt. Several subordinates, including Kordt and Spitzy, report that whenever von Ribbentrop lost his temper with them they could make him stop in his tracks by being firm with him. He became reasonable only after being confronted.

Meanwhile, preparations went ahead to solidify the Anti-Comintern Pact and on 25 November, barely a month after von Ribbentrop became Ambassador to London, D-AMY took him away to Berlin, where he signed the pact with Japan. It was a stormy, bouncy flight and the big Junkers passenger plane was tossed around, but there was no stopping von Ribbentrop,[9] and fortunately D-AMY's Captain Zivina was one of the best. Though this pact was duly signed with newly-appointed Ambassador Oshima, the AA would have no part of it. So far as they were concerned, the whole thing was a personal idea of Adolf Hitler's,

---

* The presentation was informal because the King was still uncrowned.

negotiated outside normal diplomatic channels. From the point of view of the gentlemen of Berlin's Foreign Ministry, von Ribbentrop's signature gave Japan no valid treaty, nor was the pact taken as more than a *beau geste* in Japan. Although the AA professionals in Berlin saw it as the 'adventure of dilettantes', it created many fears of some sort of future world conspiracy, particularly in Britain.

Adolf Hitler had personally attended Berlin's Japanese Embassy for the event, his first visit to a foreign mission. Suddenly the Japanese had changed from the 'culturally sterile race' of *Mein Kampf* to 'a closely related race of heroes'.[10] The pact also caused great anger in China, Japan's victim and Germany's old ally.

The Anti-Comintern Pacts were von Ribbentrop's pride until the Soviet Non-Aggression Pact of 1939. Each Anti-Comintern signing, country by country, was widely publicized, repeatedly featuring von Ribbentrop, the 'architect' of this metaphoric fortification against Moscow.

This was the first of many occasions when von Ribbentrop left his post to travel to the continent, and soon the British government took affront. In Parliament he was called the 'part-time Ambassador' to the Court of St James. *Punch*, the satirical magazine, was to describe him as 'The Wandering Aryan'. It upset Whitehall that the man who was accredited as the ambassador to Great Britain negotiated agreements, such as the Anti-Comintern Pact, which could be deemed dangerous to Britain and certainly to the allies of France and Britain.

He returned to London in December for a meeting of the Non-Intervention Committee, presided over by Lord Plymouth. The two main opponents, von Ribbentrop and the Russian Ambassador Ivan Maisky, both knew that no amount of work by the committee could stop intervention by Germany and Russia. Germany had already sent 'volunteers', the Condor Squadron, who were all Luftwaffe pilots trying out their skills and equipment practising for things to come one day, elsewhere.

The Ambassador instructed his staff to concentrate on the crisis of the King and his lady from Baltimore and on Mr Stanley Baldwin, the Prime Minister, who looked and talked like John Bull. The German Embassy 'expert' in matters concerning royalty and its affairs of the heart was 'Lu' Hessen, Prince Ludwig von Hessen, a great-grandson of Queen Victoria and a young official of the Ribbentrop Büro. The Prince was told by the Ambassador to stay as close as possible to Buckingham Palace and to report any rumours about the durability and future of the King.[11] While the British press desisted from any mention of the King's dilemma, there were no holds barred when it came to tackling the new German Ambassador. The von Ribbentrops, in return for certain Nazi gestures which were meant to impress Berlin, became targets for London's gossip press. For instance, when daughter Bettina was hurt in an accident at school, von Ribbentrop sought the advice of Professor Sauerbruch, Germany's foremost surgeon. Sauerbruch sent them to an eminent specialist in Holland, a Jew, and Bettina was registered there as a patient named Henkell. The London papers found out and gloated.

Nazi manifestations, such as the Hitler salute, the use of German language in communications, the uniformed SS guard and waiters, the vast Mercedes limousine with its swastika flags (but London licence plate CYF 3), the Jewish dentist used by the von Ribbentrops in London,[12] the well-known Junkers D-AMY which constantly ferried people between Berlin and London: all of these became the joy of gossip journalists. However, no one threw more accurate darts than David Low, the cartoonist.

The von Ribbentrops were deeply hurt by the sensationalized news coverage. Every time they left the Embassy it was on a 'mysterious mission'. Every rumour was enlarged. Every visitor was a 'mystery Nazi'. Surprisingly, for a man who had virtually grown up among English-speaking people, to von Ribbentrop this freedom of the press to publish rumour was incomprehensible. His misjudgment was probably due to some false notion of his own diplomatic immunity and of the fancied 'respect' due to the senior official of a sovereign foreign nation. Several times he complained about the press to British government officials and even to the Prime Minister. It did not help him because *they* could not help him. *Der Bo* (for *Botschafter* or Ambassador), as his staff nicknamed him, had to learn to live with it.[13]

Meanwhile, the imported SS staff could be hard on Annelies. They thought of themselves as heroes, not as skivvies. One example was SS Rottenführer (Corporal) Scharchewski, who got drunk, fell asleep on duty and then lectured Annelies on 'betraying Hitler's principles of equality'. He then told her to kiss his arse before he was arrested and flown under guard to Berlin for his punishment.[14] The SS men were bored. Guard duty was one thing, but scrubbing Embassy floors was another.

On 10 December 1936, less than two weeks after von Ribbentrop had been driven to Buckingham Palace to present his credentials to King Edward VIII, the King abdicated. It was a tremendous blow. Von Ribbentrop immediately informed Adolf Hitler and von Neurath of his view of the abdication: the very pro-German King had been forced to abdicate his throne by reactionaries and Jewish plutocrats, using the Simpson romance as a pretext. It is hard to conceive that von Ribbentrop could have believed his own fairy tale. He was well acquainted with the Emerald Cunard set and other Windsor friends like Chips Channon. Surely Rothermere and Harmsworth had told him the constitutional facts long before the abdication. On his own staff Woermann, his deputy, and Kordt, the First Secretary, were both skilled diplomats with many connections in London.

They certainly knew the truth, as did Chief of Protocol Count Dörnberg, the 'red giant', who was a cousin of the Mountbattens.

Finally, Prince Ludwig of Hesse, who was actually related to the British royal family, must have explained to von Ribbentrop the problems faced by a king who is also head of his country's Church: 'No divorce and remarriage.' Von Ribbentrop himself had wanted to rejoin the Church to please British society.

Perhaps von Ribbentrop fabricated the tale only to please his Austrian idol and then began to believe his own fabrication. He had done it before about the abortive air treaty, and about the unsuccessful attempt at postponing the disarmament conference.

On 12 December, at a meeting of the Anglo-German Fellowship in London, von Ribbentrop made his first London speech since his much noted and quoted arrival at Victoria station in October. The German delegation was headed by a devoted Nazi, the Duke of Saxe-Coburg, born the Duke of Albany, a title he had discarded. Saxe-Coburg spoke German with an English accent, but after giving up his British dukedom he became one of Adolf Hitler's blue-blooded, brown-shirted admirers. The British delegation to the meeting was manned by the usual Germanophile contingent, the Lords Mount Temple, Redesdale, Lothian and Rennell (a former ambassador to Rome), as well as the Duke of Wellington. Also present were the pacifist Lord Davis, General Hutchinson of the Liberal Party, Sir Frank Newness and Sir Horace Wilson, Neville Chamberlain's right-hand man.

Joachim von Ribbentrop, attempting a joke, committed a sledgehammer *bêtise*. He said that Lord Mount Temple was one temple which must not be destroyed because it was too useful, 'despite the Lord's Jewish wife'.[15] He then spoke unimpressively about Germany's need for the former colonies, the discarding of the 'shackles of Versailles', the danger of the Comintern and the tragic mistake of Britain and Germany fighting each other in the Great War. But, he added, if ever Germany were to re-enter the arena, 'she would not allow herself to be threatened or menaced'.

On 5 February 1937 came the famous and much publicized gaffe which shocked Britain's newspaper readers and caused anguish to Hitler's own staff members in Berlin. It was a case of tactless, tasteless behaviour, once again aimed straight at any doubting 'old party' men in Berlin. Von Ribbentrop hoped that their reaction would be that he 'was too tough' to allow those London fogeys to tell him what to do.

That 5 February had begun most decorously when the Ambassador and some of his senior staff members were driven to Buckingham Palace in the magnificent swastika-flagged Mercedes to attend His Majesty, the new King George VI, and then to present the Ambassador's credentials. The protocol was fairly strict. At the end of the formal handing-over of documents, the Ambassador from Germany, dressed in knee-breeches, hose and buckled shoes, was to leave the audience chamber backwards, stopping and bowing three times according to custom. He began to do so, but each time he stopped and bowed he also raised his right arm in a modified Hitler salute.

Twentieth-century British Court bows are not deep and never from the waist. They consist of no more than a dignified bending of the head. It was easy for the Ambassador to raise his hand. Did he also shout, 'Heil Hitler'? No one can swear to it. Apparently, the King smiled. The raised arm probably seemed a bit rum to him. But his entourage was less forgiving. They were mortified.

Reports reached the press and they loved it. The Nazi salute to the new King–Emperor! 'Ribb Heils King!'

Low drew a cartoon of Maisky, the Soviet Ambassador, in front of the King, with the Russian's clenched fist under the King's nose, since Communists saluted with a raised fist. The caption read: 'Everyone salutes his own way.'

The Ambassador's staff members were as taken aback as the King's entourage. Reinhard Spitzy, von Ribbentrop's secretary, described the immediate aftermath of the Great Saluting Crisis, after the Ambassador and his aides had returned from the Palace to the Embassy.[16]

> Von Ribbentrop rushed into his office and turned on the DO NOT DISTURB light. Those who had escorted him stormed in, demanding cognac. Something awful had happened. [Erich] Kordt and [Prince] 'Lu' Hessen fell on to couches, groaning. Then Hessen said, 'Imagine, he greeted the King of England with the Hitler salute.' Prince 'Lu' smacked his forehead with his hand. Thorner gave a hollow laugh. Kordt's arms hung straight down. Woermann quietly cursed to himself.
>
> All German journalists in London were commanded to the Embassy so they could hear the 'true story', that the King 'smiled quite contentedly'. Nevertheless, news of the gaffe quickly reached Berlin. Von Neurath was aghast. Even Hitler was critical.

During the War Crimes Trials in 1946 Göring[17] said to his prison psychiatrist Dr Douglas M. Kelley that he had told Hitler that von Ribbentrop's act was 'like the Soviet Ambassador greeting the Führer with a raised fist and yelling: "Long live the Bolshevist world revolution!"' But no one was more sensitive about British customs than London's young German professional diplomats. Yet they were not at all concerned about the thousands of German exiles and refugees who now lived hand-to-mouth in London, forced by British immigration policy to take menial jobs in order to be permitted to stay in Britain. Their fate was much more harmful to Germany's reputation than von Ribbentrop's gaffe. Architects now were manservants, and women university professors were children's nannies.

Everyone in London and Berlin took this opportunity to take aim at von Ribbentrop. He had no one to blame but himself. The international businessman, in the guise of ambassador from a violent and revolutionary government, had trapped himself through his own vanity and ambition. And those intelligent young German diplomats who worked for him and sat in judgment on him and who were paid by the same fierce master in Berlin, what of them? As Spitzy put it, 'We continued because we were ambitious and enjoyed our careers.'[18] Meanwhile, the 'Hitler salute' brouhaha went on and on. There was even an amusing question in Parliament about why the British Ambassador in Berlin should not be instructed to yell 'Rule Britannia' every time he saw Adolf Hitler.

Fear that damage might have been done to his standing with Adolf Hitler sent von Ribbentrop into panic. He was isolated from Berlin where gossip and malice could bring quick reversals to the career of a senior Nazi. For this reason, 1937 became a year of frantic cross-Channel travel to perform damage control in Berlin.

The Embassy's massive reconstruction was nearing completion just in time for a lavish ball which was planned for 12 May to celebrate the Coronation of George VI and his Queen, Elizabeth. Everyone in London was waiting to see the new Frankfurter Hauptbahnhof (Frankfurt Central Railway Station) as the Embassy was dubbed among Mayfair wags.

D-AMY became a veritable taxi. Captain Zivina brought everything from Baron Steengracht and his beautiful wife, who became Annelies' deputies and aides because they knew London society, to Rudolf Likus, and old friend of von Ribbentrop since elementary school. The semi-literate Likus became his factotum and party contact. To please his friend von Ribbentrop, Himmler made Likus an SS colonel, and he was frequently sent to Berlin as a gossip collector and spy. Dozens of friends and party bigwigs went to and fro. Captain Zivina also ferried custom-made shirts from the Berlin haberdasher Jacquet and even cologne (straw-bottled Bay Rum). But the most frequent passenger was the Ambassador.[19] Between February and December 1937 he made twelve round trips to the continent. Von Ribbentrop clutched on to his master, but his absences raised even more resentment in London, where it was felt that the Court of St James was entitled to more than a part-time ambassador.

Earlier that year, on 30 January, Hitler had made a Reichstag speech in which he emphasized that there would be 'no more surprises', but several major conflicts with Britain remained, such as those concerning the colonial question, the Spanish Civil War and the persecution of the Jews. Added to these was the increasing persecution of the Protestant clergy. On 1 July 1937 Pastor Niemöller of Dahlem was arrested for the fifth time but was not released after the usual few days of interrogation.

The Church of England launched no immediate official complaint. The Anglo-German relationship was sensitive.

The Embassy began to make more than the usual routine contacts with Germans who were resident in London but who were neither Jewish refugees nor non-Jewish political exiles. Of course, every passport-bearing German in England had to report on a strict and regular six-monthly schedule to the nearest German consulate or else their passport was cancelled, thereby invalidating their British residency visa. This applied to exiles and 'good' German citizens alike, including the hundreds of German domestic servants and waiters who were working in London's hotels, restaurants and homes. An ex-navy captain called Karlova worked as the resident SS police agent in the Embassy. He tried to organize an espionage ring of German servants who were required to report regularly to the Embassy.[20] Karlova was probably von Ribbentrop's tithe to his friend Himmler, who by then had placed SS or SD (Sicherheitsdienst) police agents in all German embassies and missions, worldwide.

Captain Karlova also contacted all German organizations which were not out-and-out Nazi groups. Several old-time German 'Kränzchen' coffee-and-cake *gemütlich* organizations were warned about dire consequences for their relatives in Germany unless they 'equalized', the Nazi term for becoming National Socialists.

There were thousands of recent German Jewish exiles in London, most of them still shocked and bewildered by the strange new English world and language, and often degraded into menial jobs. For these people, the obligatory six-monthly visits to the German Embassy were like trips to hell. Their German passports carried swastikas on the dull brown cover, and they were given no smiles of warmth from the dour German passport clerks. Yet there was no way even the refugees could avoid this unpleasant task, because an invalid passport meant the loss of their residency visa or work permit.

Still, London's refugees found their own little Germany. Undaunted by what had happened to them, they clustered together in middle-class London neighbourhoods like Hampstead, where German accents became quite common. Some began businesses. The Kempinski family, once the owners of the famous Berlin delicatessen carrying their name, opened a small restaurant in Swallow Place just off Regent Street. Several tiny, Berlin- and Vienna-style cabaret theatres sprang into life. The sons of German refugees appeared at a few of the old public schools. At St Paul's School in London Sigmund Freud's grandsons became the schoolmates of the son of old Nazi Putzi Hanfstaengl, then estranged from Hitler.

Germany's great stage star Elisabeth Bergner and Berlin's Shakespearean actor Fritz Kortner were invited to work in London. The young Lilli Palmer and the boy André Previn were among London's Germans in exile. Erich Pommer, the producer, made films in partnership with

Charles Laughton. Ludwig Stein directed films. This little London–German world stayed very much alive until 1939, when many of its members were interned, ironically as 'enemy aliens'. They included Sebastian Haffner, a lawyer and journalist, Dr G. V. Lachmann, an aerodynamicist, John Heartfield, the artist and political satirist who pioneered photo-montage, Kurt Joos, Germany's leading ballet choreographer, and Carl von Ossietsky, the general secretary of the International League for the Rights of Man. Most were soon released, but many of them were shipped to the Isle of Man, to Canada or Australia. One group was torpedoed by a U-boat on the Atlantic. Many found their way to America.

In the many memoirs written by former members of von Ribbentrop's London Embassy staff, mostly well-educated young Foreign Office or Büro members, there is never any mention of these German residents of London. Most of them were concerned only with the embarrassment von Ribbentrop was causing Germany, when the true shame for Germany lay in the refugee world all around them.

The question of Germany's former colonies was quite another matter. The return of these colonies was more hotly pursued by those who wanted to return them than by those who claimed them. Britons who advocated their return included Lord Astor, Bishop Carey, the Bishop of Southampton, Lord David Cecil in several letters to *The Times*, Gilbert Murray and Arnold Toynbee.[21] Most of these men felt that Germany's claims were just and no reason to go to war.

Two enemies of von Ribbentrop were about to be removed. On 2 February the British Ambassador in Berlin, Vansittart's brother-in-law Sir Eric Phipps, a great opponent of Nazism, was posted to Paris. Then American Ambassador William Dodd took leave of absence from his post and did not return, probably in protest against his instructions from Washington to attend the forthcoming Nuremberg party rally of 1937. Until then no Western ambassadors had attended.

On 11 May, the day before the Coronation in London, Sir Nevile Henderson, the new British Ambassador to Berlin, submitted his credentials to a very disturbed Adolf Hitler. The Führer had just learned that the airship *Hindenburg* had burned and crashed on landing in Lakehurst, New Jersey. He told Henderson that several warnings of sabotage had been received.

Now all those in London who wished to appease Hitler, but also those who wanted to delay him while Britain rearmed, had the right man. Henderson was a Foreign Office professional like Phipps, but unlike Phipps, who had clearly shown his anti-Nazi side, Henderson appeared neutral and friendly and was able to carry out a brief which some described as sympathetic to Nazism and collaborative. Others saw Henderson as the hero who held Hitler at bay while Britain rebuilt her armaments and, most of all, strengthened her will.

Sir Nevile Henderson was despised by many as Great Britain's 'Nazi Ambassador', but to others he was the twilight hero of what he himself eventually described as a failed mission. The eagle-nosed, moustached, greying Henderson was the quintessential diplomat in looks and action, calm, charming and stylish. Von Ribbentrop so dreaded any direct contact in Berlin between the new British Ambassador and the Führer that he tried at once to discredit Henderson in Adolf Hitler's eyes, even in small ways. For instance, von Ribbentrop knew perfectly well that Englishmen of the 1930s wore chalk-striped suits, brown suede shoes and carnation *boutonnières* in the style of Edward VIII. So it was an obvious act of malice to tell the unworldly Hitler that Henderson was being 'disrespectful' when he wore a carnation to meet the Führer. The Führer's limited experiences had never introduced him to the more stylish manifestations of that extraordinary species known as the British gentleman. Certainly, according to his memoirs, Henderson often *thought* disrespectfully, but he would never *dress* disrespectfully. To demonstrate how exasperated even Sir Nevile Henderson eventually became with Germany's dictator in the last days before the war, at a meeting with Hitler he once actually pounded the table. On another occasion he stood red-faced and angry in von Ribbentrop's office, ready for fisticuffs with an equally red-faced and yelling von Ribbentrop. Interpreter Paul Schmidt sat between them, wondering if it was correct diplomatic protocol to stand, too. He decided to sit until the storm had passed.[22]

But in 1937 all that was still to come, and Sir Nevile had been told to 'do his utmost to work with Hitler and the Nazi Party as the existing government in Germany'. He was quite aware that 'in democratic England, the Nazis, with their disregard of personal freedom and their persecution of religion, Jews and trade unions alike, were naturally far from popular'.[23] All the Phipps enthusiasts hated Henderson instinctively, assuming that he was sympathetic towards National Socialism, although the calm eye of time shows that this view was not entirely fair. He did have the parliamentary support of Conservative right-wingers such as Sir Harold Knox, Duncan Sandys and Victor Cazalet.[24] Meanwhile, Henderson became a new irritant for von Ribbentrop. He was an unknown quantity, an Englishman, a 'new broom', and, worst of all, he was in Berlin, where he might establish direct contact with Adolf Hitler. Certainly, von Neurath would have no compunction about bypassing his hated Ambassador in London.

Taking advantage of George VI's Coronation, von Ribbentrop then planned the great Coronation Ball at the 'new' German Embassy.

Von Blomberg, a field marshal as of 30 April, tall, grey-haired and grey-uniformed, and his aides were to represent Adolf Hitler, Germany's head of state, at the Coronation. It was a strange choice, but a clever one. Von Blomberg, Germany's top soldier, came from the sort of old German stock the British could appreciate. Titled British gentry had always found a certain kinship with their German opposite numbers. After all, the Windsors were all basically German, old Queen Victoria had married a German, and former German families like the Mountbattens (Battenbergs) were very much part of British society, and one day the Crown Princess Elizabeth would marry Philip, a Greek prince of German descent. 'German' did not necessarily mean 'evil' to the British upper classes. With the help of the Mountbattens, the German-Jewish educator Kurt Hahn, the founder of Germany's famous Salem Boys' School, was brought to Britain. He began Gordonstoun School in the north of Scotland, which later counted Prince Philip, Prince Charles and Prince Andrew among its pupils.

Somehow, quite instinctively, Adolf Hitler knew that Germany's *Adlige*, its old aristocratic families, were more like their British counterparts than like Germany's bourgeoisie or workers. The *Adligen* had a long and close bond with Germany's farmers and peasants that was almost paternal. At the level of equals they identified with the ideas, customs and manners of the families of the British counties, and they were frequently related to them by intermarriage. It became one of Hitler's many prejudices. At the end of the war many German officers who had British relatives, even wearers of the coveted Knight's Cross of the Iron Cross, were disqualified from holding any command.

On a more threatening note, von Blomberg's martial field-grey presence would serve to remind people in London that there was a new, well-run, well-armed and well-led German army.

Buckingham Palace was ready for the Coronation. So was the German Embassy.

Von Ribbentrop's aide Reinhard Spitzy in his memoirs described the Coronation on 13 May 1937, highlighting the colourful, braid-trimmed uniforms of the Empire's troops and its dignitaries, including bejewelled Indian maharajas, 'a picture from a Thousand and One Nights'. Soon he fell into the breathless German vernacular of the time:

> And then this sparkling picture is interrupted by a field-grey fog. The crowd's cheering dies down. Deeply impressed, everyone's eyes are fastened on the simple appearance of the German delegation, Blomberg accompanied by his military aides (except Admiral Wassner) all in field-grey and wearing steel helmets. They are tall men, walking with dignity. There is only slight clink of spurs and rattling of sabres. Their only decorations are those from the world war. It was like a cold gust of air which gave a hint of future battles between the two nations.

Also among the spectators there were exiles from Nazi Germany who had once worn those same field-grey uniforms in the same war. A Kafkaesque refugee story of that time was told about two former German

Jewish officers, now refugees in England. They pointed at the small, field-grey delegation from Nazi Germany. With tears in his eyes, one of the refugees said, 'Our fellows look terrific!'

The motives for the Coronation Ball given that evening at the German Embassy were tainted both with admiration and with disdain, with hatred and with longing, in fact with von Ribbentrop's very own complexes of inferiority and superiority. It certainly would never have been Adolf Hitler's own idea to invite 1,200 foreigners to London's German Embassy for a lavish fête, catered for by Horcher, Berlin's finest restaurant. Supper was flown in. Also Berlin's finest dance band and stars. Hitler's Potsdam days were far behind him. His adoration for kings and emperors had ended. He would never have chosen a royalist occasion as the reason for celebration. The anniversary of the 30 January Nazi takeover? Yes! But a royal coronation? Never! Hitler was and remained a revolutionary. Deep down he was even contemptuous of Germany's own Imperial house, the Hohenzollerns, though he still made occasional use of their pathetic Prince Auwi.

The ball was probably von Ribbentrop's idea or, even more likely, Annelies'. She had played a major part in devising and executing the whole venture. She would show Britain's society women!

Invitations to the Diplomatic Corps were sent out in German – '10$\frac{30}{}$ Uhr Anzug: Frack–Uniform–Orden'[25] (10.30 p.m. Dress: Full dress, uniforms, decorations) – with the inevitable Babel of multilingual responses. Who at the Embassy spoke Turkish or Finnish? There was a frantic search.

To assure themselves of those acceptances which were difficult to obtain, each invitation carried a handwritten note above the swastika-and-eagle escutcheon at the top: 'K. K. H. H. der Herzog und die Herzogin von Kent Haben ihr Erscheinen zugesagt' (Their Royal and Imperial Highnesses the Duke and Duchess of Kent have confirmed their acceptance).

Among others expected were Churchill, Baldwin, Eden, Halifax, the Vansittarts and the Archbishop of Canterbury. The presence of the Kents guaranteed a flood of guests, and London was in any case curious to see the inside of the renovated Embassy. The menu for the light midnight supper, again swastika-headed, was:

Langouste tail en croûte
Salad
Baby peas
Mocha and frozen dessert
Parmesan cheese croquettes
Peaches

Since it was served after 12.00 a.m., it was post-dated 14 May 1937 with typical German efficiency.

As Spitzy pointed out, 'British society laughed at the fact that the invitations went out in German.' Obviously, no one laughed hard enough to regret that they could not attend. The guest list was 'sparkling'. Beside the Duke of Kent and his beautiful Duchess, Marina, there were Prince Chichibu of Japan, General Gamelin, the French Chief of Staff, one of Ibn Saud's sons, and most of the other princes and dukes who had assembled in London for the week of coronation celebrations. Cranach's famous painting *Suicide of Lucretia Borgia* was a much admired part of the Embassy's decor and the Ambassador and his staff were convinced that the ball showed everyone that the new Germany was civilized and worldly and culturally up to the level of the other great powers.

It was probably the von Ribbentrops' final attempt to impress British society. This was their second try, after the Dahlem Olympic party, for a wide audience of the British ruling classes. Curiously, in his 1986 memoirs Spitzy reported that immediately thereafter von Ribbentrop sent anti-British dispatches to Berlin, lest the German delegation under Marshal von Blomberg throw doubts on his adequacy as Germany's representative.

But if the von Ribbentrops had not wished to solicit British good will, why would they have thrown their big Embassy party? In fact, Spitzy himself wrote that after the coronation party the von Ribbentrops' popularity was partly restored.[26]

Invitations to other functions at the Embassy were accepted at the last minute by Sir Alexander Cadogan, the new Permanent Under Secretary at the Foreign Office, and even by Churchill, whom the von Ribbentrops considered a less than gracious guest. On 21 May 1937 he came for lunch[27] and to discuss an anti-German article he had written for the *Evening Standard*. Von Ribbentrop bluntly offered a promise from Adolf Hitler to guarantee British security. An angered Churchill then growled that the Royal Navy 'had been doing that for centuries and needed no help'. Undeterred, von Ribbentrop pressed on. Germany would guard Britain's interests if Germany could have a free hand in the East of Europe. He showed Churchill a wall map, pointing at Polish, Ukrainian and Byelorussian *Lebensraum* (living space) for Germany, five times the size of her own territory. Churchill said the British would never tolerate this, even though they hated Communism. Von Ribbentrop turned away abruptly and said, 'In that case, war is inevitable. The Führer is resolved. Nothing will stop him or us.' Churchill replied, 'Do not underrate England, and do not judge her by the present administration. England is very clever. She will again bring the whole world into the war to help.' Von Ribbentrop said heatedly, 'England may be very clever, but this time the whole world won't help her.'

Churchill said privately afterwards that he had already known of the *Lebensraum* proposal 'from Vansittart's agent in Göring's office'.

During the rest of June 1937 von Ribbentrop frantically chased to and fro between Berlin and London and back to Berlin, whence came all of his support and sustenance; London was just where his duties forced him to be.

By now both of the von Ribbentrops must have realized that their dreams of acceptance socially and politically in London were never to be. There was no question that the Embassy Ball had been a great success, but it took only a few days for tensions to return. Between 5 and 28 June, von Ribbentrop's plane flew London–Berlin–London–Berlin–Dresden–London. His mind was not on London, although on the 15th he did attend a meeting of the cynically named Non-Intervention Committee, this despite the bombardment of Guernica by the Volunteer German Condor Legion on 26 April, and the bombardment of the Spanish port of Almería by the German navy. The Almería 'punitive' action was ordered because Spanish Loyalist planes had bombed the German battleship *Deutschland* while she was in their enemy's repair yard on the Franco-held island of Ibiza. Thirty German sailors were killed. News of this event reached von Ribbentrop, his family and aides while they were on a golfing holiday in Cornwall.

At this time the SS discovered that Thorner, Rudolf's former Hitler Youth superior, now von Ribbentrop's London secretary, an SS captain and Büro employee, had one-eighth Jewish blood. The frightened, shocked, pale-faced Thorner told Spitzy behind locked doors of this disaster and of his immediate discharge from the SS, which had to lead to his removal from his London post. Von Ribbentrop, who was usually loyal to subordinates, on his very next trip to attend the opening of the Dresden Autobahn on 25 June persuaded the Führer to be generous to Thorner 'due to years of party membership and Hitler Youth duty'.[28] The Führer 'graciously permitted Thorner's transfer to the Embassy in Stockholm'.

Obviously, even Hitler did not wish to interfere with many decisions of the SS, which was rapidly growing into a separate state, a reservoir of runic Teuton myth of Nibelungian proportions. The short, owlish Himmler, as unlikely a physical specimen as his Führer, was just as besotted with the myth of the tall, blond, blue-eyed 'Aryan' of fiction. As if to frustrate Himmler, even the tall, blond Reinhard Heydrich, his monstrous chief of the Gestapo, whom he considered the perfect 'Aryan' specimen, was known to have vast hips and a fat backside.

During July von Ribbentrop spent some time in Britain, because his assistants at the Embassy had heard too many rumblings from an affronted Whitehall. Meanwhile, his Japanese friends, the 'Aryans of the East' as Hitler had described them, chose that month to launch a crushing attack on China. Following an armed clash, or 'incident' as international politics would have it, on Marco Polo Bridge in Peking, they seized the old Imperial capital as well as Tientsin. Chinese troops soon abandoned the vast port of Shanghai to the Japanese, who then attacked British and American ships near Nanking. The American gunboat *Panay* was sunk with a loss of American lives. Apologies were rendered by the Japanese government and restitution was paid, but it was the beginning of Japan's road to war with the West. In London, von Ribbentrop was visited by a young Japanese diplomat, dispatched from Berlin by Japanese Ambassador Mushanokoji. Von Ribbentrop, very much out of the picture, asked, 'Will the Japanese soon defeat the Chinese?' and received a polite Japanese non-reply.

Kordt and his Foreign Ministry associates were now witnesses to a situation within the Japanese government parallel to their own. Their Japanese opposite numbers in London told them that the Japanese Foreign Ministry was rapidly losing its control of policy, while nationalist politicians and the military were taking charge. A friend of Kordt's at the Japanese Embassy in London uttered a string of uncharacteristically frank complaints about this state of affairs in Tokyo.

But von Ribbentrop remained totally unaware of these developments. He was concentrating on his empty seat 'at court' in Berlin. His old elementary schoolfriend from Metz, the simpleton party hack SS Colonel Likus, who had become a fixture at the Embassy, could only do so much to act for him *in absentia*. It was important to be physically present in the anteroom of the Chancellery in Berlin each day just before 2 p.m. Hitler usually appeared at that time and chose his luncheon companions by pointing at those waiting for 'the call'. 'You, Herr X, sit on my right, and you, General Y, on my left, and the rest of you gentlemen may choose your own seating.' Those who were specifically named were deemed to be in special favour.[29] But you had to be present to be chosen! Thus every day spent in London kept von Ribbentrop from this essential toadying.

In August the von Ribbentrops reluctantly decided to take a short holiday in Britain. No doubt the Ambassador would rather have been in Berlin. He cabled the Auswärtiges Amt:[30]

3 August 1937

TO RÜHRER [sic] AND FOREIGN MINISTER
According to permission given to me by the Führer, [I am] going to Scotland to regain my health. I intend to stay in Scotland in August to be available in case of developments in Non-Intervention matter [Spain]. End of August I shall be in London for a short stay and then go to Germany to undergo cure. Minister Woermann will represent me. Assuming that the Führer and Foreign Minister agree, I shall then give personal report in Berlin.
Ribbentrop

The family motored to Gleneagles in Scotland in two supercharged Mercedes behemoths. One of the cars developed some mechanical problems, so the three-motored Junkers D-AMY flew from London to Germany, where a Mercedes mechanic was taken aboard. Also brought on board was SS General Wolff, Heinrich Himmler's aide, requested by von Ribbentrop for 'important consultations'.[31] It must be assumed that von Ribbentrop wanted to reinforce his continuing conduit to Heinrich Himmler and that Wolff's trip was probably trumped up. The landing of D-AMY, the large, lumbering JU52 (known in the German military as 'Auntie Ju') on a small Scottish airfield, apparently caused eyes to pop. But the plane was ideal for the purpose, slow and powerful. For this reason, the JU52 became Germany's main troop transport and parachute plane.

In mid-August, unable to stay away any longer from his Führer's side, von Ribbentrop brought his family and part of his staff to the hotel at Feldafing on Starnberg Lake, near Berchtesgaden and the Berghof. They continued their holiday there until von Ribbentrop flew to the navy port of Kiel for the funeral of the recently promoted Admiral Wassner, the true architect of the 1935 Naval Agreement. The next day he travelled to Stuttgart to meet the *Auslandsdeutsche*, delegations of 'German-blooded' people from all over the world. Von Ribbentrop was busy looking busy. (These *Auslandsdeutsche*, people of German descent who lived abroad, became Hitler's constant excuse to interfere with other countries. They were all *his* Germans.)

The 1937 party rally in Nuremberg began on 8 September and, to the gloating joy of Adolf Hitler and Joseph Goebbels, the two leading Western ambassadors finally attended. After Sir Nevile Henderson, Neville Chamberlain's new Berlin 'accommodator', had signalled his acceptance; to 'keep the appearance of solidarity'. François-Poncet of France also attended. The disgusted departure of American Ambassador Dodd left the new Ambassador Hugh Wilson not yet willing to accept, though he was authorized to do so.

Henderson and François-Poncet agreed to limit themselves to two days in Nuremberg. (The full rally lasted a week.) Their reactions were quite diverse. Henderson, a newcomer to Nazi Germany, thought the rally 'indescribably picturesque, of grandiose beauty. Hess, aloof and inscrutable. Supper in the SS tent sinister and menacing. For Hitler: [the Germans showed] Idolatry.'[32]

François-Poncet was not so overwhelmed. Long familiar with Adolf Hitler and the National Socialist style, he was the 'featured' speaker at a reception for foreign diplomats at the Deutscher Hof Hotel. He told Hitler, in front of the other diplomats,[33] 'Your Propaganda Minister must be wrong, because you invited us despite the fact that Goebbels said we, the democratic peoples, are calves who chose their own butcher.'

François-Poncet was quoting from a Goebbels warm-up speech at the beginning of the rally. Goebbels fumed. Hitler grinned.

As usual, the rally had a theme, and Goebbels had named the 1937 event the Rally of Labour. It became the stage for announcing the Four-Year Economic Reconstruction and Rearmament Plan which was stated to be administered by Hermann Göring. By now the party and von Ribbentrop had learned to count on the usual visitors from Great Britain: Conwell-Evans, the Lords Mount Temple, Londonderry and Sempill.

The Embassy in London had been left in the hands of Dr Woermann, who was said to have a problem with alcohol.[34] But a drinking presence was better than none at all.

As soon as the Nuremberg party rally ended, von Ribbentrop rushed back to Berlin. His immediate plans did not include a return to London. Mussolini was on his way to pay a five-day state visit to his ally, Germany, which would precede the signing of von Ribbentrop's Anti-Comintern Pact, supposedly now a powerful bloc consisting of Germany, Italy and Japan. For von Ribbentrop the foremost aim was the building of these political power blocs. Hitler thought in terms of an ideological brotherhood of National Socialism, Fascism and Bushido. For him power-bloc thinking was reactionary and dated, but he decided to humour his touchy adviser on foreign affairs. Whitehall's patience was wearing very thin. Why should the Ambassador to Great Britain dance attendance on Italy's head of state? But von Ribbentrop paid no attention.

At 9 a.m. on 25 September the special train carrying the Duce, accompanied by his tomcat Foreign Minister and son-in-law Count Ciano, also known as the Ducellini, arrived in Munich. The train also carried Alfieri, the Fascist Propaganda Minister, and one hundred of the Duce's staff.

After a visit to Hitler's private apartment on Prinzregentenplatz, Mussolini, the man who had first used the term 'axis', was presented with an immense parade of SA and SS on the open Munich square called Königsplatz. He was trying to be 'more Prussian than the Prussians' in his newly designed, ribbon-bedecked uniform.[35] In Bologna he had bragged about the 'olive branch of peace growing from a forest of eight million bayonets'. He had seemingly overcome the disdain he had voiced in 1934 for Germany's Führer and had told John Whitaker of the *New York Herald Tribune* that he would now 'invite Hitler to make Austria German'.

There was no doubt in von Ribbentrop's mind. He simply had to be there. He had to be part of this event. This was history in the making. The stakes were high and the penalty for absence was steep. The fact that he was still Ambassador to Great Britain and that the proper escort for Mussolini and Ciano was Germany's Ambassador to Italy, Ulrich von Hassell, gave him no pause. He pursued Mussolini and his aides for the full five days of their state visit. From Munich to Essen to Berlin he chased after them by supercharged Mercedes or on one of the special trains.[36] His chauffeur Brütgam was ordered to cut in ahead of von Hassell's Mercedes when everyone was travelling in convoy. At Mecklenburg they watched army manoeuvres. At Swinemünde there were mock naval attacks. At Essen, the Krupp works displayed their weapons-building steel muscles. Von Ribbentrop was always right there. Then, finally, on to Berlin on 28 September. For the last few kilometres into the capital, Mussolini's and Hitler's special trains ran precisely side by side on twin tracks in a dazzling and theatrical demonstration of parallel Italo-German aims and loyalties.

Six hundred and fifty thousand Berliners assembled on the May Field outside the Olympic Stadium to hear Hitler and his top dignitaries declare their faith and trust, a marriage of fascio and swastika.[37] When, finally, it was Mussolini's turn to speak from the thirty-five-foot-high concrete podium, the heavens opened in a deluge of September rain. Within minutes Mussolini's notes lay dissolved in soggy tatters. His uniform was soaked and the water-logged microphones projected only high-pitched gibberish while the Roman dictator gesticulated wildly. Had they not been drenched and standing in mud, the cynical Berliners would have had a hard time suppressing raucous laughter. It was a good thing the flagpole with Hitler's *standart* was manned by sailors, who were used to the soaking.

The way back to Berlin became a nightmare of jammed traffic and mud-bespattered slipping and tottering dignitaries from generals to Gauleiters trying to find their parked, mired cars. Annelies von Ribbentrop was not even able to leave her big Mercedes, stuck in a far-away car park at the edge of the May Field. She was to have joined Joachim, but her husband went back to Berlin in a car which Spitzy requisitioned from a minor party factotum by howling at the top of his lungs in the Prussian military manner about the importance of his chief, the Ambassador Extraordinary and SS General. Among the soaked dignitaries was Franz von Papen, dressed in a Kaiser-era uniform with all his Great War decorations and sashes. On his head he wore an old-fashioned, spiked helmet. Göring greeted him with an ironic 'Heil, Herr Old Reich Chancellor!'

As honoured guest Mussolini was quartered in the former Presidential Palace, once the Crown Prince's Palais. When the shivering Duce wanted a hot bath, he found that Prussian efficiency was not infallible. There was no hot water for the lavish rococo bathtub. The drenched, freezing Mussolini had to take a frigid bath before rushing for his mountainous and regal bed.[38]

Despite this minor failure, Mussolini was deeply impressed by Hitler's ways. He returned to Rome carrying some poisonous souvenirs. He would now reshape his empire in the image of Hitler's Germany, everything from the goose-step to anti-Semitic 'blood' laws.

His oldest Fascist associates were aghast. Even the most banal of Nazi manifestations were resisted. The goose-step or *Parademarsch* now became the *Passo Romano*. His most heroic soldier, Marshal Emilio de Bono, protested, 'Since the average height of the Italian soldier is five foot five inches, we shall have an army of stiff-necked dwarfs!'[39] The advent of anti-Semitic laws raised a much bigger furor. Many Italian Jews were old Fascists and supporters of Mussolini, and Italians were by nature brotherly with their Jewish compatriots – many Italian Jewish families dated from the days of the Roman Empire. In a demonstration of protest, Marshal Balbo, Italy's air hero and one of Mussolini's closest friends, flew himself from Libya to Ferrara. In that ancient centre of distinguished Italian Jewry, he made a demonstrative point of visiting every leading Jew and then of dining with Ferrara's Jewish mayor in the city's finest restaurant.[40]

A veritable deluge of Italian decorations accompanied Mussolini's visit to Germany. Even the hall porter at the Vier Jahreszeiten Hotel in Munich was awarded a knightly cross.[41]

The von Ribbentrops and their retinue returned to London on 30 September. Once more, it was a short visit. Two matters were in the offing elsewhere: the signing by Italy of the Anti-Comintern Pact, now with Japan a three-power agreement; and a meeting with the exiled Duke of Windsor. The Ribbentrop Büro's clever von Raumer, whose research had originally produced the technicality which stopped the Anti-Comintern Pact from being a virtual declaration of war on Russia, was still the pact's chief architect.

On 4 October von Ribbentrop was in Berlin. He stormed over to London on the 15th and then immediately back to Berlin, then on to the Berghof and, finally, to Rome. The meetings with Mussolini and the Ducellini Ciano went smoothly, and all was prepared for the next Anti-Comintern gala signing, scheduled for early November in Rome.

No sooner had Rome said 'si' than von Ribbentrop rushed back to Berlin, there to protect the tenuous bond originally tied with the help of the late Ambassador von Hösch at an Emerald Cunard soirée, where von Ribbentrop had met the future King Edward VIII and Mrs Simpson, now known as the Duke and Duchess of Windsor.[42] The Windsors ostensibly wished to study social conditions in the 'new' Germany. Dudley Forwood, the Duke's aide, said that the German-speaking Duke of Windsor was fully aware of the potential for Nazi propaganda and was extremely careful.[43] He even avoided any arm gesture which might have been photographed to resemble the Nazi salute. Still, some reporters made the unlikely claim that he had rendered a full Nazi salute to Adolf Hitler and to a Death's Head SS parade.[44] True or false, the resultant uproar forced the Windsors to cancel a trip they had planned to the USA.

By the time von Ribbentrop saw them in Berlin the Windsors had already visited the Berghof for tea with Hitler. Dr Paul Schmidt, the interpreter, reported that the Duke had been noncommittal with the Führer. Forwood reported that when the Duke criticized something, an interpreter gently modified it for Hitler to avoid annoying the Führer. The Duke then shouted in German, 'Falsch übersetzt!' (Wrong translation!)[45] In Berlin the von Ribbentrops gave a dinner for the Windsors at Horcher's Restaurant. The other guests were the Himmlers, as well as Marianne Hoppe, a well-known film actress, and Gustav Gründgens, the famous actor and Nazi puppet on whom the 1980 film *Mephisto* was based. The Duke, upon being introduced, would gently tap his heels together in the old-fashioned, Imperial, pre-Nazi manner,[46] which amused some Nazi leaders. They considered it 'reactionary'.

Von Ribbentrop made a token return to London on 26 October for two events: the first was the opening of Parliament, which foreign ambassadors viewed from a special gallery. At twelve noon exactly, the slow procession of the royals, with Lord Halifax carrying the Sword of State with his one and only hand, moved through the sea of robed peers. According to Chips Channon, the King had broken his habit of stammering, and spoke well. Then came a session of the Non-Intervention Committee with its empty discussions. The die had long before been cast in Spain, and Franco was winning. Germany and Italy were helping and the Russians were withdrawing their support from the Republicans. It was a heartbreaking time for the many international volunteers like America's Lincoln Brigade, fighting on the side of the Loyalists. Reporter Ernest Hemingway learned at first hand the price paid by those who hesitated to oppose the appetites of dictators. François-Poncet once described Hitler as a *Nimmersatt*, the German word for someone who is insatiable, and Mussolini had already begun his own masticatory process in Ethiopia. Now both he and Hitler sharpened their appetites for future feasts by joining hands over Franco Spain. For these two it was to be what François-Poncet called a fatal friendship. Mussolini's early unpunished aggression in Africa encouraged Hitler. Hitler's unopposed threats to the Western powers misled Mussolini. Only Franco was and remained the enigma among the Fascist dictators. Dressed up in all the usual Nazi–Fascist trappings, including the raised-arm salute, he established an absolutist regime and kept it out of the world war. He guided it through the very decades when German, Italian and Japanese dictatorships were crushed, towards constitutional monarchy and then democracy. During World War Two he refused any major collaboration with Hitler or Mussolini, with the exception of a limited number of volunteers. He kept his borders inviolate and permitted no backdoor access to the Mediterranean, the Atlantic or to vital

Gibraltar. He had so exasperated Hitler that even Goebbels, in sheer disgust, condemned Franco throughout his diary.

To prepare the way for von Ribbentrop's Italo-Japanese Anti-Comintern plans, Hitler ordered the withdrawal of all help to Chiang Kai-shek's China. Germany was now in Japan's camp.

On 4 November, a Friday, von Ribbentrop arrived in Rome. Foreign Ministry official Prince Philipp of Hessia* had returned from the Italian capital after testing the waters for Adolf Hitler. He had succeeded with Mussolini but was still encountering some reluctance from Ciano, who was not prepared to trust this von Ribbentrop out-of-channels quasi-treaty. For the same reason, the German Ambassador to Italy, Ulrich von Hassell, had gone to Berlin to get clarification. The AA and von Neurath were suspicious of the entire Anti-Comintern Pact, afraid that Germany would bind herself to join some unknown future adventures of her new co-signatories. Besides, it was not the AA's idea, and a depressed von Hassell told Kordt that no one had been able to stem the flow of events. Hitler was in favour of the pact. Von Ribbentrop had gained his victory over the professionals. To assuage the old diplomat von Hassell, Kordt pointed out that the treaty 'contained mainly nonsense'. Von Hassell agreed. Nevertheless, he worried about the future adventures of Italy and Japan.

Among von Ribbentrop's Berlin allies for the Anti-Comintern Pact was Ambassador Walther Hewel, the charming and skilled diplomatist whom he had appointed as the Büro's liaison man at the Reich Chancellery. Adolf Hitler was extremely fond of Hewel, but Hewel stayed a loyal subordinate of von Ribbentrop, to whom he offered the reassurance that Adolf Hitler favoured the Anti-Comintern Pact in spite of von Neurath's opposition.

The pact was duly signed on 6 November in Rome, and a large state dinner followed which involved the Special Ambassador Extraordinary in a battle of precedence with von Hassell, who was technically representing Germany's head of state. To complicate things, Rudolf Hess arrived from Berlin. Hess was senior to von Ribbentrop within the Nazi Party, since the Büro was technically part of Hess's organization as deputy of the Führer.

The Italian protocol people did much gleeful hand-rubbing while watching these German titans in undignified combat over precedence. The dilemma was solved with typical Italian tact: they decided on round tables without seating by rank. These small skirmishes between old and new were constant, and Adolf Hitler relished them. He was getting

---

* Philipp of Hessia was of the minor (*Landgrave*) branch of the family of Prince 'Lu' Hessen who served in the Embassy under von Ribbentrop. Philipp was married to Princess Mafalda of Savoy and therefore the Italian King's son-in-law. He was used by Adolf Hitler as a contact with Rome. He probably had ambitions to climb above his secondary Hessian status.

his revenge over the Prussians and their aristocracy. Potsdam lay far behind.

The euphoric events of Rome made von Ribbentrop careless. On several occasions during his visit he had said publicly that he was destined to become Foreign Minister in 1938, when von Neurath's age would force his retirement. He did not know that Hitler had given von Neurath his personal assurance that in his case the age limit would be waived. Ambassador von Hassell immediately informed von Neurath of von Ribbentrop's Roman indiscretions and when von Ribbentrop returned to Munich expecting his Führer's enthusiastic congratulations, he was pointedly ignored and had to stay in his hotel, cooling his heels. The faithful Hewel had no time to warn him that a torrent of anger was about to fall on him.

When von Ribbentrop was finally ordered to report to his Führer at 9 a.m. on 8 November at the Führer's private apartment on Prinz-regentenplatz, von Ribbentrop and his secretary Spitzy, both dressed in full black SS uniforms complete with dress swords, arrived punctually. Von Ribbentrop then received a vicious and very audible tongue-lashing behind the Führer's closed study door. Hitler was furious because von Ribbentrop had bragged that he would soon be foreign minister. Hitler asked, 'Was bilden Sie sich eigentlich ein?' (the German equivalent of 'Who the hell do you think you are?') He continued, 'No, Herr von Ribbentrop. We don't behave that way! And particularly not in front of foreigners!'

A whipped, wounded and meek von Ribbentrop beat a hasty retreat to his suite in the Hotel Vier Jahreszeiten, where he immediately retired to the safety of his bed in a darkened room,[47] suffering a heavy attack of Tango Nocturno. According to Secretary Spitzy, von Ribbentrop moaned that 'it was all finished' and that he would now volunteer to fight in Spain, asking Spitzy to join him. The young SS Captain was less than anxious to seek a heroic death and gave a non-committal answer.[48] Then a lengthy phone call to Annelies in London restored some of the shaken Ambassador's equilibrium, and he returned to England the following day.

A tragedy which followed shows that Joachim von Ribbentrop still had a normal human side when his day was untouched by Adolf Hitler. His young Büro aide, Prince 'Lu' of Hessia, was about to marry an English girl in London. His whole family, all the Hessians, were to be flown by a special Lufthansa plane to London for the wedding. The Duke and Duchess of Kent had agreed to be best man and matron of honour for their young cousin.

The plane crashed on takeoff, after refuelling in Brussels, and everyone on board was killed, including a sister of the Duchess of Kent, the Grand Duchess of Hessia. Even the most cynical members of their staff said that both Joachim and Annelies were warm, supportive and sensitive in their response to this tragedy. The young couple decided to go through with the sad wedding, and the Kents, Mountbattens and von Ribbentrops helped them through the ordeal. At times, the von Ribbentrops could still muster those expected decencies which had been part of their upbringing. Within their own family, their children never lacked for affection. A human tragedy in their immediate surroundings could bring the von Ribbentrops to free themselves for the moment from the strings which made them Hitler's marionettes. But it happened only on rare occasions.

At about the time the Rome Anti-Comintern Pact was signed, Adolf Hitler had a confidential meeting with Göring, von Blomberg, von Fritsch, the army Chief of Staff, Admiral Raeder of the navy and Foreign Minister von Neurath. He was said to have outlined his plans for the takeover of Austria and the conquest of Czechoslovakia. He believed that Britain would fight Italy but not Germany. The meeting was recorded by Hitler's military aide, Major Hossbach, and his notes became well known later as the Hossbach memorandum of 5 November 1937, because they seemed to prove how early Hitler had planned it.

Early in December in London von Ribbentrop was a brief and perfunctory speaker at the London meeting of the Anglo-German Fellowship, attended by the usual group and also by the unlikely figure of Sir Robert Vansittart. Von Ribbentrop's attention was diverted by the 'private' visit which Lord Halifax, one of the participants at the dinner and, as Lord President of the Council, a member of Chamberlain's Cabinet, had just made to Adolf Hitler at the Berghof, with the hated von Neurath in attendance. Von Ribbentrop knew none of the meeting's agenda, and it took a full month before he had to embarrass himself by getting a report from von Neurath. Hitler had not asked von Ribbentrop, his 'England expert', to attend the Halifax meeting, nor did he respond to a request for an audience in early January. From November 1937 to February 1938 von Ribbentrop was clearly a man out of his master's favour, and Hitler was obviously anxious to mollify von Neurath. In fact Von Ribbentrop's days as Hitler's favourite now seemed numbered. The terrible dressing-down in Hitler's Munich apartment, the inability to obtain an audience and the Halifax–von Neurath conference at the Berghof seemed clear signals. Indeed, von Neurath was someone Hitler was not yet ready to discard. That chance would soon come, brought on by a series of events which once and for all released Hitler's deep, revolutionary hatred of aristocrats, particularly those of the Foreign Ministry. He was sure the nobles had always been his enemies. Along with Jews, Bolsheviks, Masons, his bitterest ideological enmity was for *die Reaktion*, the reactionaries. Meanwhile, though von Ribbentrop had to suffer his beloved Führer's rejections, he still refused to blame Hitler himself, and said to Spitzy, 'The poor Führer has fallen into the hands of evil advisers and saboteurs.'[49]

From the day he met Adolf Hitler to the day he died on the gallows, despite those times when he received shabby treatment, Joachim von Ribbentrop never showed a moment's disloyalty to Adolf Hitler. In his Nuremberg cell, after he had been condemned to death, he still proclaimed his eternal, personal devotion to Hitler, even after he had confessed that he was aware of Hitler's many errors. With the exception of Joseph Goebbels, he was almost unique among the top Nazis in his unwavering loyalty. It was this quality which Adolf Hitler sensed and used, and it would become von Ribbentrop's death sentence, passed on that first day in 1932 when he had met Hitler in Berchtesgaden.

Joachim von Ribbentrop was the son of an officer in the Kaiser's army, and blind loyalty was the German officer's religion. His father had ruined his own career out of loyalty to the great Bismarck. His son would lose his life for being unquestioningly loyal to an evil man.

Although von Ribbentrop decided that he had fallen from favour, he would now perform one final, great task to demonstrate his undying loyalty to Adolf Hitler, to the Reich and to the party. He began to prepare a major evaluation of the Reich's future relationship with Great Britain, a long and complicated document which was eventually titled 'Bot-schafterbericht A5522' (Ambassador's Report A5522). Annelies helped him, and it took him weeks. There are several accounts of the days when Joachim and Annelies von Ribbentrop scrambled on hands and knees on the floor of their bedroom, sorting the hundreds of draft pages.

A5522 was rambling and unfocused, but in the main it stated that Britain was trying to catch up by rearming as quickly as she could, that she thought time was on her side and that the Halifax visit was only a smokescreen. It also suggested that Britain did not trust Nazi Germany and would fight as a last resort and that Germany should maintain an open show of conciliation while continuing an Italian–Japanese coalition against Britain. He then asked rhetorically: 'Will France and Britain go to war if Germany goes to war in Central Europe?' He declared that he would prefer to make an oral report on this question directly to the Führer. He was convinced that Britain would fight if the British Isles were threatened, and he stated that Edward VIII had had to leave the throne because he was too friendly to Germany. 'Vansittart is our bitter enemy! We must think of England as our most dangerous enemy.'

Von Ribbentrop considered A5522 to be his testament. It would be his final offering, laid on the altar of his angry idol.

While he slaved over this paper, helped only by his wife, Adolf Hitler and Benito Mussolini prepared a new harsher venue for future inter-national dealings. On 11 December Mussolini's Italy withdrew forever from the League of Nations, and Hitler announced that Germany would never again return to Geneva.

TEN

EMBASSY–MINISTRY–MUNICH–KRISTALLNACHT, 1938–1939

'Will My Adorable Austria Become Nazified?'

The downhearted and pessimistic von Ribbentrops set off for Berlin on 22 December 1937 for Christmas and the New Year. They were accompanied by a substantial group from the Embassy. An expense voucher of March 1938 notes that Mitropa, the German sleeping car company, had charged the Foreign Office for thirty first-class tickets and sixteen second-class tickets. The total cost was 3,166 Marks.[1]

Christmas was spent at Sonnenburg, the new country estate the von Ribbentrops had just bought near Berlin. There was never any shortage of money. Between the von Ribbentrop Büro and the Embassy, most of their travel, entertainment and living expenses were paid, including the constant use of D-AMY. At the same time, the wine business still flourished. The von Ribbentrops were an extremely wealthy couple, though – in contrast to other party people – much of their money was earned privately and not through the party. Hitler made a vast fortune through the massive forced sales of *Mein Kampf,* and Göring earned large sums for administering his party-sponsored industrial complex, the Hermann Göring Works, and its 600,000 employees, founded in July 1937.[2]

Certainly, the purchase of a new country estate caused no financial strain, but von Ribbentrop was always careful to play down his personal fortune in front of the Nazi elite. He was quite willing to brag and boast about his political or party achievements and power, but never about his personal wealth.

A few months later, after he had become foreign minister (Reichs Aussen Minister, or RAM), he was lunching at the Führer's table in the Chancellery with a group of Nazi leaders including Dr Goebbels. Reinhard Spitzy, hovering dutifully in the background, overheard an exchange between his master and the propaganda minister.

Goebbels suddenly said, 'Herr von Ribbentrop, is it true that you have just bought a grand estate and you are now going to renovate it?'

Von Ribbentrop replied, 'Yes, the place must be straightened out agriculturally and the house should be renovated if I want to use it for some of my work as Foreign Minister, or if I should wish to holiday there.'

Then Goebbels asked, 'Oh, agriculture? Do you know anything about it? For instance, can you tell an ox from a steer?'

Grins appeared around the table while an amused, silent Hitler bent over his dish of noodles and poked around in them. Ribbentrop gave a pained laugh and tried to be a good sport.

But Goebbels returned once more to the subject. 'Herr von Ribbentrop, you seem to be making quite an investment! Is it true you are building a private golf course?'

This did not go down too well with the Nazi bigwigs around the table, who had little patience with such plutocratic affectations.

An uncomfortable von Ribbentrop said, 'Well, it's only a few holes and greens, hardly worth mentioning! I need it for those guests who like to play golf, and it relaxes me after the office routine.'

Now Goebbels went for the jugular. He said, 'And all this on a government salary?'

There was much laughter until Hitler, smiling briefly, forced a change of subject, while von Ribbentrop stared angrily at the table, and no longer participated in the conversation. He left soon afterwards.

The von Ribbentrops probably bought Sonnenburg with their own money, but why did von Ribbentrop not tell Goebbels to go to hell, and that how he spent his own money was nobody else's business? The reason was fairly obvious. He would not play the role of rich man among these revolutionaries. He wanted to be one of them and be accepted as an 'old fighter'. He had a lot to overcome: his good looks and careful grooming, his title, though 'adopted', his extensive travelling, his beautiful houses, his aristocratic friends, his rich wife and – his money. Among the Nazi Party stalwarts, he was still a complete outsider.

Goebbels once said, 'Ribbentrop bought his name, married his money and cheated himself into his job.'[3] But it was a jealous Goebbels who said so, always anxious to become Foreign Minister, always hating anyone Hitler admired.

After weeks of being ignored by Hitler, in those first days of 1938, von Ribbentrop might have thought his career was over. His great patron had turned away from him. But the fates were to do him an even worse turn, because soon they would return him to the very centre of Adolf Hitler's favour and attention.

It began on 12 January, oddly enough at a wedding. That day, in the presence of the Führer, Field Marshal Werner von Blomberg, Reich Minister for War, was married to Fräulein Eva Gruhn, his former secretary. Fräulein Gruhn was not really a suitable match for the aristocratic von Blomberg because she came from a simple, lower-middle-class Berlin background. Nevertheless, everyone sympathized with the tall, sixty-year-old Marshal, long a widower and known as a great flirt. He adored beautiful young women, and now he was about to marry one. His friends smiled and shrugged their shoulders. Why keep him from a chance to regain his youth? Even Göring had urged him to go ahead with the wedding, although Fräulein Gruhn was known to have had several affairs in the past. According to the historian Joachim Fest, Göring even paid off a rival for Fräulein Gruhn's affections, to clear Blomberg's path.[4]

Within a few days, police files revealed that the new Frau von Blomberg was not only a *femme fatale* but had actually practised prostitution and had been arrested after posing for pornographic photographs which were in the possession of a Belgian military attaché.

It was a major dilemma. The Führer had given his tacit blessing to this disastrous *mésalliance* by being present at the wedding and the military leadership of the Reich was now in the hands of a man who had shown a complete lack of judgment in the conduct of his personal life.

After originally claiming reluctance about the Nazis, von Blomberg had often demonstrated his loyalty to Hitler. He had helped to plan the Rhineland occupation and after von Hindenburg's death had approved switching the military oath of allegiance from the Reich to the person of Adolf Hitler. Hitler had always been able to count on him, but that was no longer enough. No one could help von Blomberg now. Certainly the generals, who considered Minister von Blomberg a party puppet, were not about to spring to his defence.

Like many Austrians, Adolf Hitler had always secretly worshipped all that was Prussian, hereditary, landed and military. Yet, deep inside his revolutionary's soul, he also distrusted all these aristocrats, but for the time being he still needed them to run his army, to conduct his diplomacy and to take away the radical taint of his revolutionary regime. Hitler was inhabited by three men. The conservative lower-middle-class, Catholic-disciplined Austrian; the artist *manqué* and lazy bohemian; and the revolutionary who allowed nothing to stand in his way. Now von Blomberg had offended Hitler's lower-middle-class snobberies. A German aristocrat did not marry a prostitute! And how dare von Blomberg make him, Adolf Hitler, an unwilling partner to such immorality? There also was the satisfaction of teaching all those gentry in army headquarters who was *really* in charge. He would now make the noble generals shake in their well-polished boots. If only Röhm had not been such a clumsy fool! Of course, Röhm had been absolutely right: Germany needed a new *people's* army.

But, through all the anger, the romantic Hitler's tear-filled eyes saw the 'besmirching of the noble German military spirit'. Now, fifteen days after he had witnessed von Blomberg's wedding, Hitler told his War

Minister, 'It is time for us to part,' and von Blomberg was summarily dismissed. But the von Blombergs stayed married and went off for a blissful honeymoon.

The world of the generals would undergo yet another jolt, this time in the person of General Wernher von Fritsch, the Chief of Staff of the army. Von Fritsch, one of the architects of the new German Wehrmacht, had backed Adolf Hitler in the Röhm action, but after the meeting documented by Major Hossbach on 5 November 1937, he had begun to fear that Hitler's plans for Eastern conquest were premature and precipitate. He had counselled moderation, and his influence among senior Wehrmacht officers had to be counted. Then, suddenly, came a jarring note, a Gestapo report stating that von Fritsch had engaged in 'offences against paragraph 175', the coy German way of referring to homosexual acts.

Von Fritsch stood accused by a homosexual blackmailer and prostitute who was then serving time in jail. The report had first landed on Göring's desk, and the Luftwaffe chief advised the Führer. Von Fritsch was secretly warned by Hossbach, Hitler's military aide and now a colonel, who respected the General. Of course, von Fritsch insisted on facing Hitler and Göring. He rushed to the Chancellery, where he was kept waiting for several hours. Finally he was admitted to Hitler's study to find that Göring was also waiting. As if they were small-time detectives, they now produced the accuser who had been temporarily freed for the purpose of confronting von Fritsch. 'Is this the man you saw?' they asked the shaken crook, who immediately said, 'That's the man!' No one knows what the Gestapo had done to him or had promised him.

The shocked von Fritsch did something Hitler observers judged a great mistake. Instead of howling his defiance, breaking his sword over his knee and throwing it at Hitler's feet, which would have impressed the Führer, von Fritsch calmly denied everything. Hitler never understood understatement, as the British were to learn.

Hitler immediately passed summary judgment instead of waiting for the military court of honour, which was to convene later. Von Fritsch was to retire and 'go on a long holiday'. Later, the disgraced General was acquitted by the military tribunal, but it was too late. In 1939 during the attack on Poland he was killed while leading a regiment of artillery.[5] Most German military men said he was seeking death. As a postscript, Hitler's army aide, Colonel Hossbach, who had warned von Fritsch, was dismissed.

Hitler appointed a new head of the army, General Walter von Brauchitsch, and General Wilhelm Keitel became Hitler's Chief of Staff and his perfect instrument. But now Adolf Hitler himself assumed the post of commander-in-chief of the entire Wehrmacht. Keitel, a passive, servile man, was soon called Lakeitel, a play on the German word *Lakei* meaning 'lackey'. Keitel was a cynical flunkey who never disagreed with Hitler, endorsed all measures taken by the increasingly cruel party and deserved to be hanged at Nuremberg, which he was. Oddly, he died with more dignity than he had lived.

The armed forces, always Hitler's main instrument of policy, were now entirely in his hands. All opposition had been silenced, all reason was ignored. Germany's generals and admirals could have no further illusions. They would have to be instruments of Adolf Hitler and the party. The Luftwaffe was Göring's creation.

Not all of them were automatons. There were still senior officers who opposed Hitler, and who had not buried their morality, but most leading officers of Germany's armed forces were now Hitler's property. The final step in von Ribbentrop's ascent was to come.

Hitler promoted his generals when he needed them, discarded them when they no longer suited his purpose or decorated them and even gave them cash bonuses in the manner of a feudal lord. Some generals who had managed to preserve their integrity were finally seduced when Hitler's early wartime generalship gave an impression of brilliance. Only a tiny handful remained their own masters.

Now that the Wehrmacht had been brought to heel, only the Foreign Ministry remained a stronghold of the old aristocracy. Time and again they had acted as a brake on Hitler's plans. He was sick of what he considered their air of superiority, their vacillation, their lack of flexibility and imagination. He had to persuade and convince von Neurath and his diplomats each time he wanted to step outside the path of conventional policy. From Rhineland to Naval Agreement to Anti-Comintern Pact, the Foreign Office professionals had consistently been nay-sayers.

The conciliatory year of the Olympics was now in the past. The German-friendly King of England was gone. The attempts to deal with Britain were stalled. Italy and Japan had become closer allies. France had stayed placid no matter what the provocation. Germany no longer needed the League of Nations, whose system of sanctions was ineffective.

Von Neurath had made no plans for forthcoming problems, such as the former German port of Danzig, which Hitler coveted, and for a road and a railway to guarantee access to it across that 'Versailles abomination', as he called the Polish Corridor. To drive or take the train to German East Prussia, Germans had to pass through Poland. Hitler also wanted the return of the former German port of Memel.

Von Neurath was reluctant to look East. Hitler had always insisted that that was where Germany's future lay, in Poland and Russia. In his view, Germany needed these Eastern territories as *Lebensraum*, as room to expand. Von Neurath even failed to acknowledge the alleged 'danger' which the Franco-Russian treaty had brought by way of Germany's south-eastern neighbour, Czechoslovakia.

And did von Neurath really understand the Austrian people's hunger for union with their German 'brothers'? Adolf Hitler had reason to doubt it. All of von Neurath's demonstrated allegiance to National Socialism seemed opportunistic. Hitler unknowingly agreed with André François-Poncet, the French Ambassador, who called von Neurath 'not frank, lazy, a liar and lacking in moral courage'.[6] Von Neurath did not join the party until 1937, and his general's rank in the SS was Himmler's gesture to him as a government minister. He did get involved in anti-Semitic and anti-Church measures, but that took little National Socialist conviction or personal courage.

Hitler needed a young, imaginative, flexible internationalist, someone totally loyal and aggressive who would agree with Führer-policy, Führer-plans, Führer-wishes. Since his earliest days of political combat, Hitler had always been completely sure of his own political credo. He rambled and meandered when he wrote *Mein Kampf*, but he had not changed one scintilla of his views. He now needed a new foreign policy executive.

He made an unlikely choice because he had only the narrowest list of candidates. Rosenberg had failed on his London mission in 1934. He wanted Goebbels to concentrate on propaganda. Göring was already too powerful. Most top ambassadors like von Hassell in Rome or von Dirksen in Tokyo were professional diplomats, in no way different from von Neurath. Von Papen could not be taken seriously. He was an opportunist and, as a Roman Catholic, too closely tied to the Vatican. Hess had never expressed great interest in the job. So Hitler chose von Ribbentrop, his adviser on foreign policy since 1932 and his ambassador to Germany's most important adversary.

Konstantin von Neurath was completely unaware of his imminent firing. He was quite sure that Hitler trusted him and depended on him. Hitler had time and again backed him against von Ribbentrop's attacks, although von Ribbentrop's Büro was still very active and had often pre-briefed Hitler before meetings on foreign policy. Von Neurath had put up with the Büro officials. Besides, they did much of the dirty work, like bribing foreign journalists and recruiting shady agents, and they were welcome to it. The gentlemen of the Foreign Ministry preferred to keep their hands clean.

Besides, the Führer had just celebrated von Neurath's sixty-fifth birthday by personally coming to congratulate him and to present him with a superb piece of medieval art. As von Neurath had told former AA official Paul Schwarz,

> I always respected the amount of knowledge a simple man like Hitler was able to accumulate, without the right schooling and the right opportunities. If Hitler had had the chance of travelling abroad, if he

Left: 1914: Aged just twenty-one, rehearsing for a charade in Ottawa with Miss Parker, whose family frequently received the young Ribbentrop at home parties.

Above: Annelies as a young woman.

Below: *St Louis Post Dispatch*, 18 October 1930.

VERSAILLES TREATY

Hitler's automobile mania: his own sketch of a
Volkswagen, 1933.

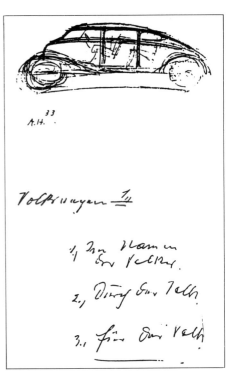

Joachim and Annelies with
Bettina in Dahlem around
1932–3.

With British newspaper publisher Lord Rothermere in Berlin, 15 December 1934.

The Special Adviser shakes hands with his delighted Chief, 1935.

"LET US EXTEND OUR HAND TO GERMANY"

'Let us extend our hand to Germany': a cartoon by David Low which appeared in the *Evening Standard*, 17 June 1935.

Ein SEKT von GROSSEM FORMAT:

- Bestechendes, elegantes Bukett
- Brillanter, anregender Charakter
- Sprichwörtliche Bekömmlichkeit

HENKELL TROCKEN

HENKELL & CO · WIESBADEN-BIEBRICH

A Henkell advertisement in the *Berliner Illustrirte*.

On the way to Buckingham Palace to present his credentials to Edward VIII, 27 October 1936: the ambassador was not in formal court dress as the King was not yet crowned.

Via Mercedes to Buckingham Palace, 1937.

The new Chief, dressed in SS uniform, greets AA staff, 16 February 1938.

had received proper education, he really would have become one of the world's great statesmen.

(In this patronizing assessment of his chief, the opportunistic von Neurath found no fault with the moral foundations of this potentially 'great statesman'.)

On the morning of 4 February 1938, von Neurath was a contented man. Lulled by the recent birthday celebration and gift, the von Neuraths had decided on a holiday on their estate, Leinfelderhof, in Württemburg, in the south of Germany. His wife began to pack for the trip. At noon that day, the Führer's State Secretary informed von Neurath that Hitler wished to see him at 3 p.m. Von Neurath then attended a long meeting with the Führer on foreign policy, with von Ribbentrop present. When it was over, von Neurath walked through some gardens to his nearby ministerial villa, accompanied by Hitler's and von Ribbentrop's best wishes for his holiday. When he arrived at home there was a message asking him to return 'for a few minutes' to the Chancellery. Hitler met him in the garden behing the Chancellery, linked his arm through his as they strolled together, and dismissed him. In gentle tones he said that von Ribbentrop would be the new Foreign Minister and that von Neurath would become President of a secret Privy Council which had just been created. 'This is my fondest wish,' said Hitler.

The stunned von Neurath returned to his villa, no longer the Foreign Minister. Two days later, Frau von Neurath was told that her servants were to report to the von Ribbentrop villa in Dahlem and that the tableware was the property of the Reich. Then von Ribbentrop's people asked when the villa would be vacated.

It is difficult to muster sympathy for von Neurath because his presence contributed so little to what remained of German sanity. Von Hassell and dozens of other aristocrats had first served their strange and vicious new master and had finally rebelled against his monstrous ways. Von Neurath simply went along. He was a man of the world. He knew right from wrong, and he willingly continued to serve the wrong. His subsequent career as Protector of Bohemia and Moravia and his occasional 'housekeeping' stints in the field of diplomacy reflected no honour on him. His fifteen-year sentence as a war criminal seemed well deserved.

Suddenly, after thirty days of abject depression during which he had received neither word nor gesture from his master, the emotionally drained and embittered Joachim von Ribbentrop, professional business-man and amateur diplomatist, now found himself Foreign Minister, and Annelies was the wife of a man of Cabinet rank. In Wiesbaden, Käthe Henkell would ask, 'Why did the most stupid of my sons-in-law achieve the biggest success?'

Many things needed to be arranged. The entire London household had to be returned to Berlin. A new ambassador had to be appointed to the Court of St James. What was to become of the Büro? The short month of February was crowded with the new RAM's unfamiliar duties. Von Neurath made absolutely no provisions for his former subordinates in the Ministry, and these gentlemen now awaited this new regime of party stalwarts with a great deal of anxiety. It fell to Kordt to handle the details of the transition as best he could. Along with Von Neurath went the dismissal of several aristocratic ambassadors such as von Hassell in Rome.

Adolf Hitler's attention now focused on his homeland, Austria. Almost as a side issue he ordered the diplomats to prepare Germany's recognition of Manchukuo, Japan's new puppet empire in China. It was also propitious that Anthony Eden, the 'difficult' British Foreign Minister, had been replaced by the easy-to-please Lord Halifax, or Lord Halali as the Berliners called him ('Halali!' was Germany's old hunting yell, and Halifax had recently been Göring's guest for the hunt.) But no matter what happened elsewhere in the world, nothing would or could divert Hitler's attention from Austria.

A week after his appointment, von Ribbentrop attended his first international meeting as foreign minister. An urgent call came from the Berghof that he was to report immediately to his Führer at the Bavarian retreat for a meeting with Austria's Chancellor Kurt von Schuschnigg and the German Ambassador to Vienna, the indestructible Franz von Papen.

Von Ribbentrop was in the dark about the state of German–Austrian affairs and quite unprepared for the meeting. Curiously, von Papen had only just been fired from his Vienna ambassadorial post along with all the other dismissed nobles, but since it was he who had arranged the von Schuschnigg meeting, he was reinstated once more. Luring von Schuschnigg to Hitler's Berghof, and into the lion's den, had been no small achievement. Von Papen deserved credit of sorts. As Sir Nevile Henderson wrote, 'Going to Berchtesgaden at all was the first of von Schuschnigg's mistakes.'

On his way south to do the Führer's bidding, the new Foreign Minister was accompanied by Spitzy, and they were joined by a party factotum and senior SS officer called Keppler, who was Hitler's expert on Austrian political and economic matters. Arriving in Berchtesgaden they also met with von Papen, who showed them his draft for an Austro-German agreement, but von Ribbentrop knew next to nothing about the subject of Austria. Nevertheless, according to Spitzy, von Ribbentrop took von Papen's draft and 'hardened' it from the German standpoint, since one 'never did oneself harm with the Führer by being aggressive'.

They arrived at the Berghof on 12 February, promptly at 10 a.m. Next came von Schuschnigg who was met halfway up the flight of stairs by his host. The pale and tired Austrian Chancellor was introduced to Hitler's associates, and the two heads of state retired to Hitler's study. Several generals, led by their newly minted Führer-supported Chief of Staff Keitel, had also been ordered to attend, supposedly to discuss Spain, but more probably to lend a military threat to the events.

February in the Bavarian Alps can be cold, grey and whipped by snow-seeded mountain winds. It must have been a threatening scene for the Austrian Chancellor and his Foreign Minister Guido Schmidt (they were accompanied by Schuschnigg's secretary, an officer of the Austrian Guards Regiment and an Austrian detective). Also on the scene, and most unwelcome to von Schuschnigg, were two semi-uniformed (they wore white stockings) representatives of the 30,000 illegal Austrian Nazis, now exiled in Germany.* Spitzy, who reported the conference, was also an 'illegal', as the exiled Austrian Nazis were called.

The paladins of both sides could do nothing but sit around and wait. Conversation between the exiled Austrian Nazis and the Austrian government officials was halting at best. No doubt their minds were not on their conversation, but on the two men locked in agreement or in combat somewhere upstairs in the sprawling half-farm, half-mansion called the Berghof. The two protagonists were both Austrians, one from a titled family, the other from the simplest of backgrounds, and they were playing poker and chess with the lives and fates of all their fellow Austrians. It is likely that it was a very harsh meeting and that von Schuschnigg was threatened and browbeaten.[7] He was forced to accept measures and conditions which were repugnant to him. Probably to ease his pain, Hitler later made a well-publicized declaration that he wished for an evolutionary solution to the Austro-German future; he also replaced the head of Austria's Nazi Party.

Von Schuschnigg was forced to add the Austrian Nazi politician Seyss-Inquart to his Cabinet. Hitler also bludgeoned him into granting an amnesty for all imprisoned Nazis in Austria, and insisted on free return for exiled 'illegal' Austrian Nazis, as well as compensation for them. At one point during the conference, Hitler made a big show of consulting privately with General Keitel just out of von Schuschnigg's hearing, but not out of sight. It was certainly an implied threat. At 10 p.m., the end of that disastrous day for von Schuschnigg, the Austrian detective bid his German hosts goodbye with 'Heil Hitler!'

After the von Schuschnigg meeting, it was back to Berlin, where von Ribbentrop now attempted to fit himself into his important new post. Fortunately for him, he got professional help in the person of Ernst von Weizsäcker, a former navy officer and AA professional. Von Weizsäcker,

---

* Austria's Nazis had been banned and could not wear uniforms. They improvised by wearing white farmers' stockings in place of brown shirts.

who had been chargé d'affaires in Switzerland and then head of the Political Department of the AA, was promoted to state secretary. If there was any future chance of conducting professional, international diplomacy, it would be due to von Weizsäcker, who had been appointed at the urging of Erich Kordt and others. Von Ribbentrop had been forced to rely on their recommendation because of his own lack of experience and training. Later, constantly battered by the insecure 'loose cannon' von Ribbentrop, by the increasingly influential Annelies and, most of all, by the objectives of Adolf Hitler, von Weizsäcker did what he could to soften the shocks, ease the pain and divert the harm. Eventually he found it impossible, and asked to be relieved. He was sent to the Vatican as ambassador at the end of the regime.

Some of the filth which splattered everything around the person of Adolf Hitler also tainted von Weizsäcker. In fact, all professional diplomats whom von Ribbentrop drew close to himself quickly became 'Ribbentrop people' in the eyes of many in the Wilhelmstrasse AA offices. Most of the AA people chose to forget that Erich Kordt and those he brought to the Office of the Foreign Minister had originally been proposed by the distinguished State Secretary von Bülow, who had hoped they would be 'observers and restrainers'. It was virtually impossible for anyone, no matter how deeply opposed to his ways, to work for Adolf Hitler without becoming part of his evil. The men who mounted an unsuccessful attempt on Hitler's life on 20 July 1944 had finally come to the conclusion that Germany herself could never survive in Hitler's filth. Yet there is strong evidence that if they had succeeded in killing Hitler, Germany might have been plunged into civil war while the Allies were still tearing at her flanks from East and West. To the very end, Hitler, who was willing to destroy every German as 'unworthy', was still adored by the majority of the people. This is one more proof of the depth of evil he had plumbed from a largely decent nation.

Von Ribbentrop witnessed the first act in Austria's eventual tragedy, without being able to contribute the slightest piece of advice or expertise. On returning to Berlin, he ordered a ceremony which must have shaken quite a few Foreign Service veterans. Everyone had to assemble for a quasi-military 'mustering' and a banal speech of loyalty to Hitler from the new Minister. By now, von Ribbentrop had worked out a makeshift persona for himself, somewhat in the imagined style of a statesman in ancient Rome: dignified, measured, stern, assured and a devoted servant of Adolf Hitler and of National Socialism. His staff at the London Embassy had often heard his dinner-time dicta, proclaiming the need for a 'new nobility' in Germany, a new elite, founded on 'Aryan' roots and on National Socialist teaching.[8] The old titled families who 'considered the AA their private club' had to relinquish command. He insisted, 'it is not so important to speak foreign languages. The others will soon have to learn German.' Both his adopted dignity and seeming assurance were soon to be put to the test. Von Weizsäcker and Kordt persuaded him to return to London in order to take his formal courteous leave of Whitehall after his sporadic and careless performance as ambassador to the Court of St James. Perhaps, they felt, a gesture of this kind might salve some wounded British feelings.[9]

On 9 March 1938, while he was back in London, he had a meeting with Lord Halifax and asked him to tone down unfriendly newspaper pieces. Amazingly, Halifax did in fact try to reason with the papers. On that same day, Kurt von Schuschnigg, unable to go through with the odious deal which had been forced on him, suddenly announced a national plebiscite to determine whether Austrians preferred their independence or wished to become part of the German Reich. Word of the unexpected plebiscite soon reached the Führer in Berlin and caused an attack of Hitlerian rage. His victim had dared to betray him! The forced deal was unravelling.

The following day von Ribbentrop appeared at Buckingham Palace to bid a formal farewell to the King, on this occasion without any Hitler salutes. At this very moment, far to the East, von Schuschnigg announced a postponement of the referendum on Austrian independence and his own resignation. It can only be assumed that von Ribbentrop had paid no attention to events in Austria. Certainly he was not informed, although Kordt, who was with him, seemed *au courant*. Exactly one month had passed since the cruel Berghof meetings with von Schuschnigg and the forced agreement. On 11 March von Ribbentrop was attending a luncheon at 10 Downing Street, hosted by Mr Chamberlain, the new Prime Minister, and his senior Cabinet ministers. Winston Churchill was also asked. Suddenly news of the German military entry into Austria was handed to Mr Chamberlain. Understandably, the luncheon soon ended, but there was no discussion of these events. Every British official present must have thought that von Ribbentrop, as German Foreign Minister, knew exactly what was happening in Austria and was playing the innocent; one can imagine their disgust and disdain for him. No one would have believed the very real possibility that von Ribbentrop had been purposely left in the dark by Hitler or that the military move had been unleashed on a sudden Hitlerian whim and that there was no way that word would have reached his Foreign Minister, who had been visiting all over London.

It seems very likely that von Ribbentrop was either ignored by Adolf Hitler or purposely not informed. Hitler knew how insecure von Ribbentrop was and wanted to prevent his sudden departure from London. Hitler, who drove into Vienna aboard a six-wheel army Mercedes, needed his 'England expert' to be near to 10 Downing Street so that he could gauge the British government's reaction to the Anschluss (literally, unification or addition) with Austria. He had virtually 'trapped' von Ribbentrop in London.

To add insult to injury, von Neurath, the hated former Foreign Minister, was instructed to be caretaker at the AA in Berlin.

Lord Halifax paid a visit to the German Embassy in London after the luncheon at 10 Downing Street and expressed his deep concern to a falsely cheerful and reassuring von Ribbentrop, who asked when next he might see Halifax in Berlin. Lord Halali answered tersely, 'I doubt if there'll be a hunting exhibition soon!'[10]

A thoroughly disturbed and anxious von Ribbentrop was now stuck in London, while his place at the Führer's side was filled by others. He had left Spitzy behind in Berlin to look after some of his interests, but Adolf Hitler's decision to reactivate von Neurath during these events seemed ominous. What did 'will take temporary charge of the Foreign Ministry' mean? Von Ribbentrop clearly was still not aware of Hitler's strategy. A letter from the Führer had been delivered by hand to Mussolini by Prince Philipp of Hessia to make sure of the Duce's friendly reaction to the Anschluss, the Duce having played Austria's 'protector' for years. Now Hitler wanted to keep von Ribbentrop in London so that Mussolini would think an accommodation about Austria was being worked out with Chamberlain.

As he had so often, von Ribbentrop felt isolated and feared he had lost the Führer's confidence. The morning after these events, he begged Kordt, almost tearfully, to fly to Berlin to 'save what he could'. Von Ribbentrop whined, 'Please see that von Neurath is no longer involved with the AA.' Kordt flew to Berlin, but von Neurath was nowhere in sight.

Von Ribbentrop finally managed to phone Spitzy, who, it turned out, had accompanied Hitler to Vienna. The young former 'illegal' Austrian Nazi could not resist his Austrian Führer's personal invitation to join him. They were now two returned patriots. Vienna's Cardinal Innitzer greeted Adolf Hitler with the raised-arm Nazi salute the day after the Führer's arrival, and assured him of Catholic support if the Church received 'the same freedom as the German Catholic churches'.[11]*

Spitzy finally obtained Hitler's permission for von Ribbentrop to leave London and to return to Berlin at once. Von Ribbentrop ordered a reception committee of the most senior Foreign Ministry officials to greet him at the airport, a contrived show of false devotion and loyalty to assuage his ill-temper. But, before leaving Britain, von Ribbentrop was forced to await the arrival of Spitzy bearing a personal order from Adolf Hitler, who wanted von Ribbentrop's equally personal report on British reactions. It was a bitter pill for the Foreign Minister to know that for

---

* He was referring to a concordat of 10 September 1933 between the Catholic Church and the Nazi regime, which was eventually to be breached by Hitler.

the moment even his young secretary was closer to the Führer than he was.

First reports of the brutal treatment of Vienna's Jews, of old Jewish men who were forced to scrub the streets on their hands and knees while the crowds jeered and spat on them,[12] soon reached London. It reduced former British sympathizers for Adolf Hitler's Germany to those who wished only to appease. What remained of British enthusiasts for Hitler soon shrank to a tiny minority. *The Times* of 15 March 1938 headlined 'The Rape of Austria' and reported the démarches against both anti-Nazis and Jews.[13] Even the pacific Lord Lothian now called for conscripted national service. Only a few diehard British apologists still carried on.[14] Lord Redesdale said in the House of Lords on 15 April, 'Hitler avoided civil war and bloodshed in Austria.' Sir Thomas Moore celebrated a 'new bloodless revolution' and Lord Londonderry blamed Britain because 'we failed to hold out the hand of friendship'. Chips Channon, now Parliamentary Private Secretary to a junior minister at the Foreign Office, heard the news in 10 Downing Street. He considered it a setback for the Chamberlain government and then, reverting to the sophisticated traveller, asked, 'Will my adorable Austria become Nazified?' And, prophetically, 'People are saying Czechoslovakia will be next.'[15]

By the time von Ribbentrop finally reached Vienna, he was part of the second wave. Hitler and Göring had already left. Only Schacht was still there to deal with immediate financial and economic problems. The Austrian official who greeted von Ribbentrop was Guido Schmidt, von Schuschnigg's former Foreign Minister who had been to Berchtesgaden with him. Schmidt was now devotedly on the side of the Germans, while his former chief was on his way to Gestapo jail and then to a concentration camp. Eventually, Schmidt was appointed to run the immense Hermann Göring Works for the fat Marshal, a profitable reward for his treachery. Von Ribbentrop quickly visited the Austrian Foreign Ministry, took charge and appropriated the great Metternich's globe for removal to his Berlin office. (André François-Poncet reported one of the most startling reactions to the Anschluss. According to him, Beneš, the Czechoslovak president, said, 'I'd rather see the Germans in Vienna than the Hapsburgs!' The months ahead must have caused him to recant these careless words.)

Ambassador Sir Nevile Henderson, the man so often accused of Nazi sympathies, now wanted to make a gesture of protest against the invasion of Austria. He decided to boycott the annual Heroes' Memorial Day parade in Berlin, a 13 March ceremony, which was usually attended by all ambassadors and foreign envoys. Instead, with Union Jacks flying from the Embassy Rolls-Royce, he had himself driven to the Austrian Mission in a show of British sympathy. He could have saved himself the trouble. The Austrian Minister, in full diplomatic uniform, was on his way to attend the German Memorial Day ceremonies, where he saluted with 'Heil Hitler!'[16]

In the first days of the Anschluss, much of Austria's population went on a rampage of anti-democratic, anti-Communist, anti-reactionary, anti-Semitic 'revenge'. Many Austrians now insisted that they had been Nazis all along. Not only did they, in the words of Dr Joseph Goebbels, 'wish to go home to the Reich', but they now delivered themselves of a shamefully amplified imitation of the wildest SA outrages of 1934. In Währing, a prosperous section of Vienna, wealthy Jewish women were forced to scrub the street while wearing their fur coats. Some of the spectators then urinated on their heads.[17] Eleven hundred Viennese Jews killed themselves after the Anschluss.

While the Viennese were committing their *vox populi* street perversions, the German SS and the Gestapo's leather-coated agents roamed throughout Austria as Himmler's angels of death, seeking anyone who had ever opposed the Anschluss or wished to protect and preserve Austria's independence as a Christian democratic nation. Even those who had compromised their democratic principles by backing the rightist semi-dictatorship of Dollfuss now became targets for the Gestapo.

This SS–Gestapo sweep produced one murder which greatly benefited the von Ribbentrop family and was counted in their disfavour by many Austrian and German nobles. The SS took over a charming lakeside castle called Fuschl, near Salzburg, after arresting its owners, the von Remitz family. Herr von Remitz, an Austrian patriot of the highest order, was then sent to Dachau and executed. Fuschl Castle was handed over to Joachim von Ribbentrop. Over the following years, Annelies, Joachim and the children used it extensively. Fuschl became the place where von Ribbentrop would usually await the call from his master at the nearby Berghof. Frau von Remitz, a niece of Fritz Thyssen, and her children were left to fend for themselves. When von Ribbentrop played host to Mussolini in 1942 at Fuschl, von Ribbentrop spoke of it as 'his father's castle'.[18]

Some Austrian Nazis were shocked because everything 'Austrian' was now systematically suppressed. Even the country's name was changed from Austria to Ostmark or Eastern province. Reinhard Spitzy, an early Austrian Nazi, bemoaned the loss of Austria's old traditions. He was not alone.

Austrians played a curious but important role in the life of National Socialism. The popular notion in Germany was that Germans made better Nazis but Austrians made better anti-Semites. Quite aside from their Austrian Führer and his Germanified brand of spoken Austrian with its rolled Rs and anachronistic style, they had a pervading influence. They were only 8 per cent of the total German population but they were 14 per cent of the SS. The Einsatzgruppen, the SS death squads, had more Austrians than Germans. Forty per cent of the extermination camp staff members were Austrians.[19] Colonel Eichmann, the SS 'Jew expert' who organized the execution of the Final Solution, was brought up in Austria. Seventy per cent of his staff was Austrian. Chief of the SS–SD (the party section of the Gestapo) Ernst Kaltenbrunner was an Austrian. Odilo Globocnik, overall commander of the death camps Treblinka, Sobibor and Belzec, was an Austrian. General Alexander Löhr, Kurt Waldheim's superior officer, a war criminal who had many Greeks, Slovakians, Yugoslavs and Jews killed, was Austrian. (There were also great Austrian heroes. Among them were Anton Schmidt, an army sergeant in Vilna, executed for helping Jews, and Ewald Kleisinger, an army officer who hid Jews in Warsaw. Fifty Austrians were declared 'Righteous Gentiles' by Israel, the highest acclaim they can give to those who braved the Nazis.)

In return for Mussolini's apparent approval of the takeover of 'his' Austria, Adolf Hitler bartered away the mostly German-speaking lands and people of the mountains of South Tyrol. This region, the domain of ancient Austro-German families like the von Wolkensteins, von Enzenbergs and von Trapps (*Sound of Music*), had been handed over to Italy in 1919 without any regard for the Tyroleans' wishes. Thousands of these people from the high mountains were forced to resettle in southern Italy or flat East Prussia. As Hitler declared on 19 May 1938, 'the Tyrolean question has ceased to exist'.

These decisions were made without so much as a moment's consultation with the new Foreign Minister. Von Ribbentrop's future appeared clear. It seemed he would never be able to initiate foreign policy or execute it independently. The external vainglory would still be his, but the policy would be Hitler's.

The first four 'problems' Hitler had originally outlined to his fledgling Foreign Minister on the day he was appointed were Austria, the Sudetenland, Memel and Danzig. Austria was now 'solved'. In his memoirs, von Ribbentrop wrote that it was always his task to offer the diplomatic solution.[20] The military people were instructed to prepare the military solution. Neither side knew the contents of the other's plans. Hitler would make the choice. This time Hitler had made the military choice. It was, in the words of von Ribbentrop, 'hard to make one's point against such a strong personality. Every man who worked for Adolf Hitler had this experience. No one could change his mind once it was made up.'

Von Ribbentrop claimed there were three separate times when he tried unsuccessfully to resign and to be transferred to the army for combat duty. Although he had become a spoiled and pampered man who loved his comforts, it is entirely possible that this was true. Someone who drove bobsleighs as a youngster, went halfway around the world to serve as a combat soldier and was willing to brave many a storm-tossed flight on

the unpressurized, primitive passenger planes of those days, probably did
not lack physical courage. What he lacked was moral courage.

However, he never lacked vanity. To von Ribbentrop, appearance
was vital, and he complained that Germany's diplomats made a poor
appearance because they had no special diplomatic uniforms like other
nations. Von Ribbentrop himself often wore his honorary SS general's
uniform, complete with sword of honour, black tunic and cap, Sam
Browne belt, black riding breeches and shiny, black riding boots. It
pleased him to wear it. It also pleased his friend, the SS chief Himmler.
However, the SS uniform would not do for many international diplomatic
occasions. It was too martial, and besides it was not the uniform of the
German Diplomatic Corps. When a forthcoming state visit to Rome was
announced, an urgent call went out to Benno von Arent, a famous
theatrical designer who had staged many Nazi events. Von Arent designed
a sort of admiral's uniform with 'piston rings' on each sleeve to denote
rank. Here, too, Adolf Hitler, the artist–architect *manqué*, had his say.
He approved it.

Until then, most members of the Foreign Ministry had appeared in
conventional tail coat and striped trousers or in white tie and tails. They
were often ordered by an angry Hitler to 'get into uniform', and for this
reason many were given honorary ranks in the SS. Kordt became an
honorary SS colonel as did Schmidt, the head interpreter of the AA.

However, for the state visit to Rome in May they now got their new
German 'admiral's' diplomatic uniform in several versions for various
occasions. In a childish act of competition, a struggle for insignia of
rank developed with State Secretary Meissner, who ran the Führer's
Chancellery. Meissner felt he was entitled to the same number of 'piston
ring' stripes as the Foreign Minister. Then von Ribbentrop designed a
special 'Eagle and Swastika over the Globe' emblem for his own sleeves,
trumping Meissner.

According to Spitzy, on the morning of 3 May when the Führer's party
of 600 was leaving for Rome, Göring saw von Ribbentrop at the railway
station wearing his new diplomatist's uniform. Göring laughed and yelled,
'Herr von Ribbentrop, you look like the doorman at the Rio-Rita Bar.'
Von Ribbentrop 'chose not to hear him'.[21] With each international event
of Hitler's making, the von Ribbentrops became less able and probably
less willing to be masters of their own fate.

A predator, in wait for the tiny gesture of helplessness which will
provoke an attack, Adolf Hitler, the master opportunist, waited for
whatever he could designate as a provocation. His every action was
preceded by the provocation he had chosen to appoint for the purpose.
The Rhineland militarization was 'provoked' by the Franco-Russian
treaty. The introduction of conscription was 'provoked' by France's
extended army duty for conscripts. Almería was bombed after a German

ship lying in a Franco harbour had been bombed for being where it should not have been. Then Austria had been invaded because Austria's Chancellor, after being bludgeoned into an impossible agreement, had decided to call for a referendum. He had consented only under duress and had a perfect right to test the will of the constituency within his own country.

Joachim von Ribbentrop had no wedge, no leverage, no strength to oppose Hitler's decisions, should he have wished to do so. His only political ally was the man he was slave to. The party's old timers still thought von Ribbentrop an interloper. The aristocrats considered him a parvenu. The army called him Hitler's puppet. He was shackled by ambition or some ill-conceived sense of duty, or both.

To keep Adolf Hitler's favour became his round-the-clock task, for even those who had long-term claims on Hitler's loyalties and gratitude could find themselves ignored or discarded without warning. Men like Alfred Rosenberg and Baldur von Schirach, the Hitler Youth leader, frequently drifted in and out of the Führer's current of good will. The Jew-baiter Streicher was now ignored as a fossil, an anachronism. Probably the four men who were most secure were Göring, Goebbels, Himmler and Hess. But even Göring was often powerless to change Hitler's mind, and despite strenuous efforts Goebbels had failed to expand his own area of influence beyond that of propaganda and the creative arts.

Himmler collected secrets about the Nazi hierarchy, like a squirrel collecting explosive nuts for the winter of Hitler's discontent, while hoping by a show of devoted Teutonism and faithfulness to dazzle his suspicious Führer. Heydrich, the cold and dangerous policeman, became Himmler's life insurance policy. Meanwhile, their emphasis was on the SS motto: 'My honour is faithfulness.' Hitler called Himmler his 'faithful Heinrich' but kept a careful eye on him.

Hess, who was one of Hitler's oldest comrades and his party deputy, would soon strike out on a dangerous venture of his own, never again to return to Adolf Hitler's favour.

While von Ribbentrop was still a young businessman in Berlin, in search of commercial success and acceptance in society, these men around Hitler had been outcasts, strange disciples of an obscure Munich political guru. While the von Ribbentrops decorated their beautiful new house in Dahlem, tried to join good clubs, hoped for invitations to prominent Berlin homes and society parties, the revolutionaries around Hitler lived the dangerous lives of political activists. They were shot at by the police, by the Communists and by the reactionaries. They were arrested, jailed, vilified in the press. They were ridiculed and denounced by most decent and serious people. Their experiences were worlds apart from those of the von Ribbentrops.

Despite his rank as foreign minister, von Ribbentrop was like a recruit in a regiment of fierce old mercenary soldiers or like a young lawyer just hired by the Mafia. He had a lot to learn, and he might never be able to catch up. Meanwhile, he was useful to Adolf Hitler and fulfilled his purpose. Every time one of the old party faithfuls criticized the RAM, Hitler, who often joked about him, rallied to his defence. Though it is probably apocryphal, several sources claim that Hitler called von Ribbentrop the 'Second Bismarck'. If true, this was either a form of self-congratulation ('Any man who works for me becomes a great man') or possibly even Hitler's sign of disdain for his nineteenth-century predecessor, Prussia's Iron Chancellor.

When von Ribbentrop had been in office a mere three months, he realized that the Foreign Ministry's organization needed some rudimentary patching. Von Mackensen, who had preceded von Weizsäcker as state secretary of the Foreign Ministry, was appointed ambassador to Rome. He was von Neurath's son-in-law, and von Ribbentrop was suspicious of him but found him pliable. Dr Woermann, who had been von Ribbentrop's deputy in London, now became head of the Political Department of the AA, replacing von Weizsäcker, who had moved up to state secretary. The bespectacled, schoolmasterish Herbert von Dirksen, who was related to the chairman of I.G. Farben Industry, Georg von Schnitzler, and came from an old diplomatic family, was shifted from the Embassy in Tokyo to the Court of St James. In London he found a difficult atmosphere. After two years of von Ribbentrop, London was suspicious of the 'new' German style of diplomacy. Von Dirksen would soon have to face the shock of events to come, such as Germany's grim November pogroms, while he tried to maintain some semblance of amity with his British hosts. In June 1938, Albrecht Haushoffer, a friend of Hess and the son of the renowned political 'guru' who had been a major influence on Hitler (and, therefore, on von Ribbentrop), sent a deeply pessimistic memorandum to the Führer and his Foreign Minister. He flatly stated that the chances for Anglo-German rapprochement were slim and fading fast.[22] His opinions were dismissed and, knowing this, von Dirksen found it more diplomatic to play the optimist for Berlin. Von Ribbentrop's ear at the Chancellery was still Hewel. Everyone liked Hewel, but he was weak and had fallen totally under Hitler's influence.

The actual running of the Foreign Ministry was the job of the new State Secretary, von Weizsäcker. Von Ribbentrop rarely attended his Ministry's morning meetings of the department heads because that was the hour when he danced attendance at the Chancellery, where the Führer usually made his first daily appearance around 11 a.m. Hitler's paladins had to be present to guard their precarious place. As Erich Kordt wrote, 'If a Minister was not present, an assignment could go to the competition.'

Of the 'problems' the 'return to the Reich' of Austria had now been achieved by its most notorious son. The 'problem' of the Sudeten Germans of Czechoslovakia came next. To Hitler, the Czechoslovak Republic represented everything he despised about the time of Versailles. This new country had been formed in 1918 out of parts and parcels of the old Austrian Empire. Czechs, Slovaks, Germans, Hungarians, Poles and Ruthenians, held together by a newly created democratic form of republic, were asked to live together in harmony. This was not an unlikely notion since the fledgling republic was comparatively rich in minerals and had strong industry and agriculture and therefore a good basis for economic existence.

In 1918, everyone tried to follow the example presented by the United States, where Americans of diverse national and religious backgrounds seemed able to live together in a brand new nation. But Europe is different. Old hatreds, both ethnic and religious, persist. Countries are small and crowded. Perhaps if the different components of Czechoslovakia had been reassembled 3,000 miles away in a vast country like America, the Czechs could have had their wish. Meanwhile, underneath the appearance of a highly successful new nation, the dream of its founder and first President, Tomas Garrigue Masaryk, was full of cracks and fissures.

Much of Czechoslovakia's German-speaking population lived in the Sudetenland, the mountains called the Erzgebirge, just south of the German border. There were ancient hatreds. During the Great War, Czechs had fought on the Allied side, while the German-speaking Czechoslovaks, who at the time were Austrians, were with Germany. The mutual dislikes of Czechoslovakia's Slavs, Hungarians and Germans were as old as their mountains. The Czechoslovak Germans were often accused of arrogance. Indeed, the city of Prague and its ancient university were jewels of the German-speaking world and a worldwide source of German pride. The Czechoslovak Germans felt they were discriminated against by the Slavic government and that they were entitled to better representation.

As is often the case in political disputes, there was some basis of truth in each of the accusations. Mutual antipathies simmered and grew. German-speaking Czechoslovak citizens, encouraged by blatant propaganda from the Nazi German side of the border, decided that their day had come. After all, they were German-speaking people and, in their eyes and in the eyes of their 'brothers' across the border, this marked them as superior people, neat, clean, conscientious, hard-working, educated – in a word, German. The German pejorative term for something slovenly and inefficient is that it is like a 'Polish farm' (*polnische Wirtschaft*). This was the classic anti-Slavic slur. Another term for a mess was to say it was like a *böhmisches Dorf*, like a Bohemian village.

The Sudeten Germans had chosen a leader, the head of the SdP, the Sudeten deutsche Partei, a former gymnastics teacher called Konrad Henlein. Under his leadership, the SdP represented the majority of

Czechoslovakia's German-speaking (non-Jewish) citizens and by 1935 had become the second-biggest party in Czechoslovakia. Czechoslovakia also had an ancient Jewish population, who spoke careful high German, unlike the regional accents of the Sudeten Germans, and were among the country's leading citizens.

Henlein's original profession of gymnastics teacher was no coincidence. Gymnastics implied much more than mere exercise. It was also political. The gymnastic movement begun by a German called Friedrich Jahn in the early nineteenth century represented a pre-Hitler, pre-'Aryan', idealized picture of the battle-hard German spartan. It was a latterday derivative of the Graeco-Roman *mens sana in corpore sano* concept and was usually blended closely with German nationalism. For Henlein, the German ideal was the Nazi, and so the SdP became a Czechoslovak Nazi party, after the Czechoslovak government banned Czechoslovakia's German Nazi Party.

Hitler fanned the flames of the dispute. He considered himself the destined champion of all Germans, no matter where, if *he* decided that they suffered what *he* defined as indignities. On 3 March 1938, Henlein paid a secret visit to the Berghof and then returned to his home country, reinforced both ideologically and financially by the Big Brother from the Berghof. As Hitler once said, 'Wherever in the world there is a fire, I shall use it to warm the German soup.' Henlein's demands increased. He insisted on self-rule for the Sudeten Germans, though still within a loose Czechoslovak federation. He also hinted broadly at threats from the big bully across the border.

The Czechoslovak government reacted harshly. There were some bloody clashes between Sudeten Germans and the Czech police, particularly in the resort town of Teplitz. Obviously Hitler had planned on interfering in Czechoslovakia.

Following another visit from Henlein in mid-March, Hitler announced on the 28th that he intended 'to solve the Czechoslovak question in the near future'. He urged Henlein to increase his demands. Von Ribbentrop had attended the Henlein meetings, and now he also entered the arena. On the 31st he informed the Czechoslovak Ambassador Mastny that Germany did not intend to interfere directly, but 'that the fate of the Sudeten Germans must change radically'. Then the Czechoslovak stew was allowed to simmer quietly on the back of the stove. There were more pressing matters ahead. On 16 April, the Italians had signed a Mediterranean naval agreement with the British. The rumour was that the French would be next. Obviously, Mussolini was still nursing the pain of the Anschluss.

The state visit to Rome by Adolf Hitler lay just ahead. Immense safety preparations were undertaken by Reinhard Heydrich of the Gestapo long before 3 May 1938, when Adolf Hitler set foot on the platform of San

Paulo station in Rome, which had been specially prepared for this visit. Six thousand suspects had been arrested by the Italian police, some of them German Jews in exile.[23] Heydrich's foreign specialist, Walter Schellenberg, was sent to Italy, where he travelled every yard of the route Mussolini and his guest, Germany's Führer, were to take. Eighty of Berlin's best Gestapo plainclothesmen were placed at key points. The preparations also gave Heydrich a chance to infiltrate Italy with German agents. Schellenberg devised teams of linguists, to travel through Italy in the guise of tourists.[24]

Hitler had accepted the new AA uniforms for the trip, but he insisted that no one in the German delegation should wear a white tunic, so that the Italians would not seem to be treated as 'exotic or colonial'.[25]

On arrival, Hitler, von Ribbentrop, Goebbels, Hess, Himmler, Frank, SS General Sepp Dietrich, General Keitel and the German press corps were met by the King and the Duce. Hitler seemed shocked and disgusted that the King and his entourage should be greeting him, while Mussolini stood off to the side in respectful attendance. Who was running Italy? This was not how Hitler had envisaged Mussolini's place in the Roman scheme of things.[26]

After Mussolini himself had greeted the Germans, Hitler stepped into the King's horse-drawn carriage ahead of the sovereign, raising the ire of the little King, who disliked having to entertain the former corporal. Without speaking, they rode through Rome, which had been lighted into an artificial ocean of flame and fire, towards the Quirinal. At the vast old palace, there were no Fascist uniforms in sight, only Court liveries and the courtiers of the royal family. This made Hitler feel most uncomfortable.

The Italian royals barely hid their dislike for these visiting German Nazis, and the more Mussolini deferred to his King, the greater grew Hitler's disdain. There was no place in his revolutionary's mind for the regal and imperial trappings of the ancient House of Savoy. Long after the visit, Hitler still complained that he was 'compelled to have contact with the arrogant idlers of the Italian aristocracy'. British diplomat Ivone Kirkpatrick wrote that whenever Hitler was accused of keeping his Italian allies in the dark, he invariably blamed it on the Italian royals and their lack of dependability.

The little King called Hitler a psychopath and spread a story that the German Führer had insisted he could not sleep unless a woman had made up his bed instead of the male servants of the royal family. So Hitler watched while a maid who had been borrowed from a nearby hotel then made his bed in the early hours of the morning.[27]

L'Osservatore Romano, the Vatican newspaper, pointedly ignored Hitler's visit. The Pope closed the Vatican to all visitors and moved to Castel Gondolfo, his summer residence.[28] 'A cross other than Christ's cross has been raised over Rome,' the Pope complained. He also felt that 'the air in Rome was difficult to breathe'. Obviously he and Cardinal Innitzer of Vienna had failed to communicate.

The next day Mussolini mounted a huge parade. Italian troops were now goose-stepping in the Italian version of the German *Parademarsch*, the new *Passo Romano*. Curiously, there were still Jewish officers among the parading Italian units.[29] Italian Jewry's arch-enemy, Roberto Farinacci, soon to be Minister of State, had not yet convinced his Duce of the 'dangers' of Italy's Jews. On 8 May Farinacci was awarded the Grand Cross of the Order of the German Eagle by his German friend, Adolf Hitler, and his star was obviously on the rise.

The vast caravan moved on to Naples, where everyone witnessed an intricate and picturesque naval review. Hundreds of Italian submarines dived and surfaced in unison. That night, an immense 'HEIL HITLER' sign shone from the Naples waterfront. Italian Fascism was very operatic.

At the end of that day came Hitler's great 'débâcle of the full-dress suit'. He attended the opera with the King. Shortly after the end of the performance he was scheduled to review a military parade. Twenty minutes and a special private room had been set aside at the Opera House, so that he could change into his Nazi uniform to review the Italian troops. Instead, the royal Chief of Protocol apologized abjectly that there was not enough time for Hitler's change of clothes, so a fuming Hitler found himself reviewing the troops while wearing his civilian, full-dress white tie and tails. Old combat soldier Hitler had wanted to present a properly martial appearance, and there he was, stuck in his embarrassing tailcoat like a gigolo at the Eden Hotel in Berlin, while the little King at his side pranced around in his Marshal's uniform with all his ribbons, sashes, medals and crosses.

Von Ribbentrop, who had stayed glued to his Führer's side during the whole trip, took the brunt of the explosion which followed. Back on their private train, he was called into Hitler's private carriage and berated for his carelessness and lack of attention to detail. He finally managed to channel the Führer's fury towards an old friend, the hapless Vico von Bülow-Schwante, the Foreign Ministry's Chief of Protocol, who was immediately relieved of his duties. Von Dörnberg, the tall, red-haired Sandro who had handled these things at the London Embassy, became the new Chief of Protocol on the spot.

On 9 May the Italian royals stayed in Rome while Mussolini, Hitler and their retinues travelled to Florence. Now that he was no longer in the hated royal presence, Hitler's enthusiasm knew no bounds. He lavished praise on Florence, Mussolini, Italy, Fascism, architecture and scenery.

While Hitler hated the royal, horse-drawn, antique carriages ('Will it take fifty years for the King to discover the internal-combustion engine?'),[30] he now admired the antiquities of Florence.

At last, Hitler was happy, if only for a while, but von Ribbentrop was not. Despite being on Hitler's leash, he had tried to use the visit to obtain a military treaty from Mussolini. During a short pause in the trip an outline for this Italo-German pact was handed to Ciano. Notwithstanding the Anti-Comintern Pact of 1937, Italy was not yet Germany's military ally. Adolf Hitler insisted that it was time to formalize such an alliance, but every attempt to discuss this matter or the forthcoming Czechoslovak 'problem' was politely sidestepped by Mussolini and his son-in-law Ciano. Even when von Ribbentrop finally stole another half-hour between banquets, parades, receptions and performances, the smiling, smooth, almost handsome Count Ciano said that surely the warm friendship between Italy and Germany made it unnecessary to sign a formal treaty. He promised, however, that he would study von Ribbentrop's proposals.[31]

Finally, another short meeting was arranged. With his usual unwavering persistence, von Ribbentrop badgered Ciano, insisting on an answer. This system usually worked for him, but this time Ciano smiled again and once more said he doubted the need for a formal treaty. It seemed to Schmidt, the interpreter, that the Italians were still numbed by the shock of the Anschluss and all the cruel things which had followed in Austria.[32] Besides, Italy was not ready to cut its bonds with the Western Allies, following the 16 April Anglo-Italian Mediterranean treaty. The disappointed and embarrassed von Ribbentrop had to return to Berlin, having failed to fulfil the Führer's greatest wish, a military alliance with Mussolini.

At the final banquet in Palazzo Venezia, Hitler said: 'It is my unshakeable will and my testament to the German people that the mountain border which nature provided for us shall never be violated.' He was speaking of the Brenner line and of the German-speaking Austrian-descended Italian citizens of the South Tyrol, whom he had permanently abandoned. Mussolini was sure of the Tyrol for the time being. How sure could he be of the future?

For Hitler, the Czechoslovak drama of early 1938 appeared on stage somewhat prematurely. Austria's Anschluss was a vast mouthful and needed some digesting.

Until May 1938, Henlein, drunk with Berghof power, had pushed and badgered Prague with an eight-point programme of demands presented at a conference in Karlsbad, the famous spa, but Czech President Beneš was in no hurry to accept Sudeten German self-government. This understandable dragging of feet caused Henlein to overwork his sense of duty to the Führer and to the Reich. He organized Sudeten German demonstrations which brought Czechoslovak governmental retaliation. Heads were broken. Blood was spilled. People were arrested. As usual in a clash between civilians and armed police, the civilians were the losers.

It made for unpleasant newspaper reading and began to embarrass the man from the Berghof who had styled himself the protector of all Germans. Goebbels' German press howled. Henlein even travelled to London, where he met with Churchill mysteriously on 13 May. Chips Channon asked in his diary, 'What is he [Churchill] up to?'

Rumours were plentiful in Prague that the German army was once more poised to repeat its Austrian blitz-action, this time towards Czechoslovakia. These whispers finally penetrated to the presidential palace up on Prague's Hradcany Hill, where they were taken seriously. On 20 May President Beneš ordered a partial mobilization of the Czech forces to counter the perceived German threat. Perhaps it was an hysterical act, or perhaps it was for internal political consumption and was meant to divert the Sudeten Germans from their Henlein-induced manifestations. Would Sudeten Germans again consider themselves fellow citizens of Czechoslovakia once they were in uniform? The horror of international dispute is that it often reflects the moods, whims and conceits of a few powerful individuals. Was Masaryk's heir, President Beneš, a great man? Probably not. But the power over Czechoslovakia lay in his hands, and he had mobilized with the approval of his Cabinet.

Officially, the Czechs had based their mobilization on reports of German troop movements near their border. In actual fact, most neutral sources denied that there were any such troop concentrations. Sir Nevile Henderson, the British Ambassador in Berlin, after a meeting with General Keitel while von Ribbentrop was absent, dispatched his military attachés to the disputed area. They found nothing to indicate that German troops were massing. Travelling separately, Attachés Colonel Mason-Mac-Farlane and Major Strong between them covered 1,200 miles of Saxony and Silesia on 21 and 22 May and came up troopless. Nevertheless, Henderson then asked State Secretary von Weizsäcker to contact General Keitel for an official denial of the invasion rumours, which von Weizsäcker then obtained. Von Ribbentrop was furious. According to Kordt: 'Sir Nevile Henderson had been instructed [by his government] to enquire officially if Germany was massing troops and to convey British warnings about any use of force.' Von Ribbentrop was outraged by this 'presumptuous' British enquiry. He treated Henderson in a decidedly unfriendly manner. Talking himself into a rising temper, he said he would 'instruct all German government officers to refuse further replies to questions of this sort'.[33]

Schmidt, who did the interpreting at the meeting, saw things less diplomatically:

On 21 May I interpreted a stormy discussion between Ribbentrop and the British Ambassador Sir Nevile Henderson, which dealt with Czechoslovakia. Von Ribbentrop began, 'You, Mr Ambassador, enquired from General Keitel *behind my back* about alleged German troop movements on the Czechoslovak border!' The Foreign Minister looked furious. They were seated in Bismarck's historic office in 76 Wilhelmstrasse. Von Ribbentrop continued, 'I shall see to it that in the future you will receive no information whatsoever about military matters.'

Henderson replied with an unusual show of temperament, 'I shall have to inform my government about that. I must draw the conclusion from your remarks that the information given to me by Keitel did not conform to the truth!' Henderson then hinted that Britain would not stand by idly if France got involved [over Czechoslovakia].

'If there is a war,' said Ribbentrop, 'then France will have provoked it and Germany will fight as she did in 1914.'[34]

Sir Nevile Henderson's own view of the contretemps is much more Britannically diplomatic. The smooth Ambassador speaks of 'a certain amount of acrimony on both sides'. Von Ribbentrop, after threatening to delay military information to the Ambassador, 'turned in wrath' to the accidental killing of two Sudeten Germans, and 'used as regards the Czechs the most reprehensibly bloodthirsty language. They would, he assured me, be exterminated, women and children and all.' 'I believe', wrote the lofty Sir Nevile, 'that the unsuitability of his language on this occasion earned for him a reprimand from his master.'[35] The rumours of German troops massing at the Czech border were not true, but the results were still calamitous.

Hitler, furious that the Western press had described him as actually pulling back because the Czechs had mobilized, flew into a rage and ordered that Case Green (the codename for the occupation of the Sudetenland) be put into readiness at once.

When this order was received on 30 May by General Ludwig Beck, the army's Chief of Staff, it did not have the effect Hitler desired. General Beck, a devoutly anti-Hitler officer, now realized that the time had come for a military revolt against the man he detested. Like many other senior officers, Beck had begun the Nazi era by enthusiastically applauding Germany's rearmament. He wanted to see his country once more become a great nation with strength and dignity. Then he came to recognize Hitler's voracious appetite for conquest, and wanted no part in supporting his ambitions. Beck now became the centre of the anti-Hitler opposition in the military. He tried to convince von Brauchitsch, the army's Commander-in-Chief, but he got a tepid response.

As soon as Hitler ordered Case Green to be readied, von Brauchitsch asked for a meeting with von Ribbentrop, from which the R A M emerged depressed and nervous. He insisted he had to see the Führer at once. Von Brauchitsch had told him that the German army was not ready for military confrontations. Kordt also begged von Ribbentrop to persuade the Führer to pull back. 'You are the Foreign Minister! You know the French and the British. For heaven's sake, tell him to keep the peace!'[36] Von Ribbentrop visibly shuddered at the idea of being made responsible for influencing Hitler's decisions. 'The Führer will know what to do!' he said. Later, he complained to others that Kordt was 'a good diplomat but lacked nerve'.

Von Ribbentrop and Kordt rushed to Munich, where Hitler was in residence. A letter arrived from Lord Halifax, earnestly urging that 'nothing irreparable be done'. Von Ribbentrop and his aide finally returned to Berlin without any notion of Hitler's plans.

Only a few Germans were openly distressed by Hitler, although the Nazis' control over 'Aryan' Germans had tightened. Many people learned to glance back over their shoulder in cafés, restaurants, theatres and hotels. Had anyone overheard what they had said? Could it be 'misunderstood'? One could get into a lot of trouble, even at a friendly dinner party.

Jewish citizens were subjected to much more painful and degrading chicanery and cruelty, and it increased with each month. This even included former combat soldiers. Their appeals for help, if any appeals could be made, were usually to former regimental comrades or commanders. The Jewish former front-line combat soldier was one of the Nazis' most pathetic victims. The percentage of German Jewish soldiers who had died in the First World War exceeded that of their Christian comrades and a large number were decorated for bravery. In a country where combat soldiering was a life-long reason for respect and admiration, former Jewish soldiers were barely able to comprehend that their sacrifices had been for nothing.[37] The figures tell the story. During the First World War, 100,000 German Jews (about 18 per cent of the total Jewish population) were soldiers, 80,000 were front-line soldiers, 35,000 were decorated, 25,000 got field promotions, of whom 2,000 became officers. 12,000 (about 12 per cent) were killed in action. Many of the remainder died in Nazi concentration camps.

During 1938, new cruelties were added to the many degradations which had existed since 1935. Jews now had to declare all foreign holdings. This also included non-Jews married to Jews. Jews could no longer attend universities. All Jews who had ever been sentenced to prison for a previous offence were arrested. Jews were barred from all financial exchanges. Jewish physicians were decertified. Newborn Jewish babies could no longer be given certain 'German' first names, such as Arnim, Siegfried or Sieglinde. Those who already carried such names had to add the name 'Israel' or 'Sarah' to their given names. Jewish lawyers were decertified. The passports of all Jews were stamped with 'J'. Even German Jewish exiles had to preserve their German passports to validate their residency as exiles in their host countries. Passports had to be revalidated (stamped) by German consulates every six months. All consulates were instructed to add 'Israel' or 'Sarah' to the passports of German Jews and to stamp the photo page with a large red 'J'. Each addition was dated and initialled by a consular clerk. This was the responsibility of the consular service of the AA and von Ribbentrop had to be aware of it. By October that year, naturalized former Polish Jews in Germany were arrested, denaturalized and expelled. There were about 15,000 of these people, released to a pathetic fate. This law was responsible for the great pogrom of 1938.

Worse things were to follow but, by the time of the Czech crisis, many Germans were aware of all these measures. They were published in the *Völkischer Beobachter*, the party paper read by almost every German. Most people realized the pain these measures would cause, but chose to shrug their shoulders because 'it was really not their concern'. Fewer than one in a hundred German citizens was Jewish. They were a small minority and what happened to them was of little concern to most German citizens. But the von Ribbentrops had Jewish relatives in the Henkell family. That should have given them pause. Probably it was Hitler's furious first reaction to von Ribbentrop's Adlon Hotel luncheon for his Jewish acquaintances in April 1933 which quashed any remaining sympathies the von Ribbentrops may have had for the fate of Jews. They were neither brave enough nor secure enough to risk the Führer's displeasure.

Austria seemed orderly and manageable. Now Czechoslovakia could finally return to the Führer's full attention. At a tense meeting on 30 May, he advised all his senior staff that it was his 'unshakeable intention to wipe Czechoslovakia from the map'.

General Beck then composed a paper which he distributed to other senior generals, expressing his disagreement with Hitler's decision and stating his anger that the army could be committed by one man in an almost cavalier manner and without consulting Germany's military leadership. By mid-July several officials of the AA also voiced their resistance to Hitler's goals. The lead was taken by von Weizsäcker, the State Secretary, and Captain Fritz Wiedemann, Hitler's wartime company commander. In an ironic reversal of roles, Wiedemann was now one of the Führer's aides. The wartime relationship gave him a certain leeway with his former company runner. To von Weizsäcker, a man of judgment and common sense, it was clear that Hitler wanted conquest, that he was willing and anxious to provoke a war and that such a war would be fatal for Germany. There was no doubt in his mind about what had to be done, only about how to do it. In the classic manner of the diplomat, he began with all the leverage available to his craft. He drew Erich Kordt into his confidence. He then suggested tacitly to Sir Nevile Henderson and to Bernardo Attolico, the respected Ambassador from Italy, that

Hitler wanted conquest. He also indicated that tough words from London and a firm 'Don't' from Mussolini might achieve excellent results. He persuaded some diplomats in Hungary of Hitler's lust for war and got their assurance that they would never help him, although the Führer had asked for their collaboration.

Von Weizsäcker also met with Generals Beck, Halder (Beck's deputy and later successor) and Admiral Canaris, the head of the Abwehr (Armed Forces Intelligence). He fed them information about his diplomatic efforts. He wanted to discredit Hitler by showing him to be the war-lusting tartar he was, and he hoped for a military boycott to back up this effort. The plan began to collapse when a conciliatory Chamberlain asked for a meeting with Hitler. The brothers Erich and Theo Kordt had done their best to stiffen London's attitude towards Berlin. At great personal risk, they had appealed to senior politicians. It was not to be.

William Manchester wrote that Henlein, on his 'mysterious' visit to Churchill in May 1938, was briefed by von Weizsäcker on how to reassure and calm British fears. This is not very likely. However, it is probable that Henlein on his own, or briefed by Hitler, played down the demands he had made on Beneš. Henlein was probably invited to London at the suggestion of Vansittart, seconded by a well-meaning von Weizsäcker. Later there was an incognito visit to London from 18 to 24 August by Ewald von Kleist-Schmenzin, a Pomeranian noble. Von Kleist took a great risk. His message from General Beck was 'If England is willing to fight, I shall end this regime!' He met with Lloyd George, Robert Vansittart and Churchill. However, his visit came to naught. Chamberlain, who did not see him and who was only briefed orally by others, would not or could not give the response General Beck had requested.[38]

Meanwhile, Beneš offered Henlein a canton-like independence, modelled on the Swiss example, but it was not enough.

Earlier that year Captain Wiedemann had made his own effort at conciliation.[39] As Hitler's aide-de-camp, he flew to London on a well-publicized fact-finding mission. He returned to say that the British were prepared to negotiate or, if necessary, to fight. Hitler and von Ribbentrop were not happy with his report. The visit had been initiated by the controversial but well-connected Princess Stephanie Hohenlohe, lover of the very handsome Captain Wiedemann and a friend of Göring. She used the good services of her friend Lady Snowden, who had Halifax's ear. The Viennese Princess Hohenlohe, the daughter of a Jewish dentist, was an ugly woman but totally charming, and an enigma. Wiedemann had lied to Hitler that the British had contacted him through the Princess, but Göring had been briefed by her with the truth, and he co-operated in ensuring that every effort was made for a peaceful solution. Wiedemann, in turn, implied to Halifax at the latter's 88 Eaton Square residence that he was there at Hitler's instigation. Everyone was used to provide leverage.

An angry von Ribbentrop, who hated these extracurricular efforts, immediately used information supplied by his friend Himmler's Gestapo to discredit Wiedemann. He felt that, as a Hitler intimate, Wiedemann was using his connections to meddle in foreign affairs. After all, Captain Wiedemann had brought a Jewish woman (Princess Stephanie Hohenlohe) into Hitler's holy, 'Aryan' presence. In fact, Hitler had spent a lot of time on several occasions in conversation with the amusing Viennese Princess 'Steph'.

On his return from London Wiedemann was immediately removed from the Führer's presence and sent to San Francisco as Consul General. Now the brothers Kordt made another desperate attempt. They assured Vansittart that there actually was an opposition to Hitler and a military one. They told him that Hitler would not hesitate to deal with the hated Stalin, but that if Britain pre-empted him by making an Anglo-Russian pact with Stalin Hitler would pull back from his schemes of conquest of Czechoslovakia and Poland. They explained that they preferred the risk of committing treason to the risk of Germany's destruction through Hitler. Vansittart assured the Kordts that Britain would 'soon conclude a pact with the Soviets', and the Kordts were relieved.

Later, at the War Crimes Trials, Vansittart attacked the Kordts and von Weizsäcker for reporting that Britain would manipulate the Soviets. But the International Military Tribunal did not accept this accusation.[40]

Even Göring made his own attempt to muzzle Hiler. He left Berlin for the Berghof, quite sure he would prevail. He returned deflated and meek, having been accused of cowardice by Hitler, his old party comrade.

Even bouncy, optimistic little Philip Conwell-Evans, von Ribbentrop's old London ally and friend in the cause of Anglo-German amity, finally saw the truth. After meeting with von Ribbentrop in Berlin in August, he told Vansittart that Hitler intended to have war in October. He urged a tough stand. Hitler's aim was to grab the Sudetenland as well as Bohemia and Moravia.[41] Historian Richard Griffiths points out the irony that Conwell-Evans was ignored by Baldwin when he was conciliatory to the Germans and by Chamberlain when he counselled a show of force. Finally, even peaceful Lord Lothian now urged a willingness to face war: 'We have strong cards in the long run and I think Hitler would hesitate.'

The effort to promote friendship with Germany was waning. Only members of the Anglo-German Fellowship, like the Lords Stamp, Hollenden and McGowan, still planned to attend the September 1938 party rally in Nuremberg with Sir Nevile Henderson. Ambassador François-Poncet once again spoke for the Diplomatic Corps attending the rally. He said he hoped that 'Hitler would do nothing to bring tears to a mother's eyes,' a hint which Hitler ignored. Other British visitors were Lord Clive, Lord Brocket and N. Hulbert MP.

Even Henlein began to have fears that the Sudeten dispute could bring

a world war. On 23 July in Bayreuth he had asked Hitler to desist from
a military solution. Hans Frank, a radical Sudeten German whom Hitler
had chosen in his usual manner to be a back-up for any deficiencies in
Henlein, likewise tried in August to prove to Hitler that war was not
necessary.[42]

Also in July a dubious initiative was taken by the British government.
Supposedly at the invitation of the Prague government, London chose a
professedly impartial fact-finder to go to Czechoslovakia, study the
Sudeten problem at first hand and report to the British Prime Minister.
The Czech government was anxious to solicit British good will but did
not commit itself to accept any of this 'ombudsman's' recommendations.
The man chosen was Lord Runciman, formerly in the shipping business,
then Minister of Trade and a member of the Liberal Party. The choice
of Runciman was pointedly ignored by von Ribbentrop as a 'British
matter', and he complained that Germany 'had not been advised'. By now
the *soigné* Sir Nevile Henderson was describing the Foreign Minister's
comments as 'ill tempered' and his manner as 'truculent'.[43] Obviously,
the two men had developed irreversible mutual antipathies.

The Runciman mission was endless and pointless. He was clearly out
of his depth, and he could do nothing to defuse the tensions or right any
wrongs. Beneš made a show of co-operation, but it lacked conviction.
The Runciman mission was a failure.

The army coup to be led by General Beck and supported by General
von Witzleben (commanding troops in Berlin-Brandenburg) was now
planned for the day Hitler had set for mobilization, 27 September at
noon. Later, when asked who were the coup's targets, Colonel Hans
Oster, an elegant and witty co-conspirator, answered 'Hi-Gö-Rib-Hi-
Hey!' for Hitler, Göring, von Ribbentrop, Himmler and Heydrich.[44] But
the military opposition to Hitler and all eventual hope for long-term
peace was undone when a cable arrived in Berlin on the morning of 14
September 1938:[45]

> In view of the increasingly critical situation I suggest that I visit you at
> once in order to attempt to find a peaceful solution. I can come to you
> by air and shall be ready to travel as of tomorrow morning. Please
> advise the earliest time when you can receive me and indicate a place
> for the meeting. I should be grateful for a prompt reply.
>
> Neville Chamberlain

By now Joachim von Ribbentrop seemed to be a vessel adrift, with
anchor dragging and no chance of catching hold while he was pulled into
deeper and deeper waters. All his judgment seemed deferred, all his
independence of action seemed abandoned. In an August discussion[46] he
told his State Secretary, von Weizsäcker, that Hitler had made the firm
decision to solve the Czech matter by force of arms. He said the final

deadline was the middle of October because thereafter flying weather would deteriorate. He was sure no other nation would lift a finger. If they did, they would be badly beaten. Hearing von Weizsäcker express doubt, von Ribbentrop insisted that 'von Weizsäcker was responsible only to him and that he [von Ribbentrop] was responsible only to the Führer, who was the only one responsible to the German people'.

And then came the credo which followed von Ribbentrop for the rest of his days. He told Erich Kordt 'that the Führer had never been mistaken and that his most difficult decisions and actions such as the Rhineland now lay behind him. One simply had to believe in his genius, as he, von Ribbentrop, had learned to do over the years.' He said 'that I would regret not accepting this if facts proved later that I had been wrong'. Von Ribbentrop also insisted that the Führer would ride into Czechoslovakia in the leading tank, with his Foreign Minister at his side, and that von Weizsäcker, not von Neurath, would run the Foreign Ministry in his absence.

Chamberlain's cable brought an instant and positive reply from Adolf Hitler. It destroyed for some time to come the notion that Britain would raise a heavy iron fist and strike at those who threatened her allies. Britain wanted to talk. *Finis* the General Beck coup, at least for some time to come. Disgusted, Beck asked to be relieved of his command on 28 August. He would soon resign.

Chamberlain's cable also brought embarrassment to all those like the Kordts, von Weizsäcker and von Kleist who had thought that Britain was done with talking. Even Conwell-Evans looked the fool.

One of Chamberlain's greatest admirers in the forthcoming months of appeasement politics was Joseph E. Kennedy, the United States Ambassador in London.* The multimillionaire Boston Irishman (stockmarket, films, liquor importing, real estate, oil, corporate acquisitions) was an early Roosevelt supporter when America's upper classes were against 'the man with the Income Tax'. Perhaps it was his revenge for many social snubs. Kennedy served Roosevelt as Chairman of the Security and Exchange Commission and the Maritime Commission. In 1937 he was appointed Ambassador to the Court of St James, an act of political gratitude.

It was a strange and careless choice. The son of a Boston Irish saloon-keeper and liquor dealer harboured instinctive and vestigial suspicions of anything British. His background had taught him to 'take care of his own' and his plans for his nine children, his personal fortune and the future of his country did not include war, certainly not on the side of the

---

* Extracts from A. Whitman, *Come to Judgement* (New York: Viking, 1980), pp. 126ff and *Webster's Biographical Dictionary* (Springfield, Mass., 1983).

English. Nor could he muster enough dislike for anti-Bolshevist Nazi Germany to warrant the drawn American sword.

Charles Lindbergh's urgent and expert warnings had made a deep impression on Kennedy, and he did his best to flood the occupant of the Oval Office with dire warnings (often via unofficial contacts). He insisted that Britain was unprepared for a fight with Germany and that America had to avoid backing a loser. He advocated strict neutrality and accommodation with Adolf Hitler. In 1939 he said in Boston, 'There is no place in this fight for us.'

Strangely, while Kennedy was Ambassador, his second son John Fitzgerald studied with Socialist professor, Harold Laski, at the left-of-centre London School of Economics. (His third son Robert attended London's Westminster School, like Rudolf von Ribbentrop.)

Ambassador Kennedy must have given much false hope to Joachim von Ribbentrop. Von Dirksen, who followed the von Ribbentrops at the Embassy in London, reported to his chief that Kennedy had shown a degree of sympathy for the anti-Semitic view of Nazi Germany.*

Joseph Kennedy resigned his Ambassadorship in 1940 to the evident relief of his President and his Chief, the Secretary of State.

Annelies and Joachim von Ribbentrop must have danced with delight. The arrogant British wanted to parley, to palaver, to shirk a fight. Once more, the Führer was right. By now there were banners all over Germany which said 'Der Führer hat immer Recht' (The Führer is always right). And what a setback it was for the reputation of the 'reasonable' top Nazis, such as Göring and Hess, not to speak of reluctant army generals like Beck, von Witzleben, Halder and even von Brauchitsch, the army's commander.

During the summer of 1938, the Westwall, later nicknamed the Siegfried Line by British wags, was built and expanded. This was a curious anachronism, since it was a *defensive* fortification, while the art of modern tank warfare being adopted by the German army was offensive, with rapid co-ordinated tank and armoured infantry movement, air support and paratrooper drops into the enemy's back. This new form called Blitzkrieg (lightning war) had nothing to do with defensive installations. Building the Westwall was probably a patronizing act in imitation of the Maginot Line, to lull the enemy. But, since the German army had never fought a Blitzkrieg, the new Westwall was also a sop for those in Germany who were thinking in old-fashioned terms.

Ironically, the demands made by the Sudeten Germans included the line of mountain fortifications in the Sudetenland which were the keystone to Czechoslovakia's defence. After the Sudetenland had been ceded to Germany, Czechoslovakia became helpless against conventional old-

---

* Strongly denied by Kennedy later.

fashioned attack. Certainly they could never have held against Blitzkrieg tactics, but the loss of their fortifications became a major morale-killer for the Czech soldiery.

Lay architect Hitler was deeply and personally involved in the design and planning of the senseless Westwall. He had to know it was a military anachronism but could not resist the siren call of the blueprint. He would see no one during the time of construction, causing von Ribbentrop once more to go into 'Tango Nocturno'.

The meeting with Chamberlain was fixed for 15 September 1938 in Munich. The ageing British Prime Minister, who had never before travelled by air, arrived in Munich on a grey, choppy day in a small, twin-engined Lockheed Electra. With him was Sir Horace Wilson, whom Churchill detested, and also Sir William Strang of the Foreign Office.

It was the consensus in Britain that Chamberlain was doing a very courageous and 'English' thing, taking the bull by the horns, getting to the heart of the matter, risking his health and his life to deal face to face with this chap Hitler. On Chamberlain's part there was the absolute conviction that if he could speak with this fellow, man to man, he could, like the good businessman he was, wring some common sense out of him. So off he went, ready, as he said later at the airport in London, to put to work the things he had learned as a small boy and 'try, try, try again'. It was a rather noble and courageous performance by a man in his late sixties, who looked much older with his unfashionably high collars. In fact, he looked like the headmaster of a second-rank public school.

There was no possible way the Austrian ex-corporal Führer could ever have penetrated past this neo-Victorian mask to the surprisingly sporting soul of Neville Chamberlain. It was difficult for Adolf Hitler to see beyond the umbrella. Nothing in his experience had taught him about this species of externally eccentric British statesman. Meanwhile, von Ribbentrop, who lumped Chamberlain with the leisurely upper-class group in Whitehall which he detested, had no intention of 'selling' Chamberlain to Hitler. But it is doubtful if he could have made any difference, or indeed if von Ribbentrop ever had more than marginal influence on the plans of the voracious Adolf Hitler.

Von Ribbentrop still had some helpers in Great Britain, people who, for wildly diverse reasons ranging from blind anti-Semitism and anti-Communism to deep British patriotism, joined groups like Sir Barry Domville's The Link. This group grew between March 1938 and June 1939 from 1,800 to 4,300,[47] but it contained many of the same names and faces which had been stalwart Anglo-Germanists since the coming to power of the Nazis. There were the Lords Mount Temple, Redesdale and Sempill, as well as members of the ineffective Anglo-German Kameradschaft. But they were only a small voice, only a small minority of votes.

Adolf Hitler had the advantage of the revolutionary. He was willing to gamble. Like the street drifter who accosts the well-dressed man, he counted on the self-protective instincts of others. Britain was tired of war and of losing her young men in battle. Her wish for peace was very real, and her leadership expressed that wish. Germany's masses were no different. They, too, wanted to live in peace, but they were dazzled by their powerful leader who had seemed to achieve everything he promised without bloodshed. Their instincts of self-preservation were dulled by propaganda and all the trappings of nationalistic success and blind faith. Hitler was their hero, their shining knight.

Yet the average roadside Münchener cheered Chamberlain with much enthusiasm because he was their *Friedensbote*, their messenger of peace.[48] Interpreter Dr Schmidt wrote that they cheered Chamberlain more than they had cheered Mussolini in 1937.

Hitler's special train came to Munich to fetch Chamberlain and his group as well as von Ribbentrop and Henderson. By coincidence or design, the train was constantly passed by armoured troop trains. Waiting in the fog and drizzle, Hitler greeted the British Prime Minister at his mountain chalet, symbolically at the very foot of the long flight of stairs, and led him from the big Mercedes up to his house. As soon as they had doffed their coats and hats and after a short period of trading halting banalities about the weather and the views from the Berghof, Hitler asked if he could speak to Chamberlain alone with only interpreter Schmidt present. This, according to Schmidt, was a ploy secretly worked out by von Weizsäcker and Ambassador Sir Nevile Henderson long before the meeting, to avoid the presence of von Ribbentrop. The plan had the full knowledge of Hitler, who feared that the Anglophobe von Ribbentrop would be a disturbing influence. It also had Göring's enthusiastic endorsement.[49]

Schmidt, the only eyewitness to the first Chamberlain–Hitler talks, described the moment when the irascible Hitler threatened to solve the Sudeten question 'one way or the other' (Schmidt's translation of Hitler's much more ominous '*so oder so*'). Then Chamberlain reacted with uncharacteristic firmness. 'As I understand it,' he said, 'you intend to move against Czechoslovakia one way or the other. In that case I might just as well return to England. There doesn't seem to be much left to be done here.' Then to Schmidt's amazement, Hitler immediately retracted. Suddenly calm, he said that he 'would be satisfied with a solution to the Sudeten problem'.[50]

That night at the Grand Hotel in Berchtesgaden, when Schmidt tried to practise a routine diplomatic courtesy by turning over a copy of his notes to a foreign negotiating partner, an angry von Ribbentrop appeared in his room and rudely told him not to give the notes to the British. 'You are no longer in Geneva where everyone was chummy. Your notes are for the Führer only!' With great regret, Schmidt had to inform Chamberlain and Henderson of his new instructions. Understandably, Chamberlain complained bitterly. For the next meeting, the British delegation would certainly bring their own interpreter.

These instructions to Schmidt were typical petty chicanery. Von Ribbentrop had been bypassed, and now he was clawing back. It was the revenge of an insecure man giving no thought to the harm it could cause in a strained relationship.

Chamberlain's plane left Munich exactly twenty-four hours after arriving there. He was on his way to ask Cabinet approval for recommending a separate Sudetenland to the Czechs.

This was the first of the three momentous September meetings, which came to be known as the Munich Conference of 1938.

The second took place at Bad Godesberg, the old Rhineside resort near Bonn. Neville Chamberlain now made the third flight of his life. He was installed high on a hill in the Hotel Petersburg, a Rhine-ferry ride across the river from Bad Godesberg's Hotel Dreesen, where Hitler usually stayed. Curiously, perhaps ominously, four days before this second meeting, Hitler had met secretly with the Polish Foreign Minister and the Hungarian Regent at the Berghof.[51] Both Poland and Hungary insisted they also had long-standing territorial claims against Czechoslovakia, because some Czechoslovak citizens had once been Poles and Hungarians.[52]

Hitler was delighted to take note of these claims on Czechoslovakia. They only served to legitimize his own demands. To add to Hitler's fuel, Sudeten Germans now began to rush across the border into Saxony, inside Germany. About 250,000 of them were temporarily, if a little disdainfully, received as 'brothers': they were not Reichsdeutsch, only Volksdeutsch, and they often spoke German with strange-sounding Slavic accents.*

Hitler had always loved the Dreesen Hotel. Most memories were good, although it was there that he had been forced to decide on the Röhm bloodbath.

Ever the old-school man, Sir Nevile Henderson described the transRhine ferry traffic from Hitler's hotel to Chamberlain's hotel as 'varsity boat race day' because of the large numbers of spectators ashore, their field glasses focused on the occupants of the ferries.

In a conference room on the main floor of the Dreesen Hotel, the German Führer and the British Prime Minister once more quickly came to grips. Chamberlain was pleased to inform Hitler of success. He had even persuaded the French to urge the Czechs to hand over the Sudeten territories to Germany. The Czechoslovaks' agreement in principle seemed assured.[53]

---

*   Today the descendants of the Volksdeutsche are still entering a much more reluctant Germany.

Chamberlain had done what he had promised in Berchtesgaden. He was therefore deeply shocked when Hitler said, 'Extremely sorry, but that is no longer acceptable!' and insisted that the claims of Hungary and Poland must now be added to the agenda. Hitler also rejected Chamberlain's timetable for the cessation of the Sudetenland, 'because of the urgent dangers now facing Czechoslovakia's Sudeten Germans'. An outraged Chamberlain soon returned across the Rhine to his hotel, accompanied by his advisers. The next morning he sent a letter rejecting Hitler's additional demands. A conciliatory note from Hitler in room 108 of the Dreesen, carried by interpreter Schmidt, soon came back across the Rhine. In their turn, Henderson and Wilson then carried Chamberlain's reply to von Ribbentrop, who had at last become involved.

At the next meeting in Hitler's hotel at 11 p.m., all the second-level participants from von Ribbentrop and von Weizsäcker to Henderson and Sir Ivone Kirkpatrick were present. It was a stormy meeting. Hitler's forty-eight-hour deadline for cession of the Sudeten territories, which Chamberlain angrily called an ultimatum, was described as 'ein Diktat' by the German-speaking Henderson. Into the midst of this angry impasse came the explosive news that Beneš had now fully mobilized the Czech army. A deep silence fell in the conference room, as the others waited for Hitler to react with his usual fury. Schmidt described it as the silence which follows the crash of timpani in a concert. Then gently, uncharacteristically, Hitler spoke: 'I shall still keep my promise to you, not to take any action.' He seemed willing to make concessions about the schedule. It was 2 a.m. They parted in a friendly way. The following day, Chamberlain and his group once more returned to London.

Sir Horace Wilson flew to Berlin on 26 September, bringing Hitler a letter from Chamberlain in which he said that, as he had warned, the Czechs had baulked and rejected the terms discussed at Bad Godesberg. Now Hitler threatened, 'The Czechs must get out by the first of October, or we shall march across the border.' Wilson calmly and firmly said that if France became involved in hostilities against Germany in consequence of her treaty obligations to Czechoslovakia, the United Kingdom would feel obliged to help France.

An angry Hitler said he took note of the statement, and then, raising his voice, said that, if France and Britain felt they had to attack Germany, he 'did not care one way or the other'. As Schmidt reported, Hitler at length almost lost control of himself. In front of von Ribbentrop, Wilson, Kirkpatrick, Henderson and Schmidt, Hitler rushed to the door of his office, yelling at the top of his lungs, 'There is no sense continuing with this!' Then he stopped and returned slowly, like a naughty child realizing that his behaviour had been unacceptable. Sir Nevile Henderson and von Ribbentrop then had their own 'heated discussion' about Beneš,[54] whom von Ribbentrop called a warmonger and terrorist. The meeting soon broke up, the mood tense and ominous, as Hitler was about to make a major speech at the Sportpalast later that day.

In that address he threatened Beneš but assured Chamberlain that, once the Czechoslovaks had dealt with the problems of their minorities, he would guarantee that Germany's involvement would cease. This was his last territorial demand. 'We do not want any Czechs!'

After the Sportpalast speech, the exchange continued. Wilson, still in Berlin, received instructions from London to state that Britain would guarantee the Czechoslovak withdrawal from the Sudetenland if Hitler guaranteed not to use force. Hitler, sensing that London was softening, turned this down, with his usual threats. But, strangely, that very night Schmidt had to translate an unexpectedly conciliatory letter to Chamberlain. What had changed Hitler's tune?

The explanation given by the majority of contemporary witnesses was that earlier on that drab autumn day, in a demonstration of martial might, or perhaps as a trial balloon, he had ordered a fully combat-ready, armoured (Panzer) division to move through central Berlin, engines roaring and tank tracks clattering on the asphalt. It made its noisy, threatening way along the Wilhelmstrasse and past the British Embassy. To Hitler's shock as he watched from a Chancellery window, the Berlin crowd was totally apathetic. He had expected wild cheers for these fierce, black-uniformed Panzer warriors in their *Balkenkreuz-* and swastika-decorated tanks and trucks, cannon and machine guns uncovered and ready for action. In 1938, Hitler's instincts had not yet been dulled by the isolation which is the fate of all dictator warlords. Hewel, von Ribbentrop's man at the Chancellery, reported that Hitler, disillusioned and disappointed by the lack of enthusiastic cheering, exclaimed, 'I cannot yet fight a war with this people.' He revised his aggressive posture.

But the mobilization date of 28 September stood unchanged. That day there was the unending coming and going of ambassadors at the Chancellery, beginning with François-Poncet, who, speaking in perfect German, assured Hitler that an attack on Czechoslovakia would set fire to all Europe.[55] Von Ribbentrop tried to interfere by urging that the Führer was right and that if war came it would be a Franco-British war, but François-Poncet dressed him down.

That day, General Beck, who had not yet resigned, and General von Witzleben were again poised for a coup, should the mobilization still go into effect.

Göring had also gone to see Hitler, along with von Neurath, who was not invited. When von Ribbentrop asked for support for the Führer, Göring yelled that he knew all about war, but if the Führer said 'March' he would be in the leading plane, provided Ribbentrop was in the seat next to him. He was said to have called von Ribbentrop a 'criminal fool'.[56]

Eventually, the key visitor arrived, the tall, heavy-set, bespectacled

Ambassador from Rome, Attolico. This respected diplomat now rushed Mussolini's message to the Führer: 'I have been asked by Chamberlain to help negotiate. Please accept me as part of the negotiating process.' Hitler, softened by François-Poncet and also not too sure that the Italians would help in case of war, was ready to talk. Besides, after witnessing the tepid Berlin reaction to the armoured division, he was somewhat subdued. When Henderson brought yet another message that Chamberlain was ready to return to Germany, Hitler told Sir Nevile that 'to accommodate the wishes of my great friend Mussolini, I have postponed mobilization by twenty-four hours.'[57]

In the Commons on the 28th, the Prime Minister told the packed House that there would probably be mobilization of Germany by 2 p.m. Suddenly a message was handed to him, and he told the hushed chamber that Mussolini had accepted his request to negotiate. In the absence of mobilization on 28 September, the Beck–Witzleben military coup was stood down once more.

The stage for the third and final in this series of conferences was now set, and the military revolt dissolved under the seemingly peaceful events which then took place in the newly finished neo-classic 'Führer Building' on the Königsplatz in Munich.

This time the number of participants in the 29 September conference was substantial, owing to the presence of the Italian group which accompanied the 'great conciliator' Mussolini and Ciano on their special train. Von Ribbentrop was only one of many participants. Unhappy with the negotiations, he was not convinced of their advantages. To show the direction he preferred, he had even ordered Diplomatic Corps uniforms in army officers' field-grey which he wanted his AA people to wear at Hitler's military headquarters in the field.[58] François-Poncet sent a message to his Foreign Ministry on the Quai d'Orsay: 'Ribbentrop is visibly urging the Führer to be obstinate.' Von Ribbentrop was obviously upset by the course of things. To the last moment he tried to create obstacles. Von Weizsäcker, Kordt and Attolico, among others, were astonished and aghast that von Ribbentrop seemed so openly anxious to save 'his' war.[59] He did not succeed. Czechoslovakia's Sudetenlands were amputated.

Munich drowned in beer when the pact was announced. As the joyous taxi driver told Kordt on his way to the Vier Jahreszeiten Hotel, 'sale of beer has been incredible ever since they announced there would be no *Schlamassel*', which was, ironically, the Yiddish word for misfortune. The street in front of the Vier Jahreszeiten, which housed senior Nazis as well as Daladier, the French Prime Minister, was besieged with crowds shouting the rhyme, 'Daladier! Vive la paix!' Daladier stood at his window overlooking the Maximilianstrasse with tear-filled eyes.

Looking into the future, Sir Nevile Henderson wrote to Chamberlain:

Millions of mothers will be blessing your name tonight ... oceans of ink will flow hereafter in criticism of your action. The day may come when we may be forced to fight Germany again. If we have to do so, I trust that the cause may be one in which the morality of our case is so unimpeachable [and] the honour and vital interests of Britain are so clearly at stake, as to ensure us of the full support of the united British people, of the Empire, and of world opinion.

Sir Nevile concluded that this would not have been the case in 1938.

Chips Channon rejoiced in the defeat of the anti-Italians in the House because of Mussolini's role as negotiator and describes Eden's 'twitching face' and 'seeming discontent'. Small wonder. It must have pained Eden to hear a British Prime Minister show pride that he had managed to enlist the help of one dictator to prevent another dictator from blackmailing the world. Channon showed a complete lack of understanding for man-of-principle Duff Cooper:

1 October. Duff has resigned in what I must say is a very well written letter, and the P.M. has immediately accepted his resignation. But we shall hear more of this – personally my reactions are mixed. I am sorry for Diana; they give up £5,000 per annum, a lovely house – and for what? Does Duff think he will make money at literature?

The reaction of Britain's far right was predictable. An October letter from the offices of their magazine *The Link* to *The Times* said: 'The Munich Agreement was nothing more than the rectification of one of the most flagrant injustices of the Peace Treaties.' The letter had twenty-six signatories. Only a few signers (like Domville and Redesdale) were actual Link members. Little attention was paid to it.[60]

Shortly before he returned to London, Chamberlain had asked Hitler at the end of the meeting in the Führerbau, Hitler's private Munich apartment, to sign a special note declaring that all future Anglo-German disputes would be resolved through peaceful negotiations. Hitler shrugged in a 'why not?' gesture and signed. It was this paper which Chamberlain triumphantly waved when he spoke the famous phrase 'peace in our time'. Spitzy reported that a short while after the note had been signed, he followed Hitler and von Ribbentrop down the stairs at the Führerbau. He was close enough to overhear them quite clearly. Von Ribbentrop petulantly criticized the agreement and the special 'paper' delivered to Chamberlain, whereupon Hitler said softly, 'Well, you don't have to take it so seriously. This paper is really of no great importance.'[61] Spitzy, a long-time Hitler devotee, was stunned.

This is the text of the famous 'Peace in our Time' paper:

We, the German Führer and Chancellor and the British Prime Minister, had a further meeting today and are agreed in recognizing that the question of Anglo-German relations is of the first importance for the two countries and for Europe.

We regard the agreement signed last night and the Anglo-American Naval Agreement as symbolic of the desire of our two peoples never to go to war with one another again.

We are resolved that the method of consultation shall be the method adopted to deal with any other questions that may concern our two countries, and we are determined to continue our efforts to remove possible sources of difference and, thus, to contribute to assure the peace of Europe.

Adolf Hitler
Neville Chamberlain

30 September 1938

In his memoirs, von Ribbentrop remembered things quite differently. He was asked at the Nuremberg Trials if 'the Führer was very unhappy' that there had been agreement at Munich, because Hitler 'did not get his war'. Von Ribbentrop said 'there is not a word of truth in that. The Führer was very satisfied with Munich and I never heard so much as a hint to the contrary from him.'[62]

Hungary and Poland were now lusting 'like jackals' (in Churchill's words) to seize the territories they had discussed earlier at the Berghof. It was the year of the political cynic. Still, Chamberlain and his hand-signed 'letter of agreement' with Hitler brought cheers from most corners of Britain. People were not ready to fight a war.

Beneš had quit. Chwalkowsky, the new Czechoslovak Foreign Minister, was a weak, conciliatory man. Czechoslovakia waited, relieved. But Hewel at the Chancellery told Kordt in confidence that the danger of war had by no means passed. Over at Admiral Canaris' Abwehr headquarters, where the anti-Hitler military conspiracy was now centred, Colonel Oster also confirmed to Kordt and his friends that planning for the military takeover of the rest of Czechoslovakia had already been ordered and initiated. Just when Kordt and the other AA staff were delighted and relieved to pack away their new, wartime grey Diplomatic Corps uniforms!

The month of October 1938, following close on the heels of the Munich Agreement, seemed to demonstrate that Hitler could count on greed and fear to motivate most nations. On the 2nd, quite unilaterally, the Poles had marched into the Olsa district of Czechoslovakia. There was no objection from Hitler.[63] At that time he still considered Poland a potential ally against Russia.

Interpreter Schmidt, present in Hitler's personal apartment when Chamberlain had asked him to sign the 'peace paper', could not understand why the Führer seemed gloomy and depressed after his negotiating triumphs. Then Hitler's fierce speech of 9 October at Saarbrücken made things clear. It destroyed the notion that the Munich Agreement guaranteed peace. Hitler was infuriated that Daladier and Chamberlain were now being heavily criticized in their own countries. He yelled, 'We are not the Germany of 1918. If Herr Duff Cooper or Herr Eden or Herr Churchill were to come to power in England, we know that they would immediately aim for war with Germany. We must maintain constant vigilance and guard the Reich!' He had no faith in the durability of a battered Chamberlain. He was angry with all those in his own camp like Göring who had counselled restraint. Von Ribbentrop had emerged as a firm and stalwart ally, while several members of his old guard had, in his eyes, seemed cowardly.

Spitzy mentions that Annelies von Ribbentrop had insisted that it was an error to 'settle' at Munich.[64] This would have been the best time for a military confrontation, with an unsure and poorly armed Britain. Several other contemporaries mention her involvement in her husband's political world. Hitler's SS aide, Heinz Linge, was sure that Annelies von Ribbentrop often saw important dispatches before her husband.[65] One of Hitler's private secretaries said that Hewel was certain Annelies von Ribbentrop played an important role behind the scenes in foreign policy and that she was her husband's evil genius.[66]

Obviously, both von Ribbentrops were convinced that Great Britain would never accept a dominant Germany. Although it is easier and more plausible to ascribe their seeming Anglophobia to hurt feelings and to their sense of social inferiority, it might also be possible that the von Ribbentrops were genuinely convinced that the Munich Agreement benefited only Britain and France.

This would contradict the interpretation put out by many of Hitler's associates and von Ribbentrop's contemporaries, who portrayed the Foreign Minister as 'Hitler's parrot', and maintained that Adolf Hitler was an easy victim of abject flattery. Eyewitnesses often reported von Ribbentrop's toadying manner, his 'Ja, mein Führer, nein, mein Führer' servility.

It was easy to hate the von Ribbentrops. They had not endeared themselves, and their arrogant style had caused much bitterness among their subordinates. Their easy success brought jealousy from equals such as Goebbels and Göring, and their tactlessness, derision from foreigners. But it would be a mistake to underrate Adolf Hitler's ability to judge others. No doubt he knew very little about the *haut monde* of Britain, France and America, but lower-middle-class Austrians were born to cynicism. It was his uncanny, instinctive ability to gauge German-speaking people, both individually and *en masse*, which had enabled this uneducated Austrian to climb to the leadership of Germany, one of the great nations of the world. He has often been described as a brilliant mimic, an actor *manqué*. Cynicism and mimicry are not the mark of the man who is easily fooled by play-acting and open flattery. There is an American expression: 'Never con a con-man.'

Something much more fundamental about the von Ribbentrops must have appealed to him in the long run and made him seek out their collaboration. Quite obviously, von Ribbentrop was not a master of statecraft, but to treat his apparent Anglophobia as a matter of personal spleen might be a mistake. It is just possible that he was convinced that an early war was the best way to solve Germany's future problems and was close enough to Hitler to back the Führer's own, similar view. Hitler's jugular instincts probably sensed the weakness of Britain and France, and he hated to let them wriggle off the hook while they were vulnerable.

Similarly, Churchill, Duff Cooper and Eden embraced the 'early war' option from their own perspective.

The fundamental differences between Adolf Hitler, the avid revolutionary, and von Ribbentrop, the pragmatic *haut-bourgeois débrouillard*, still existed, but on the subject of war with Great Britain they were in total agreement. Curiously, they both continued to be admirers of Albion, though they clearly saw Britain as the enemy. Victory over her would have been their ultimate and optimal act of faith in Germany's future.

The Poles had grabbed Olsa without much consultation. Now the Hungarian claims on Czechoslovakia still needed settling. In furtherance of this, von Ribbentrop flew to Rome and asked the Duce to let him create an Italo-German 'jury' with himself and Ciano as judges. They would decide the merits of either party's claims in the dispute. Austria's new Governor, Seyss-Inquart, was enlisted as host. Castle Belvedere in Vienna was dusted off and requisitioned. A dinner for the Italians was laid on at the restaurant on the Kobenzl mountain north of Vienna. Spitzy and his brother, who lived in Vienna, became the impresarios. The prettiest Viennese girls were produced for the flirty Ducellini, Ciano. The ladies were all required to greet the Foreign Minister with a genteel Hitler salute. Annelies von Ribbentrop, who had stayed in Berlin, quickly got wind of the festivities and expressed her displeasure on the long-distance phone.

Knowing that Hitler hated the Hungarians even more than the Czechoslovaks, von Ribbentrop more or less 'took the Czechoslovak side' in this sham of a jury, while Ciano had more sympathy for the Hungarians. Smiling ironically Ciano said to von Ribbentrop, 'If you keep defending Czechoslovak interests, Hacha [the new Czech President] will give you a medal!'[67] Between them, the Italian and German 'judges' changed people's fates and lives on whim with the stroke of a fat pencil on the large map of poor Czechoslovakia spread out before them. Eventually, Hungary received her booty, though it was smaller than she had wished.

*   *   *

On 7 November 1938 a murder took place in Paris which set off a series of events which would shock the civilized world. That day, Herschel Grynszpan, a seventeen-year-old, German-born Jewish refugee, shot and killed a Germany Embassy official called Ernst vom Rath. Grynszpan was born in 1921 in Hanover, where his Polish Jewish parents had moved to escape Polish anti-Semitism. Then, to let their son escape the Nazis, the Grynszpans sent him to Paris in 1936. The senior Grynszpans stayed behind in Germany, hoping for the best, until the Nazis passed a law that Polish-born Jews, even if they were naturalized German citizens, would be expelled to Poland. But the Jew-hating Polish government refused to readmit them. Herschel Grynszpan's parents were among those who were expelled. Thousands of these unfortunates were left to fend for themselves in the icy fields and woods of the no-man's land along the Silesian border with Poland. They were virtually non-persons, victimized by both the German and the Polish frontier policy. It was brutal and inhuman.

Young Grynszpan heard about the fate of his parents and decided to avenge them. He planned to shoot the German Ambassador in Paris. It was a grim irony that the inexperienced young Grynszpan mistook vom Rath for the Ambassador when he was shown into the minor official's office in the Embassy, and that at the time vom Rath was under Gestapo surveillance as 'politically unreliable'.

Most 1938 observers blame the incredible events which then followed on the 'poisonous dwarf' of the Nazi hierarchy, Dr Joseph Goebbels, and on the co-operation of the SA commanders. There were also some SS involved, although Himmler seemed unhappy with the spectacle of his 'black knights' performing these vulgarities side by side with the SA. He need not have been so squeamish. A year later Himmler's SS would begin to perform tasks which revolted even some top Nazis with cast-iron stomachs.

On 9 November, starting in the early morning, Nazi bands roamed throughout Germany and set fire to 171 synagogues, broke the windows of 7,500 Jewish shops and department stores, wrecked homes and apartments, murdered ninety-one Jews, arrested 26,000 others and transported them to concentration camps. The vast amounts of shattered glass in city streets from broken windows and shopfronts were the origin of the bitterly named Kristallnacht – events said to be a 'spontaneous demonstration' of the 'righteous anger of the people because of the foul murder committed in Paris'.

Jewish citizens were paid insurance compensation of about 100 million Marks, which they then had to turn over to the Reich government. Next, the sum of one billion Marks was demanded from Germany's Jewish community as 'penalty' for the murder of vom Rath.

Although several senior Nazis, including Göring and von Ribbentrop, uttered weak protests against these ugly actions, they did so only because they felt it might upset foreign business or diplomatic dealings. No one questioned the moral issue. The pogrom continued until 10 November.

Most of the Jewish men who were sent to concentration camps were battered and beaten but released later. Now even the most optimistic and proud Jews in Germany tried to flee from the country of their birth.

The pogrom is one of the ugliest stains on the honour of Germany, although it was but a gentle hint compared with things to come. Yet, according to a recently published eyewitness report, an infuriated Goebbels called in Count von Helldorf, Berlin's Police President, and howled at him that this sort of crude nonsense 'is not the way to solve the Jewish problem'. He blamed the debauches on 'that thick-necked, moronic idiot in Munich [Streicher], the schizophrenic vulgarian. Because of him Germany has made a fool of herself all over the world.'

Kristallnacht was not ignored abroad. On 15 November, Channon chronicled from Belgrave Square, 'The pogroms in Germany and the persecutions there have roused much indignation everywhere. I must say Hitler never helps, and always makes Chamberlain's task more difficult.'[68] One of the foulest of Adolf Hitler's crimes was the subversion of ordinary German decency. This report was filed by a non-Jewish, British journalist in Berlin:[69]

> By now the streets were a chaos of screaming, bloodthirsty people lusting for Jewish bodies. I saw Harrison of the *News Chronicle* trying to protect an aged Jewess who had been dragged from her home by a gang. I pushed my way through to help him, and between us we managed to heave her through the crowd to a side street and safety. Next, the object of the mob's hate was a hospital for sick Jewish children, many of them cripples or consumptives. In minutes the windows had been smashed and the doors forced. When we arrived, the swine were driving the wee mites out over the broken glass barefooted and wearing nothing but their night-shirts. The nurses, doctors and attendants were being kicked and beaten by the mob leaders, most of whom were women.

President Roosevelt recalled the American Ambassador in protest.

It was impossible for the von Ribbentrops not to have known the brutal details of Kristallnacht, but the anchor of their morality had never again caught hold. More than ever, they were now accomplices. Joachim von Ribbentrop's businessman's soul was sold to the barbarians around him.

This time there were hundreds of outraged newspaper editorials all over America. The *New York Times* of 11 November 1938 wrote about 'scenes witnessed yesterday ... which no man can look upon without shame for the degradation of his species.'

One of the few whimsical results of the terror: half-Jewish Mayor Fiorella La Guardia of New York assigned a twelve-man squad of Jewish policemen, commanded by Captain Max Finkelstein, to guard the German Consulate General.[70]

The newly-named National Conference of Christians and Jews founded the Volunteer Christian Protest Committee to boycott Nazi Germany.

Despite newspaper editorials and threats of boycott, the United States did not increase its immigration quota for German refugees (about 27,000 to 30,000 annually).

Isolationists, like the anti-Semitic, anti-Roosevelt 'radio' priest, Father Charles Coughlin, grew even stronger. Coughlin's national weekly broadcasts had a wide audience. Another clergyman, the Reverend Gerald L.K. Smith and his hate-sheet *The Cross and the Flag*, also prospered.

Eventually, in what was described as a tawdry public relations move,[71] President Roosevelt called for an international conference on the Jewish refugee problem. It convened at Evian les Bains, the old French spa, between 6 July and 14 July 1939, but the results were zero. No one agreed to accept immigrants from Nazi Germany. Each government, beset with its own economic ills, was fearful of adding foreigners to its population. Eventually, only the British admitted about 40,000. Franklin Roosevelt, the man who called the conference, also refused to antagonize his domestic opponents, the isolationists.

A curious reaction to Kristallnacht came from Reform Rabbi Ferdinand Isserman of St Louis, Mo. He called on Jews to forgive and be reconciled with Nazi Germany 'so that the minds and hearts of the persecutors may be changed'.[72]

Aligned with the America First Committee, Father Coughlin and the Reverend Gerald L.K. Smith, there was also the German American Bund.

On 29 March 1936 Fritz Kuhn, a forty-year-old Munich-born Ford worker was elected the Bund's leader. He opened a headquarters at 178 East 85th Street in Manhattan's Yorkville. The Bund had training encampments where they played at being stormtroopers. One, called Camp Siegfried was at Yaphank, Long Island, New York. Others were at Philadelphia and Pontiac, Michigan. Many of their expenses were underwritten by Berlin and doled out by the AA's Hans Thomsen, special assistant to Washington's German Ambassador Hans Dieckhoff. (The Norwegian-born Thomsen, tall, blond, very 'Aryan' and his beautiful wife Bebe, tried hard to entertain, influence and even bribe American lawmakers.)[73]

By 1938 the Bund claimed 100,000 members and sympathizers. Then, in December 1939 Fritz Kuhn was sent to Sing Sing, the Federal Prison at Ossining, for misappropriation of the Bund's funds.

America First, Coughlin, Smith and the Bund were the extreme wings of isolationism. Many other Americans, though not organized, were in full sympathy. They had no wish to focus on bad news from Europe. They listened to the new Glenn Miller band, read Hemingway's short stories, loved Nobel Prize winner Pearl Buck's book about China. Bob Hope sang *Thanks for the Memory*, Don Budge won the Grand Slam, and Orson Welles had petrified the country with his radio broadcast about an invasion from Mars.

Besides, the minimum wage was raised to forty cents an hour. Now that was worthwhile news!

Hungary, the country which had slavishly accepted its Czechoslovak booty from the Rome 'jury' of von Ribbentrop and Count Ciano, now added its signature to the Anti-Comintern Pact on 25 November. As usual, the ceremony was lavish and well publicized, with special acclaim for the creator of the pact, von Ribbentrop. On orders from the Foreign Minister, a glossy, trilingual, magazine publication was prepared in Berlin. It glorified the Anti-Comintern Pact and was called *Berlin – Rom – Tokio*. One hundred thousand copies were printed and then distributed among all German embassies and missions. Of course, it covered von Ribbentrop with 'objective' praise and flattery. The magazines were difficult to give away, but the embassies repeated the order for obvious political reasons.[74]

Early in December 1938, von Ribbentrop went to Paris on a formal state visit for the signing of a Franco-German treaty of non-aggression. To the participants, the treaty looked like a cynical, empty gesture, a holding action. Despite overwhelming French courtesy such as a special Pullman carriage, built for the British royal visit, which they sent to collect von Ribbentrop, both the diplomats and the French spectators had little faith in the enterprise. For von Ribbentrop's ceremonial wreath-laying at the grave of the 'Soldat inconnu' under the Arc de Triomphe, an immense German wreath was ready, but without its swastika-festooned ribbon, which was left behind in Berlin and had to be rushed to Paris on a Luftwaffe plane.

Though most foreigners were deeply shocked by the barbaric events which had taken place in Germany in early November, a surprising number of intelligent Germans still did not realize the enormous harm which had been done to the image and reputation of their country. An example of this was given in December 1938, a month after Kristallnacht. A senior German diplomat, a non-Nazi, insisted on speaking to Sir Ivone Kirkpatrick, then a senior official at the British Embassy in Berlin, who was being transferred back to London. In the strictest confidence, the German told Kirkpatrick that Hitler had instructed the Luftwaffe to prepare plans for a sudden, peace-time air attack on London. He did not know if or when this plan was to be carried out, but he felt that the British government had to be informed. His reason was that, 'I and my friends are appalled at Hitler's barbaric idea. Moreover, we don't believe that an air attack would be decisive. It would merely blacken Germany's name for centuries and range the whole world against her.'

Obviously, the man was unaware that the 'barbaric ideas' of November had already irreparably besmirched Germany's name.

1939 saw the publication of the aptly named *Goodbye to Berlin* by Christopher Isherwood. The world had to say goodbye to Berlin. Most foreigners had remained affectionate to the city on the Spree, often beyond their limits of patience and forebearance, while Berlin turned from a witty, ugly, affectionate, creative and cynical place which told bitter jokes about its own misfortunes, into a centre of pomposity, fear, creative sterility and government-sponsored brutality.

All this was ignored by the von Ribbentrops. Because of some differences between Goebbels and Himmler, over Kristallnacht and other matters, von Ribbentrop saw an opening to consolidate his position as a party stalwart, using his only friend in the leadership echelon, Heinrich Himmler, head of the SS. He began to 'donate' some of his own senior Foreign Ministry officials to Himmler, though only in small part. In April 1938 at the request of the Foreign Minister, von Weizsäcker and Woermann became honorary senior SS officers with the rank of colonel, though they had no specific duties in the black-coated fraternity[75] and certainly felt no affection for or loyalty towards it. Soon, several other senior Foreign Ministry officials found themselves wearing the less-than-wished-for black uniform. Of course, it was possible to refuse the 'honour', but that took men who had not yet been pushed beyond the limit of their morality. Most senior AA officials accepted SS membership, explaining that the unwanted SS rank would at least provide them with a valuable party listening post and a certain amount of leverage. Probably some of this was valid. By 1939 even the most experienced Berlin diplomats were isolated from the world's attitudes. There was no more free exchange with foreigners, be they diplomats, journalists or just friends. The number of foreign visitors from London, Paris and New York had shrunk to a trickle. Besides, any German diplomat who wore an SS uniform, no matter how rarely he did so, estranged himself from visitors from most democratic countries.

By now, through their police functions and concentration camps, the SS had become a symbol for brutality and a cause for fear even among many Germans. Fear of the SS went everywhere, even to California. There was barely a Hollywood film about the new Germany without that standard symbol for horror, the SS man. This could not be blamed on the 'Jewish film clique', although Goebbels' Propaganda Ministry trumpeted this as the explanation. The horror of the SS came from the true tales of its surviving victims and from the eyewitness reports of foreign journalists. To the world outside, an SS captain was a ruthless man, no matter if he wore 'honorary' rank like the AA diplomats or was an SD man and part of the Gestapo, with the dreaded SD 'diamond' insignia on his left sleeve. The SD, the Sicherheits Dienst (Security Service) of the SS, was the direct instrument of the Himmler–Heydrich–Kaltenbrunner triumvirate. The SD sought, arrested, held, tortured, imprisoned, condemned and executed almost at will. There were occasional hints of decency to be found among the men of its sister organization, the Gestapo, particularly among former professional policemen. There was none among the SD. Most of the world did not differentiate between the weekend-soldier Allgemeine SS and the captain of a concentration camp guard company. As a well-known German aristocrat and former army officer put it, 'One shuddered when one saw an SS uniform.'[76] Some decent men who worked for von Ribbentrop were now tarred with this brush to satisfy his party politics.

The empty drive to reassure the world continued. Following the hollow state visit to Paris, the von Ribbentrops, accompanied by interpreter Schmidt, took a special private train to Poland for a state visit with Colonel Joséf Beck, the Polish Foreign Minister and his associates. Poland was still treated as a potential anti-Russian ally. But there were certain German 'requests' on the agenda.

On 26 January 1939, the von Ribbentrops' train pulled into the swastika-festooned Warsaw main station. Flowers were presented by Mme Beck to Frau von Ribbentrop. (Mme Beck was used to making *beau gestes*. Her husband, the Colonel, had a reputation for philandering.) The German National Anthem was played, as was the Polish one, von Ribbentrop's party at the stiff Hitler salute. The RAM then inspected a smart honour guard of Polish infantry. He strode slowly and with much dignity, as suited a man of his station. A state dinner followed. Its toasts and mutual compliments were empty. Von Ribbentrop had only two aims: to obtain the return to Germany of the port of Danzig, a Polish mandate since Versailles. In exchange, Poland could use the city as a free port. The Hanseatic port of Danzig had been German until the Great War. Also, Adolf Hitler wished to have an 'extra-territorial' right of way for an Autobahn and a railway line from Germany across the Polish Corridor to German East Prussia. He virtually wanted to carve a slim strip of German territory across Polish soil so that Germany and her eastern province, East Prussia, now separated by Polish territory, could be organically connected. No more Polish frontier police, no more Polish customs, no more Polish uniforms on German trains.

The answer from Poland was a firm and polite no. On the second day of the state visit, proceedings were cut short by a 'bad cold' which Beck developed overnight.[77]

Earlier in January, Colonel Beck, unable to dodge it, had accepted an invitation to the Berghof. On that occasion, the same requests had been made by Hitler against the background of majestic mountain views from the windows. And those requests had already been rebuffed by Beck. No matter how powerful his host and how beautiful the scenery, the suave Colonel Beck made it clear that Danzig would 'stay Polish' and that cars and trains would have to submit to Polish law when crossing Polish soil. Now von Ribbentrop heard the echo of the Berghof 'nay' repeated in Warsaw.

Hitler was infuriated by these two failures, and von Ribbentrop was mortified. According to Schmidt, the RAM had already used hours of his famed perseverance at the Berghof to change the mind of Colonel Beck, but without an iota of success. He thought he could improve on his Berghof performance during the Warsaw visit, but he was to be disappointed once more. It now angered him that Hitler had supported the Polish claims against Czechslovakia and their seizure of Olsa. Was Poland still to be pampered because she was a potential ally against Soviet Russia? In von Ribbentrop's view, Poland had exhausted her credit. He had other initiatives in mind, which might involve a possible alliance with the devil, an unthinkable notion – a deal with the Soviets. Poland would then no longer be needed except as a buffer area, a margin of safety. The idea would have been inconceivable for men who had grown up with Nazi ideology and who considered *Mein Kampf* their bible, but von Ribbentrop was still enough of the international businessman to remain unhindered by such ideological instincts, and Annelies was in complete agreement. They only awaited the supreme opportunity.

According to Annelies in the von Ribbentrop memoirs which she edited after his death, on the train back to Berlin from Warsaw Ribbentrop told his staff, 'Now all that remains is to make an agreement with Russia, if we want to avoid being completely surrounded.'

Was Hitler ready for this hateful solution? Was he prepared to parley with the Satan of his nightmares, the dragon he had sworn to slay since the beginning of his political life? Or was this sort of 'power bloc' thinking only the 'businessman's' despised way of international diplomacy?

Before turning to this problem, Hitler had to deal with the correction of an error he had made in 1938: the Munich Agreement. It had not sated his appetite to solve the 'problem' of Czechoslovakia. The Sudetens were now 'free'. The Poles and Hungarians seemed to have received their territories through the Vienna 'jury'. Even the Slovaks had formed a separate republic in Bratislava on 6 October 1938 under a Slovak priest called Father Josef Tiso. Tiso had asked for and received German backing. His violently anti-Prague views led to bitter conflict with the Czechoslovak government. Employing the usual method of preparing for conquest, offences against German-speaking people of the area, true and invented, were drummed up in the German and Austrian press.

Father Tiso's rule, encouraged by Hitler, was so inflammatory towards Prague that the Czechoslovak government occupied Tiso's capital, Bratislava on 10 March 1939, and substituted another, more reliable Slovak named Sidor to head the new Slovak republic.

On 11 March in Berlin, Tiso requested Hitler's help and patronage after being persuaded by von Ribbentrop to do so. Then, 'in order to avoid further Slovak–Czech conflict and to stop further violence against Germans living in the remainder of Czechoslovakia', Hitler agreed to meet with the Czechoslovak President, a former judge called Emil Hacha, a meek, tired and ill man with the thankless task of shepherding an ailing, crippled nation. Hacha had requested the meeting through the German Chargé in Prague, who forwarded it to von Ribbentrop. Of course, the RAM received Hitler's instant agreement. When Hacha and Foreign Minister Chwalkowsky arrived in Berlin, this was the course of events according to von Ribbentrop's memoirs:

> Hacha told me the fate of Czechoslovakia was in the hands of the Führer. That very night at the Chancellery the Führer told Hacha that he intended to send his troops into Bohemia and Moravia. Foreign Minister Chwalkowsky agreed to the decision. Hacha then received telephonic approval from Prague and instructed his Cabinet to receive the German troops 'in a friendly manner'. No protest was raised from the Czechoslovak side. The occupation then took place immediately and without incident.

According to von Ribbentrop, it was as simple as that. The next day Hitler entered Prague in his usual army-grey, six-wheel Mercedes cross-country vehicle. In Prague, von Ribbentrop was ordered to read 'a proclamation which made Bohemia and Moravia into a German protectorate'. Again, according to von Ribbentrop, it was all very pleasant and calm.[78]

The truth was more brutal. At 10.40 p.m. on the night of 14 March, the train with Dr Emil Hacha, his daughter (who was his nurse–companion) and Chwalkowsky pulled into cold Berlin. Even before they had inspected a menacing-looking SS honour guard, they were told by the Czech Ambassador Mastny that German troops were already crossing the border into what remained of Czechoslovakia. They were immediately taken to the Adlon Hotel near the Brandenburg Gate, where they waited until 1.15 a.m., and were then driven through snow flurries to the newly designed Reich Chancellery. Hitler's office was an immense, lavish and gloomy wood-panelled hall with a desk at the very end of the long, thick carpet. To the side of the desk was a square of upholstered sofas and couches around a low table where they were asked to sit. Hacha and his Foreign Minister sat motionless like mummies. As Schmidt described it, 'only their eyes gave proof that they were live people'. Göring and von Ribbentrop were in attendance.

Hitler came straight to the point. 'The movement of German troops cannot be halted. If you wish to avoid bloodshed, call your Minister of War and instruct him to avoid all resistance.' That ended the conversation for Hitler, who then left. Göring took Hacha into a nearby room while telephone connections with Prague were attempted, but the lines were not open and no amount of yelling by von Ribbentrop to 'get the Reich Postal Minister out of bed to do his job' had the desired effect. While Göring tried to chat with the shaken old man, Chwalkowsky stayed with von Ribbentrop. Still no telephone connection, while the danger of a military confrontation between German and Czech troops grew. Meanwhile, the text of a document was drafted and typed, which declared that to preserve law and order the fate of Czechoslovakia had 'been voluntarily put into the hands of the German Führer. The Führer had accepted the Czechoslovak request.' Suddenly, Göring came out of the neighbouring room bellowing, 'Hacha has fainted! Fetch Dr Morell at once!'

Morell was rushed to Hacha's side. The doctor, an expert on amphetamines, injected the old man, who then recovered quickly. Telephone connections were finally established, and Hacha and Chwalkowsky, in turn, yelled into the phone in Czech, to instruct their government to accept the inevitable and avoid the loss of Czech lives. The text of the communiqué was finally signed at 3.55 a.m. by von Ribbentrop and Chwalkowsky. The exhausted participants then left the pompously grandiose, neo-classical Chancellery, which Albert Speer had probably designed for more lofty purposes than the rape of a small country and the bullying of a sick old statesman.

According to yet another view,[79] the actual signatures were given by Hacha and Chwalkowsky only after Göring and von Ribbentrop literally chased the two men around the table, holding out pens for them to use, as the pages of the agreement lay spread out before them. It was then that Hacha had his fainting spell. This is possible, though the usually reliable Schmidt mentioned only a 'calm conversation between Hacha and Göring'.

Later that day, Hitler left his special train at the border station Böhmisch Leipa, climbed into his six-wheel army Mercedes and entered Prague. That night both he and von Ribbentrop slept in the palace on the Hradcyn, and it was here that, before sleeping the conqueror's sleep, he issued the proclamation, which von Ribbentrop then read out, declaring Bohemia and Moravia a new 'Protectorate' of the Reich. Von Neurath was to be Reich Protector, although soon, in the Hitler manner, Karl Hermann Frank, a much harsher man, was to duplicate this function. Von Ribbentrop's memoirs failed to mention the last sentence of the proclamation: 'Czechoslovakia has ceased to exist.' So much for Hitler's claim that 'We want no Czechs!'

*   *   *

No British or French threats of action could be detected. No doubt von Ribbentrop slept well. Once more his master had been right.

On 17 March, the day after Hitler and von Ribbentrop awakened in Prague, a grim Neville Chamberlain made a speech in Birmingham. He asked bitterly if anyone could ever again believe any promises made by Hitler. In Paris, an angry Daladier told the German Ambassador Count Welczeck that Hitler had betrayed and made a fool of him. Schmidt doubted if Hitler ever saw the translation of Chamberlain's Birmingham speech, hinting that von Ribbentrop did not provide it or had side-tracked it. Notes from the British and French governments carried by hand from their embassies to the Foreign Ministry were discarded unread by von Ribbentrop.[80] Warnings of this sort had been delivered after the Rhineland, the Anschluss and Kristallnacht. They had come to mean very little. Besides, an Anglo-German industrial conference scheduled for the day of Hitler's proclamation in Prague went ahead as if nothing had happened. Von Ribbentrop felt only contempt, honed by long-standing British and French efforts at conciliation, and he refused to listen to any of the signals from across the Channel. The Wilhelmstrasse had also become isolated because men like von Dirksen, the Ambassador in London, declined to sound warnings which might have made him seem faint of heart and which might have displeased his chief, the RAM, or the Führer.

Friends and foes alike were shocked by the Prague invasion and by Hitler's faithlessness. To Sir Nevile Henderson, the Englishman who had been sent to Berlin to accommodate Hitler's foibles, probably the longest-suffering messenger of the policy which became known as appeasement, Hitler, von Ribbentrop and the German people had now become one and the same despicable thing. He was soon recalled to London in a gesture that could only be interpreted as Downing Street's attempt at a change of policy.

Chips Channon tried on 16 March to justify the policies of his Prime Minister: 'Never has he been proven more abundantly right, for he gave us six months of peace in which we rearmed, and he was right to try appeasement.' But even the languorous, the cynical, the sybaritic and the chic can reach their limit. He continued, 'The country is stirred to its depth, and rage against Germany is rising.' Then on the 22nd Channon chronicled, 'Memel was today ceded by the Lithuanian government under threats of invasion and aerial bombardment. Memel, not in itself very important, is the camel-breaking straw, and the Cabinet is now unanimous that "something must be done". And Lord Halifax ... is beginning to hate the devil more than his works. ...'

Memel was a port on the Baltic Sea, part of the Memel region which was independently governed but federated with Lithuania. About half of the Memel population of 140,000 spoke German, half Lithuanian, but most of Memel's legislators were German-speaking, and there were tensions with the Lithuanian government. Hitler simply ordered a warship to threaten the port, and Memel then joined the Third Reich on 23 March, one week after the end of Czechoslovakia.

Von Ribbentrop seemed absolutely puzzled by the reactions from England and France. At first, he thought London was 'reasonable and positive' because Chamberlain declared in the House of Commons that Hitler's move into Prague was no breach of the Munich Agreement. 'The guarantee was given to Czechoslovakia, but now that country has ceased to exist.' Then a few days later, influenced by the opposition, a storm broke loose. Even the peaceful Lord Halifax, so von Dirksen was finally forced to report from London, had become 'totally negative'. Later, von Ribbentrop claimed that this confirmed a prediction he had made to his Führer on 14 March. In hindsight, despite his self-imposed blinkers, he maintained that he had 'warned that there would be a penalty for the move into Czechoslovakia'.[81]

While Europe looked east, the next announcement came from the south-west. Franco, the enigmatic, uncooperative, tiny Caudillo announced that Spain was now securely in the hands of the Falange, that all Republican resistance had ceased, and a Fascist government had been installed. It was small comfort for Hitler and Mussolini. Franco had accepted their help but had given little in return. The road to Gibraltar and the Bay of Biscay remained barred behind the Spanish border. Still, in the Nazi–Fascistic view, it was also a defeat for Communism, because it denied the Communists the back door to France and the possibility of naval bases and airfields.

It is significant to note what events shocked the von Ribbentrops. The plural is indicated because by 1939 Annelies was no doubt privy to all matters of policy which reached the RAM's private office in the Wilhelmstrasse or, for that matter, the Speer-renovation of Berlin's former Reich Presidential Palace which von Ribbentrop was soon to use as his official residence. After Hitler's open breach of the 1938 Munich Agreement the RAM was shocked when Polish Ambassador Lipsky arrived with a message from Warsaw which 'brusquely' and flatly turned down Hitler's Danzig and Polish Corridor suggestions and even declared that 'any further pursuit of these German plans, particularly those about Danzig, would mean war'.[82] Von Ribbentrop gingerly told Hitler about this 'threat', but uncharacteristically Hitler asked him to put it to the Polish Ambassador that no form of settlement would be found if the word 'war' was mentioned.

When the Poles then concluded a preliminary mutual defence agreement with Britain on 6 April, von Ribbentrop was doubly shocked. After all, it was Chamberlain who had insisted on and drafted the very paper which stated that Germany and Britain would not enter future political agreements without mutual consultation.[83]

Apparently von Ribbentrop had not been listening carefully when his Führer had assured him in Munich on the steps of the Führer Building that this paper 'meant next to nothing'. But now it puzzled von Ribbentrop that Chamberlain, the man who had complained so bitterly in his Birmingham speech about the betrayal of the Munich Agreement, should have signed a Polish agreement without consultation. Britain also planned to introduce conscription, more loftily known as National Service, probably yet another blow to the closed-eyed and closed-eared Joachim von Ribbentrop. He would have been even more surprised if he had learned the convoluted untruths and failed purposes which preceded the British guarantee to Poland.

Both Lord Halifax and the Prime Minister firmly believed that Poland was a first-rate military power and quite able to rebuff any German assault. This was their first miscalculation, largely the result of the swagger of Colonel Beck, Poland's Foreign Minister. Beck also assured them that Germany had never been truly insistent about Danzig and had never contested Polish rights there; another delusion.[84] Chamberlain had also hoped that a guarantee given to Poland would mean that the Poles would also defend neighbouring Romania, but Beck would guarantee no such thing. As William Manchester wrote, His Majesty's Government 'had been had!' The fate of Britain's vast Empire from a military standpoint was now in the hands of little Poland.[85]

Worse, knowing that the eventual political guarantee against German aggressiveness would need the co-operation of Soviet Russia, Chamberlain and Halifax now discovered Beck's implacably anti-Soviet stance. His attitude was 'Fighting with Germany might cost us our land. Collaborating with the Soviets would cost us our soul.'

On 7 April, to avoid being outshone by his former protégé Hitler, Mussolini invaded Albania. It was a cheap victory against a tiny country. King Zog fled and Italy had her conquest. Mussolini could now present himself as a conqueror and could dream his dreams of invading Greece from his new Albanian base. This was his reply to Hitler's Austro-Czechoslovakian actions.

Shortly after Mussolini's Albanian adventure, one of the most acid diplomatic exchanges of the pre-war years took place. Roosevelt was anxious, once and for all, to demonstrate that the United States, though far away, was closely involved in the fate of Europe. In a personal letter to Hitler, he asked the German Chancellor to commit himself to the freedom and integrity of some thirty European and non-European countries. He named each one in his letter to the Führer. Hitler responded in a savage and bitterly ironic speech which is often shown whenever German newsreels of 1939 are broadcast. He stood in front of his adoring, party-uniformed audience, hands on hips, bobbing up and down on spread legs, pronouncing 'Herr Roosevelt' with the unmistakable sound of the German name Rosenfeld, which is often (but not always) carried by German Jewish families.* He read out Roosevelt's letter as if reading the statements of a demented person. With an ironic grin, he quoted each and every one of the thirty countries Roosevelt had listed, until the audience burst into howls of derisive laughter. Hitler then went on to say that he had taken the trouble to ask all of these countries if they felt threatened. 'In each case, the answers were in the negative and occasionally quite harshly so!' The audience roared its supercilious outrage at Roosevelt's 'presumption and impertinence'. In the same speech, Hitler announced the unilateral repudiation of the Anglo-German Naval Agreement of 1935, von Ribbentrop's first diplomatic triumph. The R A M must have flinched, but broken treaties had become the norm.

Amazingly, von Ribbentrop and most of the other senior Hitler paladins were not targets for assassination, nor is there any record of attempts on von Ribbentrop's life. In contrast, there were over forty documented attempts on Adolf Hitler's life. One of these was planned for his fiftieth birthday, on 20 April 1939. The man who conceived of the deed and wanted to execute it was Colonel Noel Mason-MacFarlane, military attaché at the British Embassy in Berlin.

The Colonel knew that a vast review of troops and party formations was planned for the Führer's birthday and that the reviewing stand would be a short 110 yards from the Mason-MacFarlane flat on Sophienstrasse 1. Enormous crowds always massed all along the route of march and they climbed on to anything from tables to tree limbs. Under the cover of these yelling crowds, the Colonel thought he could shoot Hitler from the flat's bathroom window. He had no trouble finding a hunting rifle with a telescopic sight and a silencer. Even a poor shot could not miss at such short range, and Mason-MacFarlane was an expert. Ever the loyal soldier, he went to London to seek permission from Whitehall. The idea was turned down as 'unsportsmanlike'. The details are in the Colonel's notes on deposit at the Imperial War Museum. Obviously, Chamberlain was not the only representative of the Victorian view of the world.

Probably to clear up any further designs Mussolini might have had after his first Balkan conquest, von Ribbentrop attempted to persuade Prince Paul of Romania and his Prime Minister to enter the German camp, but the Romanians managed to evade him. Next came Turkey. An even more forceful session of wooing and coercing took place at the von Ribbentrop country estate Sonnenburg. Schmidt, who was there to interpret, described the almost athletic agility with which Memenencoglu,

---

* Like Alfred Rosenberg, many Germans of both Christian and Jewish faith carried the same name.

the Turkish Foreign Minister, evaded his persistent host's thrust. Failure, failure!

Then, finally, *something* to present to the Führer: on 22 May 1939 in the Great Hall of the new Chancellery with Hitler in godfatherly attendance, von Ribbentrop and Ciano signed the ill-named Italo-German Pact of Steel.

This was Hitler's counter-move to the newly revived (by Prague) Anglo-French friendship and it probably frightened every Italian except Mussolini. Even Ciano was described as looking 'scared of his own courage',[86] and he spoke to Hitler and von Ribbentrop of 'a future peace-filled, three-year co-operation'. In what must have been a supremely cynical mood, Hitler also congratulated von Ribbentrop on the swift conclusion of non-aggression pacts with Denmark, Estonia and Latvia, probably to put the lie to the accusing hints in Roosevelt's letter. One wonders if the Latvian, Estonian and Danish governments were all living in a vacuum or had decided to ignore Hitler's breach of promise to Prague of 15 March.

Both Germany and her opponents now realized the importance of Soviet Russia, and each of them set out to 'woo the bear'. Britain needed a second-front ally, and Hitler needed a clear back.

British historian Margot Light, an expert on modern Russia, has pointed out that 1939 to 1940 was the only period of Soviet history not revised later by Stalinists. The Soviet attitudes and accounts of the time are, therefore, accurately reflected in their histories.[87] As viewed from Moscow, British and French appeasement wrecked all Soviet initiatives to create an anti-Nazi security bloc. The Soviets had not even been invited to participate in the Munich negotiations over Czechoslovakia, although their vital interests were also at stake. They tried after Hitler's 15 March seizure of Prague to invite France and Britain to another joint security conference, in fact to form a tripartite pact, but they were ignored. Britain gave Poland her guarantee, but the Soviets did not believe the British would ever honour this promise. At last in May 1939 there seemed to be some Anglo-French interest in an alliance. The Soviets also wanted to include Belgium, Greece, Turkey, Romania, Poland, Latvia, Estonia and Finland in a treaty, but the British reaction was lukewarm. Nevertheless, the Soviets invited Halifax to Moscow, but he declined. Instead, a Moscow meeting took place on 14 June between Sir William Strang, a lower-level Foreign Office official, and Vyachislav Molotov, the new Soviet Foreign Minister. Then came several weeks of stalling over definitions and responsibilities. The Soviets were absolutely convinced that the British and French were still trying to make some sort of deal with Hitler, and were using the renewed Soviet talks as leverage. Moscow became even more resentful when an Anglo-French military delegation finally arrived on 11 August, composed of delegates who had no powers to negotiate. The senior British delegate, a retired admiral called Drax, was, politically speaking, a eunuch. The Russians had given Marshal Voroshilov full powers to represent their side. The problem of defending Poland and Romania was quite self-evident: the Russians needed to enter Poland and Romania in order to defend them, but neither the British nor the French had obtained permission from Poland or Romania for this. Frustrated and then infuriated, the Russians finally called a halt to the talks.

Meanwhile, the Germans had sent urgent signals through their Moscow Embassy that they wanted to talk. Probably, the Soviets were fully aware that they could never achieve real peace with Nazi Germany and that sooner or later the Germans would attack, but they needed time to prepare themselves.

When they finally agreed to von Ribbentrop's arrival in Moscow on 23 August, there was still not an iota of progress in their meetings with the Anglo-French delegation. Anglo-French indecision brought on the Soviets' decision. This, in outline, was the Soviets' rationale for the pact with Hitler.[88]

Soviet distrust of Britain and France was probably justified. Churchill's friend 'Bob' Boothby, MP, said that with the exception of the *Daily Telegraph* the British press, led by Dawson of *The Times*, was 'bright yellow'. In fact, the BBC's Sir John Reith still barred former Ambassador to Berlin Sir Horace Rumbold and Harold Nicolson from the air because they were anti-German.

Besides, there were signs that Chamberlain was on the edge of a breakdown. After news of the Italian invasion of Albania on 7 April reached London, Under Secretary 'Rab' Butler rushed to Chamberlain's small private study at the top of 10 Downing Street, bearing the dispatch. Chamberlain was feeding the pigeons through an open window. He barely took notice of the startling news. He brushed off Butler's mention of the danger. 'Don't be silly,' he said. 'Go home and go to bed.' Then he continued feeding the pigeons like a man in a trance. William Manchester speaks of stress and of a 'personal tragedy' taking root in the seventy-year-old Chamberlain during the summer of 1939.

Poland never gained true British sympathy. Czechoslovakia, even if reluctantly sacrificed, was widely considered a democratic country. Poland was not. Historian A.J.P. Taylor points out that there was not a single demonstration in London which proclaimed 'Let's stand by the Poles!', while Czechoslovakia on the other hand always had a certain amount of popular support. It seemed to make sense to protect Poland through a Soviet alliance, but the conservative and deeply religious Halifax, among others in the British government, simply could not persuade himself to make more than a gesture towards such an alliance. In fact, the British delegation to Moscow with its French colleagues had been sent out via slow boat almost as if to prove that its presence would be half-hearted. If the Russians soon got fed up with the vague style and shallow content of the negotiations, London was not really disturbed. From their perspective, it was most unlikely that there were other 'bidders' in this particular auction. Certainly they considered Russia's arch-enemy Hitler a fairly unlikely prospect. They were wrong. The Germans were avidly anxious to bid, and Stalin was willing to listen.

The logical idea of an agreement or a pact with the Soviets had come to von Ribbentrop quite early. It might also have occurred to Adolf Hitler but only as a deeply despised but necessary final resort. No matter how often von Ribbentrop had advanced this solution, it still took an agonized decision by Hitler to set it in motion. The key man chosen to prepare the way was Germany's Ambassador to Moscow, the splendid Count Friedrich Werner von der Schulenburg, an immensely handsome and elegant silver-haired Saxonian, a professional diplomat and a great ladies' man. His appearance and manner could have served as a textbook example for young students of diplomacy. The Count was first sent to Moscow by von Neurath in 1934 to counteract some of the adverse effect of the violent anti-Soviet propaganda emerging from Germany's new Nazi government. As proof of his skills, von der Schulenburg managed to keep alive some measure of rational diplomatic dialogue between Moscow and the Wilhelmstrasse. How ironic that a right-wing, revolutionary government should dispatch a superbly mannered and trained aristocrat of the old school to deal with a left-wing revolutionary government. It was like sending a Nobel prize-winning physicist to mediate between two angry pugilists. It was not the only time a German patriot found himself serving the cause of Nazism. Usually those who did so chose to wear blinkers like von der Schulenburg and like so many of Germany's generals, who despised the *canaille* which governed Germany but were impressed with its victorious ways (and also with the many promotions it was handing out). But, unlike them, von der Schulenburg did not serve the Nazis out of opportunism. His love was for Germany, even if she had an evil master. He would have done anything to keep Germany safe from war with Russia. He probably had hopes of saving whatever he could of the country he had loved as a young man.

Four years later, when Germany's army lay bleeding in the snow on the Russian front, he joined the von Stauffenberg rebels, and they designated him to become the future Foreign Minister once they had exterminated Hitler. It was not to be. At sixty-nine, the handsome Count von der Schulenburg was hanged by his Nazi masters like a common criminal at Plötzensee prison in Berlin.

But in 1939, before war came, von der Schulenburg was overjoyed to hear a speech of Stalin's at the 18th Communist Party Congress in March which expressed Russia's unwillingness to 'pull British and French

chestnuts out of the fire'.[89] Another sign of Russia's increasing willingness
to deal with Germany was the substitution of Jewish Foreign Commissar
Litvinov with Molotov, which could have been a conciliatory gesture
towards anti-Semitic Nazi Germany. Known among Russia's elite as
Kamenaya Poposatka or Iron Arse for his dour style, the short, brush-
moustached Molotov was a member of the Politburo, and therefore closer
to Stalin than Litvinov had been. Molotov was a machine-like party
functionary who never made a decision of his own. He invariably deferred
to Stalin, which often delayed things. Adolf Hitler, an impatient long-
distance participant in the forthcoming negotiations, could not have
known that it was Molotov's deference to Stalin and nothing else which
often slowed Russian decisions.

The first real feelers were to be in the field of trade. One of von
Ribbentrop's AA trade specialists, Schnurre, was sent to Moscow. The
meetings were tentative. Molotov insisted that 'Until we have political
rapprochement, we cannot talk about trade agreements.' Also, the Anglo-
French team had only just arrived and Molotov still did not want to upset
any potential Western agreements in return for a small trade deal with
Schnurre. According to Hans von Herwarth, post-war German Ambassador in London, then a young deputy to von der Schulenburg in the
German Embassy in Moscow, it was Britain's guarantee to Poland, added
to the arrival of the Franco-British negotiating team, which had caused
Hitler to rush into full negotiations with the Soviets. Through von Ribbentrop, Hitler began to put heavy pressure on von der Schulenburg to
secure an early date for a Moscow visit by the RAM. The whole matter
was to be described to Molotov as extremely urgent and also extremely
confidential.

No one in London, Paris or Washington would have guessed that the
leopard could have changed his spots, that Adolf Hitler, Communism's
sworn enemy, was about to negotiate with Joseph Stalin, the Nazis'
bitterest foe. On the face of it, the possibility was completely out of the
question. Not so for Hitler or von Ribbentrop. Hitler saw the entire
project as vile but necessary, while von Ribbentrop saw it as necessary
and wonderful. It would be his crowning diplomatic achievement and
a stroke of genius if he could provide his Führer with safety from the
East.

Young 'Johnny' von Herwarth's conscience as an anti-Nazi soon forced
him to draw others into his confidence. Perhaps rumour could foil the
negotiators. He saw the dreadful danger of a Soviet treaty. It was bound
to bring war. He began by speaking to a friend in the Italian Embassy.
The Italian could hardly believe his ears. A pact between Hitler and
Stalin? *Non . . . mai!* Never!

But negotiations went ahead. In a secret telegram of 25 May, von
Ribbentrop assured Molotov that, even if Germany and Poland went to

war, 'Russia's special interests could be taken into consideration.' By now Ciano had also become involved, briefed by the Italian friend of von Herwarth. Then von Mackensen, the German Ambassador in Rome, reported to Berlin that even the Duce thought it was not a bad idea to conclude such a pact. Von der Schulenburg, who was in Berlin for consultations, was asked to explain how Mussolini had got wind of the whole thing, but of course he had no explanation. How could he have known that one of his own best men, Hans von Herwarth, had leaked the facts? Von Herwarth realized that such a pact would free Hitler to launch a war, and he dreaded it. But von der Schulenburg passionately wanted to retie the bonds between his country and Russia, severed by the outbreak of world war in 1914.

For a brief moment in June, von Ribbentrop hesitated out of fear that word of a treaty with Soviet Russia would upset the honorary 'Aryans of the East', Germany's new Japanese allies and Russia's enemies. But he paused only for a moment, and by July the pressure was on again. At the end of the month Hitler politely turned down an offer from Mussolini, *à la* Munich, to help negotiate a Polish pact. Hitler did not wish to offend Moscow and put Soviet sensibilities ahead of Rome's. Times were changing.

On 21 August 1939 at 10.50 a.m. a teletype letter arrived at the Berghof signed 'Stalin': 'The Soviet government has instructed me to say they agree to Herr von Ribbentrop's arrival on 23 August.' Hitler immediately ordered his press chief Dietrich to announce the forthcoming trip, exclaiming to Dietrich, 'Now we can spit in anyone's face!'[90]

On Monday, 21 August, von Ribbentrop also broke the news to his friend Ambassador Oshima of Japan that he was heading for Moscow to negotiate a treaty. Oshima was aghast, as was Tokyo when the news reached there. The German Ambassador to Japan, General Orr, was equally surprised, and unpleasantly so. At a Propaganda Ministry briefing in Berlin, the angry correspondent of the Japanese news agency Domei behaved so badly that a complaint was sent to his Embassy. Oshima, feeling he had failed to warn Tokyo, resigned.

Von Herwarth now decided to involve a non-Axis Western diplomat, his young American friend 'Chip' Bohlen, who served as a diplomat in his country's Embassy in Moscow. According to his memoirs, Bohlen immediately telegraphed a sceptical Washington. It is equally certain that Washington then briefed 10 Downing Street. The news still did not seem to stir up much action in London or Paris. The same half-hearted, slovenly efforts were continued by the Anglo-French 'negotiators' in Moscow.

Sir Ivone Kirkpatrick later believed that Anglo-French efforts to close a Soviet treaty were bound to be stillborn. For the Soviets, the Anglo-French negotiators offered the prospect of war, no discussion of the Baltic states nor of any territorial gains for Russia. In contrast, the Germans offered peace, a part of Poland and also the three vital Baltic coast countries. The German deal was much more palatable. But Kirkpatrick's view is not the majority's, though it has great validity.

On 22 August,[91] a shocked, helpless von Herwarth was ordered to fly from Moscow to Königsberg in East Prussia, to accompany Joachim von Ribbentrop on the last leg of his air journey to Moscow. They all arrived at the Soviet capital about midday on Tuesday, 23 August. Von Ribbentrop was greeted by a Soviet delegation and by the German Ambassador, von der Schulenburg, and his staff.

A German Embassy friend of von Herwarth pointed at a group of plainclothes Gestapo men who walked down the ramp of the big, four-engined German plane and were immediately greeted with many warm handshakes and fraternal smiles by a group of Russian secret policemen. Like attracts.

The streets on the drive into Moscow were decked with swastika flags. These had been hard to locate in Moscow. The Soviet protocol people were frantic. At last, somebody remembered that an anti-Nazi film was being shot in a studio near Moscow. The street sets of the film were decked out with hundreds of swastika banners. Presto! Swastika flags, hundreds of them. They were requisitioned and film shooting was suspended.

After a hasty meal at the German Embassy, the von Ribbentrop delegation was driven to the Kremlin for a meeting with Molotov. No one in the German party had slept the previous night because von Ribbentrop had kept everyone awake to help him assemble his notes.

The meetings began at once. Hilger, the AA's chief Russian-language expert, did the interpreting. Schmidt was left behind at the German Embassy, because von Ribbentrop wanted 'the fewest faces' to simplify dealing with the Russians. To everyone's surprise and even shock, Stalin appeared in Molotov's office. Even von der Schulenburg was stunned. He had served in Moscow four years but had never actually spoken to Stalin. Stalin was shorter in stature than everyone had assumed, dressed in his simple twill high-buttoned tan jacket and smoking cardboard-tipped Russian cigarettes. After Stalin's initial gesture to Molotov to lead off the meeting, Molotov deferred, and, shrugging his reluctance, Stalin took charge.

Poland was split in half like a melon, on a north–south axis, and the halves apportioned to the parties in the negotiations. Every Russian 'suggestion' was followed, and twice von Ribbentrop had to ask for telephonic permission from the Führer in Berlin, specifically about the secret 'assignment' of Finland, Estonia, Latvia and Bessarabia to the Soviets. Hitler was agreeable because he wanted to get the treaty under lock and key. He was in a hurry. Late that afternoon von Ribbentrop and his delegation went back to the Embassy for a hasty snack. The RAM was enthusiastic about the men around Stalin: 'the men with the strong faces'.

Later in Berlin, he would tell the story of his Moscow triumph and say how much he had felt at home with the men in the Kremlin. 'They were', he told several Nazi Party stalwarts, 'wonderful fellows. It was like being among old party comrades!' – which was not appreciated by the old Nazi Party comrades. The diplomat should have learned diplomacy with his own people.

After the snack, von Ribbentrop and his men returned to the Kremlin. At 6 p.m. the broad-shouldered commander of Stalin's bodyguard conducted them up some narrow tower-like stairs to the long office where Stalin and Molotov stood waiting once more.[92]

Since this was, in many ways, the apex of his career, his most important achievement, von Ribbentrop's memoirs told the story of the two days in some detail. He began by insisting that at first he had asked his Führer to send someone else to Moscow, possibly Göring, since he thought of himself as badly compromised by his years of anti-Bolshevik speeches and his own friendship with the Japanese. But Adolf Hitler insisted that von Ribbentrop 'understood these things best'. Until von Ribbentrop left for Moscow, he claimed he 'knew nothing about an alleged decision of Hitler's to attack Poland', although he acknowledges that Hitler had mentioned 'a definite solution to the Danzig and Corridor problems'. His impression was that the Polish problems would be solved peacefully through diplomacy. The outline for the Soviet pact was not sketched out until the plane ride to Königsberg and Moscow. The Russians had prepared no draft at all.

Work began again. At 10 p.m. there was a late supper for four, at which Stalin rose and spoke of a friendly new phase, as did Molotov. After much haggling and several telephonic concessions from Hitler, the treaty was finally signed at 2 a.m. on Wednesday, 24 August. The fate of Estonia and Latvia (Lithuania was eventually to follow) as 'assigned to the Soviet sphere' was contained in a separate secret protocol.

Von Ribbentrop was deeply impressed by the affable, plainly dressed and plainly spoken Stalin. During the taking of early-morning photographs by Hoffmann, Hitler's photographer, Stalin told von Ribbentrop that this was the first time a foreigner had been permitted into the Soviet Kremlin. He then refused to be photographed in the reactionary act of drinking Crimean champagne, which must have dismayed von Ribbentrop, the old champagne merchant. The next morning von Ribbentrop noticed there were faces staring at him through the open window from the building across from the old Austrian Embassy, where the Germans were quartered. He was told they belonged to the Anglo-French team.

Von Ribbentrop probably had no idea that Hoffmann, an old friend of Hitler (who first met Eva Braun when she was an assistant in the

Hoffmann studio), had special instructions from the Führer: he was to photograph Stalin's ear lobes to judge if they looked 'Aryan' (loose) or if the Georgian dictator had Jewish blood (supposedly shown by attached lobes).

Von Ribbentrop also did not mention in his memoirs that when he wanted to precede the text of the treaty with some lofty preambulant phrases of mutual admiration and respect, Stalin stopped him and said, 'We have been pouring buckets of manure all over each other for years. So let us tone down the praise.'

At a final caviar and champagne celebration, Stalin toasted Hitler 'because the German people loved him'.[93] Von Ribbentrop also shook hands warmly with Trade Commissar Kaganovich, a Jew. The Moscow citizens had created a little song to celebrate the German Foreign Minister:

> *Spassibo Jasche Ribbentropu*
> *Shto on otkryl akro w Jewropy.*
> (Thanks to dear Jakie Ribbentrop
> for opening the window to Europe.)

It was a parody of an old verse about Peter the Great. For the moment, everything German was 'ruled' popular in Moscow, even Wagner's music.

The Lithuanian section of the secret protocol of 23/24 August was not signed until 28 September, during a return visit to Moscow by von Ribbentrop.[94] Now all the Baltic states had been 'donated' to Stalin. They would stay part of the USSR for over fifty years with varying degrees of bitterness. In their hatred for Soviet Russia, many Baltic groups eventually became fruitful recruiting grounds for the SS, after the Russians had been pushed out in 1941. Many of the most cruel Death's Head SS troopers, NCOs and officers, the concentration camp guards, came from the Baltic republics. They were often found in the murderous Einsatzgruppen, the roaming SS execution battalions far behind the combat lines in Poland and Russia.

On the flight home aboard the big FW200 Condor aircraft, Joachim von Ribbentrop was euphoric. He had been in Moscow only twenty-four hours, but he had concluded one of the world's most historic treaties (he chose to ignore von der Schulenburg's enormous contribution). Von Ribbentrop would have been less ecstatic had he known what Molotov said about him once he had flown back to Berlin: 'We were immensely pleased when we found out through his chatter how stupid the Reich Minister was.'[95]

They were escorted by fighter planes of the Luftwaffe because Polish anti-aircraft guns had begun firing at Lufthansa planes.[96] To avoid the possibility of hostile Polish flak, they took a long loop out over the Baltic. Polish–German railway connections had already been suspended and war was near. They landed in Königsberg, where Erich Koch, the Gauleiter of East Prussia, hailed the RAM as a hero and presented him with a lavish amber-encrusted case which contained copies of all the treaties von Ribbentrop had negotiated. Later, Hitler was highly amused to learn that all but one of these had long been broken.

Earlier that day, at 3 a.m., after von Ribbentrop had reported via telephone that the pact was signed, Hitler put down the phone, turned and said, 'It will hit like a bomb!' He hammered the wall with his fists and yelled, 'Europe is mine. The others can have Asia!'[97] He, the tee-totaller, even sipped some champagne while his paladins toasted him.

But Alfred Rosenberg, the high-priest fanatic of the Nazi Party, the unwavering National Socialist, a Balt who gut-hated the Soviets, was deeply shocked. His diary tells of his distress: 'I had the feeling that the Moscow pact would one day turn and take revenge on National Socialism. How can we talk of saving Europe when we have to beg for help from those who would destroy it?'[98] Rosenberg remained the only senior Nazi who was a 'purist'.

This was not a step Hitler had freely taken, but a plea by one revolution made to the head of another revolution, whose defeat had been a primary goal of twenty years of struggle.

Hitler, who was at the Berghof, flew to Berlin, where he greeted his 'Bismarck'. The von Ribbentrops must have savoured their triumph. Only a short twenty months earlier, they had thought their political years were over and that their Führer had turned his face from them.

That 24 August when von Ribbentrop relished his triumph, a dis-illusioned Johnny von Herwarth asked his chief, von der Schulenburg, to release him from the diplomatic service so that he could join the army. At first, von der Schulenburg tried to dissuade him. 'Come on, now, Johnny, are you sure? Think it over!' But then the old *roué* had a moment of incisive self-chastisement. 'Perhaps you are right,' he said. 'I have tried with all my strength to work for good relations between Germany and the Soviet Union. In a way I achieved my goal. But you know perfectly well that actually I achieved nothing. This pact will bring us a second world war and plunge Germany into disaster!'[99]

While von Ribbentrop was signing the treaty in Moscow, Sir Nevile Henderson was delivering an urgent letter from Neville Chamberlain to Hitler at the Berghof. The letter stated that Britain would support Poland, but would still help to find a solution to Anglo-German differences if Germany would be prepared to open such negotiations. It added that Britain was anxious for a truce while Polish–German differences regarding the treatment of minorities were discussed and settled.

Hitler's first reaction was intemperate and negative. His second reaction was calm and negative. For the still patient Henderson, he trotted out the false allegation that 100,000 'Germans' had now fled from Polish brutality and once again presented himself as the world protector of all people he alone decided were 'Germans', no matter how remote their national or racial bonds. He said he realized it might mean war to 'protect German interests', but he would rather 'fight a war at fifty than at fifty-six'.[100] He also hinted that Britain had incited Czechoslovakia in 1938 and was doing so now with Poland. While von Ribbentrop was proposing friendly toasts in faraway Moscow, von Weizsäcker and Hewel were in the Berghof as witnesses to this display of Hitler's fierce intransigence.

Sir Nevile Henderson's memoirs treated the German Führer with more objectivity than he deserved. He wrote, 'When Hitler comes up before the bar of the Last Judgement, he will certainly argue with apparently complete self-conviction that he could have spared the horrors of war if the Poles had accepted his reasonable and generous conditions. It will, I submit, be false.' The British guarantee to Poland of earlier in the year was transformed into a full treaty on 25 August. Part of the Soviet treaty was kept hidden from the world. There was deep secrecy about the protocols relating to the Baltic countries. On 24 August, a tired von Ribbentrop swore the reluctant German Embassy staff in Moscow to absolute silence 'on Adolf Hitler's life', about the special 'deal' made for the Baltic republics.

On that same day in London, Joseph Kennedy, the American Ambassador, told Chamberlain's right-hand man, Sir Horace Wilson, that it was all useless. Poland could not be saved. 'The Poles can only fight in revenge and plunge all of Europe into destruction.'[101]

Von Ribbentrop must have been shocked when his finest achievement, which would clear the path for the Führer's master plan, seemed suddenly to be blocked by outside interference. Now that Hitler's back was secure, his partner was fading. After all the time he had spent with Ciano and the Duce, getting assurances of alliance, a letter from Mussolini to Hitler arrived at 6 p.m. on 25 August. 'This is one of the most painful moments of my life, but I must tell you that Italy is not ready for war. My Chiefs of Staff advise me that our fuel reserves would only last for three weeks. Please understand my position.'

This letter was delivered by Attolico, the Italian Ambassador, and reached the Führer at the Chancellery shortly after Henderson had paid yet another useless visit in search of some sort of accommodation. He was becoming something of a joke in Hitler's circle. Von Ribbentrop was delighted as events finally began to unfold following his Moscow diplomacy, and he gloated over Henderson's unseemly and increasing urgency. But now came the shock of that whimper from the Villa Torlonia. Hitler's reaction was cold and angry, and Attolico was dismissed like a schoolboy.

Coulondre, the successor to François-Poncet, who had been posted to the Embassy in Rome, also came to try his turn that evening, but Hitler simply yelled about the Poles. He would guard German interests, no matter what the British or French were threatening! After all, had he not given up all claims to Alsace Lorraine? He had done his best to stay friendly with France. Once more, von Ribbentrop was encouraged. His Führer stuck to his convictions, even if the Duce had turned into a weakling. Schmidt reported that Hitler said, 'The Italians are behaving just as they did in 1914!' Everyone in the Chancellery spoke of the unreliable Axis partners.

The scene there was almost operatic. The immense anteroom was crowded with Nazi courtiers. In his vast, gloomy inner sanctum, Hitler walked to and fro, meeting a constant flow of visitors and aides, pulling all the strings of events as he saw fit. He was watched by von Ribbentrop, Hewel, Schmidt. At first, Hitler had shrugged his shoulders in anger at Mussolini's cowardice, but now it finally sank in.

He shouted, 'Keitel! I want to see Keitel!' When Keitel rushed in, Hitler snapped, 'The attack must be recalled at once!' and Keitel, in turn, yelled instructions at his aides. Another downswing for von Ribbentrop. Why did his Führer suddenly pull back again? The rumour he had heard was true then. The attack had been scheduled. In the anteroom, an army major said to Schmidt, 'It's all the fault of the diplomats!' and Schmidt privately agreed. He had to rush back into Hitler's office to translate a teletype letter from the Führer to the Duce into Italian, a cold letter in which Hitler asked Mussolini to keep the fact that Italy would stay neutral a secret in order to avoid encouraging the Anglo-French allies.

Attolico soon brought Mussolini's reply: 'I promise.'

Henderson arrived with another scheme from London. Chamberlain had earlier been offered a quasi-deal by Hitler, an international 'You run your part of the world and I'll run mine, and we'll stay out of each other's way.' Now Chamberlain replied: London regretted that Britain could not accept a separate proposal. She had treaty obligations to her allies. But Chamberlain guaranteed he would produce 'a Polish representative for full discussions'. It was 28 August. Hitler immediately told Henderson that the Poles were to have their man in Berlin by 30 August. 'The barbaric treatment of Germans in Poland cries to high heaven. This cannot wait!' Sir Nevile complained strenuously. 'The Poles barely have twenty-four hours! It's an ultimatum!' Hitler then warned that 'Polish atrocities' might bring matters to a boil before then. There was no time. He yelled, 'You don't give a damn how many Germans are mauled by the Poles!' Henderson had just arrived back from London, tired and worn out. He had bathed, changed clothes and drunk a half-bottle of champagne. His limit had been reached. He finally lost his temper. He pounded the table and yelled his anger and defiance at Adolf Hitler, the man he had once tried to trust. It was to be his final meeting with the Führer.[102] Hitler would have accepted the gesture of producing a Polish negotiator, but it was not to be.

Some more interference with the RAM's area of responsibility and, as he saw it, with the Führer's own plans also came from an old von Ribbentrop enemy, the powerful Hermann Göring. An old friend of the Reich Marshal, Birger Dahlerus, a Swedish industrialist, thought he could use his London connections to defuse tensions. Von Ribbentrop was outraged by this unsolicited offer. Nevertheless, Dahlerus travelled between Berlin and London a number of times. He did his best but was generally ignored as an amateur without credentials. He began to pout and withdrew from the task but not before shopping for some special teas at Fortnum & Mason in London. This final initiative by Göring soon dissipated, leaving von Ribbentrop once more in full command of the field.

Göring was apoplectic with anger at the 'champagne salesman'. He was convinced that von Ribbentrop was the main warmonger and had an evil influence on Hitler. Göring was always willing to see the best in his old comrade Hitler and to distrust a parvenu to National Socialism and a man he believed ill-qualified to be foreign minister.

There was an avalanche of conferences, telephone calls and teletype messages in those last two days before Hitler attacked Poland. The number of events was almost uncountable by location and content. The arrival within twenty-four hours of a Polish negotiator with full plenipotentiary powers became more and more unlikely. Colonel Beck, the Polish Foreign Minister, was as stiff-necked and stubborn as the German Führer. Beck was absolutely sure of Poland's military strength and more than anxious to hold Britain and France to their promises. Hitler counted on Beck's immovable attitudes and on his arrogance, and he was right. Lipski, the Polish Ambassador to Berlin, told Dahlerus on the day before war broke out that from the Polish side there was not the slightest interest in any proposals from Berlin. After five years in Berlin, said Lipski, he knew Germany extremely well, and in the event of war 'the Germans would overthrow their government and the Polish army would then march into Berlin'.[103] So much for Polish political judgment.

Poland mobilized on 30 August. Some time that day Schmidt was suddenly asked to translate yet another final proposal from Adolf Hitler to Great Britain, France and Poland. To Schmidt's absolute amazement the draft he read was logical, reasonable, sensible and constructive. Not since the days of the League of Nations had he seen anything as conciliatory. Then he realized it was a complete sham, set against the never-to-be-observed Polish deadline, a bitter joke to make Hitler seem like a reasonable, statesmanlike, judicious man, who had proposed these just solutions but had been rebuffed. How could Hitler help it if the Poles had failed to keep their appointment? (Later, in the presence of Schmidt, Hitler said of this final, 'reasonable' treaty draft, that he needed an alibi to show the German people he had done everything in his power to avoid war.)

Late that night, just before the midnight Polish deadline, von Ribbentrop asked Sir Nevile Henderson to the Foreign Office. He then read the full text of these 'reasonable' proposals to the startled British diplomat. Henderson fancied he knew German well, but a treaty and all its technicalities, orally delivered, tested his linguistic skills. He began to interrupt and ask questions and then asked to read the paper himself. Von Ribbentrop at first refused, but then he tossed it on to the desk. Contemptuously he said, 'There! Go ahead. It's no good, though. The deadline for the Polish negotiator has come and gone!' Schmidt told the story of this, the most stormy meeting he had witnessed in his years as a diplomatic interpreter.[104] Von Ribbentrop started to yell at Henderson, who took what the German Foreign Minister was dishing out, until von Ribbentrop yelled that the matter was damned ('verdammt') grave. That breached Henderson's limit of self-control. Sir Nevile, red-faced in his turn, shouted, 'You have used the word damned. That is not the language of statesmanship in this grave situation.' It sounds somewhat mid-Victorian by today's standards, but Sir Nevile had a strict, British diplomatist's sense of what was decorous and what was unseemly in diplomatic conduct. Von Ribbentrop was literally struck dumb for the moment. This cowardly British aristocrat had dared to speak to him like a teacher to a schoolboy! Both angry men jumped to their feet, tempers flaring. Schmidt, not believing his eyes and ears, lowered his head. Courtesy demanded that he should have stood up with the disputants, but good sense dictated otherwise. Finally he heard them breathe more easily and saw them retake their seats. Schmidt, well known for his sense of humour, saw nothing funny in this moment. Too many lives were at stake.

All this took place late on the night of 30 August in the historic office of Germany's great Iron Chancellor Prince Bismarck, now inhabited by the former importer of fine spirits, Joachim von Ribbentrop.

Historians will not allow the memory of von Ribbentrop to reach far above Bismarck's ankle. Yet both men were ambitious builders of power structures. Both found war to be the final instrument of their achievements. Neither understood the strength of persuasion, the power of reason or the sanctity of life. In this sense, perhaps, Hitler was not too far off beam when he called von Ribbentrop the 'second Bismarck'.

Late in the afternoon of the following day, 31 August, the last day of peace, Ambassador Lipski of Poland went to see von Ribbentrop at the Foreign Ministry. He then expressed Poland's interest in pursuing the points of the final German proposal. He said that an answer was forthcoming from Warsaw. 'Are you empowered to negotiate?' asked von

Ribbentrop. 'No,' said Lipski. That ended the meeting, the shortest of the Polish crisis.

That same night, the 31 August, there was one final, final, final Allied attempt. Ambassadors Henderson of Great Britain and Coulondre of France asked to be jointly received by the German Foreign Minister to hand over their governments' notes. Von Ribbentrop refused a joint meeting but gave Henderson a 9.30 p.m. appointment and Coulondre one at 10.00 p.m. Henderson's note warned once more that His Majesty's Government would carry out its international obligations. The French note was almost identical. A coldly uninterested von Ribbentrop insisted on oral translations of each Ambassador's statement as if he spoke neither English nor French. He told each Ambassador that he had no right to give a reply and would refer their notes to the Führer.

One more desperate attempt came from Ambassador Attolico of Italy. This plump, elderly man rushed to and fro between von Ribbentrop's Wilhelmstrasse office and the British and French embassies. At 8 p.m. he finally gave up. No one would accept Mussolini's offer to mediate. The British and the French mobilized their armies. At 4.45 a.m. on 1 September, Case White, the invasion of Poland, was launched.

Directive OKW/WFA No. 170/39 g.k. Chefs. LI, issued in eight copies, dated 31.8.39 Berlin, marked 'Secret', issued at 12.40 p.m. was signed by Adolf Hitler as Commander-in-Chief of the Armed Forces. He states that *1*. He has decided after trying all peaceful means, to change the intolerable conditions on the Eastern frontier through the application of brute strength (*Gewaltsame Lösung*). *2*. That the attack shall be called 'Case White' and will take place on 1 September. *3*. It is to be left to the French and British to open hostilities in the West and that the neutrality of Holland, Belgium, Luxemburg and Switzerland is to be scrupulously observed. '*Air attacks against London are to be left to my discretion. Attacks on the British Islands are to be planned, ensuring that sufficient forces are involved to avoid partial success.*' Distribution: Commanders-in-Chief of Army, Navy, Air Force and General Headquarters.

A typical Hitler propaganda incident was fabricated by the chief of the SD and Gestapo, Reinhard Heydrich. An SS captain, Alfred Naujocks, and a group of SS men in stolen Polish uniforms were ordered by Heydrich to 'capture' a German radio station on the Polish border at Gleiwitz and then to broadcast a Polish-language appeal. They were even told to dress up dead concentration camp inmates in Polish uniforms (the Gestapo called the cadavers 'canned goods') and to leave them around the radio station's grounds as if they had been killed by German border police during the skirmish. The attack was made and Naujocks was the SS hero of the moment. The German police reported the attack, adding that some Polish attackers had been shot by German frontier police. The *Völkischer Beobachter* bellowed, 'Polish partisans cross German border'.

As Naujocks said much later, 'The closer you were to Heydrich, the more you learned to fear him.'[105]

What could have been Adolf Hitler's frame of mind those final days before he loosed the storm, and how did the two von Ribbentrops feel? Hitler must have been absolutely certain that his destiny was to fight this war. He was a superstitious man and a creature of whim. In the manner of a stubborn child he always resented deeply any denial, any interdiction of his pet ideas or his favourite dreams. His army aide, Major Engel, wrote in his diary on 27 August 1939 (telegraphic style): 'Führer wants to bet Hewel that England will not interfere in case of war with Poland. Hewel disagrees avidly and says verbatim: "My Führer, don't underestimate the British. When they know there is no alternative, they become stubborn and go about their business. I think I know a lot more about that than my Minister [von Ribbentrop]." Führer very annoyed. Broke off conversation.'

Hewel meant that he had dealt with the British for years while he was in self-imposed exile abroad and knew more about them than von Ribbentrop, which might have been true. Also, as a 1923 fellow fighter of Hitler's, who had been jailed with his Führer, he had a certain freedom to speak up occasionally when it mattered. But even Hewel could not budge Hitler from his point of view. The Führer resented disagreement even from an old comrade.

Hitler never lost sight of his beginnings and of his penniless days as a near-vagrant, living in public shelters, trying to sell his paintings. Later, everyone who knew him told of the evenings and nights when Hitler related stories about his army service as a simple soldier, unable or possibly unwilling to raise himself to higher rank. His commander had stated that Hitler 'was extremely courageous but could not be trusted with command responsibility'. He had won the Iron Cross First Class, which was rare among the lower ranks, and still he had stayed at the bottom of the military heap. Now he was the absolute master of an empire. He had learned that he could manipulate, command, cheer, horrify, teach, lead, destroy almost at will. He must often have asked himself what could have brought him from nothing to the very peak, and the only answer was that it had to be destiny. His every decision, it seemed to him, his every judgment had been guided by his very own fate, by the path laid out millennia before in some book that guides the gods. He had once been weak, like others, then fate lifted him above his station. Now he could recognize each weakness in others and use it against them. Nations were like men, and he sensed an 'old rich man' weakness of Britain, the country with false teeth. Their language simpered, 'Oh, I'm afraid that I . . .' Their umbrellas kept their heads out of the clean, storm-driven rain. They no longer deserved to rule the world. He, Adolf Hitler,

Reichstag, 20 February 1938: *Left to right*: Goebbels, Frick, von Ribbentrop, Hess and Hitler.

The farewell visit to London, 9 March 1938.

François Poncet and Henderson at the French Embassy, 1 August 1938.

Stalin and von Ribbentrop on 23 August 1939.

Returning triumphantly from Moscow aboard the Führer's aeroplane, 25 August 1939.

The victorious landing in Königsberg after the Soviet treaty – before reporting back to Hitler – 24 September 1939.

WHAT, NO CHAIR FOR ME ?

360 BERLINER ILLUSTRIRTE ZEITUNG 1939

Der 28. September

'What no chair for me?': a cartoon by David Low which appeared in the *Evening Standard* on 30 September 1938.

Der deutsch-russische Grenz- und Freundschaftsvertrag besiegelt. Die gemeinsame Front gegen die Kriegshetzer in Westeuropa gebildet. Ein sicheres Fundament für den Dauerfrieden in Osteuropa geschaffen. Die Dokumente vom 28. September werden unterzeichnet. Stehend von rechts: Stalin, Reichsaußenminister von Ribbentrop und der Generalstabschef der russischen Armee Schaposchnikoff, sitzend Außenminister Molotow.

The final signing of the full Soviet–German Treaty with Secret Protocols on 28 September 1939. *Left to right*: (standing) Russian Chief of Staff Shaposhnikov, von Ribbentrop and Stalin; (seated) Molotov.

Benito Mussolini confers with von Ribbentrop in Florence, during Hitler's trip to France, Spain and Italy in October 1940.

Berlin, 22 June 1941: von Ribbentrop announces to the German and foreign press that Germany has invaded the Soviet Union.

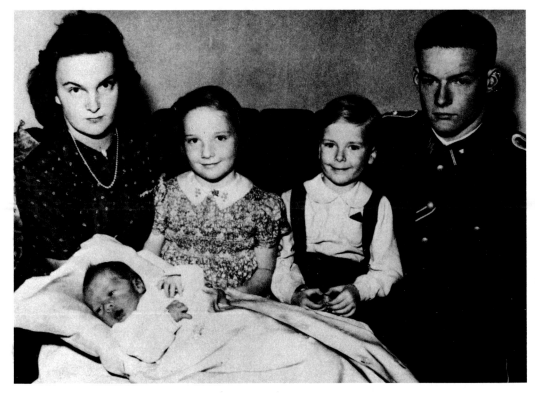

Left to right: Bettina and baby Barthold, Ursula, Adolf and Rudolf (probably early January 1942).

Rudolf, Lt SS Leibstandarte, with Knight's Cross and First Class Iron Cross, around 1942.

The War Crimes Trials in Nuremberg in 1945.

Defendant at the War Crimes Trials, von Ribbentrop takes time out from his writing in his cell at the city gaol in Nuremberg, 26 November 1945.

Von Ribbentrop's body photographed at Nuremberg, 16 October 1946.

The Munich-Solln brook where the war criminal's ashes were scattered.

and *his* Germany did! What had he said to Dahlerus? 'My people love me. When they have no butter, I'll eat no butter. They will follow me. I can outlast the others by one year, no matter how tough.' He would win. It was so written.

And the von Ribbentrops? They had now drifted so very far and they had changed so completely from the people they were only a short seven years before. They had tied their lives to this man, Adolf Hitler. There was no way out and no way back, and why would they have wanted a way out or back? They were now idealists, freed from catering to the cheap, material world. They had become one of the most powerful couples in one of the most powerful countries in the world. Joachim and Annelies, who had once longed to be invited to Berlin's 'better' homes, now commanded the presence of kings and presidents, prime ministers and captains of industry. The man who had trusted them and through whose genius they had come to this high station now wanted to make war against Poland. Surely he was right. Surely England would not interfere. Hitler was always right. The von Ribbentrops were willing to make sacrifices if need be. They, who loved their children, were willing to encourage their eldest son, their first-born Rudolf, to join the elite fighting Waffen SS as a private soldier. He was bound to be in combat soon.

Whatever had happened to Berlin's worldly, wealthy, young von Ribbentrops, who had loved being invited to *soigné* little dinners by Freddy and Lali Horstmann? Dahlem was only a short car ride from the Chancellery. To the von Ribbentrops it had become a thousand-mile journey.

On 1 September 1939 Adolf Hitler spoke to the Reichstag. The gist of what he said was contained in one sentence, which incorporates all his subversion of morality. He, the aggressor, said, 'Since 5.45 we have been returning their fire.' The *Völkischer Beobachter*, the party paper, headlined, 'The Führer Declares the Fight for the Right and Security of the Reich'.

On 2 September Sir Nevile Henderson was instructed by Lord Halifax to request 'that the United States Chargé d'Affaires [George Messersmith, Consul General in Berlin] be good enough to take charge of British interests in the case of war'.[106] All ciphers and confidential documents were burned and the Embassy staff left their normal residences and moved into the Adlon Hotel next to the Embassy. Now, in Sir Nevile's calm words, came a diplomat's equivalent of shipwreck:

> In the early hours (4 a.m.) of September 3rd I was accordingly instructed by His Majesty's Government to arrange for a meeting with the Minister for Foreign Affairs at 9 a.m. There was some difficulty in establishing contact with the Ministry at that hour, but I was finally informed

that Dr Schmidt was authorised by the Minister to accept on His Excellency's behalf any communication which I might make to him. I accordingly handed to Dr Schmidt, at 9 a.m. precisely, the final ultimatum from His Majesty's Government. ... Dr Schmidt received this communication and undertook to deliver it immediately to his chief.

The hour for war or peace was 11 a.m., as the ultimatum stated. It was close at hand.

Dr Paul Schmidt recounted in his memoirs:

On Sunday 3 September I awoke late because of the strenuous days I had behind me. I rushed into a taxi to make it to the Foreign Ministry and as we crossed Wilhelm Square I saw Sir Nevile Henderson walking into the historic entrance of Wilhelmstrasse 76. I took a side entrance, and promptly at 9 a.m. I stood waiting for Henderson in von Ribbentrop's office. Punctual to the minute, he was announced by one of the clerks. He entered, his face very grave, shook hands but refused a seat at a small table in a corner of the room. Instead he stood in a solemn, ceremonial manner in the centre of the room. In an emotional voice he said, 'I am sad that my government has instructed me to deliver an ultimatum to the German government. ...'

He then gave the terms: if there were no withdrawal by 11 a.m., a state of war would exist between Britain and Germany. Schmidt remembered, 'After these words he handed me the fateful document and said goodbye. "I am truly sorry", he said, "that I had to hand over this document to you of all people. You have always been so helpful."' Schmidt continued, 'I also expressed my regrets and directed some heartfelt words of farewell to the British Ambassador whom I had always appreciated, as I said previously.'

Schmidt then put the paper into his briefcase and walked from the Foreign Ministry to the adjoining Chancellery, where everyone was expecting him. There was much tension as he elbowed his way through the unusually heavy and visibly nervous throng of uniformed and civilian party leaders milling around in the Führer's anteroom. Several functionaries who had heard rumours shouted, 'What's the news?' But Schmidt shrugged his shoulders and said, 'No school today,' an allusion to the many informal briefings he had given in this anteroom in former days.

He stepped into Hitler's gloomy office. The Führer sat at his desk. Von Ribbentrop stood to his right near a window. Both were riveted by Schmidt's entry. They seemed tense.

Schmidt stopped some distance from Hitler's desk. He then began to translate the ultimatum quite slowly. When he had finished, there was dead silence, which seemed to Schmidt like the silence after the 'crash of the timpani' at the Godesberg Conference.

Hitler sat there, as if he had turned to stone, staring straight ahead. He did not lose his composure, as some said. He did not rave, as others would have it. He sat at his desk, completely immobile. After some time which seemed to me like an eternity, he turned to Ribbentrop, who stood frozen at the window.

'What now?' Hitler asked his Foreign Minister, with a furious look in his eyes, as if he wanted to make it clear that Ribbentrop had given him false information about the reaction of the English. Ribbentrop said in a soft voice, 'I assume that the French will give us an identical ultimatum during the next hour.'

Schmidt then withdrew. He told the surging anteroom crowd about the British ultimatum. There was deadly silence. Göring turned to Schmidt and said, 'If we lose this war, may heaven have mercy on us.' Goebbels stood in a corner looking like a drowned rat.

The French delivered their ultimatum an hour later.

BOOK III

ELEVEN

WAR, 1940

'Is He Trying to Bore Us into Peace?'

Admiral Canaris, head of the Abwehr, ran an excellent intelligence organization. There were German military intelligence agents in the most unexpected places and guises. Usually they were separatist patriots in foreign countries motivated politically, not financially. In the textbook definition, there are commercial, patriotic and coerced intelligence agents. The commercial agents are skilled but unmotivated, the coerced ones are unreliable, and the patriotic ones are amateurish but loyal. Canaris preferred patriotic agents. For instance, among his Egyptian agents were the Lieutenants Nasser and Sadat, both patriotic Egyptian anti-royalists and thereby anti-British. Canaris' organization also harboured the heart of the early-wartime anti-Hitler conspiracy and the military opposition to Hitler.

The brothers Kordt, Count Schwerin, Colonel von Kleist, State Secretary von Weizsäcker, Generals Beck and von Witzleben, Colonel Oster, all of them men who wanted to remove Hitler and avoid needless war, depended on the silver-haired Admiral Canaris to lead their effort. He, in turn, was co-operative but inactive. He was a cynic. He knew human nature and the vicious men around Himmler and the Führer. Many histories of the early days of the Second World War speak of the 1938 rebellion which was supposed to have taken place inside Germany in order to prevent war.

Joachim von Ribbentrop blamed the half-hearted German opposition groups for falsely stiffening the backs of the Chamberlain group and reinforcing the arrogance of the Poles. 'They quashed all our attempts to find a peaceful solution.'[1] It never occurred to von Ribbentrop that the world was finally ashamed of accommodating the men who had unleashed such horror in Germany, Austria and then Czechoslovakia. On 20 April he was promoted to SS Obergruppenführer, the third-highest SS rank. Perhaps this clouded his vision of that black-uniformed fraternity and its crimes – as if the outside world could endorse the subversion of individual rights, the suspension of due process, the mass arrest, torture and repression of racial minorities and the black plague of Gestapo and SS which swamped Germany and each place Germany now dominated.

Until 2 September 1939, this SS flood of horror had never followed combat troops, bombers and tanks like a pack of scavenging hyenas. Germany and Austria were wealthy, well-organized countries, and even small Czechoslovakia was wealthy, worldly and industrialized. SS and secret police functioned in these countries covertly. It was different in devastated Poland with its mud-caked villages, church-going peasants and clustered Jewish settlements, which became an SS machine-gun-controlled hell long after the Stukas had finished their bombing, the Panzers had done their mauling and the armoured infantry had mopped up and passed through. In the wake of the German army, men who wore the new Germany's eagle and swastika insignia on the right front of their uniforms, came those who wore this insignia on their left sleeves, the SS and its Einsatzgruppen. German historian Heinz Höhne, leading expert on the SS, has told the story of these ruthless groups.[2] Reinhard Heydrich, Gestapo and SD head, formed five of these Einsatzgruppen or 'attack groups'. During the Polish campaign, they were attached to each German field army. Every Einsatzgruppe contained four Einsatzkommandos of 100 to 150 men. Each small, vicious Kommando was assigned to an army corps. At first, trying to keep track of what the SS Kommandos were doing was like keeping an eye on a group of ten men in a crowded sports stadium. But soon they became extremely noticeable, carrying out their supposed mission of suppressing anti-Reich and anti-German elements. These Einsatzkommandos were often assisted by German-descended Poles taking revenge on Slavic Poles who had hounded them earlier. These 'racial German' self-defence organizations were soon shooting untold numbers of Poles and Jews. Oddly, one of their leaders was SS Colonel Ludolf von Alvensleben of the family which had once intrigued the young Ribbentrop brothers. On 20 April 1940 the first Jewish ghetto was formed in Lodz. These special SS men with the SD diamond patch on their sleeves began to commit such acts of brutality and bestiality that word soon reached the very top echelons of the army.

Then, to the deep shock of the SD and their chief Reinhard Heydrich, Colonel-General Johannes Blaskowitz, the German army commander in Poland, interfered. He would not permit the army to be complacent witnesses and passive collaborators in things which he considered abominable. He had many reports of shameful acts. He collected these and sent a written protest about the mass murders and other SD atrocities to the Chief of the Army Staff. General Blaskowitz asserted that it affected army morale to witness this SD swinishness. His memorandum was read by Adolf Hitler on 18 November 1939, and it made him apoplectic with anger. But Blaskowitz was undeterred. The field generals under his command continued to report SD atrocities all over Poland. Poles were shot arbitrarily. Jews were beaten, humiliated and killed, men, women, children and babies, sometimes in their synagogues. There was rape and looting.

Blaskowitz's next memorandum stated, 'the attitude of the troops towards SD and police alternates between abhorrence and hatred. Every soldier feels disgusted by these crimes committed in Poland by nationals of the Reich and representatives of our state.' Several generals at Hitler's headquarters joined Blaskowitz in this expression of revulsion. Army officers at Blaskowitz's headquarters would no longer shake hands with SS officers. Himmler finally had to order an investigation, but it was a sham. Blaskowitz was relieved of his command in 1940 by Adolf Hitler and never thereafter promoted. In a bitter stroke of irony, he was arrested by the Allies at the end of the war and charged with war crimes. It was too much for him to bear. He committed suicide in a Nuremberg prison in February 1948.

The era of Heinrich Himmler and the SS mass terror was at hand. They grew in power until they became an empire within the Hitler empire. The further Hitler's army ranged, the wider was the black shadow of the SS which followed them. Their Death's Head units dominated all prison systems from concentration camps to Gestapo jails. Their SD, the secret enforcement branch, also began to swallow up the old Gestapo and its functions. Beginning with Poland, the SD's Einsatzgruppen sent their bands of killers all over the East, including the Baltics and Russia. Another branch of the SD took over some espionage work. On 26 October 1939 they became part of each embassy and ministry, invading von Ribbentrop's field. In a rare conciliatory gesture, von Ribbentrop approved. After all, Himmler was powerful. The SD even asked for and got diplomatic status from the Foreign Ministry as so-called police attachés.[3] Many of these SD police attachés reported directly to Heydrich and Himmler, even to Hitler, which did not endear them to the Foreign Minister.

Eventually, this led to a showdown between the two former close friends, von Ribbentrop and Himmler. A *modus vivendi* was finally created: the SD would report directly to chiefs of mission such as ambassadors and chargés d'affaires and would avoid interfering in matters of policy.

Probably the 'purest' form of SS, or the least besmirched of the entire foul order, was the newly created Waffen SS. This organization was an expansion of Hitler's own bodyguard. It was formed into a separate army on 27 September 1939. The Waffen SS, all fiercely motivated Nazis, became a fanatical fighting army of armoured and infantry divisions. It also raised almost twenty units of volunteer non-German Nazis, mainly from the occupied countries. There were Norwegians, Belgians, Frenchmen, Spaniards, Russians, Dutchmen and even Arabs who wore Waffen SS uniforms. Many Waffen SS atrocities were to be committed against German army soldiers whom the SS deemed cowardly or shirkers. At the end of the western war, many hanged German soldiers were found by Allied troops. Usually they carried a notice pinned to the dead body such as 'This man was a coward! SS Division Das Reich.' In the last days before the total collapse, German soldiers were often more afraid of the SS than of Allied toops.

From the day Mars helped Hitler draw the sword, the need for diplomacy, statesmanship, deal-making, power-bloc-building and treaty-signing was waning fast. In war, generals do the talking and diplomatists the listening, but during the Polish campaign, at the very beginning of the long war to come, von Ribbentrop was still unaware that his days as Adolf Hitler's most precious minister and adviser would soon be over. Now the priorities shifted. Important were the air force (Göring), munitions (Todt), intelligence (Himmler), police (Himmler), party (Hess), propaganda (Goebbels) and above all Hitler's generals and admirals. Diplomacy could wait and, all too frequently, so would Joachim von Ribbentrop in the six years to come.

Most of Hitler's courtiers now moved into two special trains (Göring had his own). One was Hitler's usual private train, the *Adler* (Eagle). The other was called the *Heinrich* and was named after Heinrich Himmler. It included his own carriage, an antique. There was also von Ribbentrop's sleek, streamlined carriage and that of the durable State Secretary Lammers, who ran the Chancellery for his Führer. It must have peeved the acclaim-conscious RAM that the train had been named after Himmler. The few AA staff who accompanied von Ribbentrop were quartered in a standard civilian Mitropa sleeper attached to *Heinrich*. All meetings were held in an old, wooden dining carriage next to von Ribbentrop's vehicle.[4] Whenever the train stopped overnight on its way into Poland, von Ribbentrop spent hours in the office section of his carriage, speaking on the long-distance phone to the Wilhelmstrasse, screaming his annoyance and giving his instructions.

The train's batteries often ran down, and then candles were lighted. The 'cowardly pacifists' of the AA, as von Ribbentrop called them, thought it was like being in a combat dug-out. To the more courageous officials it looked like the chic, candle-lit Café Savarin in Berlin.

Von Ribbentrop ruled over the AA from his car, and poor Schmidt as a senior AA official had to carry out his master's instructions to phone Berlin and 'tell that horse's ass to ...' (translated into 'the Reich Minister would be grateful if ...'). At the slightest hold-up in the Wilhelmstrasse, the RAM let fly his disdain for these 'cowards', 'loafers' and 'ignoramuses' who 'did not seem to realize there was a war on'.

Each morning Schmidt, carrying a military map under his arm, had to climb across the rails and gravel of the open railway yard to the Führer's train, *Adler*, where he attended a briefing on the military situation. Schmidt then returned to *Heinrich* to give a briefing to the RAM and his AA people, using the same sweeping, strategic gestures which soon earned him the title 'Napoleon'. Reluctant AA officials were also instructed in the loading and firing of two small anti-aircraft guns at each end of *Heinrich*. Fortunately for them, their gunnery was never needed.

In Poland, Hitler's *Adler* was his temporary command post. Later, various Führer-headquarters were built, both in the west and in the east. They usually had Teuto-romantic war names like 'Wolfsschanze' (Wolf's Lair). The men around Hitler knew how to satisfy his Wagnerian taste for Germanic folk tales and myths. Other headquarters were dubbed 'Felsennest' (Rock's Nest) and 'Wolfsschlucht' (Wolf's Gorge).

There was much nighttime work on *Heinrich*. At 2 a.m. on 18 September von Ribbentrop at last went to sleep in his carriage, as did Schmidt and the other staff members in theirs. The RAM had spent hours on the phone, fighting to bar Propaganda Minister Goebbels from seizing control of the field of foreign propaganda and hunting for evidence of Goebbels' incursions into his own sacred territory. Then at 5 a.m. the tired Schmidt was awakened and told that the Russians had begun their entry into Poland towards the agreed line of demarcation between the two armies.[5] He, in turn, waited until 8 a.m. to tell von Ribbentrop, who by that time was shaving. Dressed in his underwear, the apoplectic Foreign Minister, his soap-flecked face purple, waved his razor at Schmidt and howled, 'Because you're too damn lazy to come to my bedroom, you've now interfered with history! You're too young to do that! What if there were clashes between their troops and ours?' Schmidt tried to calm him. After all, the line of demarcation was well known to both German and Russian troop commanders, but von Ribbentrop remained livid with rage – probably because he was sure the hated Goebbels had already broadcast the news of the Russian advance. That honour belonged to the press chief of his own Foreign Ministry.

On 19 September they left *Heinrich*, and temporary headquarters were established in a beachfront hotel of the Baltic Sea resort of Zoppot. They were still in Zoppot when Poland surrendered. Now that Poland was divided between Germany and Russia, Hitler turned his attention to the West. France and England were to be his next victims.

Von Ribbentrop returned to Berlin. On 26 September he flew to Moscow, this time to sign away the fate of Lithuania. It was the final section of the secret protocol to the Soviet treaty of August.

Ciano arrived in Berlin on 1 October representing the 'cowardly shirkers', Italy. At dinner in Dahlem von Ribbentrop, now very much the superior after the Soviet treaty and the Polish victory, patronized the

Ducellini, told him the tale about the 'strong faces' of Moscow and even compared the Kremlin military guards to the Duce's guards, causing the usually garrulous Ciano to sink into an icy silence. Relations between Berlin and Rome had cooled, and Ciano was obviously there to remove some of the chill. Mussolini was infuriated by the Soviet treaty, and much of the Italian public felt betrayed by it.

Back in Rome, Ciano made a speech which sent several stiletto thrusts towards Germany. On 3 January 1940 Mussolini wrote to Hitler:[6] 'You will not be surprised if I tell you that the German–Russian agreement has had painful repercussions in Spain. The earth which covers the dead – yours and ours and the Spanish – is still fresh.' He added that he realized the necessity for the pact, 'since Ribbentrop's efforts towards the non-intervention of the French and the British were not realized' – thereby having a dig at his least favourite German, the RAM. Then there followed the bitter complaints of a friend betrayed.

> But I, a born revolutionist, who had not modified his way of thinking, tell you that you cannot abandon the anti-Semitic and anti-Bolshevist banner which you have been flying for twenty years and for which so many of your comrades have died. You cannot renounce your gospel, in which the German people have blindly believed.

He suggested that Germany's territorial needs still lay in Russia and also advised reconciliation with the 'courageous Poles, liberated from the Jews'. He said he approved of Hitler's plan to concentrate these in a large ghetto in Lublin.

Almost in response, on 6 October Hitler made a lengthy speech at the Kroll Opera House in Berlin, supported by his usual audience of 'Sieg Heil!' yellers, offering European peace in the vaguest of terms. It was his usual system of following harsh measures with soft talk until the next aggressive act. It was roundly ignored by the Allies, who had finally taken the measure of his untrustworthiness. On 21 October, a statement released by von Ribbentrop declared that the Allies had ignored the Führer's offer and had thrown down the glove of challenge.[7]

Late in February 1940 there came one of those curious interludes which occur when well-meaning but unauthorized people attempt to play peacemaker. Sumner Welles, Under Secretary of State for Cordell Hull, the US Secretary of State, persuaded the President, who was a personal friend of his, to let him go to Europe on a fact-finding mission. Welles, a tall, calm diplomat from the patrician equestrian village of Bernardsville, New Jersey, soon had meetings with every available Italian and German senior official, including Hitler and Mussolini. His memoirs reflected shock that Mussolini, whom he knew, had deteriorated physically and looked bloated, clumsy and ten years older than fifty-six. He also chronicled his frustrating interviews with von Ribbentrop. The RAM was unsmiling and curt, and 'refused' to understand English, insisting on an interpreter. All the Nazi bigwigs, according to Schmidt, who interpreted these meetings, told Sumner Welles identically warlike and unconciliatory things and all in the same words. Welles returned to Washington, having learned only the truth: that Germany wanted to fight on and that Italy would probably join in.

Now it was von Ribbentrop's turn to go to Rome to patch up the spreading holes in the Hitler–Duce balloon and also to make sure that Mussolini's weakness-enforced neutrality did not grow more unyielding. To help von Ribbentrop regain Italian loyalty, the British had conveniently imposed a sea blockade of all coal shipped by Germany to Italy. It provoked great bitterness in coal-starved Italy. The Duce was in any case increasingly mortified by his own neutrality and hungry to prove himself an equal to the man in the field-grey uniform. Hitler had donned his new grey uniform jacket with a gold eagle and swastika on the left sleeve (in the SS manner) on the day Poland was invaded. 'I have', he declared in a speech, 'once more put on my favourite coat, that of the soldier, and I do not intend to take it off again until victory is won.' It sounded portentous. Actually, it was only a change in colour from his usual tan-brown Nazi Party jacket. Hitler liked symbolism.

On 10 March 1940 when in his turn von Ribbentrop arrived in Rome to woo Mussolini, his private train disgorged an entourage of thirty-five, including legal and economic experts, two hairdressers, a masseur, a doctor and a gymnastics coach. He carried an 'exceedingly long' letter[8] from Hitler which rebutted the Mussolini assertion that Germany had attacked Poland out of some sort of miscalculation about London and Paris. Instead, Hitler wrote, he wanted to involve himself in war with the West earlier rather than later, a point of view he had also presented to others. Finally, he wrote what amounted to 'Duce, all is forgiven. I understand why you could not go to war. But now it is time to share in the fight so that you can share in the spoils.' Von Ribbentrop was also sure to fan anti-British flames by expressing Hitler's outrage about the coal embargo. When the RAM was confronted once more with the Duce's earlier doubts about the Soviet treaty, he trotted out the argument he had devised for Hitler and all other senior Nazis except Rosenberg: the Soviets were no longer exporting world revolution. Stalin was just a Russian patriot, concerned with the fate of Soviet citizens. Mussolini was sceptical and ironic. Nevertheless, he had finally made up his mind. Yes, he would join Germany. But not yet! No matter how persistently von Ribbentrop tried to press him for a definite date, Mussolini remained vague. To avoid returning to Berlin empty-handed, von Ribbentrop quickly arranged a meeting between Führer and Duce at the Brenner Pass around 19 March. If this was acceptable, von Ribbentrop could cloak his inconclusive Rome efforts with a semblance of success.

It pleased Mussolini that, following the meetings with him, the German delegation was also invited to the Vatican. The conversation between Cardinal Pacelli, now Pope Pius XII, former Papal Nuncio in Berlin and well known there, seemed cordial enough. However, Cardinal Secretary Maglioni probably gave true expression to the Vatican's actual point of view. Maglioni minced no words; von Ribbentrop complained that 'if Cardinal Maglioni had continued to talk as he did, I would have stood up and left. I was ready to reach for my cap!' However, he did not reach for his cap. Instead, he probably discounted any feelings of comfort he might have received from the earlier cordial Pius XII.

Von Ribbentrop faked the results of his Mussolini meetings, but so did Mussolini. After the Germans had departed, he tried as well as he could to retreat from his promise to make war. The Italian newspapers were warned by his press aides to dampen the Duce's martial sounds and sabre-rattling. *Piano, piano!* Sumner Welles returned once more to Rome on 16 March and then reported to Washington that Mussolini seemed more at ease now that he had postponed an immediate entry into the war and 'had not determined to cross the Rubicon'.

Berlin phoned: 'Is 18 March for the Brenner Pass acceptable?' Mussolini, annoyed at being pushed, baulked but then agreed.[9] Ciano considered that by now Benito Mussolini was too cowed by Adolf Hitler to say no to him ever again. On the agreed day, the two dictators' trains stopped on neighbouring tracks in the deep snow of the mountain pass at a little station near the German–Italian border. Mussolini and Ciano welcomed Hitler and von Ribbentrop on the icy platform and then walked them to the Duce's well-heated salon carriage.

In an informal photograph of the conference, Hitler sits at a narrow table covered with a lace cloth in Mussolini's lavishly panelled custom-built carriage. At his side, the Duce's heavy-chinned, bulldog face is darkened with the shadow of the heavily bearded. Ciano, sitting across the table, is a handsome man with slick hair, who has been fattened and softened by a sybaritic life. Both of the Italians are wearing the grey uniform of the Fascist senior echelon, chests covered with decoration ribbons. They are both in black shirts and ties. Adolf Hitler, sitting between them, looks embarrassed and unwilling to be photographed. His uniform is his standard new field-grey jacket with 'gold' party badge, Iron Cross First Class and World War Combat Badge. The glittering Italians seem very much in command, but appearances in the photo are deceptive. Hitler immediately launched into an extended, unstoppable monologue to justify the Soviet pact ('Stalin had become a nationalist patriot'). If Italy wanted to be number one in the Mediterranean, she would *have* to fight England and France, whether she was ready or not. In any case, Germany would not postpone her timetable in the West. France and Britain would be attacked as planned.

Pushed hard, Mussolini finally agreed to a plan which would allot a limited number of Italian divisions to a joint attack on southern France. The entire Italian army would also enter the battle if the Germans gained early victories.

Even though Italy's senior army commanders turned it down, the plan would stand. Mussolini would become Hitler's fellow combatant, and von Ribbentrop and Ciano were to become reluctant harness-mates. Ciano hated von Ribbentrop, and his diaries fully reflect this: 'Everyone in Rome dislikes Ribbentrop.'[10]

Shortly before the Brenner meeting, SS chief Himmler met with the senior generals of Army Group A at their Koblenz headquarters, to answer their outraged complaints about the excesses of the SS in Poland and Danzig. In the case of Danzig, where Nazi Gauleiter Forster had complained that the army interfered with his brutal 'pacification' methods, army troops had been moved out so that the SS were no longer under their control. In Poland that did not apply: the army was still there and in great numbers, commanded by some very senior generals who could not be bullied. After his initial annoyance in response to Himmler's report, Hitler's final reaction to General Blaskowitz's complaint was simple:[11] how could an army command be entrusted to a man who was so childish? At Koblenz, the complaints about the SS Einsatzkommandos were brought to a painful head when Himmler told the generals, 'Everything I do is done with the full knowledge of the Führer.' The implications were inescapable. Like all German officers, the generals had sworn their personal allegiance to Adolf Hitler. If, as Himmler said, Hitler *knew* of these crimes, how could they continue to serve him? But then, having sworn their oath, how could they refuse? So they did nothing, but went away, grumbling. Besides, new glory was close at hand. They would soon shake the dust of Poland's villages from their riding boots and leave everything in the evil charge of the SS. All except General Blaskowitz. He never forgot the horror.

The curtain now rose for the next act.

The overture for the attack in the West passed quickly. While Poland was being crushed by German Panzers, infantry, bombers and Stukas, Britain did little and France, under its weak army commander, Maurice Gustave Gamelin, did even less. The attitude in Britain was curious. No one seemed to wonder why Britain had not launched bombing raids on the Ruhr industrial area nor even planned an attack on the ground, no matter how limited, while German forces were committed in faraway Poland. There was indeed a British bomber campaign, but they had dropped propaganda leaflets, not explosives. Chips Channon's 4 November entry expresses this inexplicable lack of aggressive spirit. He seemed to believe, along with others in Britain, that attacking was a

German prerogative. He wrote, 'There is no real war. Hitler is indeed shrewd. Is he trying to bore us into peace?'

One man was certainly not bored. Von Ribbentrop's enemy Churchill became First Lord of the Admiralty, and now planned the first imaginative moves, mainly an attack through Narvick in Norway on neutral Sweden to deny Germany Sweden's iron ore. The other Norwegian ports were to be mined to prevent German interference. It was all *very* Winston, very filled with drama and panache. Suddenly, he had regained centre stage. Unfortunately, some of these plans became known in Berlin. It was all the excuse Hitler needed. Pointing the finger at Churchill, a pre-emptive attack on Denmark and Norway was prepared and then executed by Hitler. Denmark was invaded – undefended – on 9 April, and this gave Hitler airfields to support German ships and troops in their invasion of Norway. To help little Norway's six divisions, British, French and Polish troops were landed on Norwegian soil, and German mountain troops and Marines were in some difficulty until the invasion of the Netherlands and France forced the withdrawal of Allied units for use on that front. Norway surrendered on 9 June. A Norwegian called Quisling, a Nazi leader whose name became synonymous with treason, was soon superseded as Norway's new chief by Hitler's own man, Terboven, the Gauleiter of Essen. King Haakon fled to England to fight on from there, as did many Norwegians. These, in outline, were the military events of early April 1940.

On the afternoon of 9 May, von Ribbentrop called together the heads of the Foreign Ministry's Press, Broadcast and Interpreter Sections and informed them quite matter-of-factly that the attack on the West 'between the Swiss frontier and the North Sea' would take place the following morning, 10 May. He told them just as calmly that the Führer had stated that anyone who caused word to leak out would be shot.[12] 'I promise you', said von Ribbentrop, 'that I would not be able to save you.' The meeting was in the opulent old Presidential Palace further down the Wilhelmstrasse which had been expensively renovated by Speer, re-mirrored, gilded and restored as the RAM's official residence, at the cost of millions of government Marks.

Very late that same night, German intelligence intercepted a message from the Dutch Ambassador to his government. It warned of the impending attack. No one knew where the leak had occurred, and von Ribbentrop was deeply worried lest someone in the AA was the culprit, but he found no one in his Ministry whom he could blame. There was even a special detective checking all the staff. Von Ribbentrop was safe.

On 10 May, he handed official notification of the invasion to the Dutch and Belgian ambassadors. Their countries were now being attacked. He boomed out this declaration to them and then to the press. The attack had been launched 'to forestall a wild act of desperation on the part of the Allies' by their 'new conscienceless leader ... Churchill!'

Winston Churchill was – at last – Britain's Prime Minister, Chamberlain having resigned after the Norway imbroglio. This was the man who ranked second only to Vansittart on the list of Joachim von Ribbentrop's leading British enemies. Churchill was now 'promoted' to the most hated. Immediately after the RAM had announced the German invasion of the Netherlands and Belgium, his mood was black. He had to listen to the radio while his bitter party foe, Joseph Goebbels, read out the very statements von Ribbentrop had just made, for the whole world to hear. How dare Goebbels pre-empt the right of Germany's Foreign Minister to announce this historic attack of 10 May 1940 by which Adolf Hitler would permanently avenge Germany's defeat and disgrace of 1918! Von Ribbentrop was furious. He screamed at Schmidt that the entire Broadcast Section of the Ministry was to be fired at once.[13]

Holland and Belgium were only the anterooms of the West. The inner sanctum was France and its army, as well as the Expeditionary Force of Great Britain on the continent of Europe. Perhaps now Chips Channon and his friends would no longer feel that Hitler was trying to bore them into making peace.

In his turn, buoyed into courage by Germany, Mussolini was finally ready to take the plunge. François-Poncet, now the French Ambassador to Rome, was asked to come to the Italian Foreign Ministry. Ciano greeted him quite formally and said, 'You can probably imagine why I asked you to call on me.' A sarcastic François-Poncet announced, 'Though I have never thought of myself as particularly intelligent, I am still able to grasp the fact that you wish to declare war on us.' Reports of this lofty reply set off some anti-Ciano glee in Berlin's Foreign Ministry.[14]

Heinrich the train was reactivated for the beginning of the western campaign.[15] It transported the same leaders, Himmler, von Ribbentrop and Lammers, and their staffs, housed in eight sleeping cars and salon carriages and two dining cars which were used as offices. The members of this triumvirate had friendly afternoon tea-meetings in the von Ribbentrop salon carriage. Tea-party chatter: Himmler was happy that the Queen of Holland had not surrendered. It would have been a nuisance if Hitler had been 'forced to be nice to the old lady'. Von Ribbentrop said the British 'would be more sensible once they had been chased back to their island'. He was upset because the Führer's new headquarters, 'Felsennest', was across the Rhine from *Heinrich*, and Göring's train, standing in a raid-proof tunnel in the Eifel mountains, was nearer to the Hitler HQ. Von Ribbentrop was also nervous that he had not been able to see his Führer often enough. He had only managed to visit him twice at 'Felsennest'.

Meantime, most old-time AA diplomats were cleared out of the

German embassies in Oslo and the Hague so that they would not embarrass the new military occupation authorities by their judicious presence.

Von Ribbentrop finally obtained clearance to join Hitler's field headquarters at the luxurious hotel Château d'Ardenne near Dinant. In some ways he would regret leaving *Heinrich*. The hotel had once been one of the continent's best, but it had fallen into disrepair. Nothing seemed to work. There was sporadic water and electricity and absolutely no service.

After the last Brenner meeting, von Ribbentrop had finally got rid of one of his *bêtes noires*, the obstreperous Italian Ambassador to Germany, Attolico, who had tried so often to preserve the peace. Attolico was transferred to the Vatican, and Dino Alfieri, an old Fascist and a close friend of Ciano, took his place.

The Germans sliced towards Paris. The French government ran away and settled temporarily in Bordeaux, and on 17 June Marshal Pétain asked the Spanish Ambassador to France, Felix de Lequerica, to mediate a request for a truce. Hitler, accompanied by von Ribbentrop, immediately flew to Munich on the 18th to meet with Mussolini, their new fellow warrior, at the Führerbau, where Chamberlain, Daladier and the two dictators had negotiated the Sudetenland handover in 1938. Schmidt translated into Italian for a surprisingly pacific Hitler, who claimed that he wanted to offer France very light armistice terms. Mussolini, suddenly ferocious, insisted on the surrender of the French fleet, but Hitler rejected this 'energetically'. 'If you make that demand, the entire French fleet will defect to the British!' Hitler also refused when Mussolini asked for a joint German–Italian negotiating team to deal with the French. Later he said to von Ribbentrop, 'Why should I burden our negotiations with Franco-Italian animosities?'[16]

The Führer was clearly in the midst of one of his post-orgiastic remissions. His 'gentle' mood extended in many directions. He had interfered directly with the High Command and had ordered the troops to hold up the attack on Dunkirk. Now he said, 'Why destroy the British Empire? It still represents a great force for world order!' And he was almost calm about the Jews! During the discussion of France's colonies and their future, he asked Mussolini, 'Why not begin an Israelitic [sic] state in Madagascar?'

On von Ribbentrop's instructions, this Madagascar idea was later promoted and pursued at length by some senior officials of the AA. Originally, it was conceived by the eccentric German orientalist, Paul de Lagarde, at the University of Göttingen. He was a pupil of one of the Grimm brothers. His convoluted racial theories were later adopted in part by Alfred Rosenberg and also became a small part of the entire Nazi credo.

His original plan to create a Jewish ghetto island-nation on French colonial Madagascar off the coast of East Africa, a plan which was being investigated by the Nazis, eventually foundered because of the Royal Navy's blockade, the Vichy government's reluctance and the difficulties experienced by the German army in Russia. Later SS Specialist Colonel Adolf Eichmann was instructed after the fatal meeting in 1942, known as the Wannsee Conference, to lead the Jews to a more final form of disposition.

Despite his bluster, Mussolini had come to Munich with empty hands. While the Germans occupied Paris on 14 June, the Duce instructed Marshal Badoglio to launch an attack on 18 June on the South of France. It was a disaster. His troops, commanded by the Italian Crown Prince Umberto, got stuck in the mountains and stopped at the small Riviera frontier town of Menton. Mussolini was not in a position to demand much at Munich, although he wanted Nice, Corsica and Tunisia. The performance of his troops had been abysmal.[17]

Taking his lead from the Führer, von Ribbentrop's bearing as a victor was also moderate, temperate, even peace-seeking. According to Ciano's memoirs, when he asked von Ribbentrop if there would now be a continuation in the war, the RAM immediately replied, 'Peace.'[18]

On Thursday, 13 June, two French officers and a trumpeter had met a German delegation at Sarcelles, a few miles north of Paris, to negotiate a truce for Paris, which had been declared an 'open city'. The French government had now moved from Bordeaux to Vichy, the old spa. On 10 July, by a vote of 569 to 80, they gave ruling power to old Marshal Pétain. It was only tenuous and involved about 40 per cent of France. It was to be called the Vichy government and it depended completely on the Germans. The fall of Paris which followed began one of the strangest chapters in von Ribbentrop's career. Although he was very much in evidence at the signing of the armistice on 22 June in Compiègne, he never set foot in Paris during the entire German occupation of France.[19] Visiting a conquered Paris should have been his second greatest personal social triumph. (The first would have been to go to a conquered London.) How much it would have meant to Annelies and Joachim von Ribbentrop to appear in Paris, as victors. Yet, for unknown reasons, he was one of the few top Nazis to stay away from the occupied city.

The overjoyed Göring made innumerable art-hunting trips to the Luftwaffe's Parisian headquarters in the Rothschild house on Avenue Marigny or to the Palais Luxembourg, where he kept a suite. But von Ribbentrop stayed away.

Perhaps it was Adolf Hitler's own unexplained reluctance to be in Paris which influenced von Ribbentrop.

Hitler visited once, on 23 June, the morning after the signing of the armistice at Compiègne. He was driven on a dawn tour of the main tourist attractions. His caravan of open Mercedes cars carrying his military aides, and also architect Speer and 'court' sculptor Arno Breker, rushed around an empty, early-morning Paris. When they reached the Opéra, Hitler told everyone he had studied the building's plans as a young man and admired it extravagantly. 'Glouglou', the Opéra's caretaker, switched on the stage lights for the Germans but turned down a tip, showing more dignity than most Parisians. By noontime, Adolf Hitler was back in his field headquarters at Bruly de Peche in Belgium.

Few *citoyens* had followed Charles de Gaulle into exile. A handful took a more lethal escape like the Mayor of Clichy, Maurice Naile, and the head of the American Hospital, Count de Martel, who both committed suicide.

The apex of von Ribbentrop's 1940 must have been to witness the Armistice with France. The ceremony took place in a clearing in the woods of Compiègne, using '2419–D', the very salon carriage of Marshal Foch, in which Germany had once hurriedly signed the surrender papers of 1918.

Hitler, Göring, Hess and von Ribbentrop sat like ramrods in the crowded carriage. The photograph has often been reproduced. The actual signing was done by the moustached General Keitel and the bitter-faced French General Huntziger. Part of the truce agreement committed France to hand over its many German exiles, a stroke of the pen which doomed thousands of German Jewish refugees who had escaped to the safety of France.

Von Ribbentrop's new Paris representative, Otto Abetz, stood outside in the clearing in front of the railway carriage with a small group of friends he had brought from Paris following an 'Armistice' luncheon at the barely reopened German Embassy on the rue de Lille. Abetz told his guests that he had already met with fifty French politicians, forty-nine of whom had asked him for extra petrol or coupons or special permits. One asked him about the fate of France.[20]

If Abetz was swamped with favour-seekers, how the Parisians would have fed the von Ribbentrops' self-esteem. They would have been the toast of *le tout Paris*. If one reads the names of those who followed Marshal Pétain's request to collaborate with the new masters, it is difficult to understand how so many can claim to have offered 'resistance'. Perhaps it is human nature to carry on living as normally as possible, even after 'L'affreuse chose c'est réalisée,' as the Paris Police Prefect put it in his diary.

The first German commander, General von Studnitz, began by giving a reception at the Hôtel Crillon for the dignitaries of the city. Next came a victory parade on the Champs Elysées which was less than formal, an entertainment rather than a drama. Later, standing in front of the American Embassy on Place de la Concorde, Robert Murphy, the deputy to anti-German US Ambassador Bill Bullitt, watched as motorized German army columns passed by. One stopped, and a young German lieutenant walked over and asked Murphy for a good hotel. Murphy suggested several, as if the German officer were a tourist. Shortly thereafter, Murphy was sent to the Crillon to 'see what was happening'. As a neutral diplomat, he was welcomed by General von Studnitz. The German army made a big show of courtesy and manners.

Many Parisians who had fled from the city before the truce now returned, but the international set had left. The Windsors hurried from their house on Boulevard Suchet. The Aga Khan, James Joyce, Daisy Fellowes, Peggy Guggenheim, the Princess de Polignac, Gertrude Stein and her friend René Clair, Louis Jouvet, Jean Renoir, André Maurois, Fernand Léger, Elsa Maxwell, Sir Charles and Lady Mendl, Nabokov, Chagall, Malraux, Matisse, Gide, had all left for the Unoccupied Zone or for other countries.

But Paris was by no means emptied of the famed, the mighty, the notorious. De Gaulle was broadcasting from London, but his appeals did not stop Sacha Guitry or dancer Serge Lifar from being acclaimed by the Germans. Lifar performed for Hitler, Goebbels and Göring during three trips to Germany. *Couturière* Coco Chanel was having an affair with a very senior Nazi (probably Walter Schellenberg, the Gestapo–SD espionage head). She 'holed up', as historian David Pryce-Jones reports it, at the Ritz with her paramour and only reappeared occasionally at parties to spew anti-Semitic tirades.[21]

The Hotel Majestic (later Eisenhower's Allied Supreme Headquarters, SHAEF) became German army headquarters; 72 Avenue Foch was turned into Gestapo and SD offices; Maxim's was run by the management of Berlin's Restaurant Horcher. Much seemed to be functioning as usual in non-Jewish Paris. Porfirio Rubirosa, the Santo Domingan playboy–diplomat later married to Doris Duke and to Barbara Hutton, was giving all-night parties to the music of Django Reinhardt's jazz and selling visas to Santo Domingo for large sums of money to wealthy refugees who needed to escape from the Nazis. And the SD chief arrived, an SS general called Helmut Knochen.

Otto Abetz, thirty-seven, who was von Ribbentrop's careful choice for ambassador to occupied France, was a believer in Franco-German amity. A Francophile since he was a very young man, he had taught art, knew France well and spoke excellent French. He was also married to a French-woman called Suzanne de Bruyker. Von Ribbentrop had recruited Abetz into the Büro before the war and had sent him to Paris, attached to the Embassy. The French expelled him in 1939 with vague accusations of espionage, which brought a storm of unpleasant newspaper publicity. His diplomatic status had saved him from jail. Now, back in Paris as ambassador, Abetz understood he was to watch over von Ribbentrop's interests, although running occupied France was actually the business of the military and of the many French collaborators.

The SD had their own harsh job: the Nazi-style boundaries of everyday life, the racial laws, the political consensus. Abetz's function eventually evolved into acting as the catalyst for society, the arts, industry, education and, above all, propaganda. He assembled a team of journalists and academics. In the former German Embassy, where he entertained so often and in such regal style, he soon became known as King Otto I.

Otto Abetz was one of the few German functionaries who admired and respected von Ribbentrop. He blamed most of the Foreign Minister's failings on the immense pressures and endless tasks which were part of the 1936–43 period. By the summer of 1942, von Ribbentrop told Abetz that he preferred his own separate field headquarters, because being near Hitler was 'too strenuous and abrasive'.[22]

Abetz's memoirs threw little light on the unexplained reason for von Ribbentrop's absence from Paris. He seemed just as puzzled.

The occupation of France, and of Paris, its convoluted life as a hunting ground for the individual conceits and vanities of various Nazi leaders and French opportunists was a labyrinth. Typical was Göring's thievery of the art assembled in the Jeu de Paume, much of it stolen from Jews and Gaullists. In Göring's view, 'They are a defeated nation! Let Herr Abetz worry about their sensibilities.'

Alfred Rosenberg, licensed by Adolf Hitler to do so, conducted his own hunt for art. Rosenberg's inventory was eventually meant to be used as a bargaining tool with the French. By 1944 21,900 pieces of art had been 'curated' by Rosenberg's staff.[23]

In 1940, the occupation was still in its infancy. Much horror, debauch and degradation, some of it self-inflicted, were yet to come. In 1940, there remained a semblance of German 'correctness' and good manners, while the true evils of collaboration were not yet apparent. The line between unwilling acceptance and enthusiastic and self-promoting co-operation with the Germans had not yet been crossed. The mass deportation of Jews, the murder of hostages, the recruiting of French volunteers for the SS and all the other French debasements were still to come. Unfortunately for those who wanted to think of France as a reluctant victim, these acts would be part of an entire new 'nationalist' (read Fascist) direction of the government. It included bitter hatred of Britain, disdain for de Gaulle and his followers, and a frantic search for union-cum-equality with Hitler's plenipotentiaries north of the demarcation line in Occupied France. There were acts of compassion and decency in Vichy France, but they were comparatively few.

While Abetz in Paris tried to maintain his chief's interests among the other paladins of Wehrmacht, party, SS, Luftwaffe and Propaganda, von

Ribbentrop became part of one of the most bizarre schemes of the war: to persuade the Duke of Windsor and his Duchess to loan their presence, if not their support, to the German cause. It is even possible that the aim was to place the former Edward VIII once more on his throne, after Britain had been invaded and defeated. But any exploitation of the Windsors, no matter how passively, was the sort of laughable plan the Berliners called a *Schnapfs Idee* (a notion someone found at the bottom of a glass of brandy).

Having left Paris to avoid the Germans, and unwilling to deal with the vagaries of 'unoccupied' France under Pétain and Laval, the Windsors arrived in neutral Spain, on Sunday, 23 June. It was the Duke's forty-sixth birthday.[24]

A portrait of Franco Spain can be given only in broad outline. General Franco seemed almost neutral, neither pro-Axis nor pro-Allies. He was careful and judicious. The second most powerful man in Spain, Interior Minister and Franco in-law Serrano Suner, was pro-Axis, but Spain's Foreign Minister, Colonel Juan Beigbeder, was in sympathy with the Allies. Representing the German side in the seething, spy-ridden, rumour-swilling Spanish capital was the Ambassador, Eberhard von Stohrer, lukewarm towards the Nazis, disliked by von Ribbentrop, despised by Hitler. Von Stohrer's beautiful, unfaithful wife, Marie Ursula, had great influence with certain gentlemen of Spanish society. On the Allied side was the new British Ambassador, former Chamberlain colleague and Foreign Secretary Sir Samuel Hoare, a man who seemed, on the surface, to be so stuffy that he was described as 'descended from a long line of maiden aunts'. He was, however, an accomplished politician and diplomat. After presenting his credentials to Franco, he wrote about the little Caudillo, 'There was obviously more in him than met the eye, or how else could this young officer of Jewish origin, little influence and unimpressive personality have risen to the highest post in the state?'[25]

Spain, an emotional country, was waiting to see some sign of the future, although the Germans had squashed France and the British had fled for their lives from Dunkirk. Spain could look back on hundreds of years of history to find abundant evidence of British resilience, but unless Churchill could convince Franco that Britain still had the will to fight, Spain might sooner or later have to ally herself with the Axis.

Hoare's brief was brutally simple: convince the Spaniards that Britain will fight and fight and fight!

The Duke's arrival could have been either godsend or disaster, depending on the ex-King's frame of mind and his devotion to his country. The Duke had been harshly treated by his brother, King George VI. The Duke also wanted a decent war job, and he wanted the royal family to accept his American Duchess as a member of the House of Windsor. How would he behave?

Hoare need not have worried. The Duke, who was very popular in Spain (he was related to the House of Bourbon through his great-grandmother, Queen Victoria), played his role to perfection. At a vast Embassy party on Saturday, 29 June for 1,000 prominent Spaniards and members of the Diplomatic Corps, the Duke exuded confidence and spread reassurance about the future of Great Britain. No matter how deep the divisions between himself and Buckingham Palace, his duty was clear and his loyalties were unshaken. Any doubts were carefully tucked away behind his suntanned, smiling face and well-tailored front.

However, Madrid was Madrid, and Madrilenos gossiped. The Duke would grumble in private, and some of his old Spanish friends would tell. Among the leakers was his old friend Miguel Primo de Rivera, a Spanish government official. The Duke was sick of the close surveillance by British intelligence, and upset by his bad treatment and the snubbing of his wife. He was also irritated that his friend Winston Churchill had not found him important war work in Britain and had sloughed him off with the governorship of the Bahamas. Perhaps the Duke's private grumbling was justified, but nothing could lead him into public disloyalty.

Three days after the British Embassy party, German troops paid 'fraternal' visits to several Spanish border towns,[26] and Spanish Foreign Minister Beigbeder, still sympathetic to the Allied cause and, prodded by the British Ambassador, launched a firm protest to Berlin. The Germans withdrew their military version of innocent tourism, but the danger seemed too near. The Windsors prepared to go to Anglophile Portugal as quickly as possible, waiting only for the departure of the Duke of Kent from Lisbon. Kent, the Duke of Windsor's favourite and youngest brother, was in Portugal for a 'show the flag' visit, and Windsor would no doubt have loved to see him for the first time in three years, but his presence in Portugal could have interfered with Kent's mission. Again, the Duke of Windsor knew his duty.

On 2 July, Kent left Portugal, and that same day the Windsors set out for Estoril and the seaside home of their friend, the banker Dr Ricardo Espirito Santo, a great British sympathizer, well known in London intelligence circles as the 'Holy Ghost'. Portuguese dictator Salazar was also pronouncedly pro-British, so the Windsors could feel safe in Portugal. To help confuse the Germans, Beigbeder had circulated the false rumour that the Duke would later return to Spain to hunt. Now the Windsors could relax temporarily while the Duke continued his long-distance struggle with London for worthwhile war work.

The German Ambassador to Portugal, Baron Oswald von Hoynigen-Huene, a distinguished and worldly diplomat, sent a most unlikely telegram to von Ribbentrop. Perhaps Hoynigen-Huene wanted to ingratiate himself with the RAM. He reported that the Duke was visiting Portugal in order to postpone his undesirable appointment to the Bahamas, that war could have been avoided had he been King, that bombing would make Britain sue for peace and that the Duke was being kept from England because he was on the side of compromise.[27] Perhaps Hoynigen-Huene was indulging in the old diplomatic ploy of 'looking busy' by sending gossip-filled, confidential dispatches to his Ministry. This time, the idle gossip raised hell. The cable reached von Ribbentrop at Fuschl, and he swallowed it completely. The RAM immediately telegraphed von Stohrer in Madrid: 'Persuade Windsor to stay in Spain. Keep him there. Tell him of peace efforts. Ask his help. Tell him he is to be assassinated in the Bahamas.'

Von Stohrer saw Suner, the Interior Minister, who was willing to send Primo de Rivera to Portugal to invite Windsor back to hunt in Spain and to warn him of a Bahamas plot. Suner thought the whole thing a bit silly, but he was willing to help von Ribbentrop in this trivial matter, to defuse their many other tensions (not least those arising out of the question 'Why did Spain stay out of the war?')

Next to get involved was Walter Schellenberg, back from Paris and Chanel. Schellenberg, a former medical and law student, a *roué* and a talented intelligence operative, was a crudely handsome thirty-year-old, multi-lingual creature of Heydrich, whose Chief of Espionage and Foreign Counter-Intelligence he was. In his memoirs, he told how one day he heard the 'sonorous voice' of the RAM on the phone. 'My dear fellow, would you please come to see me right now? No, I cannot give you details over the phone!'[28]

Anxious to avoid jealousy, Schellenberg first cleared the visit with his own wolf-faced chief, Heydrich, who regarded von Ribbentrop as an idiot but told Schellenberg to find out the details. A grave-faced von Ribbentrop, after outlining all the usual theories why the Duke of Windsor had been expelled from British favour, said that the Duke was now virtually a prisoner of the British Secret Intelligence Service, anxious to be free. Von Ribbentrop then announced that Hitler thought the Duke could be offered a sum of fifty million Swiss Francs over twenty years to sustain his friendly relations with Germany. He could live in a neutral country like Switzerland.

British intelligence were to be prevented by force from interfering with this plan and, should the Duke seem to hesitate, he could be persuaded by 'helping things along', if necessary, with a degree of force.

Schellenberg enquired about the source which had reported the Duke's dissatisfaction. He was told 'the highest Spanish circles'. Von Ribbentrop then flatly announced: 'This order is now given to you by the Führer. You will carry out this mission.'

Minutes later, on an extension phone, Schellenberg heard the unmistakable gravel voice of Adolf Hitler tell von Ribbentrop, 'Schellenberg must be sure to gauge the Duchess's attitude. She has much influence on the Duke.'

Schellenberg cleared the mission with a sceptical Heydrich and immediately flew to Spain – even Heydrich could not abort a Führer-ordered mission. In Madrid, von Stohrer confirmed rumours about the Duke's unhappiness with the Bahamas job. He offered to introduce Schellenberg to Spanish society circles so that he could get his own reading of the story. But, most of all, von Stohrer poured out his complaints about the RAM. The Herr Minister hounded him each week to urge Spain to join the war, but the Spaniards were in deep economic trouble and unable to jump into the fray. Von Stohrer had been instructed to treat the Spaniards with 'sovereign hauteur' because of their lack of comradeship. So how could he now woo them?

However, all this was not Schellenberg's problem. He went to Lisbon, where he contacted an old associate, a professional espionage agent who was a Japanese. Schellenberg needed the details about the Duke's living quarters in the borrowed home of the 'Holy Ghost' in Estoril. The Japanese agent was brilliant and provided Schellenberg with all the details. In future, not a single unreported word would be spoken by the Duke. All the house servants were 'bought'.

Schellenberg also met with Hoynigen-Huene, the chic Ambassador whose chatty report had set the whole thing in motion and who now quaked at the thought of violence and a breach in Portuguese–German relations. Totally convinced that the entire mission was nonsense, Schellenberg, with the help of his Japanese agent, then faked a few, semi-scare tactics, knowing they would not work. A stone was thrown through the window. A letter 'from an admirer' was sent, warning the ducal pair of the 'murderous' British Secret Intelligence Service, of a bomb on the ship to the Bahamas, of an assassination attempt in Nassau. Of course, there were no results. The Duke was made of firmer stuff. Although he still argued by letter with Churchill and sent back two flying boats which had been dispatched to Estoril to return the Windsors to Britain, he finally decided to accept the Bahamas governorship. 'Poor Bahamas,' Lord Halifax wrote to his Ambassador, Sir Samuel Hoare, in Madrid.

The whole sorry affair was almost brought to a head when a telegram arrived for Schellenberg to 'prepare for abduction'. Fortunately, Schellenberg seemed to have been spotted by British intelligence. Guards were tripled, and his Portuguese contacts refused to help him any further. He reported the setbacks to Berlin and was instructed to 'use his own judgment'.[29]

He had wriggled off the hook, and he returned to Berlin to face von Ribbentrop. The RAM said, 'The Führer was disappointed but approved of your decision to let the matter drop.' Later, Heydrich shrugged and said that Schellenberg should never have accepted the mission. During his 1946 War Crimes Trial at Nuremberg, Schellenberg found out, so he claimed in his memoirs, that no one in British intelligence knew of his presence in Portugal.[30] This is most unlikely to have been true.

This ended a silly episode after so many cruel ones of 1940. The final telegram sent by Schellenberg from Portugal was 'Willy [code name for Windsor] not willing' – '*Willi will nicht.*'

On 19 July 1940 von Ribbentrop alerted everyone in the AA that Hitler would give a speech in the Reichstag which was to contain an 'offer of peace'.

It contained absolutely nothing but empty verbiage. 'I speak as a victor, not as a victim, and I appeal to reason. ....' No concrete proposal, not even the suggestion of a plan. (The speech was soon forgotten, but interpreter Schmidt introduced the new radio technique of voice-over translation while the actual speech could be heard in the background.)

The speech might have contained little of substance, but for Joachim von Ribbentrop and Annelies, it was nirvana. Hitler said, 'I cannot finish this day of honour without thanking the man who made my plans into realities through years of loyal, unceasing and self-sacrificing work. The name of Party Comrade von Ribbentrop is for all time linked with the political rise of the German nation.' Was this a 'well done' or the gold watch given before retirement?

The Hungarians and the Romanians were feuding again. So on 30 August von Ribbentrop and Ciano returned to Vienna for another session of 'judging' Hungarian–Romanian frontier demands. The real crux for Hitler and Mussolini was to make sure that Romania's oilfields were secure for aircraft fuel. 'All I need', Hitler had told von Ribbentrop and Ciano at the Berghof, 'is two weeks of good flying weather to wreck the British fleet and prepare the invasion.'

New borders were drawn in Vienna and, fatefully, Germany and Italy now 'guaranteed the integrity of the Romanian frontier'. This would not please the Russians, who had already occupied some small Romanian islands in the Danube delta. Germany also sent some 'training battalions' to Romania. Tension was rising between the unconventional partners of 23 August 1939.

Relations with Germany's more natural ally, Italy, were not much easier. But, visiting Rome on 19 and 20 September, von Ribbentrop demonstrated his famous persistence.[31] Franco's lack of enthusiasm did not prevent the RAM from assuring Mussolini that Spain would enter the war very soon. He obviously wished to ignore the only concrete signal to come out of the 'Willy' embarrassment: that Franco was not about to rush to the German–Italian side.

In the same euphoric flow of wishful thinking, von Ribbentrop assured the Duce that the invasion of Britain was imminent, and so easily performed that a single German division would cause British defences to collapse. Ciano reported this exact sentence; interpreter Schmidt noted that this was a typical von Ribbentrop statement and that he, Schmidt, had translated hundreds of these. 'I got the impression that most people no longer took him seriously.' Obviously, Mussoloni was one of these. He looked at von Ribbentrop 'amusedly and incredulously'.

Shortly to replace Beigbeder as Spanish Foreign Minister, Suner came to Berlin late in September to represent his side of the Spanish Question and to prove that von Ribbentrop had been wildly optimistic. From Hitler's and von Ribbentrop's point of view, the key to the Spanish Question was the infuriating lack of enthusiasm Franco showed for combat against England and her Empire. Schmidt reports the scene in von Ribbentrop's office, in front of the windows giving on to the old park behind the Minister's newly adopted Wilhelmstrasse palace. A map of France's colonies was set on an easel, and what von Ribbentrop then said to Suner boiled down to 'Do help yourself to some colonies!' Suner was not shy. He immediately chose Oran in Algeria, all of Morocco, sizeable stretches of desert and the French West African colony of Rio de Oro. Von Ribbentrop was 'selling merchandise he did not own'. All von Ribbentrop requested for Germany were some submarine-support bases in Spain, but Suner agreed to only a few of these.

There now followed a future millstone for the German neck. In Berlin on 27 September 1940, the seventh year of National Socialism, the seventeenth year of Fascism, the ninth month of the fifteenth year of Shyova (the reign of the Emperor Hirohito), Nazis signed the tripartite military agreement between Germany, Italy and Japan. Within fourteen months it would force Germany to declare war on the USA, which was probably not von Ribbentrop's foremost wish in December 1941. Nor did Germany expect to have to send Rommel to Africa. So much for the advantages of alliances with Japan and Italy.

Another Brenner Pass, two-train meeting took place on 4 October, as before jamming all railway traffic. In a three-hour monologue, Hitler told Mussolini about his plans for the British Empire. Where to begin? To attack them in the home islands or in the Mediterranean? Once more, Mussolini was a listener, not an answerer, but at least he was kept informed this time.[32]

A 4,000-mile trip now lay ahead for Hitler and von Ribbentrop during October. Its purposes: to persuade the reluctant Franco to join the Axis powers, to persuade the reluctant Pétain to join the fight against Britain, to persuade hungry Mussolini to cancel his probable plans to attack Greece.

The trip was a diplomatic shipwreck. On 23 October Hitler awaited Franco at the small railway station at Hendaye on the border between

Spain and France. Franco was an hour late, but the good weather kept Hitler cheerful which, in turn, cheered von Ribbentrop. When tiny, fat Franco at last appeared at 3 p.m., Hitler soon offered him Gibraltar and even the conquest of its fortress by German army specialists. He also offered some African colonies. The shrunken, sombre, monosyllabic Franco was not very interested. Speaking in a low voice, he catalogued all his own problems from food to fuel. He pointed out that he would have to defend an immense coastline, would lose the Canary Islands and could never, as a Spaniard, allow foreign troops to take the fortress of Gibraltar. North Africa would be immensely difficult to attack – as an old North Africa soldier, he knew this. Britain might fall, but she would surely move her government and her fleet to North America and fight on. He said all this (as Schmidt, who interpreted, described it) in a 'quiet, near-Islamic sing-song'.

An irritated Hitler stood up at one point and, in his usual fit of temper, said there was no point in continuing the conversation. Then he sat down again, but by then the meeting had virtually ended. With the dictators dead in the water, von Ribbentrop and Suner then tried to carry on some dialogue in the RAM's private train, but this time he did not offer Suner any French colonies. Instead, Spain could have them as soon as the French could be compensated with captured British colonies. It all fell on deaf Spanish ears. There followed a formal dinner in Hitler's special banqueting car, with its brilliant indirect lighting and luxurious appointments. At table, there was some more desultory talk. The two dictators' trains then left, and the next morning, Schmidt reported, an infuriated and intemperate von Ribbentrop stayed behind to break off what had remained of any working structure with Suner.

The angry RAM then rushed to Bordeaux and barely reached the Pétain meeting by plane. The weather was foul, and Hitler's own pilot, the bibulous Captain Bauer, a veteran of many stormy landings, only just managed to get von Ribbentrop and Schmidt safely on to the runway at Tours. From there, the RAM and Schmidt rushed to the Führer's train at Montoire.

Sitting opposite Hitler, the old Marshal was tall, austere and assured, while little Laval was unsure and fidgety. Hitler went into his monologue. France would have to reconquer her own colonies if they had switched to de Gaulle, and protect the ones which had not. 'We have already won this war,' he said. 'Either France or England will have to pay the costs. It is up to you to put the burden on England.'

Pétain quickly answered that France was not in a position to fight a war and sensed that Hitler was trying to enlist France to fight Britain. The Marshal now asked for a final, formal peace agreement with Germany, so that two million French prisoners of war could return to their families.[33] Laval then said France would help in every way except fighting.

Hitler did not answer Pétain's question, and Pétain would not speak about joining the war against Britain. Schmidt claims that on that same day, 24 October, while Pétain resisted Hitler's urgent suggestions, an emissary of the Marshal, a Professor Rougier, was with Churchill in London. Rougier assured Churchill that France would never willingly do anything dishonourable towards her former ally. While the two gloom-filled special trains rolled back to Berlin, the third purpose of the trip was being pre-empted. Word came of Mussolini's foolhardy attack on Greece. In revenge for the cavalier way his German allies usually dealt with him, the Duce had not forewarned the Führer. On to Italy! Perhaps they could still persuade the Duce to draw back. The Alps were already covered with snow – not a good sign for the attacking Italian troops in moun-tainous Greece on the other side of the Adriatic. In Florence, the *pomposo* strutting Duce told them that the 'victorious Italian army has crossed the Albanian border into Greece'. Nothing was to be done. Hitler heard the news with a grim smile. He was not delighted but he kept it to himself. He and von Ribbentrop left for Berlin, back across the snowy Alps with three diplomatic débâcles to show for their 4,000 miles. If Hitler was grim, von Ribbentrop was even more so. The process of diplomacy seemed to crumble.

Von Ribbentrop was not in a victorious mood when the most important meetings of 1940 began. On the morning of 12 November, a train bearing Molotov and his staff pulled into Anhalter station in Berlin. Schmidt, there to keep the record of the forthcoming conference, drew a stern glance from von Ribbentrop when he suggested that the Russian National Anthem, which was the old Communist 'Internationale' hymn, could be sung by many of the Berliners lining the square in front of the station. It was best forgotten how many Nazis had been Communists long before Hitler came to power.

Von Ribbentrop need not have worried. The only music was a martial tune while Molotov inspected the usual honour guard. The station was decked in hammer-and-sickle emblems and banners, and the ceremony was the usual routine, including the open-car caravan into the city, but there was no cheering because no one had 'instructed' the crowd to show enthusiasm. (The young Foreign Ministry wags nicknamed Wilhelm-strasse, often lined with organized cheerers, 'Via Spontana'.)

The first conference was in von Ribbentrop's new office in the redec-orated former Presidential Palace. The RAM was immensely forth-coming, but Molotov was reluctant, and his associate, the Kremlin's Germany specialist Dekanasov, was positively taciturn.

Von Ribbentrop opened with 'England is beaten. It is only a question of time until she admits it. The Axis powers are trying to end the war as quickly as possible.'

Next, he suggested friendship with Japan, which was now looking south, not west, and would spend decades colonizing the orient. Germany, too, was looking south to Africa, not east (towards Russia, as it said in *Mein Kampf*). Why would Russia not look south towards the open sea? 'Which open sea?' asked Molotov. 'The Gulf of Persia and the Red Sea,' said von Ribbentrop. Next, he brought up a new agreement about the Dardanelles and then an invitation for Soviet Russia to join the three-nation Axis as a fourth, perhaps to be signed in Moscow by the four countries. Finally came a suggestion that there could be rapprochement between Chiang Kai-shek and Japan, mediated by Germany.

Molotov replied to none of these schemes. However, he asked for the precise meaning of the 'greater East Asian Sphere', which Japan had recently proclaimed. 'It has nothing', von Ribbentrop hurriedly assured him, 'to do with the Russian sphere.' The gong then rang for a late breakfast.

End of round one.

The afternoon discussions, this time with Adolf Hitler only, were a crushing series of questions and answers, a fierce and cold debate about conflicts of interest openly displayed and resented by both disputants. From Finland to Romania, from the Baltic to the Dardanelles, the two men disagreed on every subject and their tone was frigid.

That night there was a banquet at the lavish old Russian Embassy on Unter den Linden. The meal was ended by air-raid sirens, and von Ribbentrop had to shepherd Molotov to his own shelter. There he assured the Russian Foreign Minister, 'England has already lost the war.' Molotov was unimpressed. 'If that is so, why are we sitting in this air-raid shelter?' he said.

Von Ribbentrop's greatest achievement, the Non-Aggression Pact with Soviet Russia of August 1939, began to unravel, and Adolf Hitler found himself once more on old, familiar ground: hating Bolshevists. No doubt he felt relieved, and no doubt von Ribbentrop felt devastated.

Besides Greece, where the Italians were now floundering, 1940 brought yet another Mussolini-engineered disaster. Aiming at one of Napoleon's geographic goals, and anxious to rival his Austro-Teutonic competitor, the Duce wanted Cairo, the Suez Canal and the Nile. Across the Mediterranean in Libya was Mussolini's army of 200,000 men commanded by one of Italy's best, the tall Marshal Rodolfo Graziani. 'Attack,' said the Duce. 'Bring me Cairo!' Graziani had attacked in September, pushing east towards Egypt and Britain's troops. He did not get very far. By October his troops were bogged down only fifty miles inside Egypt near the Mediterranean at Sidi Barrani, with hundreds of miles still to go to Cairo. There they said they would stay until 1941, 'waiting for spring'. Mussolini high-handedly turned down Hitler's offer of German troops.

Hitler, still furious about Mussolini's Greek adventure, took great offence. In November he told Keitel, 'No help in Greece. No help in

Libya.'[34] By Christmas, General O'Connor, the British commander in North Africa, had rammed the Italians back to Bardiyah inside the Libyan border. O'Connor was no great military star, but he was good enough to stop the Italians with ease. Later, General Erwin Rommel seized O'Connor's captured command vehicle (along with O'Connor). He named it *Mammut* (Mammoth) and used it all through the African campaign. O'Connor's truck became as famous as Rommel's captured British visor-goggles.

By December, the Italians were hanging on the ropes, and by 22 January they had lost Tobruk, fifty miles inside the Libyan border.

The best thing to happen to the von Ribbentrops during 1940 came in the very last week. Their youngest son, Barthold, named after an earlier Ribbentrop ancestor, was born on 26 December. His godfather was the Führer. In most other ways for the von Ribbentrops 1940 had been abrasive and filled with gloomy forebodings, though it is unlikely that Annelies and Joachim von Ribbentrop wanted to listen.

TWELVE

1941–1942

'Unsung Heroes Doing the Reich's Dirty Work'

For the protagonists, most views of international politics were myopically self-serving. Von Ribbentrop began the New Year disgusted with the Italians and furious with the 'ungrateful' French. His view of the Pétain meeting at Montoire differed substantially from that of interpreter Schmidt, who had portrayed 'its abrasiveness'. Von Ribbentrop's memoirs reported it as a peaceful German offer of help to Pétain, quite open and candid. In von Ribbentrop's hindsighted view of the meetings with Suner, the Spaniard had lusted after French colonies while he, von Ribbentrop, backed by the Führer, had protected the French against the avaricious Spanish Foreign Minister. How ungrateful the French had been! In his Nuremberg memoirs of 1945, he contrasted Germany's 'honourable' treatment of the defeated French leadership with the harsh treatment later given to the senior Nazis at Nuremberg. He also insisted that it was at his own suggestion that the body of Napoleon's beloved son, l'Aiglon, was transferred from Germany to be entombed next to l'Empreur in Les Invalides. It was meant to demonstrate Hitler's chivalry. But the arrival of the SD and the Gestapo at 72 Avenue Foch had soon removed any notions of chivalry.

To von Ribbentrop's annoyance, Marshal Pétain had cancelled his promised attendance at the ceremonies held at Napoleon's tomb in early December 1940 and Abetz was delighted that Hitler had allowed them to go ahead despite Pétain's intransigence. Obviously, the many French collaborators had clouded Abetz's vision.[1] There seemed to be no major signs of adversary behaviour.

The rattled von Ribbentrop then had to face the Duce's undesirable invasion of Greece and the harm it had done to Germany's friendship with Yugoslavia. Seeing an opportunity to woo the Yugoslavs, Roosevelt had even sent Colonel 'Wild Bill' Donovan to Belgrade in February 1941.[*]

---

[*]   A. Cave-Brown, *The Last Hero* (New York: Times Books, 1982).

When the angered Yugoslavs finally joined the Tripartite Pact on 24 March 1941 it looked, Hitler said, 'like a funeral'.[2]

More trouble: the Japanese allies, whom the RAM had enticed into the Tripartite Alliance, which seemed to keep Roosevelt from threatening Germany, were causing unnecessary tensions with the USA. When Matsuoka, the new Japanese Foreign Minister, had visited Berlin all had seemed fraternal, but now Japan's policies had become a disappointment to von Ribbentrop. The Japanese had occupied French Indo-China, thereby alarming the US and also raising some eyebrows in Berlin. After all, France and her colonies were *Germany's* beaten foes. Von Ribbentrop's memoirs even agreed with the American General Marshall's on the question of Japan, and quoted him in English: 'Japan acted unilaterally and not in accordance with a unified, strategic plan.' Both of Germany's partners to the pact seemed bent on undermining its function and purpose. Poor Joachim! The French did not want to accept decent treatment, the Italians went off on disastrous rampages in Greece and North Africa and the Japanese brought the Americans closer to war on the Allied side. Next, the senior generals of the army had raised hell about the brutality of the Polish SS actions, the Spaniards did not want to risk their necks and even the Duke of Windsor indirectly refused offers of money and friendship. Worst of all, the Russians were no longer the jovial friends of 1939.

The only one of his representatives von Ribbentrop could trust was Abetz in Paris. The RAM was fed up with the old aristocrats, but the bureaucrats in the Foreign Ministry were proving difficult to discard. He had prepared retirement certificates for 200 of them (including Kordt and von Weizsäcker), but the Führer had stopped him. Once again Adolf Hitler preferred dual teams.

By now, it must have occurred to von Ribbentrop that his diplomatic efforts were faltering, that the Führer would soon be ready to scrap his crowning achievement, the Moscow pact, and that the men of the army and of the party were now in power. The army conducted the war, the party ran the conquered territories. Where could diplomacy still play its part? He should have remembered 17 April 1940, when Stalin had bitterly complained to him directly because German troops had occupied Drohobycz, an oil region in Poland, in breach of the agreed demarcation line. But the breach had been committed on purpose. When a mortified von Ribbentrop complained to the Führer, Hitler shrugged. He was on the side of the military. 'Whenever diplomats make errors in wartime they always blame the soldiers!' Hitler said. Germany's allies now were fascinated by her military victories, not by her diplomatic ones. Even Britain, Germany's only remaining intact combative enemy, would no longer accept any diplomatic overtures, no matter how precarious her position. The two greatest powers, Russia and America, loomed as possible enemies. The Russians were increasingly aggressive, Adolf Hitler was hardening his position, and America was being inexorably drawn towards conflict by the deep friendship between Roosevelt and Churchill, and also by Japan's risky forays in the Pacific. Only the forceful and sizeable isolationist movement in America deterred Roosevelt from immediate naval support for the British Isles.

On the face of it, von Ribbentrop should have relished the patriotic glory of it all: most of western Europe and Scandinavia was in German hands. Britain was being subjected to increasing air attacks and was 'nearly beaten' with much of her equipment and some of her pride left on the bombed beach of Dunkirk. All of Czechoslovakia and half of Poland were in German hands, including Danzig and the Corridor, and they had been joined by Memel. For the time being, Russia was neutralized by a treaty. Tripartite ally Mussolini was on the march in Greece, the Balkans and North Africa. The German army remained intact and powerful. The Luftwaffe was pounding British coastal ports and airfields, still seeming to prepare an invasion, and the Americans were busy worrying about Japan. The new German order, National Socialism, was being installed in the conquered nations, and Germany's 'abused' minorities abroad had been reunited with their 'homeland'.

However, it is more probable that von Ribbentrop remained too much the businessman to swallow Goebbels' advertising slogans. By early 1941, he must have sensed that National Socialist Germany's high-water mark had been reached, and that his own days as a master diplomat were beginning to run out.

Hitler grew increasingly paranoid about the Russians. Those old Nazi comrades who had warned him about the alliance with the Soviet Union became more insistent. They blamed von Ribbentrop, the *nouveau* Nazi, for the dilemma. It still infuriated Hitler that he had been 'soft' and now Latvia, Estonia and Lithuania were part of the USSR, all because of the hastily approved secret protocols. He probably blamed von Ribbentrop for having pushed him into over-hasty approval of this giveaway. Forgotten was his own haste.

Molotov's November 1940 visit was meant to defuse these tensions, but it did exactly the opposite. Finland, recently a Soviet victim, had been added as another bone of Soviet–German contention. 'In spring 1941 Hitler became much more negative about Russian questions,'[3] said von Ribbentrop in his memoirs.

On 6 April, Joachim von Ribbentrop, who was attending conferences in Vienna, was ordered to join the Führer on the nearby Führer train *Adler*. That day Hitler told his pale-faced Foreign Minister that he had decided to invade Russia.[4] The shaken von Ribbentrop offered to make one final attempt to defuse matters in Moscow. He realized that everything he had worked for was collapsing, but Hitler, in a fit of temper, forbade him. 'Any such discussion will rob us of the element of surprise!' he yelled. 'One day the Occident will understand why I attacked the East!'

Hitler's reasoning was that the USA and Britain would soon combine to attack Germany with the Russians as their ally. Britain had already begun negotiations with Russia. (Sir Stafford Cripps had visited Moscow to negotiate a trade agreement.) So far as Adolf Hitler was concerned, the time for negotiating with Russia had passed.

Like a shipwrecked sailor trying to bail out a leaking lifeboat with his bare hands, von Ribbentrop watched control slipping away. The Führer had decided on war. But first some patchwork had to be done.

As expected, Mussolini's adventures had backfired. The Greek campaign was a disaster, and the Libyan attack had turned into a débâcle. Adolf Hitler, an angry, unwilling 'I-told-you-so!' Adolf Hitler, had to come to his flabby, black-shirted ally's help. The whole thing was, as usual, dressed up in heroic terms. A secret Hitler directive of 5 February announced:

Fighting shoulder to shoulder with our allies in the Mediterranean [German troops] must be conscious of their lofty military and political mission. They have been selected to lend valuable assistance in a psychological and military way to our allies who in every theatre of war are struggling with a numerically superior army and who are insufficiently equipped with modern weapons because of Italy's limited productive capacity.

To run the campaign in North Africa, von Brauchitsch chose a tough young 'Hitler' General, Erwin Rommel, who was put in command of the DAK (Deutsches Afrika Korps). Rommel, winner of the Pour le Mérite (Imperial Germany's highest military decoration) in the First World War, was Germany's modernist, a tank man, a Blitzkrieg expert. He had once been commander of Hitler's personal army guard battalion. Rommel was Hitler's sort of general: no title, no affectations, a tough, imaginative tactician and Panzer soldier. He was a self-made man without estates or noble ancestry, much like Richard Ribbentrop. On 14 February, the first German combat troops landed at Tripoli.[5]

The fighting was going well for Adolf Hitler's soldiers, sailors and pilots, but that left little room for Adolf Hitler's diplomats. Rommel had a direct line to the Führer in the person of Hitler's military aide, Colonel Rudolf Schmundt, who flew to Tripoli with the General and then rushed back to the Berghof to report that Rommel was the perfect man for the job. Hitler congratulated himself on his own brilliant judgment. 'Anything Rommel wanted, anything at all. . . .'

The historian David Irving reports Hitler's anger at Mussolini's arrogance and impotence. 'The lunacy of it all! On the one hand the Italians are screaming about their shortages of arms and equipment. On the other hand, they are infantile and find the use of German soldiers and equipment repugnant. Mussolini probably wants us to fight in Italian uniforms.'[6]

It was the soldiers' year. Their days would wane, but in 1941 the soldiers outweighed the diplomats by far.

Two months later, on Sunday 6 April 1941, Wehrmacht HQ announced: 'Because of the penetration of British amphibious troops from Greece to the North making connections with the Yugoslav army, German troops went on the counter-offensive this morning. The Greek and Serbian frontier was crossed at several points. The Luftwaffe attacked Fortress Belgrade, and Italian fighter units successfully attacked targets in Southern Yugoslavia.'[7]

But in the spring of 1941, Hitler's mind was elsewhere. His thoughts were all geared to the codenamed Barbarossa, the planned attack on the Soviet Union.

The one ally who could have helped to take the hard edge off the immensity of this adventure was Samurai Japan, which was feared by the Russians and still admired by Adolf Hitler. On 26 March 1941, many of the Reich's leaders stood at Anhalter station, waiting for their favourite Japanese diplomat, the tiny Yosuke Matsuoka, the Emperor's Foreign Minister. The Berlin crowds had seen him before, and once again they liked his melodic name, his minuscule figure and the fact that his warlike country was on Germany's side.

Following the perfect halt of the train at the red carpet, the Japanese Minister inspected the stiff SS guard of the Leibstandarte Adolf Hitler. Then, after the two national anthems had been played and speeches had been made, he stepped into the obligatory black 'Grosser' Mercedes open phaeton for the routine 'triumphant' drive to the Chancellery through cheering (they had been primed) crowds, past rising-sun and swastika banners. At his side in full field-grey diplomatic uniform was the Foreign Minister of the Greater German Reich, Joachim von Ribbentrop. Nothing had gone wrong. Last time a fat Berliner had yelled, 'Make sure the li'l feller don't slip under the wheels!' as they climbed into the car, and recently the special train had made a jerky stop and a certain foreign dignitary had cracked his head against the frame of the train window. But this time all went well, and Yosuke Matsuoka seemed pleased. Hundreds of photographs were taken. The cheering on the 'Via Spontana' was loud. Schmidt called these events 'Gilbert and Sullivan'. Even the 100-yard-long, dark-red marble floor of the gallery which led to the Führer's office could become slippery and hazardous, and those visitors in military cavalry boots often skidded.

Unfortunately, this visit coincided with the exact moment when word arrived for the Führer that the friendly Yugoslav government had been toppled, a great setback for Germany, since Prince Regent Paul and Prime Minister Zvetkovitch were Germanophiles. Hitler had another problem in the Balkans which was coming to a head. Having given him help in Africa, he now had to bail out Mussolini's stalled and faltering troops in Greece, after the Greeks and their British allies had mounted a forceful counter-offensive. On 6 April German troops crossed into both Yugoslavia and Greece.

While Hitler dealt with the (new) Yugoslavs ('Attack them!'), von Ribbentrop now told Matsuoka, Ambassador Ott (who now headed Germany's Tokyo Embassy), and Oshima, the Japanese Ambassador in Berlin, 'I have to confess that the relationship between the Soviets and us is at present correct, but not particularly friendly.' Obviously, the RAM wanted to prevent Japan from normalizing her relations with Russia. After all, Japan's ally, Germany, was having problems with the Soviets! Von Ribbentrop cited the 'betrayal' of Cripps' recent visit to Moscow and hinted broadly that if the Russians showed any sign of hostility they 'would be smashed'.[8] This sentence startled Matsuoka no end.

The next day it was Hitler's turn to preach his usual sermon: 'Britain is beaten. When will she show enough intelligence to admit it?' He then switched to the 'Look south' motif. Russia seeks southern expansion, as does Germany and Italy. Why not Japan? How about Singapore? Matsuoka spoke in slow but comprehensible English. The gist was, 'No promises. So sorry!' to the Führer's evident disappointment. Matsuoka explained that he had to overcome the resistance of 'those British-educated and American-educated Japanese intellectuals in Tokyo'.

Astonishingly, in several earlier meetings with von Ribbentrop, Matsuoka had warned that, if Japan attacked Britain by way of Singapore, America was bound to come into the war, and von Ribbentrop kept calming him and insisting that Germany 'had absolutely no interest in war with the United States'.[9]

Matsuoka then paid a short visit to Rome and returned once more to Berlin. In a final meeting with Hitler, the Führer asked the Japanese Foreign Minister to deliver an ominous message: 'When you return to Japan, you must *not* tell your emperor that conflict between Germany and the Soviet Union is impossible.'

To Hitler's and von Ribbentrop's dismay, on his way home to Japan, Matsuoka stopped in Moscow. There he concluded a mutual non-aggression pact with the Soviets – apparently another diplomatic crash-landing for the RAM's Axis policy. The Japanese end of the Axis was being steered independently. The origins of this independence lay in events which took place two years before.

In April 1939, on the Manchurian–Mongolian (Soviet) border, there had begun a series of military confrontations, the aggressive Japanese army commanders imagining the Soviet Russians to be the weaklings of Czarist days. To their shock the Russians administered the first of a series of beatings to Japanese troops on 12 May in Mongolia. The Japanese retreated with heavy casualties. On 2 July, a Japanese counter-attack by infantry and air under General Kantogun was again repelled with heavy Japanese losses. Against orders, Kantogun then launched a major attack, almost an offensive, on 23 July. On 20 August, the Russians under Zhukov nearly destroyed the Japanese Sixth Army.

The embarrassed Japanese failed to report their defeat to the Germans. It coloured all subsequent Japanese actions and probably explains their reluctance to attack Russia's eastern flank.

It also explains why Matsuoka stopped in Moscow to sign the Russian–Japanese neutrality pact of April 1941. Russian troops released by this pact made the difference at Stalingrad, Leningrad and Moscow, and the field commander named Zhukov put his Mongolian experience to full use all the way to Berlin.

A minor scene of interest was enacted in Moscow during Matsuoka's visit. It probably failed to reassure von Ribbentrop, although Joseph Stalin had obviously arranged it to calm Berlin. In an unusual gesture, Stalin came to the Moscow railway station to bid farewell to Matsuoka. There he turned to von der Schulenburg, the old German Ambassador, put his arm around his shoulder 'in a demonstrative manner' and said to him, 'We must stay friends. Now you must do everything to ensure that.' He then said to Colonel Krebs, an assistant military attaché, 'We shall stay friends with your country in any case.' Both of Stalin's sentences were reported in breathless detail to Berlin, but von Ribbentrop must have known better. Now Japan was lost to Germany as an ally for the great Russian attack his Führer was preparing. Another hedge to a great gamble was gone. Japan's Russian treaty had reduced Germany's chances. Even a supreme optimist could hardly call Japan's action a rousing endorsement of her Teutonic allies.

So far, most of Adolf Hitler's war plans were roughly on schedule. Britain's coastal area and airfields were being pounded by Göring's Luftwaffe, and London was being hit 'in reprisal for RAF raids on Germany's cities', reportedly with good results (although, inexplicably, the RAF was growing and so were German air losses). France was vaguely under control, although Pétain was obstreperous and Laval was a slippery customer. The European 'Jew-cleansing' measures had not yet succeeded entirely, but new initiatives were being planned. German troops were stabilizing the Balkans. In Hitler's view, Rommel was performing brilliantly in North Africa. Mussolini had turned out to be a bag of hot air and his troops a failure, but then the Führer had always suspected his black-shirted friend's conceited strutting. Japan? Well, that strange alliance was another one of von Ribbentrop's notions, but Hitler was certain he could handle Stalin without the help of the samurai. The invasion of Great Britain, codenamed Operation Sea Lion? Göring would have to do better at battering the British. He would have to soften them up a lot more. At sea, Germany's U-boats had excellent hunting while trying to quarantine Britain, but so far Britain seemed to survive. Admittedly, America was a threat, but Hitler understood that there was great anti-Roosevelt isolationist opposition to entering the war, although the Americans were 'loaning' old destroyers to Britain.

Then came trouble, but from a most unexpected source. On 11 May, Rudolf Hess was reported to have flown a fast and dangerous Messerschmitt 110 fighter plane in the direction of Britain on a private peace-making mission, leaving behind a letter for Hitler. People who knew him were stunned. Could Hess fly this dicey plane? Indeed he could. He was a trained and skilled pilot. Why did he fly to Britain? Whom did he try to contact in Britain? He was trying to reach the Duke of Hamilton, who had no idea why such an 'honour' was being bestowed on him. Some people suggest that Hess was trying to reach Sir Ian Hamilton, who had been to Germany with British veterans' groups before the war. Had Hess reached his destination? As yet, no one knew.

Walther Hewel described the scene at the Berghof, as Göring, who had raced to the Führer's side by special train and fast car, rushed in to meet Hitler, a 'white-faced' von Ribbentrop, Hewel and Martin Bormann, who was Hess's Chief of Staff.[10] Hitler then thrust Hess's letter under Göring's nose. It said in effect, 'Willing to risk my life to make peace ... and end bloodshed.' Hess had always been an intimate part of Hitler's personal and political life. They had been jailed together in the 1920s. Hess had even done the secretarial work on *Mein Kampf* and had become Hitler's deputy in the Nazi Party.

Von Ribbentrop must have had his own shocked thoughts, because Hess had provided him with his first office (the Büro Ribbentrop was technically part of Hess's organization) and Hess's flight to Britain demonstratively repudiated von Ribbentrop's 'Britain is the enemy' policy. Would Hess's arrival in Britain shatter the Tripartite Alliance? Mussolini would be delighted by Hitler's embarrassment and the Japanese had already proved their lack of trust in German policy. What about the minor players, the Hungarians, the Romanians? And how would it look in France, Holland, Belgium, Denmark and Norway? Worst of all, this would surely stiffen Churchill's resolve.

Hitler had Willy Messerschmitt brought to him. He yelled at the aircraft manufacturer, 'You've allowed him to practise at your airfield. How dare you?' Messerschmitt pointed out that Hess was an important man, and that he was not in a position to say no to him. 'But you knew Hess was insane!' yelled Hitler.

It turned out that Hess had practised with guidance systems and navigation. Hitler hoped Hess would crash – Schmidt heard him say so[11] – but Hess did not crash. He parachuted into Scotland not far from the

Duke of Hamilton's estate, was arrested and never made the contacts he was hoping for, not even with the Duke, who would not see him. The Goebbels machine immediately pumped out the 'explanation' that Hess was insane. Von Ribbentrop rushed to Rome to explain to the Duce that Hess was *non compos*.

These events began the drumroll which was the prelude to the clash of cymbals at the launch of Barbarossa, the campaign which led Hitler into the hell he deserved. More importantly, hundreds of thousands of German soldiers went to their frozen death or into years of hopeless misery as prisoners of war in Russia.

First came another meeting on the Brenner Pass, this time in beautiful early-June summer weather. Not a word was uttered to Mussolini about Hitler's impending plans for the attack on Russia. It was quite clear that he was deliberately deceiving the Duce. A few days later, Marshal Antonescu, the Romanian head of state, attended a ceremony in Munich. It was a mark of Hitler's respect and trust for the Romanian Marshal that he told him the entire timetable for Barbarossa. Antonescu was delighted, particularly after he had been promised Bessarabia, which von Ribbentrop had let slip to Russia in the 1939 negotiations.[12]

A final part of the rising drumroll was a bombastic ceremony. On a sunny day in the Palace of the Doges in Venice, Croatia joined the Tripartite Agreement during a lavishly choreographed event. It was breathtaking theatre in a superb setting, all arranged for the insignificant addition of a minor nation to a crumbling alliance.

Then finally, the crash of the cymbals.

As Schmidt, an eyewitness, described the scene:

> It is just before 4 a.m. the morning of Sunday, 22 June 1941, in the Office of the Foreign Minister. He is expecting the Soviet Ambassador, Dekanosov, who has been phoning the ministry since early Saturday. Dekanosov had an urgent message from Moscow. He had called every two hours but was told the Minister was away from the city. At 2 a.m. Sunday morning, von Ribbentrop finally responded to the calls. Dekanosov was told von Ribbentrop wished to meet with him at once. An appointment was made for 4 a.m.
>
> Von Ribbentrop is deeply nervous, walking up and down from one end of his large, lavish office to the other, like a caged animal, while saying over and over, 'The Führer is absolutely right. We must attack Russia, or else they will surely attack us!' Is he reassuring himself? Is he justifying the ruination of his own crowning diplomatic achievement? Now, he had to destroy it 'because that is the Führer's wish'.

Dekanosov was punctual to the minute. He had brought his own interpreter, and he began by asking some questions Moscow wanted clarified. But von Ribbentrop stopped him. 'That's not what I wish to discuss.' He continued, 'The hostile attitude of the Soviet government towards Germany and the severe threat we perceive towards the Reich by the massing of Russian troops on our eastern frontier have forced us to take military counter-measures.' There was no mention of war or a declaration of war. Interpreter Schmidt thought that perhaps it sounded too 'plutocratic' to declare war. Also, Hitler had given instructions to avoid the use of the word. Von Ribbentrop continued: 'Such military counter-measures have been taken since this morning.' The agreement with the new 'rebel' Yugoslav government was then trotted out as one of the many sins of the Soviets.

Von Ribbentrop said he regretted he could add nothing to these statements. He himself had come to the conclusion that 'my strenuous efforts for peace between our nations were futile'. *Finis!* The gates were open. The flood was released. Dekanosov quickly took hold of himself. He said he regretted 'exceedingly' the course events had taken. It was largely due to the 'oppositional views' of the German government. 'All that remains is for your Chief of Protocol to assist us with transportation for our Embassy staff.' He stood up and made a small bow, but did not extend his hand. Then he was gone.

Valentin Bershkov, who was Dekanosov's interpreter for this meeting, tells the story a bit differently. He believed that von Ribbentrop had taken a few drinks to give himself courage for the unpleasant meeting, because his face had red blotches and his hands shook. According to this version, Dekanosov listened to von Ribbentrop's announcement and then said that Germany was guilty of criminal aggression and one day would deeply regret its action. He then strode to the entrance of the office without a parting word. Von Ribbentrop then rushed after him and Bershkov, whispering urgently that he had tried to keep the Führer from making war on Russia. He had tried to dissuade Hitler from his madness ... but he had not wished to listen. 'Tell Moscow that I was against this attack.' These were the last words Bershkov said he heard from von Ribbentrop, because Dekanosov was already on his way down the stairs.

Ever since the end of the Second World War certain German military historians have advanced the revisionist theory that Hitler's attack on Soviet Russia was actually pre-emptive. They offer in evidence that Russian troops, tanks and aircraft were deployed for attack not for defence, and that Russia had multiplied her western military strength in the six months before Barbarossa. They also offer in evidence the clearing of Russian defensive minefields in the Polish buffer zone and the disarming of explosive-charged bridges. The preamble for the Russian plan to attack Germany is said to have begun in 1939 when the Russians under Marshal Zhukov had their victorious military forays against Japan. The November 1940 Molotov meetings in Berlin at which Russia insistently demanded control of Romania (for the oil Hitler needed) then caused Hitler to begin the plans for Barbarossa on 18 December 1940. Eleven days later Moscow learned of these plans and decided to strike first. Supposedly, Hitler's attack anticipated the Soviet by two weeks.[13]

The revisionists also insist that Germany was ill prepared to attack the Soviets since German war production had been scaled back after the Western victories and partly reconverted to peacetime manufacturing. German tanks (Mark I and II) were inferior to Russian T34s and Germany was short of shells and bullets.

It is possible that, following the contentious November 1940 Berlin meetings and the subsequent Barbarossa plan, the Russians decided hastily to forestall Hitler. However, every other indication leads one to conclude that Moscow believed that the August 1939 Non-Aggression Pact would hold. Hitler, when informed of Russian troop movements, once more used anything he could deem 'offensive' (in the pejorative not the military sense) to justify his own military acts. He had done so in Czechoslovakia, Poland, Denmark, Norway, Holland, Belgium and France. It seems unlikely that he would have changed his style in the case of Barbarossa.

Barbarossa was launched at 3 a.m. on the morning of the 22 June. Artillery prepared the way across the Njemen river, which was the border between East Prussia and the Soviet Union. German bombers began to pound the Russians at daylight. As soon as the fog lifted from the river valley, the brand new 19th Panzer Division (they were originally infantry) crossed over the bridge into the Soviet Union. The time was exactly 9 a.m. They were far from their home in Hanover. Hitler's life, and thereby the lives of those who orbited him, now shifted to his headquarters, the Wolfsschanze, the Wolf's Lair, near Rastenburg in East Prussia.[14] As commander-in-chief, he had the notion that he had to be near the troops, although this was a matter more of emotion than of geography. While East Prussia was somewhat nearer to the Soviet Union, the enormous and extended Russian front could have been co-ordinated from Berlin, which was in the eastern part of Germany.

Perhaps it was the Nibelungen atmosphere of East Prussia that Hitler relished. The Wolfsschanze was in one of the deepest, darkest, most oppressive forests in Germany, a gloomy evocation of the woods in the Grimm Brothers' fairy tales. The atmosphere was haunted, foreboding and cheerless. Barrack-like cement buildings, the insides shelled in plain wood trim, were made as habitable as possible, but electric lights burned even at midday. Eventually, windowless above-ground cement air-raid bunkers augmented this network of various headquarters, connected by cement passageways. The insides of all these thick-walled bunkers were damp and resounded to the constant whirring of air-circulation pumps. Those who worked in the Wolfsschanze were prone to lasting attacks of melancholy and depression, although there was a cinema where even taboo English and American films were shown, along with the usual stereotyped Goebbels-style newsreels. Of course, the Wolfsschanze also had the latest in communications equipment.

This is where Hitler now received his foreign guests and his own associates. Foreign guests were impressed, but they were there only occasionally. Von Ribbentrop and the others around Hitler who spent much time there grew depressed.

After a state visit to the Wolfsschanze by Mussolini on 27 August 1941 during which nothing was achieved except a flood of posed photographs and pompous communiqués, Schmidt reported a typical von Ribbentropian fight for the sake of his vanity.

A final communiqué for the Duce's visit was to be issued, which dealt with the 'heroic alliance' of these two Axis giants. A message which reached the departing Mussolini's southbound train said, 'Dispatch cancelled by order of the Reich Foreign Minister.' This sent Mussolini into a tantrum at von Ribbentrop's impertinence. He wanted the train stopped. He insisted on an immediate explanation. Then the original communiqué was reinstated. Why had the RAM objected to it? It ended with 'Also participating in the military and political discussions were Field Marshal Keitel and Reich Foreign Minister von Ribbentrop.' Joachim von Ribbentrop's efforts to remain in command of his precarious status during the time of the generals now found pathetic expression. Infuriated that he was named *after* Keitel, the RAM insisted that the communiqué be held up. The matter was quickly submitted to the judgment of the Führer, who raged at von Ribbentrop's vanity but gave in. When the RAM was told that Hitler had approved the change, he said airily, 'Oh, leave it as it is.' The part of the message Mussolini saw was an internal memorandum about holding up the communiqué until the order of precedence had been settled.

Von Ribbentrop's focus of attention should have been directed towards Martin Bormann, a squat, porcine man who was gaining increasing power as 'Head of Chancellery' for the Führer. Bormann, an early Nazi and party factotum, had burrowed his way from local power to Hess's office and then, after Hess's flight to Scotland, became Hitler's creature. He held the strings to confidential purses and knew many secrets. Eventually, he would be the driving force behind the pursuit of euthanasia, the anti-Church campaign and most anti-Semitic measures.

Earlier, Bormann had been helpful to von Ribbentrop in persuading Hitler to allow the removal of Gauleiter Bohle from the AA. Bohle was chief of the Auslandsorganisation, the Foreign Agency of the Nazi Party, and a constant irritant to von Ribbentrop. Bormann soon became everybody's distasteful key to the Führer's door.

The winds of war had blown away many of Joachim von Ribbentrop's favourite dreams. No longer could he forge alliances of powerful nations and bring diplomatic pressure to bear on those who would oppose Germany. No longer could he taste the triumph of successful diplomacy or feel pride when the old powers kowtowed to the new player on the diplomatic field. Now success was counted in men killed, prisoners taken, tanks destroyed, planes shot down and ships sunk. Maps were marked with the symbols of military units, with arrows of advance or retreat and not shaded into new colours by the horse-trading of diplomatic negotiators. He had built a large, worldwide organization to deal with Germany's diplomatic business, and he feared that it would now be dismantled by his warlord master. How could he make himself needed? What functions could the Foreign Ministry's staff of thousands now perform to please Adolf Hitler in war? Von Ribbentrop decided on an answer which would eventually be fatal for him. His commitment, probably made with the shielded eyes of the unquestioning disciple, was to order the Foreign Ministry to help with the so-called Final Solution. It was not a sudden walk into quicksand. The whole thing began much earlier. Reinhard Heydrich, the Gestapo and SD chief, 'received his orders' from Reich Marshal Göring to 'find a *Gesamtlösung* [total solution] for the question of European Jewry'.

Actually, according to historian David Irving, at 6.15 p.m. on 31 July 1941 Heydrich had drafted the entire order on a faked-up letterhead of Göring's and got the harried Marshal to sign it without much attention to detail because he was rushing to meet his wife at the station.

Eventually, on 29 November 1941, Heydrich wrote to Martin Luther, the von Ribbentrop import from Dahlem, now a senior official in the AA, requesting his help in this matter and enclosing a photocopy of the Göring 'order'.[15]

Von Ribbentrop's first personal contact with this cruelty came through a department of his Foreign Ministry called 'Deutschland', which dealt with the Nazi Party side of the AA. Von Ribbentrop had appointed Martin Luther, his Nazi Party 'expert', to take charge of Department D (for 'Deutschland') with the rank of deputy state secretary (von Weizsäcker was State Secretary).

Luther, the clever, loud-mouthed Berliner, was absolutely ruthless and, like a lot of old party hands, almost anti-SS. He had always been loyal to the SA, the Brown Shirts, and had never got over the shock when the SS executed Röhm. Luther knew his way around the circle of 'old fighters' close to the Führer. Most of them had once been SA stormtroopers, and they did not like Himmler or the SS.

The section of Department D which handled Jewish matters was DIII, and its head was a former lawyer named Rademacher. It was Rademacher who had once avidly promoted the Madagascar solution, until it dissipated in 1941. This was the first time that a branch of von Ribbentrop's Ministry had been directly connected with SS actions involving the Jews.

(Madagascar was meant only for 'Western' Jews. 'Eastern', that is Polish and Russian, Jews were to be handled differently.)

Luther's next contact was through the Einsatzkommandos in the Baltics, Romania and Russia. Here are excerpts from Einsatzkommando reports in the Archives of the AA (all September 1941): 'The finishing of 4,000 Jews in Jussy [Romania]'; 'Many snipers and functionaries, mainly Jews, were liquidated [Einsatzgruppe A, action near Riga, Latvia]'; 'In the environs of Riga 459 people were shot, among them were 237 mental patients from Riga and Migan. In all, in this territory there were 29,246 persons liquidated'; 'The Jewish persons liquidated by one Sonder-kommando increased to 75,000'; 'In the districts of Roskiskis, Sarzai, Perzai and Prienai, the figure of those executed rose to 85,000. These dis-tricts are now cleansed of Jews.'[16] All of these SS–SD reports were passed on to the Foreign Ministry's Department Deutschland, Division DIII.

Dr Georg Bruns, a lawyer for the AA, a nephew once removed of von Weizsäcker, reported in 1976 that Ribbentrop did not like to see the Einsatzgruppen reports passed through to the Foreign Ministry.[17] Was it that von Ribbentrop knew the horror and wanted to sweep it under the carpet? Was it that he himself was horrified? Was it that he did not want to be compromised? Was it all of these? However, it did him no good to try to dodge the issue. Heydrich would not permit it. After the first five Einsatzgruppen reports had been ignored by the AA, Heydrich sent a personal report (No. 6) dated 25 November 1941 on Einsatzgruppen activities and their situation in the USSR with a request for acknowledgment, and Dr Bruns, the legal expert, was forced to 'receive acknowledgment from the RAM'.

There followed other atrocious reports, 'the Liquidation [*Liquidirung*] of 3,000 Jews in Witebsk. More than 33,000 Jews executed [*hingerichtet*] in Kiev, 3,000 Jews shot in Shtomir, and east of the Dnieper River nearly 5,000 Jews shot'. (These are on file in the Archives of the AA.) One secret report (DII 211 g.Rs. 10.12.1941) says: 'All male Jews over 16 with the exception of physicians and the elders.' State Secretary von Weizsäcker (and it is assumed a sickened von Weizsäcker) saw report No. 6 before Luther had a chance to show it to von Ribbentrop. Von Weizsäcker's initials were on the document but he made no marginal comments on the report. Usually such communications are initialled by each reader.

How could von Ribbentrop not have been aware of this shameful business, even though he strenuously denied any knowledge of the murders, using the official euphemisms 'removal, resettlement, dis-placement' as proof that he could never have guessed that they meant mass murders. Yet the Einsatzgruppen reports seemed explicit enough.

It is entirely likely that for the first time in his career he withheld information from his wife. This is one matter in which she might not have been the 'tougher of the two' (Hitler). By 1942, rumours of these murders were rampant among many senior Foreign Ministry officials, particularly because men like Martin Luther insisted that Einsatz-kommando reports be widely circulated among those functionaries who were entitled to classified information.

The SD people charged with the task of killing considered themselves unsung heroes patriotically doing the Reich's dirty work with iron resolve and a stomach for bloodshed.

Nothing in von Ribbentrop's background could have trained him for such bloody business. However, like the man in the dinner jacket who sees a derelict lying on a park bench, he hurried on to the dinner party. There was probably little he could have done to stop the SS murders. He was too involved, too committed, too dependent. Eventually, this was to cost him his life.

The Russian campaign began with a comprehensive rout of the Soviets. By 9 July 1941 German troops had taken 320,000 Russian prisoners; by October the figure had risen to over 1.2 million.

In North Africa, Rommel and his new Africa Korps were still on their triumphant advance after their April defeat of the British at Bardia, Derna and Halfaya inside Egypt. Not until December was Rommel to suffer a setback, but it was only temporary. By January 1942, he was back on the attack.

This was not the case in Russia. The Moscow government had moved to Kuibischev, but then the German attack ground to a halt on 1 December 1941, sixteen miles from the Kremlin.[18] By then German losses in the campaign were 158,773 dead, 31,191 missing, 563,082 wounded; 2,093 aircraft lost. The Russians now blocked the way with fresh troops released from their eastern areas by the Japanese Non-Aggression Pact. With this treaty, Germany's diplomatic loss meant a loss of lives. But all that was no longer in von Ribbentrop's hands. All he could do was to listen to the reports of the military. On 5 and 6 December 1941, the Russians launched a massive winter offensive against German troops which were ill-equipped to handle such an attack in 50-degrees-below-zero weather in their summer uniforms. Back in Germany people were asked to contribute their fur coats. The lack of winter combat gear was a scandal.[19] It was the first time the German footsoldier, the *Landser*, was to taste the bitter brew of Hitler's personal strategic generalship. Stalled on the rim of Moscow that December, 286 German tanks were lost, 305 artillery pieces and their tractors. Men retreated in near panic for 100 miles. The myth of German invincibility was gone.[20]

On 19 December, Marshal von Brauchitsch, the official commanding general in Russia, was discharged without so much as a handshake, and Hitler took personal tactical as well as strategic charge. Now, behind his back, Hitler was often called the *Gröfaz*, pronounced in English

'Groefuts'. It sounds as slanderous in Berlinese as it does in English. Gröfaz is an acronym in German which means 'the greatest warlord of all time'.

Within hours of the beginning of the Russian offensive, on 6 December 1941, the Japanese navy's aircraft carriers launched their attack on Pearl Harbor, and the USA then declared war on Axis partner Japan. The fat was in the fire. Now the Tripartite Treaty would oblige Hitler to declare war on the United States, the very thing von Ribbentrop had tried for so long to avoid. What a diplomatic shambles!

The Führer's aggressive plans had wrecked von Ribbentrop's grand designs. The Russians, confident that they were safe from attack by Japan because of the Matsuoka–Molotov treaty of 4 April, now had fresh troops. Then the United States, whom the Germans had wanted to keep out of the war, were attacked by Japan because the Japanese now felt safe from Russia. How to explain all this to Italy? Or was it worth explaining anything to Italy? According to Ciano's diary, the Duce had already said he hoped that the Germans might 'lose a lot of feathers' in Russia.[21] In his memoirs von Ribbentrop insisted that neither he nor Japanese Ambassador Oshima had any inkling of the impending carrier attack on the American fleet in Pearl Harbor. If so, Ambassador Oshima must have felt deeply betrayed by Tokyo, and his urge to commit *seppuko*, what foreigners called *harakiri*, must have been strong.[22]

Meanwhile, Heinrich Himmler's empire, the dark world of the SS, took deepening hold. Vengeance was theirs. A large number of AA department heads held SS ranks ranging from major to general, although these were often so-called 'honorary rank', given at the request of von Ribbentrop. The gifts might have been only a gesture, but now a certain degree of leverage could be brought to bear by Himmler. Even 'honorary' SS were, after all, SS.

In Russia, the SS continued its rampage. At the beginning of the war, orders had been given to shoot without trial any Soviet commissars captured with the Russian army. This so called Commissar Order brought much resentment among German officers, who considered it to be against their code. But that was only the beginning. Rudolf Christoph von Gersdorff, an officer of traditional Prussian background, tells this story. The staff of the Middle Army had their headquarters a few miles from Smolensk.

A Silesian friend, Nanne von Heydebrand, came into my room, chalk-pale. I thought he had been airsick on the flight to headquarters so I offered him some brandy. He told me that the Junkers 52 transport which had brought him back to the front from home leave made a stop at Borisov. He heard pistol and machine-gun fire near the airstrip and, when they took off, they flew at low altitude over a dreadful execution scene. Thousands of people, probably Jews, had dug deep ditches and were then shot with machine guns and pistols. The next shift had to step on top of the fallen, dead or alive, and they were then shot in their turn. Also, babies and naked women, begging for their children. Everyone died in a hail of bullets.

The SS men, it turns out, were Latvians. The whole matter was investigated and found to be true. Commander-in-Chief General von Bock ordered the field commander of the Borisov area to report to him at once. The man shot himself on the way to headquarters.

This massacre and others like it created a nucleus of officers who planned to kill Adolf Hitler.[23] Many of them belonged to Potsdam's legendary 9th Infantry Regiment, which had descended from the Kaiser's Guards Regiments. The officers of the 9th were usually the sons of the Kaiser's Guards officers. Many of them were to die after their attempt to kill the Führer on 20 July 1944 when Colonel Claus von Stauffenberg tried to blow up Hitler but did not succeed. In all, the attempts on Hitler's life in the eleven years between 1934 and 1945 numbered forty-two.

The Einsatzgruppen, the packs which scavenged after combat troops had passed, were only a primitive first attempt at mass slaughter. Soon the SS had prepared more efficient ways to eliminate 'undesirables', such as Jews, homosexuals, gypsies, freemasons, Jesuits, Poles, Jehovah's Witnesses, the terminally ill or the mentally disabled. Forming a new category were the *Nacht und Nebel* (Night and Fog) prisoners. They were arrested without warning for any true or fancied enmity to the Reich.

One of the original camps, Ravensbrück, was for women only. The camps, which had begun as prisons for political opponents, became harsh labour camps and eventually death camps. The mortality rate from overwork, starvation and disease was immense, but the murders at the eventual killing 'factories' dwarfed these 'natural' deaths.

Lest the army be portrayed as totally averse to Einsatzgruppen violence, it should be noted that certain army commanders, either opportunists or Nazi believers, approved SD actions. In an order to Sixth Army Group, Field Marshal Walter von Reichenau told his troops that 'they were the standard bearers of an inexorably popular concept' and that they 'must have full comprehension for the necessity of this severe but justified atonement required from the Jewish sub-humans'.[24]

One Einsatzgruppe reported that Army Group Centre had liquidated 19,000 'partisans and criminals' (mostly Jews). There were so many requests from local army commanders for liquidation by the Einsatzgruppen that an SS major called Lindow complained that 'the Gestapo was not the Wehrmacht's hangman'.[25] When these murders were dressed up in governmental definitions, party cant, Hitler's views, army orders, oaths of office, 'honour of loyalty', even decent men were capable of seeing the victims as criminals and using the expediency of war to circumvent morality.

Most of these acts were primed in Berlin by officials dubbed 'desk murderers'.

At the other end of the disaster of the Einsatzgruppen was the SS's expectation that they could appeal to their people on the basis of duty and honour. Ideologically, the murders were described as 'cleansing, surgical' acts. 'Judaism in the East is the source of Bolshevism and must therefore be wiped out in accordance with the Führer's wishes.' The Einsatzgruppen believed they were entitled to the sympathy and thanks of all good Aryans. 'The job is not a pretty one!' said SS General Turner. Attached to the legality of it all, this was the vocabulary for these murders: 'special action', 'special treatment', 'elimination', 'cleansing', 'resettlement', 'transported elsewhere'.

Not all SS functioned the way Heinrich Himmler and Reinhard Heydrich had wished. Several top SS leaders requested transfers from Einsatzgruppen duties. Among the best known were SS General Nebe, a former senior police officer, who soon beat a hasty retreat back to Berlin. Another of Himmler's top SS officers, General von dem Bach-Zelewski, was taken to the hospital with a nervous breakdown. This was multiplied in the ranks.

Himmler himself once insisted on trying to watch as 200 Jews were shot in Minsk. SS General Wolff, his deputy, barely kept him from collapsing. Himmler turned green when a piece of human brain flew into his face.[26] The shootings had sickened the SS chief, and he insisted that a new and better system be found for the extermination of unneeded or undesirable human beings, namely the gas van. Huge closed trucks were built. Each one held dozens of victims. At one point, the truck was stopped and the exhaust gases were switched by lever from the outside to the inside of the locked rear compartment, killing the victims. The trucks were then unloaded and washed out. The victims were mass-cremated or buried in secret mass graves.

In January 1942 Rommel gathered his forces and counter-attacked the British. By the 30 June, he had pushed them past Benghazi and Tobruk to El Alamein, well on the way to Cairo. It was to be the zenith of Rommel's efforts in Africa.

During that summer of 1942, Hitler temporarily moved his head-quarters east into the Ukraine near Winniza, and von Ribbentrop opened a separate headquarters nearby. This was Hitler's choice because he did not want the RAM underfoot, 'bothering him with all sorts of matters'.[27] In East Prussia von Ribbentrop established headquarters a short distance from the Wolfsschanze at Castle Steinort on the edge of a lake called Schwentzeitsee, owned by the von Lehndorff family. Another part of the

Minister's staff was at the other end of the lake in a hotel.

There was a constant coming and going of staff from Berlin to these orbital headquarters. Each night a train of luxury sleeping cars waited at the Schlesischen railway station in Berlin ready to leave for Hitler's advanced field headquarters, and it took over two laborious days to reach Winniza. On the way it stopped at 3 a.m. to discharge foreign diplomats who were visiting von Ribbentrop at his separate headquarters. After lunch he would fly to Winniza with his guests for a Führer monologue, then back by car over bouncing, gutted roads to his own headquarters and eventually on to a small station where the Winniza train stopped on its way back to Berlin. This visit by foreign diplomats, a voyage of three days and four nights, often accompanied by AA staff, was an exercise in futility, empty ceremony and needless expense. Probably it was von Ribbentrop's way of 'looking busy' or as Spitzy put it, 'reigning'.

During this time, to show his utter devotion to his Führer, von Ribbentrop's organization became even more deeply involved in the action which was to be known as the Final Solution, through Martin Luther, head of the AA's Deutschland Department. The AA's first official involvement came in an 8 January 1942 letter dictated in Prague, signed by Heydrich, addressed to 'Dear Party Comrade Luther!' It said that the conference first scheduled for 9 December 1941 dealing with the final solution of the Jewish question had had to be postponed because of 'well-known events' (the Russian winter offensive and Pearl Harbor). This conference, with an early meal to follow, was now set for 12 noon, 20 January in Berlin, am Grossen Wannsee 56–8. The original guest list had stayed unchanged. The letter was stamped as having been received by AA Department DIII on 12 January, was marked Secret and identified as no. 181. Each ministry involved was represented by a senior official. Among the five Gestapo and SD officers, there was their 'Jewish specialist', an SS lieutenant-colonel called Adolf Eichmann.

Wannsee is a sparkling, peaceful lake west of Berlin, a large inland bay, surrounded by resort villas, woods and a beach. Berliners sailed on Wannsee, motorboated on Wannsee, flirted and made love and played tennis and danced and got sunburned and drank champagne or beer, and it was a most unlikely venue for planning mass murder. The luxurious and secluded lakeside house chosen for the conference had earlier been requisitioned by Berlin's Criminal Police for their own use.

The core of the ten-page agenda for the conference was this. We have attempted to remove Jews from Germany's life and lands. We have tried to cajole, force and even help them to emigrate, and we have managed to get rid of about 537,000 from Germany, Austria and Czechoslovakia. The Jews were told to finance their own emigration. We even had them pay for their impoverished brethren. Besides, 9,500,000 American dollars were put at our disposal by foreign Jews. Now the time has come to shove the remaining Jews into the eastern territories. This concerns about eleven million European Jews.

Page six of the agenda contained this listing:

Land	Zahl (totals)
A. Altreich [Germany]	131.800
Ostmark [Austria]	43.700
Ostgebiete	420.000
Generalgouvernement [Poland]	2,284.000
Bialystok	400.000
Protektorat Böhmen und Mähren (Czechos)	74.200
Estland [Estonia] – judenfrei – [free of Jews]	0
Lettland [Latvia]	3.500
Litauen [Lithuania]	34.000
Belgien	43.000
Dänemark	5.600
Frankreich/Besetztes Gebiet [occupied]	165.000
Unbesetztes Gebiet [Vichy]	700.000
Griechenland [Greece]	69.000
Niederlande [Netherlands]	160.800
Norwegen	1.300
B. Bulgarien	48.000
England	330.000
Finnland	2.300
Irland	4.000
Italien einschl. Sardinien	58.000
Albanien	.200
Kroatien [Croatia]	40.000
Portugal	3.000
Rumänien einschl. Bessarabien	342.000
Schweden	8.000
Schweiz [Switzerland]	18.000
Serbien	10.000
Slowakei [Slovakia]	88.000
Spanien [Spain]	6.000
Türkei (europ. Teil)	55.500
Ungarn [Hungary]	742.800
UdSSR [Soviet Russia]	5,000.000
Ukraine	2,994.684
Weißrußland ausschl. Bialystok [White Russia excl. Bialystok]	446.484
Zusammen [Grand Total] über	11,000.000

This was the beginning of 1942. The Jews of England (Britain), Ireland, Finland, Portugal, Sweden, Switzerland, Spain and Turkey were listed, although these countries were by no means in German hands or under German control. It was just taken for granted that soon they would be.

Estonia had already made itself 'free of Jews' through some of the harshest Einsatzgruppen action, aided by native Estonian auxiliary police. On page nine of the agenda, Luther, there to represent the AA, was quoted as suggesting that actions should be delayed in the 'difficult' Nordic states (Norway, Denmark) but that the Foreign Ministry anticipated no problems in the Eastern countries.

Not mentioned in the agenda or during the conference was the fact that the extermination camps Auschwitz, Chelmno, Belzec, Sobibor, Majdanek and Treblinka were already being constructed. Whatever co-operation Heydrich obtained from the participants at Wannsee would send men, women and children straight into the work gangs, gas chambers and ovens of these newly built outposts of hell.

Had von Ribbentrop heard of the extermination camps? It was most likely, in part because of the constant in-fighting among the Nazi leaders. Sooner or later someone had to tell the tale of the evils of the SS. Certainly von Ribbentrop's plenipotentiary in that distasteful field, Martin Luther, had to be aware. And von Ribbentrop's only semi-ally in Hitler's immediate circle was Heinrich Himmler, whose SS built and administered these extermination camps. Did von Ribbentrop prefer not to credit his own ears? Did he prefer to shut these ugly things out of his mind so that he truly believed he knew nothing about them?

Page 276 of von Ribbentrop's memoirs contains this paragraph about his Führer: 'Never, until 22 April 1945 when I saw him for the last time at the Reich Chancellery, did he speak a single word about the killing of the Jews. To this day, I cannot believe he ordered the extermination of the Jews. So, I must conclude that Himmler presented him with a *fait accompli*.' An opposite view was offered by Walter Schellenberg, Himmler's Chief of Espionage. He reported that after Heydrich's death some British contacts had been established with Churchill's approval. Schellenberg asked Himmler if he might follow these up. Himmler turned down the idea because 'I am sick of working against the Führer. You will just have to accept that!' Schellenberg stated that for Himmler Hitler's every word was law, even to the horror of the Jewish massacres. According to Schellenberg, these were originally not Himmler's idea, but Hitler's.[28] Still, he reports that after a warm reception by Latvian children in Riga, a touched Himmler heard that the Latvian and Estonian auxiliary police were holding 200 Jews for 'sabotage, espionage and extortion'.

'Shoot them,' said Himmler.

Himmler did hedge some of his bets. That same summer of 1942 he obtained a 26-page medical report that Hitler was suffering the creeping after-effects of syphilis and would eventually be paralyzed. One day Himmler asked Felix Kersten, his medical practitioner and masseur, if the Führer, who was also a Kersten patient, was mentally ill. Kersten said Hitler belonged in a hospital for mental diseases, not the Chancellery. Kersten was one of the men, like Kube, who discovered the need to save Germany by saving the Jews. He frequently made attempts to get life-saving information or to cause Himmler to change some harsh measures.

By 1942 Britain was supposed to have been a conquered nation, Russia was to have been a battered bear. Rommel was supposed to have reached Cairo, with the Suez Canal in the Wehrmacht's hands. Spain was to have been a firm ally, putting the Mediterranean under Hitler's control. Göring's Luftwaffe, after smashing Britain's military and emotional defences, was to have administered a similar fate to Russia. Japan would own the Orient and Germany the Occident.

Instead, Britain was stubbornly unbeatable. Rommel was being held at bay and in danger of being chased back to Libya. In Russia, Germany was trying one final time to break through, lest winter came before success. The United States was gaining in its battles against Japan, and a vast flow of American men and *matériel* was on its way to Britain. Supplies were also going to Russia, and the U-boats could not stop them. And Mussolini? The Duce was not even worthy of mention.

The only progress Hitler could measure visibly was in his fight against the Jews and the Poles, against the mentally ill and the incurables.

No wonder that a minor, probing attack on the French coast was publicized as a major battle. On 19 August 1942 a small force of Canadians and British troops landed at Dieppe and did some damage before being killed or captured. It was a strange action, hard to explain in retrospect, since it had few chances of success. The rationale ranged from 'morale' to 'rehearsal', from 'deception' to 'plain miscalculation'.

On 2 November 1942 a new British general, Montgomery, took back El Alamein from the Afrika Korps, and thereafter most of Rommel's North African campaign unravelled fast. He lost almost all the ground he had gained. The British captured 30,000 prisoners and the fortress Tobruk, which Rommel had taken from them earlier in the year. A few days later the Allied landings in Morocco, Operation Torch, put the Afrika Korps totally on the defensive.

Hitler at once called a meeting in Munich at the old 'Chamberlain' hall with von Ribbentrop, Laval and Ciano. The subject was the total occupation of the Vichy government area for 'combined vigilance against attack' following the Allied landings in French North Africa. A depressed Laval tried to persuade Hitler to hold back. He failed and soon left the meeting. Ciano looked bored and von Ribbentrop kept quiet.[29] The resulting proclamation issued on 11 November spoke of the French army and the German Wehrmacht combining to protect the French frontier and also 'to shield the African possessions from criminal attacks'. The occupation of Corsica and Tunisia was also announced.

When Göring then tried separately to persuade the French General Juin to help to hold Rommel's defensive line against the British, Juin said, 'I cannot expect my officers to do that while there are still French prisoners of war in Germany.' Late in December 1942, there was another such conference in the gloomy Wolfsschanze in East Prussia. This time Göring was also present. Ciano brought a message from Mussolini: 'Stop all offensive operations in Russia. Hold the line with fewer men and assign troops to North Africa.' Hitler merely accused the Italian troops of being the weak link which had brought about the disaster at Stalingrad and Laval was assailed with a catalogue of French sins. There were no recorded comments either from Göring or from von Ribbentrop. These silences became quite usual.

The occupation of the Unoccupied Zone was the end of collaborative France under Pétain. Three days earlier Hitler had enquired if the French were willing to fight on Germany's side against Britain and America, but he had received no assurances, even though he had promised the French an alliance 'through thick and thin'. Supposedly, on 11 November Pétain secretly instructed Admiral Darlan in North Africa to make peace with the Allies and to fight once more against the Axis. That also failed, and Darlan was relieved on 16 December and then assassinated by a de Gaulle agent, Bonnierd la Chapelle, a student.

Now Abetz in Paris was even more helpless than before. All of France was run by the military, the party and their police. Von Ribbentrop's influence was minimal.

Then Rommel fell ill on 22 September 1942 and set off for convalescent leave in Germany and Austria; the remainder of the Afrika Korps under General von Arnim had no future. Nevertheless, Abetz sent a senior AA official called Rahn to represent the Ministry at von Arnim's headquarters in Tunisia.

In November, after the occupation of Vichy France, Abetz was recalled by von Ribbentrop. It was a strange recall because Abetz had never been accredited as ambassador to France. There was never a peace treaty between Germany and France.[30] Abetz knew he was now in disfavour although he did not understand why. He had seen neither Hitler nor von Ribbentrop for a full year. He had been consulted only once, when a French volunteer Waffen SS unit called 'Charlemagne' was formed. In his memoirs, Abetz assumes that he was considered 'too Francophile' and that his constant warnings about the loss of the French fleet and the loss of the French North African colonies were a thorn in the side of von Ribbentrop, particularly now that they had turned out to be correct. The scuttling of the French fleet at Toulon on 27 November 1942 had ensured that they would not join the Axis.

However, this was among the smallest of Adolf Hitler's many problems. His offensive launched towards Stalingrad in August had stalled. The entire German Sixth Army under the newly promoted Marshal Paulus was now encircled by the Soviets and anxious for the Führer's permission to break out. From his headquarters, Hitler gave von Paulus his answer: no retreat. There was no possible way the frozen German soldier, short of ammunition and food, could hold out. Göring's promise to supply them by air was empty. Hitler should have sensed that Mars had turned his face from him. And Joachim von Ribbentrop?

He spent as much time as he could near his Führer, mostly in East Prussia. As 1942 went on, his hatred for those 'rigid creatures' of the AA in Berlin intensified. Martin Luther, his 'spy', his Wannsee deputy, now became his watchdog in the Wilhelmstrasse. At the AA, Luther would have to concern himself more with the possibilities of negative attitudes than with the danger of actual rebellion. It was extremely difficult for a professional member of a senior German ministry to convince himself that the time for active revolt had come. The AA officials were held together by the decency and steadfastness of the Ministry's State Secretary, Ernst von Weizsäcker, the chief of staff running the Ministry for its usually absent Minister.

The State Secretary's dilemma was insurmountable. He hated his chief, von Ribbentrop, as well as Adolf Hitler. He could not stomach the Foreign Minister's arrogant dilettantism, his lack of diplomatic skills and his lack of courage in dealing with Hitler. But von Weizsäcker's immediate concern was for the men working in the Ministry, most of whom he considered honourable. He also wanted to 'preserve' the German diplomatic service as a vague legacy for post-war Germany, though he obviously misjudged the amount of bitterness the world would feel for this very legacy. In the execution of his own duties, he could not help but sign papers and orders of atrocious content, often the results of Under Secretary Luther's collaboration with the SD. Luther's ruthless alliance with those who executed the Final Solution was performed at the request of the insecure von Ribbentrop, to 'help me preserve the Wilhelmstrasse'. Originally, von Weizsäcker, like the Kordt brothers and other professionals whom von Ribbentrop had brought into the AA, had been tainted as a 'Ribbentrop creature', but by 1942 he had gained the respect of the Ministry's staff and had the confidence of anti-Hitler people in other ministries. Still, no matter how strenuously he tried to distance himself from the RAM and to block the party collaboration of Luther's Department Deutschland, he himself still had to wade in the mud of the regime. His initials on deportation orders, which became virtual death warrants, would haunt him to his last days.

Decency was not enough, but revolt was suicide. It is unlikely that he was more afraid of death than any other patriot, but if he died who was to act as buffer for the 'helpless' officials of the AA? This, in all probability, was the crux of his misjudgment. It was also the direct result of the creed of German officialdom: Obey! If von Weizsäcker could have persuaded himself that each and every official of the Ministry was individually responsible for the fate of Germany, he could have climbed down from his undesirable perch. The blinkers worn by many members of Germany's diplomatic service were astonishing. For instance, Dr Paul Schmidt,[31] who had been an official and chief interpreter of the AA for over twenty years, since early Weimar days, said of the bombing of his native Berlin: 'I had listened to Goebbels' jubilant announcement in the autumn of 1940 of the bombing of London with a heavy heart. Now, after the bombings of Berlin, I would be able once more to look my English friends in the eye.' He considered the Berlin bombings a *quid pro quo* for most evils and, therefore, a return to normality: '*They* could take it, and *we* could take it.' He failed to take account of the absolute revulsion that German murders and atrocities had caused in the outside world, barbarities which could never be sanitized or negated by the bombardment of cities.

Joachim von Ribbentrop's place at the end of 1942 was precarious. His Führer was stumbling and demanded more blind loyalty than ever, but he no longer required the advice of his expert on foreign policy. That need had long passed. To preserve his Ministry in Berlin, von Ribbentrop had to depend on Ernst von Weizsäcker, whom he disliked but could trust, and on Martin Luther, whom he neither liked nor could trust. Von Ribbentrop's eyes were firmly closed against the future. He must have worried about his son Rudolf in the Waffen SS. No father can be immune to fears about a soldier son. Rudolf was their firstborn, and Annelies and Joachim von Ribbentrop were devoted to him.

As part of the programme to help the SD in their evacuations for the Final Solution, an SS General called Dr Werner Best, an SD officer of proven brutality, was dispatched as governor general to stubborn little Denmark. Best became one of the most controversial figures on both sides of the war. He was one of the original organizers with Heydrich of the Gestapo and SD and had then become part of the AA under von Ribbentrop's command. In Denmark Best decided to turn a blind eye to the very successful efforts of the Danish resistance to smuggle Denmark's Jews to safety in neutral Sweden. Known for his brutality to members of the resistance in France, it is still difficult to understand Best's decision to allow the Danes to save their Jews. Once word got back to Berlin he was severely criticized but was allowed to continue in office. As a result of the work and the courage of the Danish resistance, 7,906 Danish Jews and part-Jews, or people married to Jews, were saved. 492 were sent to the Theresienstadt concentration camp. 423 survived. 113 Danes were executed under Best, though not in connection with the save-the-Jews action. (As in all such events, nothing is pure or clear. Some Danes even confessed to being anti-Semitic. 'We saved the Jews because they were *our* Jews. No one could tell us what to do with *our* Jews. Disliking them was *our* business, not theirs!')

After he had ignored further orders to institute severe reprisals against mounting Danish resistance, Best was summoned to Berlin by von Ribbentrop. Hitler, in a screaming fit, refused all reasonable explanations by Best about the ineffectiveness of harsh reprisal measures in stubborn Denmark. 'I will not listen!' he howled.[32] A few hours later von Ribbentrop told Best, 'Do what you think is right and sensible, but the Führer's orders must be carried out.'

Probably the document which most closely reveals the interlocking machinery of the AA as a newly adopted instrument of mass deportation (and thereby eventual murder) is the following[33] issued before the Danish evacuation of their Jews:

Berlin, 24 September 1942
SECRET

Memorandum

The RAM instructed me on the telephone today to expedite the evacuation of Jews from the various countries of Europe, because it is certain that Jews everywhere are maligning us and must be held responsible for acts of sabotage and assassination. After informing me about the current Jewish evacuations from Slovakia, Croatia, Romania and the occupied territories, the RAM ordered me to approach the Bulgarian, Hungarian and Danish governments to inform them that they are to initiate the evacuations of Jews from their countries.

Regarding the Jewish question in Italy, the RAM has decided to reserve decision. This subject is to be discussed personally between the Führer and the Duce or between the RAM and Count Ciano.

Remitted to the State Secretary [von Weizsäcker] with request for personal acknowledgment.

All written documents will be submitted to you for approval.

Signed
Luther

Everyone featured in this document became involved, from von Ribbentrop to von Weizsäcker to Luther. It also concerned Best in Copenhagen and his opposite numbers in Slovakia and Bulgaria. This document was a clear demonstration of von Ribbentrop's struggle to stay in every way possible within reach of his Führer's desires and plans.

THIRTEEN

1943–1944

'Prussian Marshals Do Not Mutiny'

On 13 January 1943 a cursing, screaming Adolf Hitler heard news of the imminent disaster of the Battle of Stalingrad. On 14 January, Churchill and Roosevelt met at Casablanca, and Roosevelt for the first time unilaterally uttered the words 'unconditional surrender'. This term was greeted with great joy by Goebbels since he thought he could now use it to wring unconditional efforts from tired Germans to win the war.

On 2 February, a stunned Hitler heard that Marshal Paulus ('But I have only just promoted that coward!') had surrendered with his surviving 90,000 men. ('Why did he not shoot himself dead?') Paulus then founded the anti-Hitler organization called 'Free Germany' and appealed to German troops still fighting in Russia to surrender.

In April it was Joachim von Ribbentrop's turn to taste treachery. Under Secretary Luther, his deputy for the Final Solution, was arrested by the Gestapo for insubordination to his superior, relieved of his office and sent to Sachsenhausen concentration camp, where he stayed as a prisoner with certain special privileges until the end of the war, although von Ribbentrop had asked for his execution. His arrest was preceded by some convoluted events.

Luther's original anti-SS stance slowly eased during the time of his collaboration with the SD following the Wannsee Conference. In August 1942 he had a confidential discussion with Himmler about the anti-British mania of von Ribbentrop, which he claimed had forced Germany into a two-front war. Himmler then instructed Schellenberg, the SD's espionage head, hero of the unsuccessful Duke of Windsor caper, to investigate through his network the possibility of putting out peace feelers to the West. Schellenberg told Luther, with whom he was to liaise, that he was sure von Ribbentrop had a disastrous influence on the Führer and asked him to provide documentation to speed the fall of the RAM.[1] Luther was delighted. He and von Ribbentrop had been at each other's throats, in part because of a deep mutual dislike between their wives. Another matter of contention was the von Ribbentrops' expensive tastes. For example, in 1942 in the middle of war the wallpaper in the Dahlem villa was changed four times to please Annelies. Luther, who had special access to party funds, had been able to supply the money for the von Ribbentrops' recent financial appetite, but now these matters had to come to a halt.

Himmler still liked von Ribbentrop, but Heydrich and the SD had always hated him. One of the points of friction between Heydrich and von Ribbentrop was that the SD wanted to install their own secret service in the various embassies and ministries of the AA. Of course, von Ribbentrop insisted that these would have to be controlled by him, and a major contest about areas of competence soon developed. Eventually, through Luther, a deal was made which showed the SD's strength. SD agents became part of most AA missions. They were carried as members of the AA but were not directly responsible to the RAM. For instance they would use special green envelopes because their mail was to remain uncensored. Special radio transmitters were to be built for them, but not inside embassies. In certain emergency cases, the SD could use the broadcast facilities of the AA missions. (In May 1942 Heydrich was assassinated in Prague by two British-trained Czech secret agents. He was succeeded as head of all German police by the scar-faced Ernst Kaltenbrunner.)

During this SD–AA struggle, Schellenberg reported to Professor de Crinis, a well-known SS medical adviser, that von Ribbentrop's face tended to slacken on one side whenever he got tired,[2] and Dr de Crinis claimed that these disfunctions were due to von Ribbentrop's kidney problems, and would get worse.

According to Schellenberg's memoirs, Luther's attack on his own minister was meant to ingratiate him with Himmler after years of not being beloved by the black-shirted fraternity. Probably, Luther sensed that von Ribbentrop was sliding while Himmler was growing in power. At first, when Schellenberg had brought Luther's accusations about von Ribbentrop's extravagance and diplomatic incompetence to Himmler, the Reichsführer SS was tempted to take action, but his aide SS General Wolff, the man von Ribbentrop had once flown to Scotland, came to the RAM's defence. Wolff said, 'You cannot allow SS General von Ribbentrop, one of our highest functionaries, to be wrecked by this miserable crook Luther.' Himmler, who had been sitting on the fence, finally agreed, particularly after Wolff correctly pointed out that Adolf Hitler would never dismiss his 'Bismarck' on the basis of accusations by Luther, a nobody.

The next day a feared senior Gestapo official named Müller questioned several shaking AA subordinates of Luther. A week later Luther was arrested, and von Ribbentrop was given the file of accusations Luther had made against him. The RAM took these to Adolf Hitler, pointing out that Luther had committed treason by criticizing the Führer's own foreign policy. He demanded that Luther be hanged for 'defeatism'. Hitler thought that excessive for an old party comrade, so he ordered that Luther be jailed in Sachsenhausen concentration camp. In 1945 Luther was freed by the Russians. Some say he was shot by them. Others report that he died of a heart attack. The file of accusations against von Ribbentrop remained locked in Himmler's desk. He need not have worried. Von Ribbentrop was now umbilically linked to the SS.

In Rome, for instance, he reprimanded an AA head of mission, Consul Eitel Moellhausen, for interfering with the SS. The Consul wanted to warn the RAM that 8,000 Jews were to be deported from Rome by the SD for liquidation in Mauthausen concentration camp. On 10 October 1943 the Consul was told 'to leave things in the hands of the SS and not to interfere'. Great offence was taken by the AA in Berlin that the Consul had used the word 'liquidation' in his cable.

It could not have failed to reach the ears of the von Ribbentrops that there was a small but growing anti-Hitler resistance movement. It was probably strongest among certain army officers, most of them from titled families. Other resistance groups formed around the newly founded 'confessing Christians', who refused to accept the official Nazi-tainted Protestant 'Reichs Church'.

The most professional anti-Hitler cell grew around Admiral Canaris, the head of the Abwehr, or Armed Forces Intelligence, and several of his senior officers. These men were connected to General Beck, who had wanted to take over the government just before the Munich Conference in 1938. Although there were sure to be rumours about these resistance cells, there had been no arrests.

More than ever, Germans, particularly the upper strata with a history of international connections, looked over their shoulders, in fear of the ever-growing strength of the SD and the Gestapo. The SS, like a bull terrier which would rather drown than relinquish its hold on a swimming victim, committed its horrors until the very moment the Allies poured through the walls of its camps and jails.

On 10 May the North African campaign collapsed in Tunis. Von Arnim surrendered to Montgomery. It was the beginning of the avalanche.

In 1943 the bombings of Germany intensified. The RAF continued their night attacks, and now the American Eighth Air Force added saturation daylight bombing raids with their large new B17 Flying Fortresses. The old building of the Foreign Ministry suffered severe damage, but the staff kept working, although the top floors were now gone. There was no heat that cold autumn and winter, and the thick carpets were covered with pools of water whenever it rained. Each chandelier became a fountain, and windows were haphazardly nailed shut. Von Ribbentrop's own office had been 'moved' by the bombers to the floor below its usual location.[3]

The RAM had stayed as long as he could in East Prussia, lambasting his Berlin staff from a distance, exhorting them to greater efforts in the Führer's task of resettling people to suit his vision of the future. Meanwhile Berlin was bombed day and night, and the ruined Kaiser Wilhelm Memorial Church stands to this day at the end of the Kurfürstendamm, preserved in its grotesque 1943 agony.

Probably the heaviest loss of human lives in 1943 through aerial bombing came in Hamburg, which was attacked twice during July by over 1,200 British bombers: 30,480 people were killed, 277,330 apartments burned out, twenty-four hospitals destroyed, 220 schools and fifty-eight churches were razed. This was only a token of the terrible destruction yet to come.

The Luftwaffe was no longer able to keep its enemies at bay. The industrial Ruhr district was smashed, its capital Düsseldorf flattened by 2,000 tons of bombs, and two vast dams in the valley were breached, drowning thousands. Nuremberg, Hitler's Mecca, was blasted in March and a day later the birthplace of the movement, Munich, suffered the same fate. Göring took to his bed and then to various of his homes, isolating himself from the truth that Germany was not able to keep up the air contest. Even young General Galland's visit, when the fighter ace told him about the fantastic new Messerschmitt jet pursuit craft, the Me262, had failed to rouse Göring from his daydreams of shopping and collecting *objéts*. Hitler barely spoke to him, and Göring did not seek contact with the Reich's leaders. His only moments of joy came when he was introduced to the V1, the self-propelled, jet-powered bomb later known as the buzz bomb in England. Revenge! 'V' for *Vergeltung* (Vengeance).

Von Ribbentrop's activities in 1943 were limited. In February, he had the dubious joy of travelling to Rome to explain the Stalingrad disaster to a cynical Duce and his less than sympathetic son-in-law, Ciano, who was about to lose his own job (he was sent to the Vatican) and, less than a year later, his life.

Early on 10 July, the Allies landed in Sicily, and the Duce himself was only fifteen days from being deposed. After a meeting with the King he was arrested by the Carabinieri, ushered into a waiting ambulance and taken into confinement at a Carabinieri barracks.

It became von Ribbentrop's task to meet with Badoglio's new regime at Tarvisio, near the Austrian border. The RAM tried to save some semblance of Axis solidarity, but just to make sure that he would not be kidnapped he was accompanied by a bodyguard of machine-pistol-wielding SS. Guariglia, the new Italian Foreign Minister, swore solidarity, but Ambrosio, the new army Chief of Staff, tried to stem the flow of German troops now crossing the border to 'protect' Italy. There followed two hours of lie-filled, desultory statements. At the end, no Italian raised an arm in the old Fascist salute as von Ribbentrop's train pulled out. Schmidt, who had interpreted for the RAM, was amused to see the embarrassed grins on the non-saluting Italian officials, the same people he had worked with in their salute-filled Mussolini days. On 8 September, Italy surrendered to the Allies, and Mussolini was put under arrest by his king, the man Hitler despised.[4]

In 1943, with everything nearing disaster, von Ribbentrop must have realized that the worst was yet to come, that the Allies would soon invade the heart of Europe from Britain and from Italy, that the Russians would drive west and that Germany was doomed.

The German army, which had been mauled so fiercely in Russia, had not yet faced the mighty invasion force massing in Britain. The Luftwaffe was helpless to stop the bombers. The U-boats had failed to destroy the enormous American expeditionary force and its mountains of supplies. How could the truth have failed to impress von Ribbentrop? Was he still hoping for the Japanese to finish the job? They were being pushed back across the Pacific, and Tokyo was under heavy bombardment. Did he believe Hitler's talk of miracle weapons? What remained of the inventive worldly businessman who had joined forces with Adolf Hitler?

On 12 September an unshaven Mussolini, tears streaming down his face, was rescued from confinement in the resort hotel Campo Imperatore high up on Gran Sasso mountain. 'I knew my friend Adolf Hitler would not abandon me!' He pulled a black overcoat over his blue suit and followed his rescuer, SS Colonel Otto Skorzeny, and the group of German parachutist commandos to a small plane.[5] The overloaded little Fieseler Storch aircraft groped its way down a rock-strewn meadow and barely got airborne with the load of three men, its pilot, behind him Benito Mussolini and then the six foot three inch Skorzeny, the huge SS man who was Hitler's favourite tough guy and secret agent. They made it only because the pilot, one of the Luftwaffe's best, ran the plane off the side of the mountain and then used the thousand-metre drop into the valley below to gain airspeed. When he pulled out of the dive, the plane barely cleared the trees below. Mussolini, who fancied himself a good pilot, was white-faced. Skorzeny grinned. He had pulled it off! They connected with a larger plane and flew on to Vienna.

In the Imperial Hotel in the suite reserved for the Duce, Skorzeny was decorated with the Knight's Cross ('tin necktie') by an army colonel who had been ordered by the Führer's personal phone call to take off his own Knight's Cross and hang it around Skorzeny's vast neck. Adolf Hitler still had a sense of drama, but in effect the whole wastefully dangerous act of saving Mussolini was only a sop to Hitler's vanity. It also became the final nail in the coffin of Mussolini's self-esteem.

Himmler was delighted. The rescue was an SS operation, and the Black Knights had received another enormous boost in prestige, though one asks oneself, 'For what?' Surely the Reichsführer of the SS must have known that the Reich's days of glory were ending.

There were to be a few more moments of elation, a few fleeting hours when Adolf Hitler's stubborn belief in his own destiny would seem nearly justified, but not in 1943 during that September.

The Duce was then flown to the Wolfsschanze. After landing he was reluctant to leave the plane to meet Adolf Hitler. His disgrace was too immense, and he was once more in tears when he finally shook hands with the Führer. He thought perhaps his dignity could now be restored, but he soon learned his new place in Hitler's scheme of things. He was quickly accused of being a failure. He was asked, 'What is this Fascism that it melts like snow under the sun?'[6] Hitler wanted Mussolini to head a new Italian state and to announce that the monarchy was abolished. Ciano, held in a Munich Nazi Party guest house, where Mussolini had just heard his son-in-law make an extraordinary confession before flying to the Wolfsschanze, was to be executed. Mussolini was aware that Ciano had betrayed him, by making contact in March–May 1943 (while he was ambassador to the Vatican) with the anti-Mussolini Fascist resistance and voting in their Grand Council on 25 July 1943 to depose the Duce. But he had not known he wanted to go as far as executing him? Aghast, he said to Hitler, 'This is the father of my grandchildren!' 'Duce, you are too good,' said Hitler. 'You can never be a dictator.'

On 25 September from a borrowed chalet in Bavaria, Mussolini tried on a priority Führer-phone to gather a cabinet of old Fascist collaborators, all scattered in exile and safety from Madrid to Bucharest and Bern, but each one of them turned him down.

So he flew back to Italy. His chief new associate was Marshal Graziani, the African failure, who hated Badoglio, now Italy's new head of state. Graziani also hated the Germans and he barely put up with Mussolini. Nevertheless he accepted when he was created the senior minister in Mussolini's new mini government.

The Germans installed the patched-up Duce in a villa on Lake Garda near the town of Salo. On 27 September he had his first pathetic Cabinet meeting. He was a puppet, and he was to live only two days less than Hitler the puppeteer. Shot, hanged, kicked, splashed by urinating women, the carcasses of Mussolini and his mistress Clara Petacci were hung upside down, pour *épater la canaille*, from the beams of a garage on 28 April 1945 in Milan.

And von Ribbentrop? Did he truly believe that the ruined Duce and his false new regime could once more run Italy? Was he delighted to see the end of his old sparring mate, the vain satyr Count Ciano? The old playboy was handed over to an Italian tribunal of the newly named Republic of Salo, and executed on 11 January 1944.

In his memoirs, von Ribbentrop called Ciano vain and jealous, unreliable and tricky, and careless with the truth. He accused him of betraying his father-in-law, Mussolini. According to von Ribbentrop, Mussolini complained that Ciano had lied to him for years, and von Ribbentrop claims that Ciano forged his own diaries to accuse the German Foreign Minister of being a warmonger.

Ciano's diaries were indeed used against von Ribbentrop during the War Crimes Trials. Von Ribbentrop referred to an entry for 1 October 1939, following the Polish campaign. Italy was still reluctant to join the battle. Hitler had pointed out at length that Italy should join to 'satisfy her aspirations' in the Mediterranean. Now, von Ribbentrop, according to Ciano, said, 'I am of the opinion that in the present circumstances Germany must proceed forthwith to settle the situation by means of force.' Hitler replied, 'Many people think like Ribbentrop. Particularly the army. ...' It was Joachim von Ribbentrop's opinion that this entry was faked long after 1 October 1939 to compromise him, specifically, as a warmonger.

The bombings of Berlin continued without let-up. On a trip to report to Adolf Hitler about events in Turkey, Franz von Papen, then Ambassador in Ankara,[7] told how he sat in the cellar under his family's mansion in Berlin's distinguished Unter den Linden district near the Hotel Esplanade, while bombs fell throughout the night. The family's house burned above them, and the Wilhelmstrasse was in complete ruins. They finally fled into the neighbouring hotel for the night because all windows and doors in their own house were gone. All of Berlin's railway stations had been smashed, but an occasional train still ran on the few tracks left intact or quickly patched by railway engineers.

The von Ribbentrops spent part of late 1943 in Fuschl. The RAM must have felt absolutely useless in East Prussia near his Führer. According to his memoirs, late in 1943 he had advised Hitler by memorandum to make peace with Stalin as quickly as possible, but in reply he received a message through Ambassador Hewel, his own AA liaison man at Hitler's headquarters, that 'there is no compromise in the fight against Bolshevism. I cannot accept von Ribbentrop's "businessman's politics". This war cannot be won by diplomatic means.'

When the Allied bombing of Berlin intensified, von Ribbentrop returned to the capital. What drove him voluntarily to expose himself to this danger and discomfort? The anti-Hitler conspirator Count Helmut James von Moltke wrote in his diary on 28 November 1943, 'All the military officers are alike. They [only] think of making their lives more comfortable and are indifferent to everything else. On the other hand Ribbentrop and

Goebbels, for whom I have no love, concern themselves with everything: they visit the wounded and bombed-out, inspect the damaged sections of their offices and see to it that their office functions again. Ribbi in particular refuses to return to East Prussia and remains firmly in Berlin.' Von Ribbentrop probably preferred the danger and sense of purpose of being near his Ministry in bombed Berlin to the ignominious treatment Hitler had been handing him.[8]

On 5 December von Ribbentrop had one of the few diplomatic duties of the month, following a very severe raid on Berlin. Tough reprisals for anti-German resistance had been taken against Norwegian students in Oslo with widespread arrests. The Swedish government had protested to the German government. Although even Hitler agreed that these measures were too indiscriminate, von Ribbentrop was instructed to answer the Swedish protest 'in the sharpest language'.[9]

That same day came the terrible raid on Leipzig, one of the most destructive of the war. It ruined the splendid baroque city and made hundreds of thousands homeless. And still, no one in the party admitted the end was near. Instead, Joseph Goebbels kept mentioning 'British fears of reprisals' because of their 'bad conscience'. One wonders where the Minister of Propaganda got his information about Britain.

The following day in Berlin there was another confrontation between von Ribbentrop and the Swedish Chargé about the Oslo affair. Harsh words were said by both. Von Ribbentrop, who was probably less than convinced by his own words, was a good and faithful servant. To Goebbels, the whole Norwegian affair 'stank', and the Führer was angry about the way it was handled by Norway's Nazi government. Himmler was especially upset (and this is proof of the poor judgment of the Reichsführer SS) because he had planned to recruit 40,000 to 60,000 volunteers in Norway for SS Division Viking, which was composed of the shredded remnants of earlier volunteer SS regiments. These units were 'Nordland' (Danes and Norwegians), 'Westland' (Dutch and Flemish), 'Germania' (Germans and Baltics) plus a battalion of Finnish volunteers. He was sure that the arrest of the students had ruined this.

On 9 December, Goebbels' diary describes an apocalyptic fight between himself and Joachim von Ribbentrop. The conflict was over who was to conduct propaganda in Paris. Von Ribbentrop felt it was the AA's function, and he tried to get the army in Paris to back him up, but Hitler seemed to side with Goebbels. The Reich Propaganda Minister wrote of the Reich Foreign Minister in his diary, 'If Ribbentrop is as clever in his foreign policy as he is towards his colleagues in matters of internal politics, I can well understand why we don't achieve any notable successes in our dealings with foreign nations.'[10]

A social note about that same time from Sir Henry ('Chips') Channon in London. His diary of 11 January 1944 gives vent to his pique-filled *tristesse* about the loss of a potential dinner guest.[11]

> Ciano has been shot. ... He was forty-one. ... I knew him and always found him gay, fashionable and painstaking: he was pro-Fascist certainly, but not anti-English. He three times invited me to luncheon and once I went, a grand affair at the Palazzo Barberini. He was shot on Mussolini's orders, and I find it rather shocking to shoot one's son-in-law.

Beginning in 1944, von Ribbentrop created a 'new' AA. Because of the Luther affair he eliminated Department Deutschland and handed over its duties to two other departments directly under the RAM's control.[12] Von Weizsäcker was then fired from his post as state secretary and assigned to the Vatican as ambassador. His place as state secretary was taken by a nonentity called Baron Adolf Steengracht von Moyland, who had once worked for von Ribbentrop in the Embassy in London. Steengracht was weak and inconsequential, but he had an extremely beautiful wife who had embellished many Embassy parties. Now he was von Ribbentrop's 'parrot', and the sometimes obstreperous von Weizsäcker was safely out of the way. Yet even the most complaisant of Hitler's creatures could at times prove they had a conscience. Steengracht had once added a zero to the number of Hungarian Jews who were permitted to emigrate. Now there were 4,000 instead of 400, saving 3,600 lives.[13]

Germany's efforts on the Russian front were shaking, ready to collapse. On 28 January 1944 Hitler ordered all his senior commanders to the Wolfsschanze. A stormy meeting followed in a large, converted barracks.[14] Hitler berated the generals like schoolboys until his greatest commander, Marshal von Manstein, interrupted him. Hitler had melodramatically spoken of 'fighting on alone, surrounded by only a few of his generals who remained loyal'. Then a furious von Manstein yelled, 'You're right, my Führer! That's exactly the way it will happen!' as if to point out that the Führer would certainly be alone unless he stopped interfering.

His punishment was not long in coming. On 30 March 1944 one of Hitler's own four-engined Condor planes landed near Lemberg, the southern headquarters of the Russian front, to bring Marshals von Manstein and von Kleist to the Berghof, there to be relieved of their commands. The mood on the plane was one of deep gloom.

They stayed at the Berchtesgadener Hof Hotel near the Berghof complex. In the dining room they had to witness a raucous, drunken group of senior SS officers who were partying with some young Luffwaffe girls. 'A birthday party', they were told. It was in sad contrast to the miserable freezing men on the Russian front. But the two marshals and their aides said nothing. They were in Berchtesgaden, strictly Nazi Party territory, where even marshals kept their mouths shut.

The next day at the Berghof, von Manstein was handed one final decoration. The Führer then read a *laudatio*, and that ended the career of Hitler's most valuable military tactician. The reason he gave was ludicrous: the time for 'operational knowledge' was over. Now one needed 'only to defend'.

Why did von Manstein not rebel? 'Because', as he had often explained, 'Prussian marshals do not mutiny.'[15]

How could Hitler still have believed? Even before the fatal invasion from across the Channel his house of cards was ready to tumble. Nowhere and in no way could he have found a single hopeful sign. Perhaps he was banking on the buzz bombs and the new V2 high-altitude rocket missiles. Or perhaps it was the new Messerschmitt jet-engined fighters which were supposedly going into immediate production. Obviously, Hitler was an avid reader of his own Wehrmacht's reports.

The Russians were gathering for the final offensive into Germany. Allied bombers were devastating her cities. Anglo-American forces were in complete command of North Africa, Sicily, Crete and the lower boot of Italy, and, most ominously, even the tightest security could not hide the gathering of millions of heavily armed troops in Britain, ready to invade Europe. The Axis alliance was gone, with Italy now a 'co-belligerent' of the Allies, Hungary about to defect and Japan fighting her own desperate battles in the Pacific area.

What, then, was Hitler's cause? How did he keep faith? No matter what the setbacks he still believed in his own destiny and the destiny he had chosen for Germany.

Meanwhile, the slaughter of thousands in the eastern camps continued with mounting savagery, and in Germany itself the SD and the Gestapo hounded any sign of opposition. Many who were physically or mentally handicapped were disposed of under a regulation codenamed T4 because the location of the office administering this horror was on the *Tiergarten Strasse No. 4*.[16] Everything was channelled into bureaucratic form. Nazi Germany could even make its victims pay financially for their own beheading by dunning their relatives posthumously.

This is a government bill sent to the family of a man who was arrested for the crime of *Wehrkraftzersetzung*, loosely translated as 'subversion of the will to fight'. The accused, a lawyer, was overheard by someone on a tram and denounced to the police for what he said. This was his fatal statement: 'When the Italians formed a new government after Mussolini's fall, the Führer should have stepped down because we can no longer win and we'll all be burned alive.'

For this opinion he was condemned to death and executed. His arrest was on 24 December 1943. He was beheaded on 8 May 1944. This is the bill which was then sent to his wife.

Reichsanwaltschaft   Nj 84
beim Volksgerichtshof
– Staatsanwaitschaft –
Geschäftsnummer: 3 J 301/44

Kostenrechnung
in der Strafsache gegen . . . . . wegen Wehrkraftzersetzung

Lfd Nr.	Gegenstand des Kostenansatzes und Hinweis auf die angewandte Vorschrift	Wert des Gergenstandes RM	Es sind zu zahlen RM	Rpff
1	2	3	4	
	Gebühr für Todesstrafe		300	—
	Postgebühren gem. § 72 GKG . . .		2	70
	Geb. für den Rechtsanwait		81	60
	Haftkosten gem. § 72 GKG			
	f.d. Unters. Haft v. 24.12.43 bis			
	28.3.44 = 96 Tg. á 1,50		144	—
	f.d. Strafhaft v. 29.3.44 bis 8.5.44			
	= 40 Tg. á 1,50		60	—
	Kosten der Strafvollstreckung			
	1) Vollstreckung des Urteils		158	18
	Hinzu Porto für Ubersendung der			
	Kostenrechnung		—	12
			746	60

Left-margin annotations (English translations):
- Fee for death penalty
- Mailing cost
- Legal fees
- Detention costs
- Investigate detention
- 24.12.43 to 28.3.44
- Punitive detention
- 29.3.44 to 8.5.44
- Cost of execution
- Mail charges for this bill

Several anti-Nazi groups had existed over the years in vague forms since before the beginning of the war. Most of them wanted to assassinate Hitler and to institute a new anti-Nazi government which would negotiate with the onrushing enemies of the East and the West. Would the Allies have halted their attacks? Probably not. But Germany would have removed Hitler's gang before the Allies could.

Would there have been sympathy among Germans for the killing of Hitler and the removal of Göring, Goebbels and Himmler? The conspirators did not concern themselves with this question. They were sure that no matter who agreed or disagreed with them they were right and their duty, popular or not, was clear. It had to be done.

The conspirators, mostly officers and descendants of old titled families, had been planning the coups for years and months and had been forced to abort several earlier attempts. Hitler was a bohemian, and his schedule was often changed at his whim.

One attempt, a bomb which was placed on Hitler's plane, failed because the fuse was faulty. Retrieving it unexploded from the aeroplane and getting it out of sight of the SD was extremely dangerous, but was done with some *élan* by one of the conspirators. 'Where's that bottle of cognac I was promised? Ah, that must be the briefcase. . . .' The plotters included two field marshals and several generals and also many young captains and lieutenants who were aides and adjutants. It finally centred around the magnetic person of a colonel called Claus Schenk von Stauffenberg,

These were typical days in Hitler's life.[17]

	1943		1944		1945	
	25 Nov.	25 Dec.	27 Nov.	25 Dec.	25 Jan.	28 Feb.
Wake up	10.30	10.30	11.30	11.45	12.00	13.00
Situation conference	12.35	12.30	15.00	15.00	16.25	16.15
Lunch	14.15	14.30	14.15	14.00	14.00	14.30
Situation conference	22.00	22.00	–	0.15	0.50	1.15
Tea	1.10	24.00	0.50	2.00	2.10	2.30
Bed	2.45	2.00	5.00	4.00	4.00	5.15

Any man who keeps these strange hours was hard to pin down.

a badly wounded, heroic man, a soldier–intellectual, an athlete and horseman, a southern German and a Catholic. The task eventually fell to him because he had access to Adolf Hitler and it had to be done with a bomb because von Stauffenberg had been so badly crippled during the Africa campaign that only three fingers remained of his ten and these on his one remaining hand. He could not hold a pistol. He was often in the presence of Hitler because his distasteful army job was to provide reserve units by scavenging what remained of Germany's manpower and of foreigners willing to volunteer.

There were also civilians among this group of conspirators, Carl Goerdeler, a former Mayor of Leipzig, Count Helmut James von Moltke and Adam Trott, both government officials. There were clergymen and businessmen among the plotters. Probably the key man in this action was Erwin Rommel, who had finally come to understand how low Hitler had brought Germany.

What sort of a post-Hitler government were these men planning? The outline was ready. It was to be anti-Nazi and anti-Communist. It was to be democratic, though not clearly so. Goerdeler, who was to be Chancellor, envisaged a semi-democracy, run by a semi-elite. Curiously, although he had clearly protested against the Nazis' anti-Semitism, he wanted to treat the post-Hitler Jews as honoured strangers in Germany without returning them to their former German citizenship.

The entire von Stauffenberg group distanced itself from an earlier and much larger resistance group which the Gestapo had codenamed the Rote Kapelle, or Red Orchestra, which dealt directly with Moscow. They were not Communists in the true sense of the word, but they found that the Soviets were their most accessible, potent and trustworthy anti-Hitler sponsors. The German members of the Rote Kapelle conducted some espionage for Moscow, wrote propaganda pamphlets and were eventually joined by some German army officers. By the time of the von Stauffenberg attempt, most of the Rote Kapelle had been executed or jailed.

Von Ribbentrop was not top of the resistance movement's list for elimination. By this time, just a few months before the invasion, he no longer mattered enough to be a factor.

Many of the von Stauffenberg resistance people were well known to earlier members of von Ribbentrop's own staff. General Beck, one of the key officers, had collaborated with the Kordt brothers as early as the 1938 Munich crisis, and many of Canaris' Abwehr intelligence men like General Oster were known by the Kordts. Even Reinhard Spitzy, once von Ribbentrop's adjutant and then his secretary, had found a place working with Colonel Oster. It is unlikely that von Ribbentrop could have remained completely in the dark. He must have known that there was some organized opposition to Adolf Hitler. There were too many connections, in both his diplomatic and his social life.

However, had he been in possession of some solid information, there is no doubt that he would have warned the Führer. By 1944 his life was so closely linked to his Führer's that losing him through an assassination was unthinkable. Everything in Joachim and Annelies von Ribbentrop's life focused entirely on Adolf Hitler. All other bonds had been cut long before. The von Ribbentrops' pre-war social connections, several with Jewish friends, had not endured. Their family ties had been ruptured. The Henkells seemed to stay away from them. Their friendships abroad had long faded in the harsh war. Certainly there was no one inside the Nazi Party whom they could call 'friend'. The one man on whom Joachim von Ribbentrop had relied, the only one von Ribbentrop called by the familiar 'Du', Heinrich Himmler, was no longer a friend. All that remained were people like the weak-willed Steengracht, since he was now state secretary. Even the Führer kept the von Ribbentrops at arm's length.

Only their children were a genuine source of affection. Rudolf was an officer in the SS Panzer Division which carried Adolf Hitler's name. He was a combat man in a combat unit and he won the Knight's Cross.

Hammerblows kept raining on Germany. On 4 June Rome fell to the Allies. On 6 June Rommel, who was in command of the Seventh Army on the French Channel coast, was home in Germany, reassured that there would be no immediate Normandy invasion. It was unlikely, considering that the navy had predicted rough seas in the Channel and the meteorologists looked for poor flying weather. But, despite poor conditions, in the ugly, stormy dark, at 1.30 a.m. on 6 June came the invasion. The Wehrmacht's report of that day in 1944, usually so laconic, began with a trumpet call.[18] 'Special Report! *Sondermeldung!* The long-expected attack by the British and North Americans against the French coast began last night. A few minutes after midnight, after a heavy bombardment, enemy airborne troops landed in the Seine estuary. Other troops were landed from the sea.'

How could von Ribbentrop in Fuschl have guessed at the incredible errors which then followed, precipitated by the Führer's own bohemian schedule and the fear he instilled in everyone near him, even in generals who had been decorated for personal bravery? When the invasion was still precariously balanced between success and disaster, Hitler was asleep and could not be disturbed!

From Fuschl to the Berghof is only a short drive, but even if von Ribbentrop had known the true nature of the events it is unlikely he would have awakened the Führer. The days when he would have braved the fury of Adolf Hitler had long passed. He was to record in his memoirs that in 1941 he had once violently disagreed with Hitler, who had grabbed at his heart and feigned a coronary crisis.[19] 'Don't ever do that to me again, Ribbentrop, disagree with me so vehemently.' Von Ribbentrop, guilt-ridden, never forgot it. In fact, this father image lasted until the very end when he told the Nuremberg prison psychiatrist that killing Hitler would have been 'like killing my own father'.

At 6 a.m. Rommel's Chief of Staff, General Speidel, called Rommel at his home in Germany. The night had been wasted because General von Rundstedt, Commander-in-Chief of German forces in the West, thought the Normandy attack was only a feint. Rommel drove back as fast as he could. Because Allied fighter planes dominated the skies, Marshal Rommel, like all senior generals, had been forbidden by Hitler to fly. He arrived in Normandy late in the afternoon after cancelling his Berghof visit.

That day Hitler slept until 3 p.m. This meant that certain available Panzer divisions which might possibly have thrown back the invasion on the beaches could not go into action. No one could commit them without Hitler's express personal permission. At 4.55 p.m. on 6 June Hitler issued an impossible order from the Berghof: 'The beachhead must be cleaned up no later than tonight!'[20] Of course, it could not be done. The bridge-heads were held and consolidated. Rommel forced Hitler into a meeting in northern France near Soissons on 17 June in a concrete bunker which had been built as advance Führer headquarters for the victory in France. Rommel came straight to the point. 'The battle is hopeless. Let us take the troops back and regroup beyond the naval guns.' He then continued his doomsday scenario. The western campaign was lost, as was that in the east. *Make peace!* Hitler's cold reply was, 'Just take care of your invasion front. I shall take care of the future of the war.'*

---

* William Shirer reports these events from the memoirs of Rommel's Chief of Staff, General Speidel.

On 20 June the Russians launched their next offensive and, in the west, von Rundstedt was fired after telling Keitel to 'Make peace, you fool!'

More bad news was to follow. Trying to crisscross his patched-up command, Rommel was gravely wounded on 17 July when his staff car was machine-gunned on a Normandy road by an Allied fighter plane. His skull was fractured in several places. He was never to recover completely, robbing the von Stauffenberg comspiracy of a great central figure, who, if healthy, might have converted that failure into some semblance of success.

The attempt on Hitler's life, codenamed Valkyrie after the legendary Nordic goddesses who floated high above a battlefield to point at those who were to die, finally took place on 20 July 1944 at the Wolfsschanze in Rastenburg. It failed. The bomb, set to go off at a conference table, killed and injured several men, but Hitler was only superficially wounded. Probably the key error was to depend on Adolf Hitler's death as the central element and to have no army units at hand which could have breached the many concentric rings of SS guards at the Wolfsschanze and taken charge. The entire machinery of the revolt faltered the moment it became clear that Hitler had survived. The SS then kept him safe and there was no alternative plan to take over his headquarters and arrest his closest henchmen.

Hitler, the captive at bay, like Mussolini, might have been as impotent as Hitler dead, and probably more so.

But the average German was still slavishly devoted to him and had been taught to link the defence of Germany against impending catastrophe with a paradoxical adoration for the Führer, the very man who had brought Germany to that position. Germans clutched on to the person of Adolf Hitler as their shield against the vengeance of the advancing Soviets. He would still save them. One always had to trust the Führer.

On 21 July the revolt was finished. By daybreak, von Stauffenberg, his immediate associates as well as General Beck, the earliest of the highly placed conspirators, were dead. They were shot in the courtyard of army headquarters in the Bendlerstrasse in Berlin. The firing squad's targets were illuminated by the headlights of army cars. Above the crash of rifles came von Stauffenberg's shout, 'God save our holy Germany!' Beck had tried but failed to kill himself in his office and was shot there and then.

Today, that street is called Stauffenberg Strasse, and the men of the resistance are national heroes to all but a handful of ultra-conservatives. As many as 200 others would die barbarically, strangled by ropes while being hoisted on meat hooks mounted from beams of the execution hall at Plötzensee prison. Camera crews sent by Goebbels to film the executions for the Führer were sickened and had to abandon their task. To this day, this brick-walled building is a national shrine.

About 11,000 others were arrested by the Gestapo and SD as co-

conspirators or simply relatives. All this happened less than a year before Hitler committed suicide and Germany collapsed. Vengeance and cruelty continued even as the enemy's guns could be clearly heard near by. Among those executed were twenty-one generals, thirty-three colonels, two ambassadors, seven senior diplomats, one minister of state, three secretaries of state. In 1944, 5,764 were arrested, and in 1945 another 5,684.

At the Wolfsschanze on that fateful 20 July, a shaky and stunned Hitler, his right arm temporarily out of action, one eardrum shattered, his legs singed, was lucky to be alive. Some of his aides were badly wounded and near death. His valet helped him dress in a clean uniform to go to the small nearby terminal where the puppet Mussolini was arriving by train. Hitler reached out with his left hand to shake the shocked Duce's right hand and conducted him on a tour of the devastated headquarters, as if to prove that the fates had made him immortal. During tea at 5 p.m., Mussolini was witness to quite a scene. Admiral Dönitz, head of the navy, attacked Göring for his Luftwaffe's failures. Then the fat Marshal blasted von Ribbentrop (who had rushed to the Wolfsschanze on hearing of the assassination attempt) for his disastrous foreign policy and almost struck him with a raised marshal's baton, screaming, 'Ribbentrop, you lousy little champagne pedlar!' Von Ribbentrop shouted back, 'I am still the Reich's Foreign Minister and my name is *von* Ribbentrop!'[21] Mussolini was embarrassed. Hitler was not listening. He was deep in his own thoughts, his ears stuffed with cotton wool, sucking lozenges. He paid no attention to his squabbling paladins or to his Italian guest until someone mentioned Röhm and his treason. Then Hitler came to furious life. He yelled for bloody revenge on the conspirators, their wives, relatives and children. He used his very survival as proof, to himself, to his subordinates and to every last German in the armed forces or civilian life that he was *fated* to lead Germany. The very fact that he had survived proved that God, whose name he used only in the face of momentous events, had chosen him for the task.

The German people still believed him. They suffered more bombs and fought on. Hitler's survival also stiffened the resolve of the SS, men who had 'steeled' themselves to do the cruel business which 'had to be done by those of courage' in the concentration camps and the killing camps.

Obviously, Joachim von Ribbentrop also seemed reinforced by the 'judgment of God and the proof of His benevolence to Germany's Führer'. Oddly enough, the man whom the conspirators had planned to have as the future Chancellor, Carl Goerdeler, had been against assassination and also called Hitler's survival 'the judgment of God'.

The question is often asked why the German resistance movement was so belated and why Germany's leading classes originally endorsed Hitler's anti-Semitism. Many titled and *haut-bourgeois* Germans were anti-Semitic in the old-fashioned, conservative 'social' way. In this respect they did not differ from their British, French or American counterparts. 'One invited' only a few Jews. 'One married' them only if one could explain that they were the wealthy daughters of titled Jewish banking families. Hitler's early anti-Semitism fell on understanding ears among many in Germany's upper classes who accepted anti-Semitism as a *specific* manifestation, not as a *symbolic* one. They could not or would not see that the attack on Jews was a signal of forthcoming attacks on all things which differed from the National Socialist standard such as Catholics, Masons, artists, millionaires, eccentrics, cynics, homosexuals, derelicts, avant-gardists or recluses.

Pastor Niemöller is said to have confessed 'When they came to arrest the Jews, I said nothing. I was not Jewish. When they came to arrest the Catholics, I said nothing, I was not Catholic. When they came to arrest the Communists, I said nothing. I was not Communist.

'When they came to arrest me, I had nothing left to say.'

The German 'gap' seemed to be that missing link of protective reaction to be found in (often anti-Semitic) upper-class Britain, which allowed a Jew to take his oath in Parliament wearing his hat and without reference to Jesus, which appointed a Jewish (by descent) Prime Minister and a Jewish Viceroy of India. These appointments were too important to be discounted as mere tokens. The British seem to have a built-in alarm system which rings whenever they perceive a genuine threat to individual liberty. It has been part of British thinking since Runnymede.* The French, equally, if not more anti-Semitic than the Germans, also had a Jewish Prime Minister and, before him, Emile Zola and *J'accuse* and the redress of the slanderous treatment of Captain Dreyfus. Before Zola, there were Voltaire and Rousseau who spoke out for individual liberty.

Why had Germany's upper strata not developed this litmus test of 'wrong to one, wrong to all'? Their recognition of the evil may have been delayed, but once they understood it their courage was immense.

The Hitler of old would never be again. From 20 July 1944 onwards, he was a sick man, unsure of his step, slower of speech and reaction, and increasingly under the spell of the treatments of Dr Theo Morell, the man who had once revived the tired, ill, old President Hacha of Czechoslovakia in 1938 in Berlin after Göring had frantically called for a doctor. Morell, who began his career as a young ship's doctor, had set up practice in Berlin. An expert in the use of injected stimulants and sedatives, he soon developed a large circle of famous patients. Hitler, who was frightened of stomach cancer, was only suffering psychosomatic stomach cramps, but he became one of Morell's most devoted patients. Karl Brandt,

---

* Americans, who certainly have their well-known problems with all sorts of racial prejudice, are positively hysterical in their immediate reaction to an attack on personal liberties. For every hundred admitted offences against citizenship and decency there are a thousand screaming protests.

another Hitler doctor (sentenced to death in 1948 for euthanasia and other SS medical murders), dubbed Morell the 'Reich Injection Master'.[22] There was hardly a day when Hitler would not have his rendezvous with Morell.

There is a theory that Hitler introduced Morell to Göring and von Ribbentrop. Göring was a life-long morphine addict since his days in Sweden after the war when he was battling the pain of a war wound.[23] Von Ribbentrop, who had a cast-iron stomach for alcohol, probably part of his pre-Hitler business life, had never been addicted to drugs, although he was always a highly-strung man. During that last abrasive year of the war, when his own world was shaken by Hitler's cold reserve, it is possible that he asked Dr Morell for help. It would explain some of the sleepwalking apathy and unawareness of the imminent dangers and his final collapse at the beginning of his imprisonment at Nuremberg.

Adolf Hitler wanted to mount one final military thrust while he waited for the supposed flood of Messerschmitt jet fighters and the devastation which was to be caused in London and elsewhere by Wernher von Braun's newest ballistic rocket missile, V2, first launched against London on 8 September 1944. There would be over a thousand more. Over 2,000 were launched that year against Brussels and Antwerp from V2's Peenemünde pads.

Hitler's surprise offensive was a blitz attack against the Americans in the Ardennes mountains, which was later to be called the Battle of the Bulge.

A large Panzer army, most of it robbed from the Russian front, aimed to punch through the Americans and rush to the Channel coast to outflank them. The attack was to be spearheaded by German soldiers in American uniforms, trained to act the part of GIs by Hitler's favourite secret agent, SS Colonel Otto Skorzeny.

On a grey, cold, mist-shrouded winter day early in December 1944, they attacked the unsuspecting GIs at Stavelot in hilly south-west Belgium, and for a short while confused them with fake US MPs who misdirected traffic and carried out other disruptive activities. However, the US 101st Airborne Division under General McAuliffe rushed to Bastogne to block the German troops. When the snow and foul weather lifted on Christmas Day, the US Air Force did the rest, combined with part of General George Patton's Third Army which sped reinforcements into the Bulge.

In the final western assault, the Germans lost 120,000 dead, wounded and missing, 1,600 planes, 600 tanks and assault vehicles and 6,000 vehicles.

The Americans lost 8,000 killed, 48,000 wounded, 21,000 captured and missing, 733 tanks and tank destroyers. Even in its last gasps, mortally wounded, the German army still had a fierce clout.

That was Hitler's last military adventure. It was mounted against the advice of some of his best generals – Blumentritt, Model, Manteuffel. Even SS General Sepp Dietrich, commander of the SS Leibstandarte Adolf Hitler, a man who had begun as one of Hitler's street toughs, was reluctant. Hitler ignored them all. 'I need no advice from you, gentlemen,' said a bent and shaking Führer, his left arm twitching, one leg dragging. 'I have commanded the army for five years. I have read Clausewitz and Moltke.'*

During the last days of January some of Marshal Zhukov's troops reached the Oder river. The Russians were now a short peacetime car trip from Berlin, about fifty miles away.

Reading the Wehrmacht reports for the weeks between Christmas 1944 and 1 February 1945 is to learn the art of creative writing. While history tells us that US and British troops advanced towards Germany, each day's *Wehrmacht Berichte* brought news of thousands of burned American tanks, tens of thousands of prisoners. Each attack by the Allies, east or west, was 'beaten back in a bloody manner'. Only the map shows that each 'victory' is closer and closer to the heartland of Germany. No doubt Germany's soldiers and airmen were courageous, but the writers at the Oberkommando der Wehrmacht matched them in sheer audaciousness. One detects the usual 'dead messenger' syndrome of dictatorship: Don't hand 'the Man' bad news in the raw. Dress it up to look positive.

---

* General Manteuffel reported these words, according to William Shirer.

FOURTEEN

1945

'Justice from the Bomb Bay of a Boeing's Belly'

On 20 November 1944 Adolf Hitler left his Wolfsschanze, the dark, gloomy cement fortress in the forest where fate had once spared his life, and returned to the rubble of his capital city and the scarred Chancellery. Then on 10 December he moved on to another block of cement bunkers, this time in the Friedberg area of Hessia. Those who had not seen him since 20 July 1944 were shocked by his deterioration.[1]

On 16 January 1945 with the Russians nearing the Oder river Hitler returned from the safety of Hessia to his Chancellery in Berlin.[2] He was never again to leave it or the bunker beneath it except for a few short sorties into the rubble and bomb-craters of the ruined Chancellery gardens and the neighbouring Foreign Ministry garden.

That 30 January brought a harsh reminder of what might have been. It was the twelfth anniversary of Hitler's coming to power in 1933, and of the oath of office taken just a few houses away, down the bombed Wilhelmstrasse in the old Presidential Palace.

The Wilhelmstrasse's neo-classical buildings, once the seats of power, were now scarecrows or skeletons. First there was Speer's masterpiece, Hitler's Chancellery, once *faux* Graeco-Teuton. Next came von Ribbentrop's Foreign Ministry and, across the street, the Deutsche Bank. Then diagonally from there stood the Prusso-Imperial Presidential Palace, also von Ribbentrop's. Alongside the Presidential Palace stood the Ministry of the Interior, where Frick, the jurist of the regime, had devised the Nuremberg Racial Laws, and then came the British Embassy, where Sir Nevile Henderson had fought that losing battle with his own good manners. At the Unter den Linden corner was the Hotel Adlon, Berlin's finest, with its special air-raid cellar reserved for Nazi and foreign dignitaries. Herr Adlon, the owner, was still in residence, managing his battle-weary establishment. Unter den Linden, the wide boulevard, was named after its linden trees, which had long disappeared, either splintered by bombs or chopped down for the stoves of Berlin's shivering survivors.

The great Tiergarten Park beyond the Brandenburg Gate looked like any forest after armies had fought for its possession, although the Russians were still fifty miles away.

The Führer's bunker under the Chancellery was large, built on two levels, with many bedrooms, kitchens, bathrooms, conference rooms, dining rooms and offices. About twenty of its rooms were in use. Underground passages connected the Chancellery bunker with two others: that of the Foreign Ministry next door and a large one under the Voss Strasse.

By now, Adolf Hitler was shaking and uncoordinated. He could read only from the pages his secretaries typed in so-called 'Führer script', an extra large typeface, and he seemed to have trouble standing and walking.[3] But this was deceptive. Whenever his Chief of Army Staff General Guderian suffered Hitler's rage and anger, whenever Hitler screamed his bitterness, he seemed physically in complete command of himself. No one knew if his disabled appearance was play-acting, or if the Morell injections caused these violent swings in mood and physical co-ordination. Perhaps Professor de Crinis' diagnosis of Parkinson's disease was correct. It is astonishing that the people around him still listened, feared and believed. Perhaps they felt trapped and beyond redemption. Had the Russians been physically and directly *ante portas*, it might have stirred them into some act of self-preservation. Perhaps it was Martin Bormann whose threatening presence held them together so long.

On 24 January General Guderian told von Ribbentrop in private at the crippled AA offices that the war was lost and asked him to persuade Hitler to make peace. How could Guderian have known that von Ribbentrop had absolutely no influence on Hitler, but welcomed this chance to bring himself to the Führer's attention by repeating Guderian's statements to him?

Two hours later, during his daily situation conference with Guderian in attendance, Hitler raged at all those who talked defeat. 'Come and tell me, but I forbid you to tell anyone else! It is high treason!'[4] This was the last meeting in Hitler's large office in the above-ground Chancellery. Thereafter, they were held in the bunker. Also, from that day on, Kaltenbrunner, head of the SD, usually hovered in the background of all these meetings.

Everyone was still frightened and cowed by the shaking, palsied Adolf Hitler. The man was a wreck. He confessed to Speer on the 18 January that his hand shook so badly that no one could read his writing, while he handed Speer a birthday present, an inscribed photograph. Speer checked the dedication, and Hitler was right. It was barely legible. Speer had been deeply shocked six days before when Hitler had calmly issued orders to destroy most things which would enable the German people to rebuild their lives after the war. The Führer wanted scorched earth. 'If

Germany is a weak nation, it deserves to die! Only the inferior would survive. . . .'[5]

Perhaps Hitler's Germany was collapsing, but its viciousness continued without let-up. In the People's Court Building the men who had planned Hitler's death in July 1944 were still on trial. Their prosecutor was Roland Freisler, President of the Court. A converted former Communist, who became the Reich's Torquemada, Freisler had spent the day berating the accused Ewald von Kleist-Schmenzin, the man who had visited London in 1938 in the hope of persuading Chamberlain's people to stem Hitler's tide. Von Kleist proved to be a tough man to frighten, so Freisler temporarily switched his attack to another prisoner, Fabian von Schlabrendorff, a lawyer and officer. Von Schlabrendorff, who despised Hitler, was the man who had placed the (faulty) bomb on his plane.

Freisler was shouting, 'You are a traitor!' when the air-raid sirens sounded. The prisoners were shackled hand and foot and taken to the cellar, and the prosecutor and his staff rushed to follow them as the first American Flying Fortress bombers came overhead. Justice was then dealt from the bomb bay of a Boeing's belly at 27,000 feet. The prosecutor who had berated, belittled, insulted and humiliated so many courageous men now had only seconds left to live. Then a heavy beam crushed his chest. He died still clutching von Schlabrendorff's folder. The victim was alive and the prosecutor dead. When the prisoners were returned to Gestapo headquarters on Prinz Albrecht Strasse, that building too was on fire.

Von Schlabrendorff was one of the few survivors of the plotters. Most of the others lost their lives even though Freisler was dead. Hitler could not win a war against Germany's enemies, but he won his victory against many patriotic Germans.

At the end of January 1945, von Ribbentrop got up the courage to ask Hitler for permission to establish unofficial contact with the Russians. He even offered the services of Annelies, who would fly to Stockholm, there to make contact with Mme Kollontay, the powerful Soviet Ambassador to Sweden. Annelies would claim to be a divorcee to gain the Russian woman's sympathies and then would offer to contact the Führer. When Hitler turned down the scheme, von Ribbentrop then offered to take his family to Moscow and to leave them there as hostages while peace was being negotiated. Hitler again shook his head. 'Ribbentrop, don't give me any troubles like Hess!' he said.[6]

Von Ribbentrop should have remembered the time after Mussolini's final visit to the Wolfsschanze when the Italian had received his 'instructions' as a puppet dictator. For some reason, Hitler told Mussolini he might make peace with Moscow. Later, an amazed von Ribbentrop tried to see Hitler to pursue this idea, but he was rebuffed and insulted for even mentioning it. Afterwards, Hitler came to his quarters, seemingly contrite, and said, 'If I made peace with them today, I'd fight them again tomorrow. I can't help myself.' For Hitler, the idea of another treaty with the Soviets was too repugnant to consider.

The world outside became more and more remote for the Führer and most of the others in the bunker. Hitler would occasionally take his Alsatian dog Blondie for a walk in the shattered gardens but always came back grim-gaced.[7] He took refuge in his dreams. Speer and he often studied the model of a redesign of his hometown of Linz which had been set up in one of the bunker rooms.[8] By now, the truth had finally penetrated. Hitler knew that the end was near, and his brain was beginning to create the apocalyptic scenes to come.

Although von Ribbentrop could now clearly see into the grim future, the AA still functioned, and its Department II, successor to Luther's Deutschland, was more helpful to the SS than ever. It had full charge of 'Jewish matters', and, until the very final days, it helped to expedite the remaining Jews to their fiery death. The machinery of hatred and destruction continued until the very moment when an Allied soldier, American, British, Russian or French, stood at the gate of a concentration camp or the door of a Gestapo prison.

Department II of the Foreign Ministry, under Eberhard von Thadden and Horst Wagner, had condensed its immediate task into:

1. The dilatory treatment or rejection of all neutral intervention regarding deported Jews.
2. The blocking of enemy reports as 'horror propaganda'.
3. Refusal to give information to chargés or to international organizations [e.g. Red Cross] about the fate of deported Jews.
4. The prevention of the emigration of several thousand Jewish children to Palestine.
5. Personal and propagandistic support for the deportation of Slovakian, Greek, Romanian, Hungarian and stateless Jews into the [extermination] camp Auschwitz.[9]

After the German defeat Horst Wagner outlined the duties and responsibilities of Department II for the American authorities without even mentioning its close association with the SS. When his outline turned out to be a lie, Wagner fled to South America. He returned to Germany in 1952 under a false name as correspondent for an Argentine newspaper and was finally indicted by the court of Essen for complicity in the murder of 356,642 Jews. Legal manoeuvres and illnesses postponed his trial. He died on 13 March 1977 without having been tried.

To prove how crushing was the continuing machinery of Hitler's revenge, on 2 February Goerdeler, the former Mayor of Leipzig and resistance fighter, was executed even as Himmler was trying to make contact with Sweden. Goerdeler's younger brother was executed on 1 March 1945.

Even the trial of von Kleist-Schmenzin, interrupted by the death of Freisler, continued. Freisler had died on 3 February. He was buried without ceremony. Hitler himself insisted there be no semblance of a state funeral. But von Kleist was still executed on 9 April while Hitler and his entourage cowered in the bunker and their enemies were within artillery range.

Equally harsh retribution was handed out by hastily convened kangaroo courts of the army field police or roving SD and Waffen SS. Any soldiers or officers who were deemed deserters or civilians whose identification papers were suspect were often hanged on the spot from trees or lampposts. According to Wehrmacht figures, the number of executions by formal courts martial and firing squads added to lynchings by roving squads was 14,500.

On 7 March the Americans crossed the bridge at Remagen over the Rhine, and with them came the deluge of Western troops into Germany.

After Hitler's orders to Speer to destroy everything, Speer there and then decided to put an end to the man. He planned to pump poison gas into the bunker but was foiled by someone who had raised the level of the air intake well above shoulder height, probably to avoid smoke from the nearby government buildings.

On 19 March, Eva Braun, Hitler's long-time paramour, arrived in the bunker from her safe haven in Bavaria. She stayed with Hitler despite his half-hearted protestations.

Von Ribbentrop lived in his own bunker, close to his Führer. Annelies and the family were in Fuschl, but she had rented a small villa near Dachau, the notorious Munich suburb, should she have to leave the castle. On 25 March he decided to ask the former Japanese Military Attaché, his old friend Oshima, to initiate some peace feelers in Stockholm through the Japanese Embassy there. A Japanese military attaché then flew from Stockholm to Berlin on 28 March but was sent back because von Ribbentrop had acted on his own. Hitler listened to his 'idea' but turned it down categorically. He actually told von Ribbentrop, 'I am absolutely convinced I will win final victory. . . .'[10] Could von Ribbentrop believe him? Still, he asked the Japanese to cancel his request for peace tacks.

This was von Ribbentrop's second Stockholm contact within the month. Earlier, he had had an inconclusive visit from Count Folke Bernadotte, cousin of the King of Sweden, who came to negotiate for the release of millions of Jews in return for certain possible political offers to Germany. Bernadotte's dealings began with Himmler, who was hiding out at a clinic at Hohenlychen near Berlin, where he was receiving treatment for 'stomach disorders'. Once more the mission was aborted since Hitler was not involved. The disgusted Swedish Count later described von Ribbentrop's one-hour monologue at their meeting as filled with arrogant banalities. Again, Morell's injections?

On 28 March, the hot-tempered, truthful General Guderian was fired, and his place was taken by General Hans Krebs, a devoted Nazi and a friend of Bormann. The only thing left for Krebs to do was to listen to Adolf Hitler's impotent daydreams about units which no longer existed. He would witness Hitler's last testament to the German people. Guderian's eventual survival was ironic, since he was a member of the military tribunal which had been formed after the 20 July assassination attempt. He had channelled many victims towards Freisler's tender mercies.

During this period came the great raids on Dresden which devastated the rococo city and killed tens of thousands. Hitler now proposed to his circle in the bunker that 'harsher measures' would have to be taken against Allied troops. According to historian David Irving, two nerve gases, Tarin and Sabun, were ready for use,[11] but Göring, von Ribbentrop and Admiral Dönitz were bitterly opposed to the use of these gases. Only Goebbels approved, but in the end they were never used.

This was not the time for claustrophobics. All who lived in the bunker, or who had to go there for Hitler's eternal meetings, spoke of the dank, damp air, the monstrous hum of air compressors and generators, the unvarying artificiality of electric lights and the cement-cushioned shocks of the hammer blows on the city overhead. Von Ribbentrop mostly stayed in his own nearby bunker, isolated from his wife, his children, his Führer. The others, the men who had always been his enemies, were now constantly beside the Führer, although Göring, the man of empty promises, was in deep trouble with his chief.

Goebbels came into the bunker on 10 April, crowing his delight. *Roosevelt was dead*! For a moment Hitler thought this finally was the long-promised sign from Providence, but on the 16th the Russians slammed their way across the Oder: there was little now between them and Berlin. Providence had lied. Everyone had lied, even the SS. Just before his birthday he gave Guderian a final distasteful task: order the Leibstandarte Adolf Hitler to remove its sleeve band with his name. Guderian refused. He said only Himmler could do so. Sepp Dietrich, old Nazi fighter and SS Leibstandarte commander, personally went to the bunker to complain about the undeserved insult. Hitler cancelled the order.[12]

Hitler's last birthday came on 20 April. That morning he went to the desolate garden to decorate a group of young boys for their fighting courage, for attacking tanks and lobbing mortar shells at tough Soviet troops. The last-known photograph and film of Hitler was taken on this occasion.

Later, back in the bunker, in the crowded situation room Hitler took his seat at the small map table. Göring was wearing a new, olive-coloured,

American-style uniform.* He and everyone around the table said that
Berchtesgaden should become the new headquarters, but Hitler refused.
'How can I ask troops to fight for Berlin, and then I withdraw to safety?
I shall leave it to fate.' His words were prophetic.

Göring said he would leave, but Hitler barely paid attention.[13] There
and then he split command of Germany into north and south. Admiral
Dönitz was to command the north from Plön, twenty kilometres south-
east of Kiel, and Göring the south from Berchtesgaden, near the Berghof.
Göring left at once for his nearby home, Karinhall, where he collected a
vast load of artworks and other belongings on the way south via his
private train. He then ordered Karinhall destroyed.

Dönitz left for the north to take up his command.

Speer was one of Hitler's final visitors in the bunker, and Bormann
asked him to persuade Hitler to go south, but instead, once alone with
Hitler, Speer said, 'It seems to me better, if it must be, that you end your
life here in the capital rather than in your weekend house.'[14]

Those who saw Hitler in the bunker during those last days spoke of
his spotted uniform, his slovenly appearance, his total apathy. Only once
was he roused from it. A telegram arrived for von Ribbentrop from
Göring in Berchtesgaden:

To Reich Minister von Ribbentrop

I have asked the Führer to provide me with instructions by 10 p.m., 23
April. If by this time it is apparent that the Führer has been deprived
of his freedom of action to conduct the affairs of the Reich, his decree
of 29 June 1941 becomes effective, according to which I am heir to all
his offices as his deputy. By 12 midnight, 23 April 1945, if you receive
no other order from the Führer or from me, you are to come to me at
once by air.

Göring. Reich Marshal

Bormann yelled, 'Treason!' and an apoplectic Hitler at once stripped
Göring of the succession. He was to resign 'for reasons of health'. The
original fury was followed by a final, overwhelming outburst of anger
and self-pity. Speer, who witnessed it all, was amazed when Hitler raged
about Göring's corruption and neglect of the Luftwaffe. Then the storm
had passed. Hitler collapsed. 'Let Göring negotiate the surrender. It's
over anyway.'

Nevertheless, Göring resigned by telegram, 'due to coronary illness'.
Bormann then told Hitler that von Ribbentrop was waiting for an audience. Hitler was irritable. 'I've already said several times I don't want to
see him.' Bormann persisted. He said, 'Ribbentrop said he won't budge.
He'll wait there like a faithful dog until you call him.'[15]

---

* A. Speer, *Inside the Third Reich*, Macmillan, New York, 1970.

Finally Hitler allowed Bormann to admit von Ribbentrop. They spoke alone. They discussed some Czech engineers who wanted permission to surrender to the Americans instead of falling into Russian hands. Speer had told Hitler of their plight and how painful it would be to lose them to the Russians. When von Ribbentrop finally left Hitler, he saw Speer in the hallway and said, 'About those Czechs, that's really a matter for the Foreign Ministry. But all right, if you mention that it is with the approval of the Foreign Minister, I shall indeed approve it.' Ever the man to guard his empire! Shortly thereafter von Ribbentrop left the bunker and Berlin, as did Dr Morell.

Von Ribbentrop never again saw Hitler. His Führer went on to marry Eva Braun, and the newlyweds then committed suicide, on 30 April, after Hitler had poisoned Blondi, his dog. Executed on the 28th, Mussolini preceded his former protégé by two days. The house of cards kept collapsing. Dönitz became Germany's short-term head of state on 1 May, and Berlin surrendered to the Russians on 2 May. Bormann was killed trying to escape the city. General Krebs shot himself. Goebbels and his wife committed suicide in the bunker after poisoning their children. Looking at photographs of the prisoners in the dock at the Nuremberg War Crimes Trials, it never fails to amaze how many of the leading figures of the Nazi era survived nevertheless. Of the men at the top only Goebbels and Himmler killed themselves before the trials, Goebbels in loyalty, Himmler in treason.

Sebastian Haffner, the great German journalist, pointed out that the German people were besotted with *the man* Hitler, not with his political theories. This was also true of the men and women who were his closest associates. His death cut them adrift and, with the exception of a few internationalists like Schacht, they stayed adrift. Many of the old guard (party number under 100,000) and old fighters (under 300,000) had spent the major part of their adult lives attached, devoted to, working for, propagating, saying prayers for, and often to, Adolf Hitler. Now they had only themselves and each other, and, more often than not, they found it insufficient. Most adults have experienced that same sense of finality after leaving a graveside. A wooden coffin can be more impenetrable than a steel safe. Hitler's men, those who survived, were in deep shock. The author witnessed Hermann Göring's first press conference after his capture in the garden of a villa in Augsburg. Göring behaved like the fat little boy who had lost his daddy at the zoo. He was sweating, shaking, nervous, dressed up in light blue with gold trim for the sad costume party.

Later, removed from drugs and distanced from the time of Hitler's death, he seemed to gather himself into a semblance of the cohesive and intelligent fighter pilot he had once been. Göring was always one-third big mouth, one-third gallant, one-third coward. Others, like Hess, never regained their equilibrium. In the case of von Ribbentrop, the period of post-Hitler shock was lengthy. He became, in turn, a bon-vivant boulevardier in Hamburg, a frazzled and frayed wreck as a prisoner in Nuremberg and then, at the very end, a man of some courage and bearing.

After Berlin, his first destination was north, towards Hamburg and Kiel where Dönitz had his headquarters in nearby Plön. During those weeks in Hamburg he effected a strange return to the international world of business and the boulevards. Was he looking for old friends from his business days?

> As a businessman I was interested in politics but not anxious to take an active part. But when I saw that Germany was aiming for the abyss during 1931 and 1932, I tried hard to help with the formation of an alliance between the conservative parties and the National Socialists.[16]

Annelies von Ribbentrop, in her notes to his memoirs,[17] wrote: 'He joined the Nazi Party after his first meeting with Adolf Hitler.'

The enormity of his decision to join Hitler can be gauged only when it is put into context. Joachim von Ribbentrop was wealthy and successful, on the threshold of social acceptance in the snobbier segments of the capital. No doubt he was desperately anxious to show a socially impeccable conservative face and to conduct his life in a most conventional manner. In contrast, the Nazi Party was seen by most upper-class Berliners as a radical group of dangerous and violent men who brawled and pushed their way into national prominence. Their figurehead and leader was a former Austrian and a nobody. Some people of 'good' family joined the Nazi Party, but most of these were black sheep. To make common cause with this noisy, boisterous and rowdy mob from the beer cellars of Munich was not the best way to reassure Berlin society and its industrialists. But, despite all, Joachim von Ribbentrop joined the Nazi Party and endangered his own credentials as a successful man of commerce in order to take his place alongside these revolutionaries. He explained: 'Even on first meeting him, Adolf Hitler made such a strong impression on me that I was convinced only his party could save Germany from Communism.'

Thirteen years had passed since that first meeting on the Obersalzberg, when von Ribbentrop had been a handsome, well-groomed, self-assured thirty-eight-year-old entrepreneur. Now he was a worn-out fifty-two-year-old, deserted by everyone but his wife and children.

Von Ribbentrop gives a hint about how he left Berlin after that final meeting in the bunker. He wrote: 'I often thought it would have been better if they had sent back the Storch to Nauen, and I could have taken part in the final battle for Berlin.'[18] Hitler must have ordered him to be flown out of Berlin by a Storch, a little Fieseler aircraft which resembled the British Moth or the American Piper Cub. Several of these planes were the final air link from the city, since they could land on the remaining pieces of road near the Brandenburg Gate. They flew low and slowly and were elusive targets for fighter aircraft.

Grand Admiral Dönitz had returned to his navy headquarters at Plön where word of Hitler's death reached him via a telegram from Bormann. Now he was Hitler's heir, the head of state, and he moved to Flensburg, the little coastal town on the Danish border, to form a makeshift government. He made his headquarters on the ship *Patria*. On 1 May 1945, he issued a declaration to the German people, still filled with Nazi jargon, proclaiming 'deep respect and sorrow for the dead Führer and for his life's mission to protect the world from the storm flood of Bolshevism'.

He followed it with a similar appeal to the armed forces, explaining that he must continue his fight against the English and Americans 'as far and as long as they hinder me in the execution of the battle against the Bolshevists'. He informed the people and the armed forces that as head of the Reich 'the oath of loyalty which you gave to the Führer is now due from each one of you to me, as the Führer's appointed successor'. It took weeks for Dönitz to distance himself from Hitlerian ways and language.[19]

Von Ribbentrop, waiting not far away in the Friesian district near Plön, was contacted by Dönitz's adjutant, Lüdde, who wanted to locate von Neurath for Dönitz (Dönitz was not known for his tact). Von Neurath was in the Alps, so Dönitz had to choose another man for foreign minister. Von Ribbentrop then came to see him, and the Admiral informed him that he had almost chosen Count Schwerin von Krosigk, the former Finance Minister, but, to get rid of von Ribbentrop and purely as a gesture, he then asked for other suggestions. Von Ribbentrop telephoned the following day, offering only one name: von Ribbentrop.[20] Dönitz declined his offer, and he returned to Hamburg.

On 3 May, Kiel and Flensburg were declared open cities. Shattered, scarred Hamburg was trying to return to life. As if to mock its legendary neo-British style ('When it rains in London, everyone in Hamburg opens umbrellas. ... Hamburg is the only British city Germany ever held'), on 4 May Hamburg was occupied by British troops.

Von Ribbentrop had rented a flat on the fifth floor of one of the few remaining apartment houses. He was in his near-somnambulant flashback stage, trying to contact old friends and to open some form of social life. He was described as 'making the rounds of the city, dressed in a double-breasted blue suit and homburg hat, reviving old acquaintances'.

Then early in the morning of 14 June he was arrested by British troops. He was still in bed.[21] The son of one of his old acquaintances had tipped off the British authorities. Did he now remember a conversation he had held in 1944 with Fritz Hesse, once the London Bureau Chief of the German wire service DNB, and a quasi-publicist for the Embassy?

Hesse had said that something had to be done to save Germany from total destruction. 'It is quite clear', he said to von Ribbentrop, 'that even then you might not be able to save your life. You know what the Allies plan to do to the leading National Socialists!'

Von Ribbentrop stared at him. 'Do you really mean', and he faltered, 'that they intend to hang us all?'

'Why not?' said Hesse.

'What have I done? Do you really believe Lord Simon's statement in the House of Lords?' Lord Simon, usually a mild man, had spoken of hanging all German leaders. Von Ribbentrop continued, 'Do you think that's really true? But why? After all, I only did my duty like any patriot, and I can assure you I did what I could to soften the Führer's harsher decisions.'[22]

Hesse had brought up the subject to punish a man who had frequently been impatient and unkind to him, and it must have raised cold fear in von Ribbentrop. Could he guess the full extent of the crimes in which he had somehow participated? He had often complained about those who 'pampered the enemy' and who failed to 'take a hard stand when it is needed', but did he understand the consequence of his Ministry's co-operation with the SS in 'displacing, relocating, resettling, cleansing' and all those other euphemisms? Could he conceive of murder and extermination by those 'courageous men (and women)' of the SS who 'had to steel themselves to do the Reich's foul work to save the German people from mongrelization and moral decay'?

There was a curious passage in a 1943 book about von Ribbentrop by a former AA official called Dr Paul Schwarz, an exile living in New York. The book was of course completed long before the Nuremberg War Trials and their consequences. It was therefore uncanny in its forecast. This is the final paragraph of the final chapter.[23]

> My sleep is usually undisturbed. But in the days when I finished this manuscript [1942–3], the Old German Foreign Office appeared in my dreams. I was walking along beside the old Chancellery, and finally I reached the entrance to No. 76, the entrance which is called the *Ministertreppe*, the staircase reserved for the minister and his visitors of diplomatic rank. Old Schmidt, the doorman with the white beard, greeted me. He was friendly, as he has always been. He pointed to the tall lamppost which flanked the entrance on its left, and there I saw a body hanging, Ribbentrop's body dressed in the uniform which he had introduced for the Foreign Service. I woke up, shuddering. But, thinking it over, I must confess that I knew that this lamppost would do!

The arrested von Ribbentrop was taken to Luxemburg, where a large number of the Reich's surviving *altesses* were interned at the Palace Hotel in Mondorf-les-Bains (Bad Mondorf), a spa on the French border. It must have been cold comfort to see that the men he had despised for years were now his fellow prisoners. Göring, Frank, von Papen, Daluege, Darré, Frick, Funk, Marshals Jodl, Keitel and Kesselring, Speer, Ley, Rosenberg, Streicher, and even Admiral Dönitz, who 'could not use him as Foreign Minister'.

For years he had looked down on nearly all these men as unworldly drifters, parvenu opportunists, dreamers or, in the case of Streicher and Ley, vulgarians. They had always reciprocated heartily. Only von Papen came from von Ribbentrop's old Berlin circle, and they had fought often. The old luxury hotel was stripped of most comforts. It was a quasi-prison under the command of a discard US cavalry colonel named Burton C. Andrus, a heavy-set, moustached, bespectacled, 'spit and polish' American career officer and an imitation George Patton. Some prisoners were held at Neuheim in the Taunus mountains at a castle called Kransberg which had once been renovated for Göring by Speer, but the Palace Hotel at Mondorf, nicknamed the 'Ashcan', held most of the senior Nazis.

Around 16 August 1945 the Allies began to transfer them to Nuremberg, where their trials were to be held in the restored and patched Palace of Justice, which had large, attached prison wings. The Nuremberg cells were sparse, cold and uncomfortable, but the food was adequate. Many in defeated Germany were starving, but not those accused of war crimes. The prison guards were young American soldiers, filled with movie-style ideas about these evil Nazi bosses, ideas that sometimes turned the GIs into petty tyrants. In the middle of the night they made as much noise as they could, and they used contemporary cartoon descriptions for the prisoners ('Send up fat stuff' meant Göring was needed). Like most young Americans they were good-natured but disrespectful, and the Nazi prisoners, all men of standing in their own dubious world, were often more upset by disrespect than they would have been by harsh measures. There were classic German complaints about treatment 'unsuitable to a field marshal or to a senior minister'. The oil of American military informality and the water of German military and bureaucratic pomposity often failed to mix.

Most of the prisoners were accustomed to comfort if not luxury. They were not young men, and even the soldiers among them had led cosseted generals' lives with military servants, aides and adjutants. For Joachim von Ribbentrop, who had continued to live as the internationalist, *l'homme du monde*, with custom-made clothes and haberdashery in the care of good valets, the change must have been acute. The cell walls were covered with stained, peeling whitewash. There was one small barred window about five foot from the floor. An army cot covered with a brown US Army blanket stood against one wall, flanked by a small, wooden table. It was too weak to carry the weight of a potential suicide. Against the other, shorter wall stood a rickety wooden chair, cushioned with another folded-up blanket. This chair was also deliberately flimsy. Göring usually sat on his cot. One wall contained a small alcove, like a narrow fireplace, which housed a toilet. A window and peephole in the heavy wooden door guaranteed that each prisoner could be under twenty-four-hour surveillance. Most prisoners kept their washing gear and personal books and papers on the small table or on the narrow ledge over the toilet-alcove. It was a sparse and probably odoriferous life, yet one reads few complaints in von Ribbentrop's memoirs. By contrast, Speer, the only one of the prisoners who acknowledged his criminal guilt by association with the actions of the Nazi regime, complained of discomfort and occasional maltreatment. Yet he began as a young architect with few of the luxuries of life when Hitler first reached out for him.

Perhaps von Ribbentrop's acceptance of prison conditions can be credited to absolute, complete and uncomprehending shock. Nuremberg photographs and eyewitnesses depict the boulevardier gone to seed, with stringy, rumpled grey hair, crushed clothes and an air of complete disorganization. He spent his Nuremberg prison term in cell number 7, between those of Keitel and Jodl, on the lower level of the prison wing.

As a defendant, he was the exact opposite of Speer. Speer accepted his total guilt and had written to his wife of 'the truth about the whole madness'.[24]

Von Ribbentrop, from the beginning to the end of the trial, never cast a moment's doubt on his allegiance to Adolf Hitler. He had believed in the man. He had followed him and carried out his wishes. He did not question them. He could not conceive of the horrors he was now learning from films or eyewitnesses about the camps or the Einsatzgruppen. He was deeply shaken, particularly by some of the films.

He never disavowed Hitler and would not accept any personal guilt as a result of this great act of faithfulness. He admitted all signatures on all incriminating documents. He had followed his Führer's orders.

He would not acknowledge that the attack on Poland had been an act of aggression. He had accepted Hitler's view of a spiteful country brutalizing German minorities. Nor did he acknowledge aggression against Denmark or Norway. (They were pre-emptive attacks to forestall Churchill.)

His plea? 'In the sense of the indictment, not guilty.' Of which categories of crimes were they to be accused? 1. Crimes against Peace. 2. War Crimes. 3. Crimes against Humanity. Or the launching of premeditated military aggression, the maltreatment of prisoners of war and acts of brutality against conquered people, as well as Jews, Masons, gypsies, the medically incurable and others.

None of these was acknowledged by von Ribbentrop. In fact, he stated he knew of only two concentration camps, Oranienburg and Dachau. Dönitz concurred, for he too knew the names of only two camps. Sir David Maxwell-Fyfe, the British prosecutor, was baffled and outraged.

Von Ribbentrop was the only defendant to send the Russian prosecutors into fury. By asking Ambassador Gaus, the AA's legal head, who had accompanied him to Moscow in 1939, to testify in detail about the friendly meetings with Stalin, he saw to it that the entire course of events relating to those days of Nazi–Bolshevist collaboration was told openly. Even the secret protocols relating to the Baltics were read into the record. It caused no end of embarrassment to the Western judges on the bench.[25] Yet, when von Ribbentrop returned to his seat on the defendants' bench between Hess and Keitel after this testimony, he received no praise or acknowledgment from his fellow accused. The disturbed-looking and -sounding Hess was barely present, and Keitel still hated his cell neighbour, the 'champagne salesman'.

Meals were served in the Palace of Justice's dining hall, and prisoners were seated in groups of four to avoid the influence of Göring and his open attempts to 'forge cohesion'. Göring had made grandiose promises to several accused that he would take their guilt upon himself. But after an initial few gestures he ended up distancing himself from guilt by implicating others.

Almost a year was spent shuttling between the prison cells and the large courtroom, which looked like a ship's nave, with a rising set of benches on one side for the judges and another rising set of benches on the other for the accused and their lawyers. Towards the stern stood the prosecutors, and towards the bow was the witness stand. In the belly of the ship, astern of the courtroom, were rows of seats for the world's press. Proceedings began each morning at nine and were recessed at noon for lunch. Court resumed between 2 p.m. and 5 p.m. in the afternoon. Most prisoners then conferred with their lawyers or occasional visitors and took care of their personal chores, such as the barber (German, supervised), the dentist (extractions, only; no treatment) and the shower (once a week).[26] They could get their civilian or uniform suits pressed. These they wore only in the courtroom and to meals. The rest of the time they wore prison fatigue uniforms. Clergymen and psychiatrists conducted fairly frequent rounds of visits, the clergy to help the prisoners, the psychiatrists to help themselves. There were even Rorschach 'experts'.

Annelies von Ribbentrop and several of the other wives obtained permission to visit the accused, although they did not see the trials. The women met their husbands in small glass-partitioned, side-by-side booths in the inhibiting presence of American guards.

Towards the end, after his father had been sentenced, Waffen SS Captain Rudolf von Ribbentrop, who was a prisoner of war, was temporarily released to accompany his mother on her final visit to her husband.

Did Joachim von Ribbentrop ever plan to commit suicide? According to Colonel Andrus and his men, the day the trials began some pills, wrapped in tissue paper, were found inside one of von Ribbentrop's garters.[27] However, these could have been old Morell pills to calm his nerves. They were never analysed, and nowhere in his memoirs did von Ribbentrop speak of taking his own life.

The men in the dock were natural targets for journalists and psychologists. Everyone wanted to 'know the inside', to understand these men who had administered a regime of such bestiality and brutality. They were to be disappointed. These were men like any others. Adolf Hitler, the true genius of evil, the Satan who had sparked all the horror and stood back to watch while others administered it, lay dead in the garden above the bunker, doused with petrol and set on fire. His most vicious associates were also dead, Heydrich assassinated, and Himmler a suicide. Another suicide was the man who helped him to spread his poison, Goebbels.

Also in the Nuremberg dock sat the last head of the Gestapo, Kaltenbrunner, a man whose vulpine looks were deceptive. He was only a pale replica of Heydrich. Kaltenbrunner was ill during most of the trials, a wreck in a wheelchair. No one was too sorry for him. Streicher, the former schoolteacher who became the Nazis' chief vulgarian and Jew-baiter, had once invented the very style of stereotyping the Jew. When arrested, bearded and with a black hat, he looked like one of his own anti-Semitic stereotypes. Hitler had discarded him long before, and the men in the dock looked down on him and ignored him. His type of Nazi bully had gone out of Nazi fashion since the early days of the regime.

It might be indicative that of the twenty-one major war criminals whose IQ was tested, Kaltenbrunner and Streicher took the bottom two spots. Von Ribbentrop came tenth. These were the scores:[28]

1.	Schacht 143	12.	Speer 128
2.	Seyss–Inquart 141	13.	Jodl 127
3.	Göring 138	14.	Rosenberg 127
4.	Dönitz 138	15.	Von Neurath 125
5.	Von Papen 134	16.	Funk 124
6.	Raeder 134	17.	Frick 124
7.	Frank 130	18.	Hess (estimate) 120
8.	Fritzsche 130	19.	Sauckel 118
9.	Von Schirach 130	20.	Kaltenbrunner 113
10.	Von Ribbentrop 129	21.	Streicher 106
11.	Keitel 129		

Dr G. M. Gilbert, a psychiatrist assigned to the trials, published his memoirs in 1947, a year after the executions. He interviewed Göring in his cell on 11 November 1945 and quoted him as complaining about von Ribbentrop's 'tactlessness in England', just as he had earlier complained to Dr Kelley. He then trotted out the usual two examples: the newly appointed Ambassador's anti-Soviet speech upon arrival at the train station and the Nazi salute to King George VI. 'I told Hitler', said Göring, to his own vast amusement, 'how would you like it if the Russian Ambassador greeted you with "Long live the Communist revolution!"' Göring also said that Hitler had never travelled and thought von Ribbentrop 'had connections with English aristocrats'. At the signing of the Axis pact, von Ribbentrop had wanted Göring to stand behind him for the photographs. Göring said he had told von Ribbentrop that '*he* could stand behind *me*! I was the number-two man in the Reich! I had not read the treaty. Who knows? I did not really want to be there!'

Apparently nothing the 'number-two man in the Reich' said could unseat von Ribbentrop as German Foreign Minister. Long before his Luftwaffe failed to hold off the Allied bombers, Göring had often overestimated his own power. No doubt he now tried to make up for the last few years of disdain from Hitler by displaying his newly detoxified virtuosity at Nuremberg.

On 8 and 9 December 1945 Gilbert interviewed von Ribbentrop in his cell. The subject turned to anti-Semitism and the accusation that the former RAM had made certain anti-Jewish statements. Von Ribbentrop protested, 'I could not have said those anti-Semitic things! Impossible! *Ausgeschlossen!* I always thought the anti-Semitic policy was *madness*. But I was a loyal follower. Hitler had a very magnetic personality. I still cannot shake it off, six months after his death. He *overwhelmed* Chamberlain and Daladier at Munich. Himmler and Goebbels increased his anti-Semitism. I once asked about Majdanek [extermination camp], and he told me to mind my own business.' So he had heard about a camp other than the two he mentioned!

One morning a film about Hitler was shown in court, a composite of old newsreels. Later, at lunch von Ribbentrop, quite overwhelmed, wept. 'Can't you see the strength of his personality? How he swept people off their feet? It [the film] was shattering [*erschütternd*], as if a dead father had returned to life.'[29] He added that if Hitler were to walk into his cell and 'if he said, "Do this!" even now I would do it.'[30]

Then followed this question-and-answer interval with Gilbert.[31]

Gilbert: 'Was Hitler crazy? At the end of his life?'
Von Ribbentrop: 'No. You can't say that.'
Gilbert: 'Neurotics flare up when contradicted.'
Von Ribbentrop: 'Well, after I argued with Hitler in 1940, I never again had a calm discussion.'

Von Ribbentrop insisted that Hitler did not become rigid and fixated until the end of the war. After his escape on 20 July 1944, one of Hitler's eyes seemed cloudy, and his face and hands were very pale. Was it lack of sleep? Or perhaps Morell's injections? Von Ribbentrop suggested these but had no sure answers.[32]

The only time von Ribbentrop amused the court, involuntarily, was during cross-examination about the famous Berlin meeting with Czech President Hacha, during that snow-swept night early in 1939. Von Ribbentrop insisted that Hacha had never been threatened. Sir David Maxwell-Fyfe then asked, 'How can you threaten a man beyond bombing his capital and invading his country?' Von Ribbentrop answered, 'War, for instance.' The courtroom rang with laughter.

On 2 April 1946, to the hypothetical courtroom question, 'Would you have helped to assassinate Hitler if you had known the full content of the extermination camps?' von Ribbentrop answered, 'I could never have killed him. I could never repudiate him now or renounce him. I don't know why.'[33]

About the famous personal argument with Hitler, when the Führer nearly 'had a coronary attack': von Ribbentrop told Gilbert in May 1946 that it had been about the Jewish question, and that it took more courage to face Hitler on the Jewish question than to face an atom bomb. He said, 'I told Hitler he was lining up yet another power against us, added to England, France and Russia, now the Jews. As for world Jewry starting the war, that is nonsense!'

He was still puzzled why Britain should have fought over 'reasonable' demands that Poland should return Danzig and grant a right of way through the Corridor in exchange for certain concessions.[34]

Eventually, von Ribbentrop was indicted and convicted on four main counts which emerged from the millions of words, in the tens of thousands of pages.

1. His 2 January 1938 memorandum to Hitler, describing England as the arch-enemy which had to be fought.
2. His participation in the Sudeten crisis.
3. His part in the attack on Poland.
4. His orders to the AA's full staff everywhere to help with the deportations which were inherent in the Final Solution. Also, his participation in crimes against the people of the occupied countries and Vichy France.

On 1 October 1946 these brought the sentence of death by hanging. The entire trial of the twenty-three men and the absent Martin Bormann had lasted ten months. There were twelve sentences of death, three of life imprisonment. There were prison sentences of ten to twenty years for four defendants, while three of them, von Papen, Schacht and Fritzsche, were acquitted. Three names were missing – Ley committed suicide, Krupp was too ill to stand trial, Bormann was sentenced *in absentia*. Von Papen, who had shepherded Hitler's beginnings, and Schacht, who had made it possible for him to succeed economically, both seemed unlikely culprits to escape scot-free, but they did. Fritzsche, Berlin radio's chief announcer, was only the empty, pompous voice of Germany on the world's radio sets, Goebbels' spokesman, who dispensed bombast without having written it.

There were many rumours about the place chosen for the execution. It turned out to be the gymnasium of the Palace of Justice. A gallows and trap doors were built on to a platform which was mounted via an eerily symbolic thirteen steps.

The executioner was almost typecast by Hollywood, a crude, bulky Texan master sergeant called John C. Wood, who wore his 'overseas' cap with the jaunty 'twin peaks' favoured by American garrison and rear-line troops. In the US Army they were called 'latrine lawyers'. Sergeant Wood maintained that he had never lost any sleep carrying out his gruesome speciality. It had to be done by a military executioner, because it was a military tribunal which had condemned the prisoners. The journalists attending the trials had devised a form of pool to bet on the odds of who would be hanged, and their list of death sentences was headed by Göring, von Ribbentrop and Kaltenbrunner.

On the morning their sentences were to be pronounced, the prisoners assembled in a large room in the basement of the Palace of Justice. Most of these men had spent their lives together in the stream of the National Socialist revolution, its victories and final defeat, and with few exceptions they were never to see each other again. Von Ribbentrop was handcuffed to an American MP, who wore the usual white helmet, Sam Browne belt and leggings. They went to a small lift he had never seen before, ascended two floors and then walked a few steps. A door opened, and now they stood on a small platform in the courtroom, facing the judges. After von Ribbentrop had been freed of his handcuffs, a headset was handed to him and he fumbled it into place over his ears.

Then he heard the mechanical impersonal voice of an interpreter delivering the most personal words of von Ribbentrop's life. 'You are to be executed by hanging.'

He held himself together. He and his guard turned towards the small lift and back to his cell through strange new passages. It was done. It was over.

Most people who saw him after the sentencing noticed how he had aged. His cheeks sagged, his hair was wig-like and lifeless, his eyes rimmed in red like those of the sleepless. And yet he held together. The next days would find him writing last notes, memoirs and last letters. His mind functioned well. He was quite clear now. Earlier, Göring had said to Colonel Amen, the chief interrogator, that 'Ribbentrop was cracking up.'[35] He need not have worried. Von Ribbentrop stayed intact, surprisingly so for such a brittle man.

Quite calmly, he wrote a quasi-protest against the proceedings which had brought him to this no-escape end. This was his Don Quixote rebuttal.[36]

1. The jury could not be impartial. It consisted only of victors.
2. The court was based on a statute written *after* the alleged crimes. Therefore, it could not be legal.
3. He had disputed and disproved that he had ever 'conspired' to make war.
4. If he was accused of waging 'offensive war', how about the USSR (Poland and its partition according to the Molotov–Ribbentrop treaty)?
5. Many documents he wanted to submit regarding foreign policy had not been admitted.
6. About the atrocities: those who had committed them were dead. Most of those who survived had been kept in the dark (except Kaltenbrunner). And the Russians had committed equal atrocities.
7. Every convicted German in the trials would stand in the way of German reconciliation with the West.

He also presented the following.

As a believer in the Geneva Convention, I brought about the unshackling of Western POWs and prevented the branding of Russian POWs. I also prevented the shooting of 10,000 POWs, particularly airmen, after the Dresden bombings, although Hitler wished to cancel the Geneva Convention in protest against these terror bombings. I tried to change anti-Jewish laws, when no one in the party had the mental strength to approach Hitler [on this subject]. I found it obvious for humanitarian reasons. I also tried through the whole war to reopen peace talks. I never heard Hitler speak of world domination, but Hitler was convinced that the defence against eastern Bolshevism depended on Germany alone.

How can anyone blame Germany for her government when it was the Versailles Treaty which produced such a government? We were willing to compromise. Look at the Fleet Agreement and Alsace Lorraine [which Germany had decided not to claim]. But England would not go along [with our efforts]. She saw the 'balance of power' disturbed. There was no peace to be made with Russia. Hitler said there can be no compromise with Bolshevism. A contented Germany is the best guarantee for peace in Europe. The victorious powers have hopefully learned this lesson.[37]

These memoranda were later edited and published by Annelies following her husband's death. They are a classic résumé of self-justification, since few ever acknowledge that they have done evil things. In a letter to

Annelies, written on 5 October, five days after he was sentenced to death, he said:

> If Hitler were alive, his testimony would clear me. I did not wish to air my many strong disagreements with Hitler, or the German people would say what kind of a man is this who now opposes Hitler for his own selfish reasons in front of a jury of foreigners?
>
> History will show that Hitler awakened Europe to the danger of Bolshevism.

On 6 October he described himself as 'ground up by the millstones of history'.

The last two letters released by his wife were written by a father and husband. To Rudolf von Ribbentrop, the young Waffen SS officer, himself a prisoner of war, he wrote on 14 October:

> I shall walk the last steps sure that I was a patriot and did everything I could. I always did what I thought was right, although Adolf Hitler would not accept much advice about foreign policy. My thoughts and my workdays and nights were only for the good of Germany. The truth will out one day.
>
> It is very hard to part from you, but it must be, and we must not complain. Stick together through good and bad, and know that I shall always be among you and will surround you with all my love.
>
> I embrace you my dear son. . . .

Then, on 15 October, the night before his execution, he wrote this final letter to his wife:

> . . . I tried to help Adolf Hitler to build a strong flowering Germany. But the Führer and his people failed. Millions died. The Reich was destroyed and our people lie prone. Is it not right – not because of the Nuremberg verdict by foreign judges – but because of some higher judgment, that I, too, should fall?
>
> I am calm and shall face what comes with head high, which I owe to the history of my family and to my own as German Foreign Minister.
>
> You, my beloved wife, must now give your courageous heart and all the love you once had for me to the children. I know I can depend on you completely. You must know this is my final comfort.
>
> I shall go on my way with pride and belief in eternal life.
>
> Once more I take your beloved face in my hands and look deep into your eyes with all the love one human being can give to another.
>
> Farewell . . . I shall see you again in another world. God help you.[38]

At 1 a.m. on 16 October 1946 Joachim von Ribbentrop, handcuffed between two American soldiers, took his last walk into the converted gymnasium where he was to die. He was accompanied by an Evangelical

chaplain named Gerecke, assigned to those condemned who were Prot-
estants. Von Ribbentrop showed all the wear and tear of the last year of
defeat and trial. At the bottom of the stairs, his hands were tied behind
his back with a black cord. He was asked to state his name. He walked
upright when he was led up the thirteen symbolic steps of the scaffold
where a black hood was pulled over his head. Sergeant Wood then pulled
the loop of the hanging rope around his neck. His legs were tied at
the ankles. Because Göring had committed suicide in his cell after the
sentencing (with a cyanide capsule), von Ribbentrop was the first condemned man to be hanged.

After the trap door had been sprung, it took ten minutes for life to
leave him. Those who were experts said the hanging had been bungled.[39]

Joachim von Ribbentrop's last words, both in his memoirs and also as
recorded shortly before his death were:

> God protect Germany.
> God have mercy on my soul.
> My last wish is that Germany should stay united and that East and
> West will reach agreement about this.

The bodies of the executed men were laid out on cots and marked with
name tags. They were then photographed both dressed and naked and
finally placed into wooden coffins. The ropes used for their hangings were
put into the coffins with the bodies.

Arrangements for immediate cremation had been made earlier, and the
ashes were scattered by US Army personnel.

Annelies and the children who were with her returned to their rented
Dachau house. Rudolf was a prisoner awaiting processing by the
Americans.

Notes

Chapter 2: Wesel to London, 1893–1910 – 'No Violin for Christmas'

1. Dr Paul Schwarz, *This Man Ribbentrop* (New York: Julian Messner, 1943), p. 39.
2. *Ibid.*, p. 40.
3. Joachim von Ribbentrop, *Zwischen London und Moscow*, ed. A. von Ribbentrop (Leoni am Starnberger: Druffel, 1953), p. 20.
4. *Ibid.*, p. 11.
5. *Ibid.*, p. 12.
6. Ernst Hanfstaengl, *Zwischen Weissem und Braunem Haus* (Munich: R. Pieper, 1970), p. 320.
7. J. von Ribbentrop, p. 13.
8. Author's interview with Dr Franz Werner Michel, Mainz, Germany, 21 September 1990.
9. Author's interview with Jacques Français, New York, USA, 1 October 1990.
10. J. von Ribbentrop, p. 13.
11. Reinhard Spitzy, *So Haben Wir das Reich Verspielt, Bekenntnisse eines Illegalen* (Munich: Langen-Müller, 1988), p. 92, and H.J. Döscher, *Das AA im Dritten Reich* (Berlin: Siedler, 1987), p. 146, n. 7.
12. Schwarz, p. 41.
13. *Ibid.*, pp. 33–4.
14. Spitzy, p. 92, and Döscher, p. 147, n. 7.
15. J. von Ribbentrop, p. 12.
16. *Ibid.*, p. 14.
17. *Ibid.*
18. *Ibid.*, pp. 14–17.
19. *Ibid.*, p. 16.
20. *Ibid.*
21. *Ibid.*, p. 17.
22. Sir Henry Channon, *Chips: The Diaries of Sir Henry Channon*, ed. Robert Rhodes James (London: Weidenfeld & Nicolson, 1967), p. 36.
23. Schwarz, pp. 42ff.
24. John Norris, *Strangers Entertained* (Vancouver: Centennial Committee, 1971), pp. 101ff.

Chapter 3: Canada, 1911–1914 – 'The Wild West'

1. J. von Ribbentrop, p. 19.
2. Schwarz, p. 44.
3. *Ibid.*
4. J. von Ribbentrop, p. 19.
5. Schwarz, p. 43.
6. Norris, p. 102.

7. J. von Ribbentrop, pp. 20ff.
8. Douglas Glen, *Von Ribbentrop Is Still Dangerous* (London: Rich & Cowan, 1941), p. 17.
9. J. von Ribbentrop, p. 21.
10. Schwarz, p. 48.
11. *Ibid.*, p. 40.
12. J. von Ribbentrop, p. 24.
13. *Ibid.*
14. *Ibid.*, p. 25.
15. Christian Zentner and Friedemann Bedürftig, *Das Grosse Lexikon des Dritten Reiches* (Munich: Südwest, 1985), p. 246.
16. J. von Ribbentrop, p. 22.
17. *Ibid.*, p. 23.
18. *Ibid.*
19. André François-Poncet, *The Fateful Years: Memoirs of a French Ambassador in Berlin, 1931–1938*, trans. Jacques LeClercq (New York: Harcourt Brace, 1948), pp. 60ff.

Chapter 4: War – 'The Hussar'

1. Richard Knötel, Herbert Knötel and Herbert Sieg, *Uniforms of the World* (New York: Scribner, 1980), p. 131.
2. *Ibid.*, p. 150.
3. Joachim Fest, *Hitler* (New York: Vintage, 1975), pp. 68–9.
4. Schwarz, p. 51, and Wolfgang Michalka, *Ribbentrop und die Deutsche Weltpolitik, 1933–1940* (Munich: Wilhelm Fink, 1980), p. 25 n. 9.
5. Glen.
6. J. von Ribbentrop, p. 28.
7. Schwarz, p. 52.
8. J. von Ribbentrop, p. 29.
9. Schwarz, pp. 52ff.

Chapter 5: Berlin, 1919 – 'The Champagne Salesman'

1. J. von Ribbentrop, p. 30.
2. *Ibid.*
3. Schwarz, pp. 10ff.
4. *Ibid.*, p. 11.
5. *Ibid.*, pp. 55–6.
6. *Ibid.*, pp. 68ff.
7. Daniel Koerfer, 'Ernst von Weizsäcker im 3. Reich' in *Die Schatten der Vergangenheit* (Frankfurt: Propyläen, 1990), p. 382; cited in *Die Weizsäcker Papiere 1933–1950* (Berlin: Propyläen), p. 71.

Chapter 6: Berlin – 'He Could Walk over Dead Bodies'

1. J. von Ribbentrop, p. 31.
2. *Ibid.*
3. Hanfstaengl, p. 320.
4. Michel interview; and Spitzy, p. 87.
5. Michel interview; and Schwarz, pp. 16, 57.

6. Spitzy, p. 81.
7. Schwarz, p. 13.
8. *Ibid.*, p. 12.
9. Michel interview.
10. Schwarz, p. 16.
11. *Ibid.*, p. 12.
12. PEM, *Heimweh nach dem Kurfürstendamm* (Berlin: Lothar Blanvalet, 1962), p. 150.
13. Schwarz, p. 66.
14. J. von Ribbentrop, p. 33.
15. Schwarz, p. 58.
16. *Ibid.*, pp. 60–1.
17. *Ibid.*, p. 63.
18. *Ibid.*, pp. 63–4.
19. *Ibid.*, p. 66.
20. Michel interview.
21. Lali Horstmann, *Nothing for Tears* (London: William Clowes & Sons, 1948), p. x.
22. Marie 'Missie' Vassiltchikov, *The Berlin Diaries, 1940–1945* (London: Chatto & Windus, 1985), p. 25.
23. Spitzy, p. 93.
24. Schwarz, pp. 66–7.
25. François-Poncet, p. 20.

Chapter 7: Hitler to 1934 – 'Hidden Fantasies'

1. François-Poncet, p. 23.
2. J. von Ribbentrop, p. 36.
3. *Ibid.*, p. 37.
4. Döscher, p. 148.
5. Ivone Kirkpatrick, *The Inner Circle* (New York: Macmillan, 1959), p. 72.
6. François-Poncet, p. 55.
7. Schwarz, p. 73.
8. *Ibid.*
9. *Ibid.*, p. 76.
10. *Ibid.*, p. 77.
11. *Ibid.*, p. 78.
12. *Ibid.*, p. 102.
13. Nevile Henderson, *Failure of a Mission: Berlin, 1937–1939* (New York: Putnam, 1940), pp. 42ff.
14. François-Poncet, p. 289.
15. Heinz Höhne, *Die Machtergreifung* (Hamburg: Spiegel-Buch, 1983), p. 242.
16. *Ibid.*, pp. 244–6.
17. Alexander Stahlberg, *Die Verdammte Pflicht: Erinnerungen 1932 bis 1945* (Berlin: Ullstein, 1987), p. 28.
18. Höhne, *Die Machtergreifung*, pp. 248ff.
19. Konrad Heiden, *Hitler: A Biography* (London: Constable, 1936), p. 279.
20. Höhne, *Die Machtergreifung*, pp. 254–5.
21. *Ibid.*, pp. 256–7.
22. Stahlberg, p. 32.
23. *Ibid.*, p. 34.

24. Schwarz, p. 67.
25. Kirkpatrick, *The Inner Circle*, p. 53.
26. Stahlberg, p. 44.
27. François-Poncet, p. 65.
28. *Ibid.*, p. 79.
29. J. von Ribbentrop, pp. 44ff.

Chapter 8: Büro to Embassy, 1934–1936 – 'The German People's Supreme Judge'

1. Kirkpatrick, *The Inner Circle*, p. 52.
2. Erich Kordt, *Nicht aus den Akten* ... (Stuttgart: Union Deutsche, 1950), p. 51.
3. Schwarz, p. 95.
4. H.A. Jacobson, *Nationalsozialistische Aussenpolitik* (Frankfurt: Metzner, 1968), p. 253.
5. Michalka, p. 78 n. 46.
6. Jacobson, p. 253.
7. *Ibid.*, pp. 254ff.
8. Schwarz, p. 99.
9. Kordt, pp. 62–3.
10. Jacobson, p. 265 n. 6.
11. Kordt, p. 70.
12. *Ibid.*, pp. 76–7.
13. Heinz Höhne, *The Order of the Death's Head: The Story of Hitler's SS*, trans. Richard Barry (London: Pan, 1972), p. 94.
14. *Ibid.*, p. 85.
15. *Ibid.*, p. 88.
16. *Ibid.*, p. 114.
17. *Ibid.*, p. 117.
18. *Ibid.*, p. 66.
19. John Toland, *Adolf Hitler* (New York: Doubleday, 1976), p. 263.
20. Kirkpatrick, *The Inner Circle*, p. 56.
21. Franz von Papen, *Der Wahrheit eine Gasse* (Munich: Paul List, 1952), pp. 379f.
22. Ivone Kirkpatrick, *Mussolini: A Study in Power* (New York: Hawthorn, 1964), p. 294.
23. *Ibid.*, p. 296.
24. *Ibid.*
25. Jacobson, p. 793.
26. François-Poncet, p. 156.
27. Kordt, p. 82.
28. *Ibid.*, p. 84.
29. Griffiths, p. 117.
30. *Ibid.*, p. 124.
31. *Ibid.*, p. 14.
32. *Ibid.*, p. 40.
33. *Ibid.*, p. 54ff.
34. *Ibid.*, p. 52.
35. *Ibid.*, p. 53.
36. *Ibid.*, p. 55.
37. *Ibid.*, p. 65ff.

38. *Ibid.*, p. 81.
39. Interview with Franz Werner Michel, Mainz, 1990.
40. Schwarz, pp. 130ff.
41. Dr Paul Schmidt, *Statist auf Diplomatischer Bühne, 1923–1945* (Bonn: Athenaum, 1951), p. 315.
42. Richard Griffiths, *Fellow Travellers of the Right: British Enthusiasts for Nazi Germany, 1933–1939* (London: Constable, 1980), pp. 129–30.
43. *Organisationsbuch der N.S.D.A.P.* (Munich: Franz Eher, 1943), p. 566.
44. *Ibid.*, p. 568.
45. Kordt, p. 122.
46. Michalka, p. 114.
47. Schmidt, p. 327.
48. J. von Ribbentrop, pp. 141ff.
49. Channon, p. 108.
50. William Manchester, *The Last Lion: Winston Spencer Churchill*, vol. II: *Alone, 1932–1940* (Boston: Little Brown, 1988), pp. 92–3.
51. Sir Robert Vansittart, *The Mist Procession* (London: Hutchinson, 1958), p. 445.
52. *Ibid.*, p. 524.
53. *Ibid.*, p. 526.
54. Channon, p. 73.
55. *Ibid.*, p. 78.
56. J. von Ribbentrop, p. 90.
57. Schwarz, p. 189.
58. Kordt, p. 151.
59. Schmidt, p. 332.
60. Schwarz, p. 193.
61. Jacobson, p. 824.
62. J. von Ribbentrop, p. 94.
63. Channon, pp. 106ff.
64. Griffiths, pp. 221–2.
65. J. von Ribbentrop, pp. 96ff.
66. *Ibid.*, pp. 98ff.
67. Dodd, p. 245.
68. James Bentley, *Martin Niemöller, 1892–1984* (New York: The Free Press, 1984), p. 89.
69. Schwarz, pp. 36–7.
70. *Ibid.*, p. 216.
71. Michalka, p. 155.
72. Griffiths, pp. 225ff.
73. *Ibid.*, p. 230.

Chapter 9: Embassy, 1936/1937/1938 – 'Our Fellows Look Terrific'

1. Kordt, p. 154.
2. Schwarz, p. 34.
3. *Ibid.*, p. 35.
4. Interview with Spitzy.
5. Kordt, p. 154.
6. Schwarz, p. 217.
7. Interview with Spitzy.

8. Kordt, p. 160.
9. Spitzy, p. 87.
10. Kordt, p. 156.
11. Spitzy, p. 98.
12. Schwarz, p. 70.
13. Spitzy, p. 111.
14. Schwarz, pp. 194ff.
15. *Ibid.*, p. 208.
16. Spitzy, p. 102.
17. Heinz Günther Sasse, *100 Jahre Botschaft in London* (Bonn: Foreign Office, 1963), pp. 74ff.
18. Spitzy, p. 88.
19. Michalka, p. 157 n. 36.
20. Schwarz, p. 216.
21. Griffiths, p. 254.
22. Schmidt, p. 458.
23. Henderson, p. 7.
24. Griffiths, p. 282.
25. Interview with Spitzy.
26. Spitzy, p. 153.
27. Manchester, *The Last Lion*, vol. II, pp. 256ff.
28. Spitzy, p. 164.
29. *Ibid.*, pp. 124ff.
30. AA Archive, Bonn.
31. Spitzy, pp. 167ff.
32. Henderson, pp. 66ff.
33. François-Poncet, p. 212.
34. Schwarz, pp. 196ff.
35. Richard Collier, *Duce!: A Biography of Benito Mussolini* (New York: Viking, 1971), p. 134.
36. Spitzy, p. 173.
37. *Ibid.*, pp. 173ff.
38. *Ibid.*, p. 176.
39. Collier, p. 149.
40. *Ibid.*, p. 147.
41. Spitzy, p. 177.
42. Griffiths, pp. 272ff.
43. Michael Bloch, *Operation Willi* (New York: Weidenfeld & Nicolson, 1984), pp. 36ff.
44. Griffiths, pp. 273ff.
45. Bloch, *Operation Willi*, p. 37.
46. Spitzy, p. 178.
47. *Ibid.*, pp. 185ff.
48. *Ibid.*, p. 188.
49. *Ibid.*, p. 186.

Chapter 10: Embassy–Ministry–Munich–Kristallnacht, 1938–1939 – 'Will My Adorable Austria Become Nazified?'

1. AA Archive, Bonn, 9 March 1938.

2. Zentner and Bedürftig, p. 488.
3. Döscher, p. 158 n. 3.
4. Fest, *Hitler*, pp. 542ff.
5. Zentner and Bedürftig, p. 195.
6. François-Poncet, pp. 29ff.
7. Henderson, p. 120.
8. Spitzy, p. 229.
9. Kordt, p. 194.
10. *Ibid.*
11. George E. Berkley, *Vienna and Its Jews: The Tragedy of Success, 1880–1980s* (Cambridge, MA: Abt Books, 1988), p. 323.
12. *Ibid.*, p. 259.
13. Griffiths, p. 292.
14. *Ibid.*, pp. 295ff.
15. Channon, p. 151.
16. Henderson, p. 128.
17. Berkley, p. 259.
18. Schwarz, pp. 237ff.
19. Berkley, p. 315.
20. J. von Ribbentrop, pp. 125ff.
21. Spitzy, p. 260.
22. Griffiths, p. 360n.
23. Meir Michaelis, *Mussolini and the Jews: German–Italian Relations and the Jewish Question in Italy, 1922–1945* (Oxford: Clarendon Press, 1978), p. 147.
24. Walter Schellenberg, *Memoiren* (Cologne: Verlag für Politik und Wirtschaft, 1956), pp. 56ff.
25. Spitzy, p. 261.
26. Kirkpatrick, *Mussolini*, pp. 366ff.
27. *Ibid.*
28. *Ibid.*, p. 367.
29. Michaelis, p. 148.
30. Collier, p. 139.
31. Schmidt, p. 388.
32. *Ibid.*
33. Kordt, p. 225.
34. Schmidt, pp. 389ff.
35. Henderson, pp. 138ff.
36. Kordt, pp. 226ff.
37. Ulrich Dunker, *Juden in Preussen: Ein Kapital Deutscher Geschichte* (Dortmund: Harenberg, 1981), p. 352.
38. Stahlberg, p. 115.
39. Rudolf Stoiber and Boris Celovsky, *Sie Liebt die Mächtigen der Welt: Stephanie von Hohenlohe* (Munich: Herbig, 1988), pp. 167ff.
40. Kordt, pp. 315ff.
41. Griffiths, pp. 301ff.
42. Heinz Höhne, *Canaris: Patriot im Zwielicht* (Munich: Bertlesmann, 1984), p. 287.
43. Henderson, p. 145.
44. Höhne, *Canaris*, p. 329.
45. Schmidt, p. 394.

46. Ernst von Weizsäcker, *Die Weizsäcker Papiere, 1933–1950* (Berlin: Propyläen, 1974), p. 136, 19 August 1938.
47. Griffiths, pp. 307ff.
48. Schmidt, p. 395.
49. *Ibid.*
50. *Ibid.*, pp. 397ff.
51. Kordt, p. 261.
52. Henderson, p. 155.
53. *Ibid.*, p. 158.
54. Schmidt, p. 408.
55. *Ibid.*, p. 411.
56. Henderson, p. 168.
57. Schmidt, p. 413.
58. Kordt, pp. 273ff.
59. *Ibid.*, pp. 275ff.
60. Griffiths, pp. 329ff.
61. Spitzy, p. 320.
62. J. von Ribbentrop, p. 145 and n.
63. Spitzy, p. 324.
64. *Ibid.*, p. 322.
65. Heinz Linge, *Bis zum Untergang*, ed. W. Maser (Munich: Herbig, 1980), p. 151.
66. A. Zoller, *Hitler Privat* (Düsseldorf: 1949), p. 219.
67. Schmidt, p. 422.
68. Channon, p. 177.
69. Leonard Baker, *Days of Sorrow and Pain: Leo Baeck and the Berlin Jews* (New York: Macmillan, 1978), pp. 231ff.
70. LBI lecture 32, New York, 1988.
71. Baker, p. 226.
72. LBI lecture 32, New York, 1988, Alfred Gottschalk, p. 11.
73. Higham, p. 1ff.
74. Schwarz, pp. 180ff.
75. Döscher, pp. 186ff.
76. Interview with Karl Max von Schaesberg, Munich, 1990.
77. J. von Ribbentrop, pp. 160.
78. *Ibid.*, p. 150.
79. Manchester, *The Last Lion*, vol. II, p. 303.
80. *Ibid.*, p. 396.
81. J. von Ribbentrop, p. 152.
82. *Ibid.*, pp. 162ff.
83. *Ibid.*, p. 163.
84. Manchester, *The Last Lion*, vol. II, p. 408.
85. *Ibid.*, p. 409.
86. Schmidt, p. 437.
87. Margot Light, 'The Soviet View', in Roy Douglas (ed.), *1939: A Retrospect Forty Years Later* (London: Macmillan, 1983), pp. 74ff.
88. *Ibid.*, pp. 74–86.
89. Hans von Herwarth, *Zwischen Hitler und Stalin* (Frankfurt: Ullstein, 1982), pp. 162ff.
90. Charles Whiting and Friedrich Gehendges, *Jener September: Europa beim Kriegsausbruch 1939* (Düsseldorf: Droste, 1979), p. 9.

91. Herwarth, pp. 185ff.
92. J. von Ribbentrop, pp. 177–84.
93. Schmidt, pp. 445ff.
94. Walter Hofer, *Der Nationalsozialismus Dokumente, 1933–1945* (Frankfurt: Fischer, 1988), pp. 234ff.
95. *Der Spiegel*, No. 47, 1966.
96. Kordt, p. 447.
97. Donald Cameron Watt, *How War Came: The Immediate Origins of the Second World War, 1938–1939* (New York: Pantheon Books, 1989), p. 462.
98. Hofer, p. 236
99. Herwarth, p. 188.
100. Henderson, p. 270.
101. Whiting and Gehendges, p. 15.
102. *Ibid.*, p. 22.
103. *Ibid.*
104. Schmidt, pp. 458ff.
105. Whiting and Gehendges, pp. 44ff.
106. Henderson, pp. 298–9.

Chapter 11: War, 1940 – 'Is He Trying to Bore Us into Peace?'

1. J. von Ribbentrop, p. 203.
2. Höhne, *The Order of the Death's Head*, pp. 273ff.
3. *Ibid.*, p. 261.
4. Schmidt, pp. 466ff.
5. *Ibid.*, p. 469.
6. Kirkpatrick, *Mussolini*, pp. 441ff.
7. Schmidt, p. 474.
8. Kirkpatrick, *Mussolini*, p. 448.
9. *Ibid.*, p. 451.
10. Count Galeazzo Ciano, *The Ciano Diaries, 1939–1943*, ed. Hugh Gibson (New York: Doubleday, 1946), p. 294.
11. Jochen von Lang, *Der Adjutant: Karl Wolff: Der Mann Zwischen Hitler und Himmler* (Munich: Herbig, 1985), pp. 140ff.
12. Schmidt, pp. 482ff.
13. *Ibid.*, pp. 483ff.
14. *Ibid.*, pp. 484ff.
15. Kordt, pp. 387ff.
16. Schmidt, pp. 484ff.
17. Kirkpatrick, *Mussolini*, p. 467.
18. *Ibid.*, p. 469.
19. David Pryce-Jones, *Paris in the Third Reich: A History of the German Occupation, 1940–1944* (New York: Holt, Rinehart & Winston, 1981), pp. 12ff.
20. *Ibid.*, p. 38.
21. *Ibid.*, p. 25.
22. Otto Abetz, *Das Offene Problem* (Cologne: Greven & Bechtold, 1951), p. 300.
23. Pryce-Jones, p. 90.
24. Michael Bloch, *The Duke of Windsor's War: From Europe to the Bahamas, 1939–1945* (New York: Coward-McCann, 1983), pp. 76ff.

25. *Ibid.*, p. 76.
26. *Ibid.*, pp. 89ff.
27. Bloch, *Operation Willi*, p. 96.
28. Schellenberg, pp. 108ff.
29. *Ibid.*, pp. 116ff.
30. *Ibid.*, p. 118.
31. Schmidt, p. 496.
32. *Ibid.*, p. 498.
33. *Ibid.*, p. 504.
34. David Irving, *The Trail of the Fox* (New York: Dutton, 1977), p. 63.

Chapter 12: 1941–1942 – 'Unsung Heroes Doing the Reich's Dirty Work'

1. J. von Ribbentrop, pp. 217ff.
2. *Ibid.*, p. 224.
3. *Ibid.*, p. 237.
4. *Ibid.*, p. 238.
5. Roger J. Bender and Richard D. Law, *Uniforms, Organization and History of the Afrika Corps* (Mountain View, CA: R.J. Bender, 1973), p. 20.
6. Irving, *The Trail of the Fox*, p. 69.
7. *Wehrmacht Berichte, 1939–1945* (Cologne: GLB, 1989), 6 April 1941, p. 467.
8. Schmidt, p. 531.
9. *Ibid.*, pp. 537ff.
10. David Irving, *Göring* (New York: Morrow, 1989), p. 323.
11. Schmidt, p. 538.
12. *Ibid.*, p. 539.
13. *Criticon* (Munich, May–June 1991), Walter Post, p. 119; Joachim Weber, p. 125.
14. Schmidt, pp. 544ff.
15. Döscher, p. 221.
16. *Ibid.*, pp. 246–7.
17. *Ibid.*, p. 247.
18. Zentner and Bedürftig, p. 508.
19. Schmidt, p. 551.
20. Will Berthold, *Die 42 Attentate auf Adolf Hitler* (Munich: Goldman, 1981), p. 176.
21. Ciano, p. 373.
22. J. von Ribbentrop, p. 326.
23. Will Berthold, pp. 178ff.
24. Höhne, *The Order of the Death's Head*, p. 85.
25. *Ibid.*, p. 339.
26. Von Lang, *Der Adjutant*, p. 172.
27. Schmidt, p. 553.
28. Schellenberg, pp. 295ff.
29. Schmidt, pp. 564ff.
30. Abetz, pp. 258ff.
31. Schmidt, pp. 558ff.
32. Höhne, *The Order of the Death's Head*, p. 460.
33. Döscher, p. 251.

Chapter 13: 1943–1944 – 'Prussian Marshals Do Not Mutiny'

1. Döscher, pp. 256ff.
2. Schellenberg, p. 211.
3. Schmidt, p. 559.
4. *Ibid.*, p. 569.
5. Glenn Infield, *Skorzeny: Hitler's Commando* (New York: St Martin's Press, 1979), pp. 40ff.
6. Collier, pp. 270ff.
7. Von Papen, p. 577.
8. Helmut James von Moltke, *Briefe an Freya, 1939–1945* (Munich: Beck, 1988), p. 368.
9. Joseph Goebbels, *The Goebbels Diaries*, trans. Louis Lochner (New York: Popular Library, 1948), 5 December 1943, p. 613.
10. *Ibid.*, 9 December 1943, p. 618.
11. Channon, p. 384.
12. Döscher, p. 261.
13. Daniel Koerfer, 'Ernst von Weizsäcker im Dritten Reich', in *Die Schatten Der Vergangenheit* (Frankfurt: Propyläen, 1990), p. 396.
14. Stahlberg, pp. 356ff.
15. *Ibid.*, p. 372.
16. Zentner and Bedürftig, p. 21.
17. Werner Maser, *Adolf Hitler: Das Ende der Führer Legende* (Düsseldorf: Econ, 1980), p. 139.
18. *Wehrmacht Berichte*, 6 June 1944.
19. Maser, *Adolf Hitler*, p. 142.
20. William L. Shirer, *The Rise and Fall of the Third Reich* (New York: Simon & Schuster, 1959), p. 1038.
21. *Ibid.*, p. 1056.
22. Maser, *Adolf Hitler*, p. 140.
23. Irving, *Göring*, pp. 82–3.

Chapter 14: 1945 – 'Justice from the Bomb Bay of a Boeing's Belly'

1. Jochen von Lang, *The Secretary: Martin Bormann – The Man Who Manipulated Hitler*, trans. Christa Armstrong and Peter White (New York: Random House, 1979), p. 295.
2. Fest, *Hitler*, p. 724.
3. Toland, *Adolf Hitler*, pp. 727ff.
4. Albert Speer, *Inside the Third Reich*, trans. Richard and Clara Winston (New York: Macmillan, 1970), p. 423.
5. *Ibid.*, p. 440.
6. J. von Ribbentrop, pp. 266ff.
7. Pierre Galante and Eugene Silianoff, *Voices from the Bunker: The True Account of Hitler's Last Days*, trans. Jan Dalley (New York: Putnam, 1989), p. 138.
8. Walter Laqueur and Richard Breitman, *Breaking the Silence* (London: Bodley Head, 1986), p. 139.
9. Döscher, p. 294.
10. John Toland, *The Last 100 Days* (New York: Random House, 1966), pp. 306–7.
11. Irving, *Göring*, p. 454.

12. Roger J. Bender and H. P. Taylor, *Waffen-SS*, vol. II (Mountain View, CA; R. J. Bender, 1971), p. 71, and Günter Fraschka, *Mit Schwertern und Diamanten* (Munich: Universitas, 1989), p. 188.
13. Speer, *Inside the Third Reich*, p. 475.
14. *Ibid.*, p. 479.
15. *Ibid.*, pp. 483ff.
16. J. von Ribbentrop, p. 35.
17. *Ibid.*, p. 37.
18. *Ibid.*, p. 298.
19. Peter Padfield, *Dönitz: The Last Führer* (New York: Harper & Row, 1984), pp. 411ff.
20. Count Lutz Schwerin von Krosigk, *Es Geschah in Deutschland* (Tübingen: Rainer Wunderlich, 1951), p. 239, and Karl Dönitz, *10 Jahre und 20 Tage*, p. 446.
21. Werner Maser, *Nuremberg: A Nation on Trial*, trans. Richard Barry (New York: Scribner, 1979), p. 50.
22. F. Hesse, *Das Vorspiel zum Kriege* (Leoni am Starnberger: Druffel, 1979), pp. 296ff.
23. Schwarz, p. 298.
24. Speer, *Inside the Third Reich*, p. 517n.
25. Maser, *Nuremberg*, pp. 126ff.
26. *Ibid.*, pp. 63–7.
27. Ben E. Swearingen, *The Mystery of Hermann Goering's Suicide* (New York: Harcourt Brace Jovanovich, 1985), p. 42.
28. G.M. Gilbert, *Nuremberg Diary* (New York: Farrar, Straus, 1947), p. 31.
29. *Ibid.*, p. 66.
30. *Ibid.*, p. 68.
31. *Ibid.*, p. 108.
32. *Ibid.*, p. 130.
33. *Ibid.*, p. 236.
34. *Ibid.*, p. 438.
35. Irving, *Göring*, p. 484.
36. J. von Ribbentrop, pp. 294–5.
37. *Ibid.*, p. 297.
38. *Ibid.*, pp. 303–6.
39. Swearingen, p. 55, and Maser, *Nuremberg*, p. 253n.

Addendum

Since the publication of the hardback edition the following information has come to light:

Chapter 6, page 27

The allegation that the von Ribbentrops failed to help their sister in law has been disputed by Rudolf von Ribbentrop, their eldest son. He stated that his parents did manage to obtain the freedom of his aunt. He also offered the notarized testimony of Ernst Kaltenbrunner, last head of the RSHA, given at Nuremberg, dated 8 July 1946. The author offers this rebuttal in the interest of fairness.

Chapter 10, page 151

The author believes that Dr Guido Schmidt harboured sympathies for the *Anschluß*. In rebuttal, Dr Guido Schmidt's son Guido Schmidt-Chiari of Vienna, has disputed this allegation and has offered in evidence the results of a trial conducted in Vienna in 1947 by the *Volksgericht Wien*, which absolves the former Austrian *Staatssekretär* of High Treason or complicity in High Treason. Herr Schmidt-Chiari's views are published in the interest of fairness.

Select Bibliography

Abetz, Otto, *Das Offene Problem*, Cologne, Greven & Bechtold (1951).

Agee, Joel, *Twelve Years: An American Boyhood in East Germany*, New York, Farrar, Straus, Giroux (1981).

Allen, Peter, *The Windsor Secret*, New York, Stein & Day (1984).

Anger, Per, *With Raoul Wallenberg in Budapest*, New York, The Holocaust Library (1981).

Angolia, J.R. and A. Schlict, *Uniforms and Traditions of the German Army* Vol. 2, San Jose, CA, Bender (1984).

Archives of the Auswärtige Amt, Bonn

Arenhövel, Alfons, *ARENA der Leidenschafter, 1910–1973*, Berlin, Willmuth Arenhövel (1990).

Aster, Sidney (ed.), *British Foreign Policy, 1918–1945: A Guide to Research and Research Materials*, Wilmington, DE, Scholarly Resources (1984).

Schaber, Will (ed.), *AUFBAU: Dokumente einer Kultur im Exil*, New York, Overlook Press (1972).

Bach, Jurath Arne, *Franz von Papen in der Weimarer Republik*, Düsseldorf, Droste (1977).

Bailey, George, *Germans: The Biography of an Obsession*, New York, World Publishing (1972).

Baker, Leonard, *Days of Sorrow and Pain: Leo Baeck and the Berlin Jews*, New York, Macmillan (1978).

Barnett, Correlli (ed.), *Hitler's Generals*, New York, Weidenfeld & Nicolson (1989).

Bender, Roger J. and H.P. Taylor, *Waffen-SS* Vol. 2, Mountain View, CA, R.J. Bender Pub. (1971).

Bender, Roger J., H.P. Taylor and Richard D. Law, *Uniforms, Organization and History of the Afrika Corps*, Mountain View, CA, R.J. Bender Pub. (1973).

Bendt, Vera, *Wegweiser durch das jüdische Berlin: Geschichte und Gegenwart*, Berlin, Nicolai (1987).

Bentley, James, *Martin Niemöller, 1892–1984*, New York, The Free Press (1984).

Berber, Friedrich, *Zwischen Macht und Gewissen*, Munich, C.H. Beck (1986).

Berkley, George E., *Vienna and Its Jews: The Tragedy of Success, 1881–1980s*, Cambridge, MA, Abt Books (1988).

Berliner Illustrirte Zeitung 1892–1945, ed. Christian Ferber, Berlin, Ullstein (1985).

Berliner Stadtbilder aus zwei Jahrhunderten, Berlin, AGO Galerie (1987).

Berthold, Eva and Norbert Matern, *München in Bombenkrieg*, Düsseldorf, Droste (1983).

Berthold, Will, *Die 42 Attentate auf Adolf Hitler*, Munich, Goldman (1981).

Bielenberg, Christabel, *The Past is Myself*, London, Corgi (1984).

Bloch, Michael, *The Duke of Windsor's War: From Europe to the Bahamas, 1939–1945*, New York, Coward-McCann (1983).

Bloch, Michael, *Operation Willi*, New York, Weidenfeld & Nicolson (1984).

Bock, Helmut (ed.), *Sturz ins Dritte Reich*, Leipzig, Urania (1983).

Bohlen, Charles E., *Witness to History, 1929–1969*, New York, Norton (1973).

Bower, Tom, *The Pledge Betrayed: America and Britain and the Denazification of Postwar Germany*, Garden City, NY, Doubleday (1982).

Bower, Tom, *Klaus Barbie: The Butcher of Lyons*, New York, Pantheon (1984).

Bracher, Karl Dietrich, *The German Dictatorship: The Origins, Structure and Effects of National Socialism*, trans. Jean Steinberg, New York, Holt, Rinehart & Winston (1970).

Breitman, Richard, *The Architect of Genocide: Himmler and the Final Solution*, New York, Knopf (1991).

Brown, Anthony Cave, *The Last Hero: Wild Bill Donovan*, New York, Times Books (1982).

Burdick, Charles, Hans-Adolf Jacobson and Winfried Kudszus (eds), *Contemporary Germany: Politics and Culture*, Boulder, CO, Westview (1984).

Busse, Horst and Udo Krause, *Lebenslänglich für NS-Verbrecher: Der Fall Schmidt*, Pfaffenweiler, Centaurus (1989).

Buxa, Werner, *Der Kampf am Wolchow und um Leningrad, 1941–1944: Eine Dokumentation in Bildern*, Dorheim, Podzun (1969).

Campbell-Johnson, Alan, *Viscount Halifax*, New York, Ives Washburn (1941).

Cartarius, Dr Ulrich, *The German Resistance Movement, 1933–1945*, Stuttgart Exhibition (1988).

Channon, Sir Henry, *Chips: The Diaries of Sir Henry Channon*, London, Weidenfeld & Nicolson (1967).

Churchill, Winston S., *The Second World War: Closing the Ring* Vol. 5, New York, Houghton-Mifflin (1948–1953).

Ciano, Conte Galeazzo, *The Ciano Diaries, 1939–1943*, ed. Hugh Gibson, New York, Doubleday (1946).

Coats, Peter, *Of Generals and Gardens: The Autobiography of Peter Coats*, London, Weidenfeld & Nicolson (1976).

Collier, Richard, *Duce!: A Biography of Benito Mussolini*, New York, Viking (1971).

Craig, Gordon A., *The Germans*, New York, Putnam (1982).

Davis, B.L. and P. Turner, *German Uniforms of the Third Reich*, New York, Arco (1980).

Deacon, Richard, *A History of the British Secret Service*, London, Granada (1985).

Deakin, F.W., *The Brutal Friendship: Mussolini, Hitler and the Fall of Italian Fascism*, New York, Harper & Row (1962).

Deighton, Len, *Blitzkrieg: From the Rise of Hitler to the Fall of Dunkirk*, New York, Knopf (1980).

De Jonge, Alex, *Stalin and the Shaping of the Soviet Union*, New York, Morrow (1986).

D'Este, Carlo, *Decision in Normandy*, New York, Dutton (1983).

Dirksen, H. von, *Moscow, Tokyo, London*, London, Hutchinson & Co. (1952).

Dodd, Martha, *Through Embassy Eyes*, New York, Harcourt Brace (1939).

Dönitz, Karl, *Zehn Jahre und zwanzig Tage*, Frankfurt, Athenäum (1964).

Döscher, H.J., *Das A.A. im Dritten Reich*, Berlin, Siedler (1987).

Douglas, Roy (ed.), *1939: A Retrospect Forty Years Later*, London, Macmillan (1983).

Dumbach, Annette E. and Jud Newborn, *Shattering the German Night: The Story of the White Rose*, Boston, Little Brown (1986).

Dunker, Ulrich, *Juden in Preussen: Ein Kapitel Deutscher Geschichte*, Dortmund, Harenberg (1981).

Eckhardt, Wolf von and Sander L. Gilman, *Bertolt Brecht's Berlin: A Scrapbook of the Twenties*, New York, Anchor Press (1975).

Eliach, Yaffa and Brana Gurewitsch (eds), *The Liberators: Eyewitness Accounts of the Liberation of Concentration Camps – Liberation Day* Vol. 1, New York, Center for Holocaust Studies (1981).

Emery, Edwin, *The Story of America as reported by its Newspapers, 1690–1965*, New York, Simon & Schuster (1965).

Engelmann, Bernt, *Germany Without Jews*, trans. D. J. Beer, New York, Bantam (1984).

Englemann, Bernt, *In Hitler's Germany: Everyday Life in the Third Reich*, trans. Krishna Winston, New York, Schocken (1986).

Essame, Hubert, *Normandy Bridgehead*, New York, Ballantine (1970).

Everett, Susanne, *Lost Berlin*, London, Bison (1979).

Fest, Joachim C., *Hitler*, trans. Richard & Clara Winston, New York, Vintage (1975).

Fest, Joachim C., *Das Gesicht des Dritten Reiches*, Munich, R. Pieper (1988).

Ford, Corey, *Donovan of OSS*, Boston, Little Brown (1970).

François-Poncet, André, *The Fateful Years: Memoirs of a French Ambassador in Berlin, 1931–1938*, trans. Jacques LeClercq, New York, Harcourt Brace (1948).

Friedrich, Otto, *Before the Deluge: A Portrait of Berlin in the 1920s*, New York, Harper & Row (1972).

Fromm, Bella, *Blood and Banquets*, New York, Birchlane Press (1990).

Galante, Pierre and Eugene Silianoff, *Voices from the Bunker: The True Account of Hitler's Last Days*, trans. Jan Dalley, New York, Putnam (1989).

German Resistance Movement, 1933–1945, Catalog, Institut für Auslandsbeziehungen, Stuttgart (1988).

Gerwin, Robert (ed.), *Wie die Zukunft Wurzeln schlug*, Berlin, Springer (1989).

Gilbert, G.M., *Nuremberg Diary*, New York, Farrar, Straus & Giroux (1947).

Gillman, Peter and Leni Gillman, *Collar the Lot*, London, Quartet (1980).

Gisevius, H.B., *Bis Zum Bittern Ende*, Zurich, Fretz & Wasmuth (1946).

Gladwyn, Hubert M.G.J., *The Memoirs of Lord Gladwyn*, New York, Weybright & Talley (1972).

Glen, Douglas, *Von Ribbentrop is Still Dangerous*, London, Rich & Cowan (1941).

Glendinning, Victoria, *Vita: The Life of Vita Sackville-West*, New York, Knopf (1983).

Glueck, Sheldon, *War Criminals: Their Prosecution and Punishment*, New York, Knopf (1976).

Goebbels, Joseph, *The Goebbels Diaries*, trans. Louis Lochner, New York, Popular Library (1948).

Goldmann, Nahum, *Mein Leben als deutscher Jude*, Munich, Langen-Müller (1980).

Gordon, Leonard A., *Brothers Against the Raj*, New York, Columbia University (1990).

Griffiths, Richard, *Fellow Travellers of the Right: British Enthusiasts for Nazi Germany, 1933–1939*, London, Constable (1980).

Gross, Leonard, *The Last Jews in Berlin*, New York, Simon & Schuster (1982).

Grubel, F., *Catalog of the Archival Collections: Leo Baeck Institute*, Tübingen, Mohr (1988).

Grunfeld, Frederic V., *The Hitler File: A Social History of Germany and the Nazis, 1918–1945*, New York, Random House (1974).

Gun, Nerin E., *Eva Braun: Hitler's Mistress*, New York, Meredith (1968).

Haffner, Sebastian, *Anmerkungen zu Hitler*, Frankfurt, Fischer (1987).

Haffner, Sebastian, *Von Bismarck zu Hitler: Ein Rückblick*, Munich, Knaur (1989).

Hanfstaengel, Ernst, *Zwischen Weissem und Braunem Haus*, Munich, R. Pieper (1970).

Hansen, Thorkïld, *Der Hamsun Prozess*, Hamburg, Knaus (1979).

Harris, Robert, *Selling Hitler*, New York, Pantheon (1986).

Hassell, Fey von, *Hostage of the Third Reich: The Story of My Imprisonment and Rescue from the SS*, ed. David Forbes-Watt, New York, Scribner (1989).

Hassell, Ulrich von, *Die Hassell-Tagebücher 1938–1944: Deutscher Widerstand 1937–1945*, Berlin, Siedler (1988).

Hastings, Max, *Das Reich: The March of the 2nd SS Panzer Division through France*, New York, Holt, Rinehart & Winston (1981).

Hastings, Max, *Victory in Europe: D-Day to V-E Day in Full Color*, photog. George Stevens, Boston, Little Brown (1985).

Haupt, Werner and J.K.W. Bingham, *Der Afrika Feldzug, 1941–1943*, Friedberg, Podzun (1968).

Heiden, Konrad, *Hitler: A Biography*, London, Constable (1936).

Heilburt, Anthony, *Exiled in Paradise*, New York, Viking (1983).

Henderson, Nevile, *Failure of a Mission: Berlin 1937–1939*, New York, Putnam (1940).

Henry, Frances, *Victims and Neighbors: A Small Town in Nazi Germany Remembered*, South Hadley, MA, Bergin & Garvey (1984).

Herwarth, Hans von, *Zwischen Hitler und Stalin*, Frankfurt, Ullstein (1982).

Herzstein, Robert Edwin, *The Nazis*, Alexandria, VA, Time-Life Books (1980).

Hess, Wolf R., *Rudolf Hess Briefe 1908–1933*, Munich, Langen-Müller (1987).

Hesse, F., *Das Vorspiel zum Kriege*, Leoni am Starnberger, Druffel (1979).

Higham, Charles, *Trading with the Enemy: An Exposé of the Nazi-American Money Plot, 1933–1949*, New York, Delacorte Press (1983).

Higham, Charles, *American Swastika*, Garden City, NY, Doubleday (1985).

Hildebrandt, Fred, *. . . ich soll dich grüssen von Berlin, 1922–1932*, Munich, Ehrenwirth (1966).

Hillesum, Etty, *An Interrupted Life: The Diaries of Etty Hillesum, 1941–1943*, trans. Arn O. Pomerans, New York, Pantheon (1983).

Hinze, Rolf, *Die 19. Panzer-Division, 1939–1945*, Friedberg, Podzun-Pallas (1979).

Hitchens, Marilynn Giroux, *Germany, Russia, and the Balkans: Prelude to the Nazi–Soviet Non-Aggression Pact*, New York, Columbia University (1983).

Hitler, Adolf, *Mein Kampf*, Munich, M. Muller & Sohn (1927).

Hofer, Walter, *Der Nationalsozialismus: Dokumente, 1933–1945*, Frankfurt, Fischer (1988).

Höhne, Heinz, *The Order of the Death's Head: The Story of Hitler's SS*, trans. Richard Barry, London, Pan (1972).

Höhne, Heinz, *Die Machtergreifung: Deutschlands Weg in die Hitler-Diktatur*, Hamburg, Spiegel-Buch (1983).

Höhne, Heinz, *Canaris: Patriot im Zwielicht*, Munich, Bertlesmann pb. (1984).

Horstmann, Lali, *Nothing for Tears*, London, William Clowes & Sons Ltd (1948).

Hubmann, Franz, *Das Deutsche Familienalbum*, Vienna, Molden (1972).

Infield, Glenn B., *Hitler's Secret Life*, London, Hamlyn (1979).

Infield, Glenn B., *Skorzeny: Hitler's Commando*, New York, St Martin's (1981).

International Military Tribunal Vols XII and XIII, Nuremberg (1949).

Irving, David, *The Trail of the Fox*, New York, Dutton (1977).

Irving, David, *Göring*, New York, Morrow (1989).

Jacobson, H.A., *Nazionalsozialistische Aussenpolitik*, Frankfurt, Metzner (1968).

Kahn, Leo, *Nuremberg Trials*, New York, Ballantine pb. (1972).

Keegan, John, *Six Armies in Normandy: From D-Day to the Liberation of Paris, 6 June – 25 August 1944*, New York, Viking (1982).

Kehr, Helen and Janet Langmaid (eds), *The Nazi Era, 1919–1945*, London, Mansel (1982).

Keneally, Thomas, *Schindler's List*, New York, Simon & Schuster (1982).

Kiaulehn, Walther, *Berlin*, Munich, Biederstein (1958).

Kirkpatrick, Ivone, *The Inner Circle*, New York, Macmillan (1959).

Kirkpatrick, Ivone, *Mussolini: A Study in Power*, New York, Hawthorn (1964).

Knötel, Richard, Herbert Knötel and Herbert Sieg, *Uniforms of the World*, New York, Scribner (1980 rev. edn).

Koch, Hannsjoachim W., *Volksgerichtshof: Politische Justiz in 3. Reich*, Munich, Universitas (1988).

Koch, Peter-Ferdinand (ed.), *Die Dresdner Bank und der Reichsführer-SS*, Hamburg, Facta-Oblita (1987).

Koerfer, D., 'Ernst von Weizsäcker im Dritten Reich' in U. Backes, E. Jesse and R. Zitelmann, *Die Schatten der Vergangenheit*, Frankfurt, Propyläen (1990).

Konsalik, Heinz A., *Stalingrad: Bilder vom Untergang der 6. Armee*, Bayreuth, Goldmann (1979).

Kordt, Erich, *Nicht aus den Akten . . .*, Stuttgart, Union Deutsche (1950).

Krüger, Horst, *A Crack in the Wall: Growing Up Under Hitler*, trans. Ruth Hein, New York, Fromm International (1982).

Lang, Jochen von, *The Secretary: Martin Bormann – The Man Who Manipulated Hitler*, trans. Christa Armstrong and Peter White, New York, Random House (1979).

Lang, Jochen von, *Der Adjutant: Karl Wolff – Der Mann zwischen Hitler und Himmler*, Munich, Herbig (1985).

Lange, Annemarie, *Berlin in der Weimarer Republik*, Berlin, Dietz (1987).

Laqueur, Walter, *Weimar: A Cultural History, 1918–1933*, New York, Putnam (1974).

Laqueur, Walter, and Richard Breitman, *Breaking the Silence*, London, Bodley Head (1986).

Leber, Annedore, Willy Brandt and Karl Dietrich Bracher, *Das Gewissen Steht Auf 1933–1945*, Mainz, von Hase & Koehler (1984).

Leo Baeck Institute, *Yearbook* Vols 29/1984, 31/1986, 33/1988, 34/1989, 35/1990, London, Secker & Warburg.

Lester, Elenore, *Wallenburg: The Man in the Iron Web*, Engelwood Cliffs, NJ, Prentice-Hall (1982).

Lêvai, Jenö, *Raoul Wallenburg*, trans. F. Vajda, Univ. of Melbourne, Australia (1989).

Levenstein, Aaron, *Escape to Freedom: The Story of the International Rescue Committee*, Westport, CT, Greenwood Press (1983).

Linge, Heinz, *Bis zum Untergang*, ed. W. Maser, Munich, Herbig (1980).

Lorant, Stefan, *Sieg Heil!: An Illustrated History of Germany from Bismarck to Hitler*, New York, Norton (1974).

Lucas, James S., *Last Days of the Third Reich: The Collapse of Nazi Germany, May 1945*, New York, William Morrow (1986).

Lyons, Graham (ed.), *The Russian Version of World War II*, Hamden, CT, Archon Books (1976).

MacDonald, Callum A., *The Killing of SS Obergruppenführer Reinhard Heydrich*, New York, The Free Press (1989).

Macksey, M.C., *Afrika Korps*, New York, Ballantine (1972).

Manchester, William, *Krupp: Chronik einer Familie*, Munich, Wilhelm Heyne (1978).

Manchester, William, *The Last Lion: Winston Spencer Churchill – Alone 1932–1940* Vol. II, Boston, Little Brown (1988).

Marrus, Michael R. and Robert O. Paxton, *Vichy France and the Jews*, New York, Basic Books (1981).

Maser, Werner, *Nuremburg: A Nation on Trial*, trans. Richard Barry, New York, Scribner (1979).

Maser, Werner, *Adolf Hitler: Das Ende der Führer Legende*, Düsseldorf, Econ (1980).

Mechow, Max, *Die Ost- und Westpreussen in Berlin*, Berlin, Haude & Spencersche (1975).

Metcalfe, Philip, *1933*, Sag Harbor, NY, Permanent Press (1988).

Michaelis, Meir, *Mussolini and the Jews: German–Italian Relations and the Jewish Question in Italy, 1922–1945*, Oxford, Clarendon Press (1978).

Michalka, Wolfgang, *Ribbentrop und die deutsche Weltpolitik 1933–1940*, Munich, Wilhelm Fink (1980).

Moltke, Helmut James von, *Briefe an Freye 1939–1945*, Munich, Beck (1988).

Mosley, Diana Mitford, *A Life of Contrasts*, New York, Times Books (1977).

Neave, Airey, *Nuremburg*, London, Hodder & Stoughton (1978).

Nelson, Walter Henry, *The Berliners: Their Saga and Their City*, New York, David Mckay (1969).

Norris, John, *Strangers Entertained*, Vancouver, Canada, Centennial Committee (1971).

Organisationsbuch der N.S.D.A.P., Munich, Franz Eher (1943).

Padfield, Peter, *Dönitz: The Last Führer*, New York, Harper & Row (1984).

Papen, Franz von, *Der Wahrheit eine Gasse*, Munich, Paul List (1952).

Paucker, Arnold, Sylvia Gilchrist and Barbara Suchy, *Die Juden im National-sozialistischen Deutschland 1933–1943*, Tübingen, Mohr (1986).

PEM, *Heimweh nach dem Kurfürstendamm*, Berlin, Lothar Blanvalet (1962).

Persico, Joseph, *Piercing the Reich*, New York, Viking (1979).

Persico, Joseph, *The Spiderweb*, New York, Crown (1979).

Peters, A.R., *Anthony Eden at the Foreign Office, 1931–1938*, New York, St Martin's (1986).

Picker, Henry and Heinrich Hoffmann, *Hitler Close-up*, trans. Nicholas Fry, New York, Macmillan (1973).

Piekalkiewicz, Janusz, *Spione Agenten Soldaten*, Munich, Herbig (1988).

Poliakov, Leon, *Geschichte des Antisemitismus: von der Antike bis zu den Kreuzzügen* Vol. 1, Worms, Heintz (1977).

Pollack, Wolfgang (ed./trans.), *German Identity: Forty Years After Zero*, Sankt Augustin, Comdok (Friedrich Naumann Foundation) (1987).

Pomrehn, Arno, Hans Sänger and Dr Hans Joachim Schaeffer, *Der Weg der 79 Infanterie Division 1939–1945*, Dorheim, Podzun (1971).

Pryce-Jones, David, *Paris in the Third Reich: A History of the German Occupation, 1940–1944*, New York, Holt, Rinehart & Winston (1981).

Reichel, Sabine, *What Did You Do in the War, Daddy?: Growing Up German*, New York, Hill & Wang (1989).

Reider, Frederic, *The Order of the SS: How Did It Happen?*, Tucson, AZ, AZTEX Corp. (1981).

Ribbentrop, Annelies von, *Die Kriegsschuld des Widerstandes*, Leoni am Starnberger, Druffel (1975).

Ribbentrop, Joachim von, *Zwischen London und Moscow*, ed. Annelies von Ribbentrop, Leoni am Starnberger, Druffel (1953).

Richarz, Monika (ed.), *Jüdisches Leben in Deutschland*, Stuttgart, Deutsche Verlags-Anstalts (1982).

Riess, Curt, *Goebbels*, Munich, Universitas (1989).

Ritter, Gerhard, *Carl Goerdeler und die deutsche Widerstandsbewegung*, Stuttgart, Deutsche Verlags-Anstalt (1954).

Roters, Eberhart, *Berlin, 1910–1933*, New York, Rizzoli (1982).

Russell, Francis, *The Secret War*, Alexandria, VA, Time-Life Books (1981).

Sasse, Heinz Günther, *100 Jahre Botschaft in London*, Bonn, Foreign Office (1963).

Sayer, Ian and Douglas Botting, *Nazi Gold*, London, Congdon & Weed (1984).

Schaumburg-Lippe, F.C., *Dr Goebbels*, Kiel, Arndt (1990).

Schellenberg, Walter, *Memoiren*, Cologne, Verlag Für Politik und Wirtschaft (1956).

Schmidt, Dr Paul, *Statist auf diplomatischer Bühne, 1923–1945*, Bonn, Athenaum (1951).

Schmitz, Gunther, *Die 16 Panzer Division*, Friedberg, Podzun-Pallas (1979).

Schwarz, Dr Paul, *This Man Ribbentrop*, New York, Julian Messner (1943).

Schwerin von Krosigk, Count Lutz, *Es geschah in Deutschland*, Tübingen, Rainer Wunderlich (1951).

Sellenthin, H.G., *Geschichte der Juden in Berlin und des Gebäudes Fasanenstrasse 79/80*, Berlin, Jewish Community of Berlin (1959).

Shirer, William L., *The Rise and Fall of the Third Reich*, New York, Simon & Schuster (1959).

Siewert, Curt, *Schuldig?: die Generale unter Hitler*, Bad Nauheim, Podzun (1968).

Smith, Truman, *Berlin Alert: The Memoirs and Reports of Truman Smith*, ed. Robert Hessen, Stanford, CA, Hoover Center (1984).

Sonnleithner, Franz von, *Als Diplomat im 'Führerhauptquartier'*, Munich, Langen-Müller (1989).

Speer, Albert, *Inside the Third Reich*, trans. Richard and Clara Winston, New York, Macmillan (1970).

Speer, Albert, *Spandauer Tagebücher*, Frankfurt, Propyläen (1975).

Speer, Albert, *Infiltration*, trans. Joachim Neugroschel, New York, Macmillan (1981).

Spitzy, Reinhard, *So haben wir das Reich verspielt*, Munich, Langen-Müller (1988).

Squadron Signal Publications Nos 2004, 3001, 3002, 3004, 6101, Carrolton, TX (1972, 1973, 1980).

Staden, Wendelgard von, *Darkness Over the Valley*, trans. Mollie Comerford Peters, New Haven, CT, Ticknor & Fields (1984).

Stahlberg, Alexander, *Die verdammte Pflicht: Erinnerungen 1932 bis 1945*, Berlin, Ullstein (1987).

Stoiber, Rudolf and Boris Celovsky, *Stephanie von Hohenlohe*, Munich, Herbig (1988).

Studnitz, Hans-Georg von, *Menschen aus meiner Welt*, Berlin, Ullstein (1985).

Swearingen, Ben E., *The Mystery of Hermann Goering's Suicide*, New York, Harcourt Brace Jovanovich (1985).

Tetens, Tete Harens, *The New Germany and the Old Nazis*, New York, Random House (1961).

Titzenthaler, Waldemar, *Berlin: Photographien von Titzenthaler*, Berlin, Nicolaische (1987).

Tokayer, Marvin and Mary Swartz, *The Fugu Plan*, New York, Paddington Press (1979).

Toland, John, *The Last 100 Days*, New York, Random House (1966).

Toland, John, *Adolf Hitler*, New York, Doubleday (1976).

Toland, John, *Hitler: The Pictorial Documentary of His Life*, New York, Doubleday (1978).

Tutas, Herbert C., *N.S. Propaganda und deutsches Exil, 1933–1939*, Meisenheim, Anton Hain (1973).

The Twentieth Century, Television Series, Arts & Entertainment Network (February 1990).

Urdang, Laurence (ed.), *The Timetables of American History*, New York, Simon & Schuster (1981).

Vansittart, Sir Robert Gilbert, *The Mist Procession*, London, Hutchinson (1958).

Vassiltchikov, Marie 'Missie', *The Berlin Diaries, 1940–1945*, London, Chatto & Windus (1985).

Volkswagen in *Automobile Quarterly* Vol. 18, No. 4, pp. 340–61, Princeton, NJ (1980).

Vormann, Nikolaus von, *So begann der Zweite Weltkrieg*, Leoni am Starnberger, Druffel (1978).

Warlimont, Walter, *Im Hauptquartier der deutschen Wehrmacht, 1939 bis 1945*, Augsburg, Weltbild (1990).

Watson, Francis, *Dawson of Penn: A Biography*, London, Chatto & Windus (1950).

Watt, Donald Cameron, *How War Came: The Immediate Origins of the Second World War, 1938–1939*, New York, Pantheon Books (1989).

Webster's New Biographical Dictionary, Springfield, MA, Merriam-Webster (1983).

Wehrmacht Berichte, 1939–1945, Cologne, GLB (1989).

Weizsäcker, Ernst von, *Die Weizsäcker Papiere, 1933–1950*, Berlin, Propyläen (1974).

Werbell, Frederick E. and Thurston Clarke, *Lost Hero: The Mystery of Raoul Wallenburg*, New York, McGraw-Hill (1982).

Werlich, Robert, *Orders and Decorations of All Nations*, Washington, DC, Quaker Press (1974).

Westphal, Uwe, *Berliner Konfektion und Mode 1836–1939 die Zerstörung einer Tradition*, Berlin, Hentrich (1986).

Whiting, Charles and Friedrich Gehendges, *Jener September: Europa beim Kriegsausbruch 1939*, Düsseldorf, Droste (1979).

Willett, John, *The Weimar Years: A Culture Cut Short*, New York, Abbeville Press, (1984).

World Guide, New York, Rand-McNally (1953).

Wortmann, Michael, *Baldur von Schirach: Hitlers Jugendführer*, Cologne, Bohlau (1982).

Wykes, Alan, *Goebbels*, New York, Ballantine (1973).

Zentner, Christian and Friedemann Bedürftig, *Das Grosse Lexikon des Dritten Reiches*, Munich, Südwest (1985).

Ziemke, Earl F., *Battle for Berlin: End of the Third Reich*, New York, Ballantine (1968).

Zoller, Albert, *Hitler Privat*, Düsseldorf (1949).

Index

AA, *see* Auswärtiges Amt
Abetz, Otto, 228, 229–30, 241, 242, 263–4
Afrika Corps, *see* Rommel, Erwin
Albania, invasion by Italy, 192
Alfieri, Dino, 131, 226
Allen, Commandant Mary, 85
Allen of Hurtwood, Lord, 87, 89
Alvensleben, Alvo and Eno, 10–11
Alvensleben, Ludolf, 216
Alvensleben, Werner, 56
Ambrosio, Italian soldier, 271
America First Committee, 101–2
Anglo-German Fellowship, 88–9, 98, 137, 167, 171
Anglo-German Group, 86–7
Anglo-German Naval Agreement, 93–4, 193
Anglo-Italian Mediterranean Treaty, 158, 161
Anschluss (Austrian), 149–50, 152
Anti-Comintern Pact, 97, 108, 110–11; and Hungary, 184; and Italy, 131, 133, 135; and Japan, 116–17, 242
Anti-Semitism: in Austria, 151, 152; in Britain, 85–6, 283; in France, 283; in Germany, 282–3; amongst Jews, 39; and the Nazis, 37, 95–6, 98, 108; in Poland, 216–17; in USA, 183–4; *see also* Final Solution; *Kristallnacht*; ss atrocities
Antonescu, Marshal Ion, 249
Appeasement policy, 169; *see also* Munich
Apsley, Lord, 112
Arent, Benno von, 154
Armistice 1918, 20
Arnim, General Jurgen von, 263, 269
Arnold, Lord, 88
Attolico, Bernardo, 165, 175–6, 203–4, 207, 226
August Wilhelm, Prince ('Auwi'), 16, 126
Auslandsdeutsche, 130
Austria, 79–80, 146–7, 149; German entry (*Anschluss*), 149–50, 152; and Adolf Hitler, 137, 146–7, 149–50, 153
Auswärtiges Amt (AA), German Foreign Service, 23, 35, 58, 59, 73, 97, 107, 253–4, 268; and the ss, 62, 154, 256

Bach-Zelewski, General Erich von dem, 258
Badoglio, Marshal Pietro, 227, 270, 272
Balbo, Marshal Count Italo, 133
Baldwin, Stanley, 71, 82, 91, 93; and Germany, 100, 117

Balfour, M. G., 86
Baltic countries, and the German/Soviet Pact, 199, 200, 201, 203, 243, 299
Barthou, Jean Louis, 70–1, 74, 89
Bateman, Arthur, 86
Battle of the Bulge, 284–5
Beck, Colonel Joséf, 186–7, 192, 205
Beck, General Ludwig, 95, 281; and Czechoslovakia, 163, 165, 166; against Hitler, 163, 168, 169, 175, 176, 269, 279
Beigbeder, Colonel Juan, 231, 232, 236
Belgium, 97, 224
Beneš, Eduard, 151, 161, 162, 166, 168, 174, 178
Berlin, between the wars, 22–3, 29–32; bombing of, 273–4, 286–7
Bernadotte, Count Folke, 290–1
Bershkov, Valentin, 250
Best, ss General Werner, 265–6
Bethmann-Hollweg, Theobald von, 10
Bismarck, Prince Otto von, 8, 102, 112, 206
Blaskowitz, Col-General Johannes, 216–17, 223
Blomberg, General Werner von, 56, 69, 70, 81, 124–5, 140–1, 142; and the Rhineland, 98, 99; and Röhm, 74, 75
Blum, Léon, 99, 105–6
Bock, Field Marshal Fedor von, 257
Bohle, Gauleiter, 252
Bolshevism, *see* Communism
Bormann, Martin, 248, 252, 287, 292–3; death and after, 293, 302
Bose, Herbert von, 75
Brandt, Karl, 284
Brauchitsch, General Walter von, 142, 163, 255
Braun, Eva, 201, 290, 293
Brauweiler, Roland, 72
Brenner Pass meetings, 222–3, 236, 249
Brinon, Count Fernand de, 71, 74
Britain, *see* United Kingdom
British Legion visit to Hitler, 95
British Union of Fascists, 84–6
Brüning, Friedrich, 39–40
Bruns, Dr Georg, 254
Brunswick, Duke of, 108
Bülow, Bernhard von, 58, 63, 106, 148
Bülow-Schwante, Count Vico, 48, 49, 160
Büro Ribbentrop (later Dienststelle Ribbentrop), 68, 72, 94, 144, 146, 248

Cadogan, Sir Alexander, 127
Canaris, Admiral Wilhelm Franz, 166, 178, 215; opposition to Hitler, 269, 279
Casablanca, meeting at, 267
'Case Green', 163
'Case White', 207
Chamberlain, Austen, 81–2, 83, 114–15
Chamberlain, Neville, 103, 149, 190, 192, 195, 204–5; and Hitler, 166, 168–9; and Munich, 171–3, 176, 177–8, 179
Channon, Sir Henry 'Chips', 10, 87, 88, 105, 108–9, 134, 151, 162, 177, 190, 223; on Ciano, 274–5; on Ribbentrops, 102–3
China, and Germany, 117, 135
Churchill, Winston, 224–5, 238; meeting with Henlein, 162, 166; and Mussolini, 83; and Ribbentrop, 127, 149; and Roosevelt, 243, 267
Chwalkowsky, 178, 188–9
Ciano, Count Galeazzo, 131, 133, 135, 180, 203, 274–5; and Ribbentrop, 219–20, 223, 235, 273; German-Italian military treaty, 161; and Munich, 176; Italo-German Pact, 194; and German-Soviet Pact, 198; meetings with the Germans, 222, 235, 262–3; declaration of war on France, 225; sent to the Vatican, 270; death, 270, 273; views on, 273, 274–5
Clive, Lord, 167
Communism, German fear of, 33, 37–8, 97, 108, 114; and Ribbentrop, 304–5; *see also* Anti-Comintern Pact
Concentration camps, 62, 95, 257, 260; and Ribbentrop, 260, 298
Connaught, Arthur William, Duke of, 13, 14
Conwell-Evans, Philip, 82, 87, 88, 89, 94, 98, 103, 111, 131, 167, 169
Cooper, Duff, 103, 104–5, 112, 177
Coronation of George VI, 115, 124, 125–6
Coulondre, 204, 207
Craigie, Sir Robert, 93
Crinis, Professor de, 268, 287
Cripps, Sir Stafford, 244, 246
Croatia, joins Tripartite Agreement, 249
Cunard, Emerald, Lady, 10, 88, 93, 102
Czechoslovakia, 143, 151, 156–8, 161–2; and Adolf Hitler, 137, 156–8, 161, 163; and Ribbentrop, 158, 162–3; mobilized, 162, 174; invaded by Poland, 178; Hitler enters Prague, 188; German occupation, 188–90; and Hungary, 173–4, 178, 180, 187

D'Abernon, Lord, 35
Dahlerus, Birger, 205
Daily Mail interviews with Hitler, 80, 89
Daladier, Édouard, 74, 176, 179, 190
Danzig, 92, 143, 186, 223
Darlan, Admiral Jean Louis, 263
Davidson, J. C. C., 71, 82

De Bono, Marshal Emilio, 133
Dekanosov, Ambassador, 238, 249–50
Democracy, questioned in UK, 83
Denmark, 194, 224, 265–6
Deutsche Volks Partei (DVP), 45
Deitrich, SS General Sepp, 76, 159, 198, 285, 291
Dirksen, Herbert von, 156, 170, 190, 191
Dodd, Martha, 109
Dodd, William E., 78, 95, 101, 123
Dollfuss, Engelbert, 79–80
Domville, Admiral Sir Barry, 89, 112, 171
Dönitz, Admiral Karl, 282, 292, 293, 295, 298; and Ribbentrop, 295
Donovan, Colonel 'Wild Bill', 241
Doran, Edward, 86
Dörnberg, Freiherr Alexander von, 49, 119, 160
Doumergue, Gaston, 74–5
Drax, Admiral, 195
Duelling in Germany, 39

Ebert, Friedrich, 22, 29
Eden, Anthony, 72, 81, 98, 99–100, 146, 177; visits to Hitler, 70, 90
Edward VIII, 98, 116, 117, 118, 234; and Nazism, 87, 88, 105, 112; meets Ribbentrop, 93, 116, 133; meets Hitler, 133–4; attempted recruitment of him as Duke of Windsor, 230–5
Ehrhardt Brigade, 28, 76
Eichmann, SS Colonel Adolf, 152–3, 227, 259
Einsatzkommando reports, 254–5
Eltisley, Lord, 88
Engel, Major, 208
Estonia, 194, 260

Falkenhayn, General Erich von, 19
Farinacci, Roberto, 160
Fascism:
in Britain, 84–6, 88–90; in Italy, 159–60; in Spain, 191; *see also* Nazism
'Final Solution' (*Endlosung*), 253, 259–60
Finland, and Soviet Union, 243
Fitzpatrick, Sir Charles, 13
Flick, Friedrich, 52
Forgan, Dr, 85
Forster, Albert, 69, 92, 223
Forwood, Dudley, 133–4
France: military service, 90; quiescence on Rhineland, 99, 100; ultimatum 1939, 211; invasion, 225, 226; and Adolf Hitler, 227, 228; Vichy government and Armistice, 227; occupation of Unoccupied Zone, 263; French fleet scuttled, 264
Franco, General Francisco, 105–6, 112, 134, 191; neutrality, 231, 236–7; meeting with Hitler, 236–7
Franco-Soviet Pact, 92, 98, 99

François-Poncet, André, 40, 54, 59, 69, 78, 151, 204; on Hitler, 50, 134; on Nazism, 65; at Nuremberg Rallies, 130–1, 167; on von Neurath, 144; and Czechoslovakia, 175; in Italy, 225
Frank, Hans, 159, 167–8
Frank, Karl Hermann, 189
Freisler, Roland, 288, 290, 291
Frick, Dr Wilhelm, 54, 59, 63, 95–6
Fried, Susie, 35
Fritsch, Werner Freiherr von, 99, 142
Fritsche, radio announcer, 302–3
Fuschl Castle, 152

Galland, General Adolf, 270
Gamelin, General Maurice Gustave, 127, 223
Gaulle, General Charles de, 228
Gaus, Ambassador, 299
Geneva disarmament conference 1933, 69–70
George v, 87, 92, 98
George vi, 115, 124, 125–6, 134; and Ribbentrop, 119–20, 149
German American Bund, 183–4
German colonies, 123
German Embassy, London, 110–11, 115, 118, 121; Coronation Ball, 124, 126–7, 128
German Hospital, London, 115
German-Italian Pact of Steel, 194
German-Soviet Pact, 199–200, 239; and Hitler, 239, 242, 243
Germans exiled in UK, 120, 122–3
Germany: post World War i, 21; post World War ii, 21–2; economic problems, 33, 38; re-armament, 69–70, 72–3, 89–90; economic agreements, 90, 193–5; and Denmark, 194, 224; military agreement with Italy and Japan, 236; declaration of war with USA, 236; invasion of Soviet Union, 243–4, 245; Soviet campaign, 250–1, 255, 264, 267, 275; bombing of Britain, 247; bombing of, 269–70, 273, 286–7, 291; invasion of, 279–80
Gersdorff, Rudolf Freiherr von, 256
Gilbert, Dr G.M., 300–1, 302; interview with Ribbentrop, 301
Glen, Douglas, 19
Globocnik, Odilo, 153
Goebbels, Dr Josef: and Ribbentrop, 139–40, 219, 225, 274; close to Hitler, 50, 155; in 1933, 56, 57, 59; Minister for Enlightenment and Propaganda, 64; at Geneva, 69; and foreign press, 83; Olympic Games, 109; party rally 1937, 131; anti-Franco, 135; in Rome, 159; and *Kristallnacht*, 181; on Britain, 274; life in the bunker, 291; suicide, 293, 300
Goerdeler, Carl, 278, 282, 289
Göring, Reichsmarshal Hermann: and Ribbentrop, 120, 154, 175, 205, 282; on Ribbentrop, 300–1; and Hitler, 66, 73, 155; and Helldorf, 47; meeting with Hitler and others, 54, 56; importance, 59; and sa, 60; Prussian Minister-President, 63; and Röhm, 76; Jewish godfather, 96–7; cautious on Rhineland, 99; and Olympic Games, 109; Four-Year Plan, 131; wealthy through industrial plant, 139; and von Blomberg, 141; and Prince Stephanie Hohenlohe, 166; and Czechoslovakia, 167, 179, 189; and Jewish pogrom, 181–2; and Poland, 205; and France, 227, 228, 230; and Final Solution, 253; and Juin, 263; depression, 270; attacked by Dönitz, 282; addiction to morphine, 284; in the bunker, 291–2; possible succession to Hitler, 292; after Hitler's death, 293–4; at Nuremberg, 297, 299; suicide, 306
Grandage, Dr, 9
Graziani, Marshal Rodolfo, 239, 272
Greville, Mrs Ronnie, 88, 98
Gröner, General, 40
Gruhn, Eva, later von Blomberg, 140–1
Grynszpan, Herschel, 181
Guariglia, 271
Guderian, General Heinz, 287, 291
Gürtner, Dr Margarete, 86–7
Guttmann, Herbert, 26

Hacha, Dr Emil, 180, 188–9, 284, 302
Haffner, Sebastian, 293
Halder, General Franz, 166
Halifax, Edward Frederick Lindley Wood, 1st Earl of, 134, 137, 164, 166, 190, 234; Foreign Secretary, 146, 149, 209; and Austria, 150; and Czechoslovakia, 191; and Poland, 192, 196; and Soviet Union, 194
Hamilton, Douglas Douglas-Hamilton, 14th Duke of, 248–9
Hanfstaengl, Ernst 'Putzi', 19, 61, 67
Harmsworth, Esmond, Lord, 82, 84
Harzburg Congress 1931, 41
Hassell, Ulrich von, 73, 132, 135, 145
Haushofer, Albrecht, 156
Haushoffer, Professor Karl, 111
Helldorf, Count Wolf Heinrich von, 15, 37, 47, 48, 56, 182; and sa, 61, 63, 64
Henderson, Sir Nevile, 103, 123–4; and Ribbentrop, 124, 162–3, 168, 206; and Hitler, 49, 123; at Nuremberg rallies, 130, 167; and Austria, 146, 151–2; and Czechoslovakia, 162–3, 165; Munich, 172–3, 174, 176–7; recalled after Czechoslovakia, 190; and Poland, 202–3, 203–5, 206, 207; recognition of war, 209–10; and Paul Schmidt, 210
Henkell, Käthe, 27–8, 49, 145
Henkell, Otto, 24, 27
Henlein, Konrad, 157–8, 161, 166, 167–8
Herwarth, Hans von, 109, 197, 199, 202

Hess, Rudolf, 52, 59, 89, 111, 130, 135, 155, 159; French Armistice, 228; mission to UK, 248–9; at Nuremberg trials, 299

Hesse, Fritz, 295–6

Hessen, Prince Ludwig von ('Lu'), 117, 119, 120, 136–7

Hessia, Prince Philipp of, 135, 150

Hewel, Walther, 135, 156, 175, 178, 179, 203, 208, 248, 273

Heydrich, Reinhard, 62, 69, 128, 155, 158–9; and Ribbentrop, 233, 268; and Röhm, 75–6; Naujocks incident, 207–8; and Poland, 216; and the Final Solution, 253, 259; and ss, 258; assassination, 268, 300

Himmler, Heinrich: and Ribbentrop, 78, 113, 154, 217, 185, 217, 268, 279; and Hitler, 155, 261–2; at political meetings 1933, 52, 54; importance, 59; and Röhm, 75–6; network in Britain, 122; and Aryanism, 128; in Rome, 159; and Jewish *pogrom*, 181; and Polish atrocities, 217, 263; and the ss, 256, 258; and massacre of Jews, 260–2; Western contacts, 267; rescue of Mussolini, 272; and Bernadotte, 290; suicide, 293, 300

Hindenburg airship crash, 123

Hindenburg, Colonel Oskar von, 54, 56, 80

Hindenburg, Field Marshal Paul von: and Ribbentrop, 71; and Hitler, 16–17, 40, 47, 57, 64; elected President, 29; and Brüning, 39; re-elected President 1932, 40; and Nazis, 40; and von Papen, 51; potential scandals, 55; and von Schleicher, 55–6; death, 80

Hilter, Adolf: and Ribbentrop, 9–10, 16, 37, 45–7, 65, 68, 70, 71–2, 120, 121, 136, 180, 261, 298, 301; and the Imperial house, 16, 126; and Hindenburg, 16–17, 40, 47, 57, 64; in World War I, 18; and motor sport, 32; challenge for Presidency, 40; approached by Ribbentrop for coalition, 45–7; wooed by Annelies Ribbentrop, 48–9; spell of, 49–50, 53, 301; appointed Chancellor, 52; prophecy about, 52; negotiations with von Papen, 54; gaining of full powers, 63–4; admits Ribbentrop to friendship, 65, 71–2; character, according to Ribbentrop, 65–6; uses Ribbentrop as envoy, 65, 68, 70–1; and disarmament, 70; interview with *l'Information*, 71; court around, 73–4, 129; and Röhm, 75–7; interviews with *Daily Mail*, 80, 89; 'divide and rule' policy, 91, 97; use of Berchtesgaden, 94; sends troops into Rhineland, 99; interview with *Paris Midi*, 99; Peace Proposals 1936, 99–100; desire to visit Britain, 100; views on black athletes, 109; and Anti-Comintern Pact, 110–11, 117; and Edward VIII, 116, 133–4; and Ribbentrop's London gaffe, 120, 121; and Sir Nevile Henderson, 123–4; anger with Ribbentrop, 136; plans for Austria and Czechoslovakia, 137; earnings through *Mein Kampf*, 139; and Von Blomberg scandal, 141–2; and Austria, 137, 146–7, 149–50, 153; and Czechoslovakia, 137, 156–8, 161, 163; state visit to Rome, 158–61; invasion plans, 168–9; and Munich, 171–4; Berlin war display, 175; possible coup against, 163, 168, 169, 175, 176; the Munich note, 177–8; anger after Munich, 178–9; relations with Ribbentrop, 180; possible pact with Soviet Union, 187; enters Prague, 188, 189; ironic reply to Roosevelt, 193; attempts on his life, 193; and Soviet Union, 196, 197, 199–200, 202; and Poland, 200, 204; proposal to Britain, France and Poland, 205–6; invasion of Poland, 207; belief in British inaction, 208; view of his destiny, 208–9; speech 1 September 1939, 209; reception of 1939 Ultimatum, 211; wartime rail HQ, 218–19; 'offer of peace', 220, 235; Brenner Pass meetings, 222–3, 236, 249; and fallen France, 227, 228; plans war on British, 236, 247–8; meets Franco, 236–7; to Soviet Union, 239; anger with Mussolini, 239, 244; and Soviet Pact, 242, 243; invasion of Soviet Union, 243–4, 245; comes to aid of Italy in North Africa, 244–5; and Hess mission, 248–9; attack on Soviet Union, 250–1; new HQ for attack, 251–2; as Gröfaz, 255–6; opposition to, 257, 277–8; attempts on life of, 257, 277, 281; new field HQ at Winniza, 258–9; not believed by Ribbentrop to have ordered Jewish deaths, 261; mental health questioned, 262, 301–2; meeting with France and Italy after Rommel's defeat, 262–3; 'no retreat' order, 264; and Stalingrad, 267; and Martin Luther, 269; anger with generals in Russia, 275; anti-Hitler groups, 277–8; daily schedule, table, 278; attempts on life, 277; 20 July 1944, 281; conspirators shot and rounded up, 281–2; injured, 282; physical state after attack, 283–4, 287; attack on Ardennes, 284–5; back in Berlin, 286; in the bunker, 287, 291; refusal to accept defeat, 287; last days, 50–1, 289; in favour of nerve gas, 291; last photograph, 291; final collapse, 292; people's loyalty to, 293; suicide, 293; Ribbentrop still loyal to, 298, 301

Hoare, Sir Samuel (later Viscount Templewood), 98, 231

Hoffmann, Heinrich, 200–1

Hohenlohe, Princess Stephanie, 166–7

Hortsmann, Freddy and Lali, 36

Hösch, Leopold von, 72, 91, 92, 97, 100, 101, 133

Hossback, Major Friedrich, memorandum, 137, 142

Hoyningen-Huene, Baron Oswald von, 232–3, 234

Hugenberg, Alfred, 41, 56, 65
Hulbert, N., 167
Hungary: and Czechoslovakia, 173–4, 178, 180, 187; signs Anti-Comintern Pact, 184; feud with Romania, 235; defection from Axis, 277
Huntziger, General, 228

IMPREGROMA, 34
Imperial family: and Hitler, 16, 126; and Ribbentrop, 16
Imperial Fascist League, 86
Industrialists, and Nazi Party, 52–3
Innitzer, Cardinal, 150, 159
Irving, David, 244, 253, 291
Italo-British Naval Agreement, 158, 161
Italo-German jury on Czechoslovakia, 180
Italo-German Pact of Steel, 194
Italy: Anti-Comintern Pact, 131, 133, 135; withdrawal from League of Nations, 138; Mediterranean Treaty with Britain, 158, 161; not ready for war, 203; relations with Britain after Poland, 220–1; to join the Axis in war, 222–3; in the war, 226; in trouble in Greece and Libya, 244; surrender to the Allies, 271; now an Ally, 276

Jacobson, H. A., 70
January Club, 85
Japan: overtures to, by Ribbentrop, 97, 108, 111; signs Anti-Comintern Pact, 116, 242; attack on China, 128–9; puppet state, 146; and German-Soviet Pact, 198; discussed by Soviet Union and Germany, 238–9; and USA, 242; occupies French Indo-China, 242; discussions in Berlin and Rome, 245–6; non-aggression pact with Soviet Union, 246–7; pre-war defeat by Soviet Union, 246–7; attack on Pearl Harbor, 256; US declaration of war, 256; decline during war, 276
Jews: Ribbentrop and, 21, 24, 35–7, 61, 181–2, 253, 254–5, 259, 260–1, 266, 298, 301; and the Nazis, 60–1, 63; treatment in 1938, 164–5; in World War I, 164; *Kristallnacht*, 181–2; in USA, 60–1, 182–4; massacred near Smolensk, 256–9; list of, by country, 260–1; saved in Denmark, 266; to Mauthausen camp, 269; further persecutions, 289; *see also* Anti-Semitism; Final Solution
Jungk, Edgar, 75, 78, 79

Kaiser, *see* Wilhelm II
Kaltenbrunner, Ernst, 153, 268, 287, 300
Kantogun, General, 247
Kapp *putsch*, 28
Karlova, Captain, 122
Keitel, General Wilhelm, 142–3, 147, 159, 162, 204, 281; and France, 228; at Nuremberg, 299

Kemsley, James Gomer Berry, Lord, 101
Kennedy, Joseph E., 101, 169–70, 203
Kent, George, Duke of, 87, 126–7, 136, 232
Keppler, Wilhelm, 146
Kersten, Felix, 262
Kirkpatrick, Sir Ivone, 159, 174, 184; and German-Soviet pact, 198–9
Kleist, Marshal Paul von, 169, 275
Kleist-Schmenzin, Ewald von, 166, 288, 290
Knickerbocker, H. R., 61
Koch, Erich, 202
Killontay, Mme, 288
Kordt, Erich, 72, 73, 77, 81, 82, 92, 93, 94, 100, 106–7, 114, 118, 129, 135, 154, 156, 162, 163–4, 165, 166, 167, 169, 178, 242; in London, 115, 120; under Ribbentrop as Foreign Minister, 146, 148, 149
Körner, 54
Köster, Ambassador, 70–1, 74
Krebs, General Hans, 291, 293
Kristallnacht, 9 November 1938, 181, 182
Krosigk, Count Schwerin, 295
Krupp von Bohlen und Halbach, Gustav, 53, 302
Kuhn, Fritz, 183–4

La Guardia, Fiorella, 182–3
Latvia, German non-aggression pact, 194
Laval, Pierre, 89, 91, 94, 237, 247, 262–3
League of Nations, 70, 90, 100–1; and Italy, 95, 138
Lebensraum, 127–8, 143
Leese, Arthur, 86
Ley, Robert, 69, 302
Likus, Colonel Rudolf, 121, 129
Lindbergh, Charles, 101–2, 170–1
Link, The, 171, 177
Lipsky, Ambassador, 191, 205, 207
Lithuania, 219
Lloyd George, David, 111, 112, 166
Lockhart, Robert Bruce, 86
Löhr, General Alexander, 153
Londonderry, Charles Stewart Henry, 7th Marquess of, 88, 102, 131, 151
Lörzer, Bruno, 87
Lothian, Philip Henry Kerr, 11th Marquess of, 82, 87, 88, 89, 108, 119, 151, 167
Low, David, 115, 118, 120
Lubbe, Marius van der, 63
Lüdde, 295
Lüdecke, Kurt, 66–7
Luftwaffe, 89, 184–5
Luther, Martin, 110, 114, 253–4, 255, 259, 260, 264, 267–9
Luttman-Johnson, Captain H. W., 85
Lutze, Victor, 77–8

McAuliffe, General, 284
MacDonald, Ramsay, 71, 83

McGowan, Lord, 167
Mackensen, Ambassador von, 156, 198
Madagascar, proposed as Jewish state, 226, 253–4
Maglioni, Cardinal, 222
Maisky, Ivan, 117
Manstein, Marshal Fritz Erich von, 275–6
Marshall, General George C., 242
Mason-MacFarlane, Colonel Noel, 162, 193
Mastny, Ambassador, 158, 188
Matsuoka, Yosuke, 242, 245–6, 246–7
Maxwell-Fyfe, Sir David, 298, 302
May, Karl, 7
Meissner, Otto, 54, 56, 71, 81, 154
Memel, 153, 190, 191, 243
Memenenocoglu, 194
Mitford, Unity, 85, 112
Moellhausen, Consul Eiten, 269
Molotov, Vyachislav, 194, 197, 199, 200; in Berlin, 238–9, 243; on Ribbentrop, 201–2
Moltke, Count Helmut James von, 273–4, 278
Monsell, Sir Bolton Eyres, 93, 108
Montgomery, General Bernard, 262
Moore, Sir Thomas, 112, 151
Morell, Dr Theo, 189, 283–4, 287, 293
Moscow, Ribbentrop visits to, 195, 198, 199–201, 219
Mosley, Sir Oswald, 84–5, 86, 90
Mount Temple, Lord, 98, 103, 108, 112, 119, 131, 171
Moyland, Baron Adolf Steengracht von, 275
Munich talks, 171–4, 176, 177, 179
Murphy, James, 83
Murphy, Robert, 228
Mushanokoji, Viscount, 111, 129
Mussolini, Benito, 58, 73; and Ribbentrop, 221–2, 235–6, 270; and Hitler, 159, 222–3, 226, 236, 249, 252, 263, 282, 288; and Dollfuss murder, 80; appreciated in Britain, 83–4; and Mosley, 84; and Ethiopia, 89, 95, 134; to Germany, 131–3; and Spain, 134; and *Anschluss*, 150, 158, 161; Hitler's visit to Italy, 159–61; possible treaty with Germany, 161; and Czechoslovakia, 165; Munich, 176, 177; invasion of Albania, 192; and German-Soviet Pact, 198, 220; not ready for war, 203–4; mediation offered on Poland, 207; physical deterioration, 220; meetings with Ribbentrop, 221–2, 235–6, 270; meetings with Hitler, Brenner Pass, 222–3, 236, 249; visit to Munich, 226; attack on Greece, 238, 239; in Libya, 239–40; visit to Hitler's HQ, 252; on Germany's attack on Russia, 256; advice to Hitler on strategy, 263, 288; arrested, 271; rescued, 271–2; return to Italy, 272; death, 272, 293

Nadolny, 69
Naujocks, Captain Alfred, 207–8

Naumann, Max, 39
Nazi Party (NSDAP): Ribbentrop joins, 47, 294; election successes 1930, 38; ban on SA, and its removal, 40, 51; and the Jews, 60–1, 63; in Auswärtiges Amt, 73; and Röhm *putsch*, 75–7; rallies at Nuremberg, 82–3, 95, 112, 130–1, 167; not appreciated in Britain, 83; British sympathisers, 84, 86–8; recruitment in Britain, 122; Austrians exiled, 147; nature in early days, 294
Negrin, Prime Minister of Spain, 105–6
Netherlands, German attack planned, 224
Neurath, Baron Konstantin von, 58, 59, 61, 65, 70, 89–90, 150, 175; and Ribbentrop, 91, 95, 97, 106–7, 137; on Hitler, 144–5; directive on Jewish question, 97–8; cautious on Rhineland entry, 99; and racial policy, 108; and Henderson, 124; Anti-Comintern Pact, 135; Hitler's weariness with, 143–4, 145; Reich Protector of Bohemia/Moravia, 189; and Soviet Union, 196; Dönitz' choice as Foreign Minister, 295
Newnes, Sir Frank, 112, 119
Nicolson, Harold, 84, 195
Niemöller, Pastor Martin, 28, 110, 121–2, 283
Non-Intervention Committee, 112, 117, 128
Norway, and Germany, 224, 274
Nuremberg Laws, 95
Nuremberg rallies, 82–3, 95, 112, 130–1, 167
Nuremberg trials, 297–304

O'Connor, General, 239–40
Olympic Games 1936, 105, 107, 108–9
Operation Barbarossa, 243–4, 245
Operation Sea Lion, 247–8
Opfermnann, Herr, 35
Oshimas, Lt-Colonel, 97, 111, 116, 198, 246, 256, 290
Oster, Colonel Hans, 168, 178, 279
Osthilfe scandal, 55

Papen, Franz von: and Ribbentrop, 19, 20, 35, 58; and Hitler, 51–4, 79, 80–1; Chancellor 1932, 45, 51; Vice-Chancellor, 57, 65, 75; at German/Italian talks, 132; Ambassador to Vienna, 146; Ambassador to Turkey, 273; acquitted at Nuremberg, 302
Paris: visits by Ribbentrop, 70, 184, 227; occupation, 227–9
Patton, General George, 284
Paul, Prince of Romania, 193
Paulus, Field Marshal Friedrich, 264, 267
Pearl Harbor, 256
Pétain, Marshal Henri Philippe, 226, 227, 228, 241, 247, 263; meeting with Hitler, 237–8
Phipps, Sir Eric, 70, 100, 103, 104, 123
Platen-Hallermund, Count Oskar von, 35
Plymouth Lord, 117

Poland: and Hitler, 200, 204, 205–6; claims on Czechoslovakia, 173, 174, 178, 180, 187; German interest in, 186, 200; Ribbentrop's visit to, 186–7; agreement with Britain, 191–2; UK's general lack of interest, 195; German/Soviet division of, 199; UK's recovery of interest, 202–5; mobilisation, 205; German invasion, 207; ss in, 216–18, 223; surrender to Germany and Soviet Union, 219; source of displeasure to Stalin and Hitler, 242

Polish Corridor, 143

Pope Pius xi, 159

Pope Pius xii, 221–2

Potsdam meeting, Hitler and Hindenburg, 64

Press, British, and the Nazis, 82–3, 112

Price, George Ward, 80, 81, 82, 89

Race laws, 95–6; *see* Anti-Semitism

Rademacher, 253

Rath, Ernest von, 181

Rathenau, Walter, 29

Raumer, Dr Hermann von, 108, 110, 133

Redesdale, Lord, 119, 151, 171

Redesdale, Lady, 112

Reichenau, Field Marshal Walter von, 257

Reichstag fire, 47, 63

Remitz, Herr von, 152

Reparations, payment of French, 51

Rhineland, German troops sent into, 98–9, 100

Ribbentrop, Adolf von (son), 110, 114

Ribbentrop, Annelies von (wife): good mother, 8; editor of husband's memoirs, 16, 304; ambitions, 27, 34; wish to entrap Hitler, 48; and Nazism, 77; Channon on, 102, 103; and Niemöller, 110; in London, 113, 118; Coronation Ball, 126; working help to husband, 138; with Mussolini in Berlin, 132; political involvement, 179, 191; displeasure, 180; and Soviet agreement, 187; expensive tastes, 268; offered as visitor to Soviet Union, 288; whereabouts at the end of the war, 290; visits husband in prison, 299; after husband's execution, 306

Ribbentrop, Barthold von (son), 240

Ribbentrop, Bettina von (daughter), 28, 114, 117–18

Ribbentrop, Gertrud von ('aunt'), 7–8

Ribbentrop, Ingeborg (sister), 4

Ribbentrop, Joachim von: and Hitler, 9–10, 16, 37, 65, 68, 70, 71–2, 120, 121, 136, 180, 261, 298, 301; birth and family, 4–5; and father, 5, 6, 9; and the British, 5–6, 9–10, 15; schooling, 6, 7; character, 6, 25; love of music, 7; interest in languages, 7; acquires title 'von', 8; as father, 8; early visit to London, 9–10; visit to Canada, 10, 12–14; good looks, 10; jobs in Canada, 12, 13; not a volunteer in the army, 12–13; illness, 13;

to Germany for World War I, 14–15; and German Imperial house, 16; in Torgau Hussars, 18; awarded Iron Cross, 19; in Constantinople, 19–20; resignation of commission, 20; in Berlin, post-war, 21–5; champagne merchant, 23–4; and the Jews, 21, 24, 35–7, 61; ability on world scene, 25; textile salesman, 26; pays off debts, 26; meets Annelies Henkell, 26; close marriage, 26–7, 28; wealth, 28, 39–40; and motor cars, 32; wine firm, 34; social climbing, 35, 38; joins Union Klub, 35; approached by Nazis, 37; interest in politics, 37–8; send by Von Papen to see Hitler, 45–7; joins Nazis, 47; house used for crucial meetings, 53–4; snubbed in 1933, 57–8; joins ss, 59; on Hitler, 65–6; used as foreign affairs adviser, 65, 68, 70–1; to Paris, 70; to London, 71, 72; appointed Plenipotentiary for Matters of Disarmament, 71–2; description of, 72; to Rome, 73; courts, Hitler, 73–4; and French, on disarmament, 74; full ss uniform, 77, 78; and Röhm *putsch*, 77; and Himmler, 78, 113, 154, 185, 268; to London for naval agreement, 81, 89, 91, 92–3; view of British sympathisers, 87–8; and Nazism, 91, 140, 155; Extraordinary Ambassador of the German Reich on Special Mission, 91; Junkers plane D-AMY, 92, 118, 121, 130; crude tactics on naval agreement, 93; luncheon in London, 93; reports back to Hitler, 94; to Belgium, 97; and Rhineland, 98–9; to London 1936, 99; Ambassador to the Court of St James, 102, 106–7, 112, 113–16; difficulties in London, 102–5; Vansittart's view of, 104; and Spanish Civil War, 106; Olympic Games, 108; promotion to ss General, 113; lampooned as Brickendrop, 115, 118; irritant to British Government, 117, 121; view of Abdication, 118; presentation of credentials to George VI, 119–20; speeches and gaffes, 119; Hitler's view of, 120, 121; trips abroad, 121, 128; and Sir Nevile Henderson, 124, 162–3, 168, 206; Coronation Ball, 126–7; and Churchill on war, 127; not in Hitler's entourage, 129; holiday in Scotland, 129–30; pursues Hitler and Mussolini, 131–2; not close to Hitler, 136, 137, 140; ambitions to be Foreign Minister, 136; sympathy with Prince Lu, 136; total loyalty to Hitler, 138, 209, 298, 301; report to Hitler on Britain, 138; wealth, 139–40; ill at ease with Nazis, 140, 155; appointed Foreign Minister (ram), 145, 147–9; and Austria, 146, 152; to London, 149; acquires Fuschl Castle, 152; attempt to resign, 153; ss and diplomatic uniforms, 154; and Czechoslovakia, 158, 162–3; Hitler's visit to Rome, 159, 160; with royalty, 159,

Ribbentrop, Joachim von – *contd*
160; military treaty with Italy, 161; and
Mussolini 161; and Henderson, 162–3, 168;
and Munich, 172–3, 174, 176, 178; and
Hitler, 180; and Britain, 180; and
Hungary/Poland/Czechoslovakia plans,
180; and Jewish *pogrom*, 181–2; Anti-
Comintern Pact, 184; to Paris for Franco-
German Treaty, 184; and Himmler and ss,
185; to Poland, 186; possible Soviet deal,
187; invasion of Czechoslovakia, 189, 190–
1; and Romania, 193; and Turkey, 193–4;
and Italo-German Pact, 194; to Moscow,
195, 198, 199–201; and Soviet Union, 196,
197, 198; Molotov on, 201–2; row with
Henderson, 206; adherence to Hitler, 209;
reception of British Ultimatum, 211;
promotion in ss, 215; versus Himmler, 217;
decline in influence, 218; wartime HQ in
railway carriages, 218–19; and Goebbels,
219, 225; to Moscow, re Lithuania, 219;
and Ciano, 219–20, 223; to Italy, 221–2;
meets the Pope, 221–2; and Madagascar, 226; and
France, 227, 228, 230; and the Windsors,
230–1, 233–4; thanked by Hitler, 235;
meeting with Ciano on Romania, 235;
meeting with Mussolini, 235–6; not taken
seriously, 236; meeting with Franco, 236–7,
241; meeting with Pétain, 237, 241; and
Hitler's invasion of Soviet Union, 243–4;
and Japanese, 245; Hess's flight to Britain,
248–9; meeting with Dekanosov, 249–50;
and Bormann, 252; and the Final Solution,
253, 259; search for new role, 252–3; and
Jewish deaths, 254–5, 260–1, 266; new field
HQ at Castle Steinort, 258–9; meeting after
Rommel's defeat, 262–3; absence from
Auswärtiges Amt, 264–5; insecurity, 265;
fall of Luther, 267–9; connection with ss,
269; and anti-Hitler movement, 269, 279; to
Italy, 270–1; on Ciano, 273; advice to Hitler
on Soviet campaign, 273; in Berlin during
bombing, 273–4; and Sweden, 274, 290–1;
row with Goebbels, 274; new Auswärtiges
Amt created, 275; not on the hit list, 279;
unable to oppose Hitler, 280; attacked by
Göring, 282; asks Hitler to contact Soviet
Union, 288; life in the bunker, 291; sees
Hitler at the end, 292–3; after Hitler's death,
294–5; effect of events on, 294; refused as
RAM by Dönitz, 295; arrested, 295; to
Luxembourg, 296–7; to Nuremberg, 297; in
prison, 297–8; still loyal to Hitler, 298, 301;
indictments, 298; claims no knowledge of
atrocities, 298; tells all about German-Soviet
Pact, 299; denies anti-Semitism, 301; on
Hitler's alleged madness, 301–2; not a
plotter against Hitler, 302; disagreement
with Hitler, 302, 304, 305; convicted on four
counts, 302; ageing at Nuremberg, 303;
writing memoirs, 304; self-justification, 304–
5; letters to Annelies, 304–5; executed, 306;
ashes, 306; last words, 306
Ribbentrop, Karl Barthold von (uncle), 8
Ribbentrop, Lothar (brother), 4, 5, 7, 10, 12–
14
Ribbentrop, Olga Margarete (stepmother), 7
Ribbentrop, Richard (father), 4, 5, 6, 7, 8, 15;
and Hitler, 49; and Nazism, 91
Ribbentrop, Rudolf von (son): birth, 28; and
ss, 62, 209, 265, 279; at British school, 67,
114; to Nuremberg, 299; father's last letter
to, 305; prisoner of war, 306
Ribbentrop, Sophie, née Hertwig (mother), 4–
5, 6–7
Ribbentrop, Ursula von (daughter), 114
Rieth, Dr, 79
Röhm, Ernst, 54, 56, 58, 59–60, 74, 75, 141;
downfall, 75–8; and Hitler, 75–7
Roman Catholic church, and Nazis, 150; *see
also* Pope
Romania, 193, 125, 251
Rome, Hitler's visit to, 158–61
Rommel, General Erwin, 236, 240, 244, 255,
258, 262, 279; plotter, 278, and the invasion
of Germany, 280; wounded, 281
Roosevelt, President Franklin D., 60; and
pogrom, 182–3; challenge to Hitler, 192–3;
and Yugoslavia, 241; and Churchill, 243; at
Casablanca, 267; death, 291
Rosenberg, Alfred, 66, 67–8, 87, 97, 144, 202,
230
Rote Kapelle, 278
Rothermere, Harold Sidney Harmsworth,
Lord, 81, 82, 86, 101, 103, 108
Rumbold, Sir Horace, 195
Runciman, Walter, Lord, 168
Runstedt, General Karl Rudolf Ferd von, 280
Russia, *see* Soviet Union

SA (*Sturmabteilung*), 61, 62–3, 75–6; *see also*
Röhm, Ernst
SD (*Sicherheitsdienst*), 62, 186, 216–17, 254–5,
257, 268
SS (*Schutzstaffel*), 60, 61–2; Ribbentrop as
member, 59, 77, 78, 113, 154, 185, 215, 269;
strength in Austria, 152; encouragement by
Ribbentrop, 185–6; atrocities by, 181, 185–
6, 215–16, 253–4, 256–8; Baltic recruits, 201;
in Poland, 216–18, 223; in Soviet Union,
256–7; recruits expected in Norway, 274;
still pursuing Jews, 289; Waffen ss, 62,
217
Saar plebiscite, 70, 89
Salazar, Antonio de Oliviera, 232
Sassoon, Sir Philip, 105
Saxe-Coburg and Gotha, Duke of, 112, 119

Schacht, Dr Hjalmar, 41, 61, 74, 151; and Hitler, 49–50; acquitted at Nuremberg, 302

Schellenberg, General Walter, 62, 159, 229, 233–5, 261, 268; Western contacts, 267

Schlabrendorff, Fabian von, 288

Schleicher, General Kurt von, 45, 46; Chancellor, 51, 53; and Hindenburg, 55–6; death, 76, 78

Schmidt, Guido, 147, 151

Schmidt, Paul Otto, 92, 107, 124, 134, 154, 161, 162–3; on Ribbentrop, 235–6; at Munich, 172, 174, 175, 178; and Poland, 186, 205–6; and Czech invasion, 189, 190; and Turkey, 194; and Henderson, 210; and the Ultimatum, 210–11; wartime working for Ribbentrop, 218–19; and Sumner Welles, 220; voice-over technique, 235; and Spain, 236; and France, 237; and Soviet Union, 238; Ribbentrop/Dekanosov meeting, 249; guilt, 265

Schmundt, Colonel Rudolf, 244

Schnurre, 197

Schröder, Baron Bruno, 115

Schröder, Kurt von, 52, 115

Schulenburg, Count Friedrich Werner von der, 196–7, 198, 199, 201, 202, 247; death as rebel, 196

Schurman, Jacob Gould, 34–5

Schuschnigg, Kurt von, 146–7, 149, 151

Schwarz, Dr Paul, 23, 24, 91, 92, 94, 101, 106, 296

Schwerin von Krosigk, Count Lutz, 65, 74

Seeckt, General Hans von, 20, 41

Sempill, Lord, 131, 171

Seyss-Inquart, Arthur, 147, 180

Shaw, George Bernard, 82, 83

Simon, Sir John, 70, 71, 72, 81, 88, 90, 93, 296

Simpson, Mrs Wallis, later Duchess of Windsor, 93, 116

Skorzeny, SS Colonel Otto, 271, 284

Slovak Republic, 187–8

Sonnenburg estate, 139–40

Soviet-German Non-Aggression Pact, *see* German-Soviet Pact

Soviet Union: and Hitler, 187, 196, 197, 199–200, 202; economy in 1920s, 33; doubling of military budget, 99; relations with Britain, 168, 194–5; wooed by Germany and others, 194; and Germany, 195, 196, 235; invasion of Poland, 219; occupation of Romanian islands, 235; invasion of, by Germany, 243–4, 245; pre-war defeat of Japanese, 246–7; German attack, 250–1; Stalingrad, 264, 267; belief in Non-Aggression Pact, 251; nearing Berlin, 285, 291–2

Spain, Fascist, 191: not joining the war, 233, 234, 235–6; offered colonies, 236; talks with, 236–7

Spanish Civil War, 105–6, 128

Spartakus revolt, 22

Speer, Albert, 82, 113, 189, 224, 287, 289, 290, 292, 293; in prison, accepting guilt, 298

Speidel, General Hans, 280

Spitzy, Reinhard, 36, 114, 120, 121, 125, 127, 136, 146, 147, 150, 152, 154, 177, 180, 259, 279

Squire, Sir John, 85

Stalin, Joseph, 58, 196, 197, 199, 200–1, 222, 299; complaint on occupation, 242; affection for Germans, 247

Stalingrad, 264, 267

Stamp, Josiah Charles, Lord, 167

Stanhope, Lord, 72

Starhemberg, Prince, 80

Stauffenberg, Colonel Claus, Count Schenck von, 257, 277–9, 281

Steengracht, Baron, 121, 279

Stohrer, Eberhard von, 231, 233, 234

Strang, Sir William, 171, 194

Strasser, Gregor, 51, 54, 76, 78

Strauss, Ottmar, 23, 24

Streicher, Julius, 65, 90, 182, 300

Studnitz, General von, 228–9

Sudetenland, 153, 156–7, 161, 163, 167, 172, 173, 174, 176

Suner, Serrano, 231, 233, 236, 237

Sweden, 224, 274; and Ribbentrop, 274, 290–1

Tennant, Ernest W., 71, 82, 88, 98, 103

Tennant, W., 82

Thadden, Eberhard von, 96–7, 289

Thomas, Sir Nigel, 87

Thomsen, Hans, 183

Thorner, Herr, 114, 120, 128

Tiso, Fr Josef, 187–8

'Torgau' Hussars, 18

Trott, Adam, 278

Turkey, and Germany, 193–4; Ribbentrop's visit, 19–20

Tyrol, ceded to Italy, 153, 161

Umberto, Crown Prince of Italy, 227

United Kingdom: appeasement politics, 169; bombing by Germany, 247; Ultimatum on war, 210; lack of early action in 1939, 223–4; Hitler's plans for, 236; bombing of Berlin, 239

United States: and Jews, 60–1, 182–4; declarations of war, 236, 256; bombing of Germany, 269; troops in Germany, 290

V-1 missiles, 270

V-2 missiles, 276, 284

Van der Lubbe, Marius, 63

Vancouver, German community, 10–11

Vansittart, Sir Robert, 72, 100, 103–4, 108, 109, 137, 166, 167; on Ribbentrop, 104

Versailles, Treaty of, 33, 34, 86, 93
Victor Emanuel III, King of Italy, 159, 160
Voroshilov, Klimenti Efremovich, 195

Waffen ss, 62, 217
Wagner, Horst, 289
Waldeck und Pyrmont, Prince Josias, 73
Wall Street crash, 38
War criminals at Nuremberg, 297–306; IQ tests,
   300
Wassner, Captain, later Admiral, 91, 92, 130
Waugh, Evelyn, 112
Wehrmacht, and Hitler's power, 142–3
Weimar Republic, end, 51–2
Weinhandlungsgesellschaft, 34
Weizsäcker, Ernst von, 24, 147–8, 156, 162,
   169, 203, 242, 264–5; against Hitler's
   Czechoslovakia plans, 165–6; and Munich,
   172, 174; and the ss, 185; and the Jews, 254;
   Ambassador to Vatican, 275
Welles, Sumner, 220–1, 222
Wesel, Ribbentrop's birthplace, 4
Westwall, 170–1

Wied, Prince, 48
Wiedemann, Captain Fritz, 165, 166–7
Wilhelm II, the Kaiser, 5–6, 8, 20, 22, 30n
Wilson, Sir Horace, 119, 171, 174, 203
Wilson, Hugh, 130
Windsor, Duke of, *see* Edward VIII
Winterbotham, F. W., 68, 87
Wise, Rabbi Stephen, 61
Witzleben, Marshal Erwin von, 168, 175
Woermann, Dr Ernst, 91, 100, 115, 118, 120,
   131, 156, 185
Wolff, ss General Karl, 130, 258, 268
Wolfsschanze, 251–2
Wood, John C., 303, 306

Yeats-Brown, Francis, 85, 86
Yugoslavia, 241–2, 245–6

Zeeland, van, Prime Minister of Belgium,
   97
Zhukov, Marshal Georgy Konstantinovich,
   247, 250, 285, 292
Ziniva, Captain, 116, 121